A Gathering of Grand Canyon Historians

Ideas, Arguments, and First-Person Accounts

Proceedings of the Inaugural Grand Canyon History Symposium, January 2002

Compiled and Edited by

Michael F. Anderson

GRAND
CANYON
ASSOCIATION

Grand Canyon Association
PO Box 399
Grand Canyon, AZ 86023-0399
(800) 858-2808
www.grandcanyon.org

Printed in the United States of America
Edited by Todd R. Berger
Designed by Rudy Ramos

10   09   08   07   06   05 1   2   3   4   5   6

ISBN: 0-938216-83-X
Monograph Number 13

Library of Congress Cataloging-in-Publication Data

Grand Canyon History Symposium (1st : 2002)
  A gathering of Grand Canyon historians : ideas, arguments, and first-person accounts : proceedings of the inaugural Grand Canyon History Symposium, January 2002 / compiled and edited by Michael F. Anderson.— 1st ed.
      p. cm. — (Monograph / Grand Canyon Association ; no. 13)
   Includes bibliographical references and index.
   ISBN 0-938216-83-X
  1. Grand Canyon (Ariz.)—History—Congresses. 2. Grand Canyon National Park (Ariz.)—History—Congresses. I. Anderson, Michael F. II. Title. III. Series: Monograph (Grand Canyon Association) ; no. 13.
   F788.G7465 2002
   979.1'32—dc22
                                 2005015968

Cover background photograph courtesy Emery Kolb Collection, Cline Library, Northern Arizona University, Flagstaff (NAU.PH.568.2816). Cover inset photograph courtesy Grand Canyon National Park Museum Collection (#10455)

Inset photographs courtesy of Grand Canyon National Park Museum Collection:
      pages vii (#20836), 19 (#11041), 23 (#17700), 63 (#15003), 73 (#3973E), 87 (#2339), 129 (#17227), 137 (#17262), 163 (#14737)
Courtesy of Grand Canyon National Park Museum Collection, photograph by Mike Quinn: pages 1, 39, 43, 49, 69, 111, 123, 171, 177, 181, 190
Courtesy of the National Park Service, photograph by Mark Lellouch: page 7
Courtesy of the National Park Service: page 33
Courtesy of the U.S. Fish and Wildlife Service: pages 53, 105
Courtesy of Bill Bishop: page 57
Courtesy of Todd R. Berger for the Grand Canyon Association: page 99
Courtesy of Richard D. Quartaroli: page 155
Courtesy of Northern Arizona University, Cline Library, Special Collections, Flagstaff: page 163

It is the mission of the Grand Canyon Association to cultivate knowledge, discovery, and stewardship for the benefit of Grand Canyon National Park and its visitors. Proceeds from the sale of this book will be used to support the educational goals of Grand Canyon National Park.

DEDICATION

In Memoriam
Dr. Robert Clark Euler
August 8, 1924–January 13, 2002

Dr. Robert Clark Euler, of Prescott, Arizona, was born in Brooklyn, New York. He was a decorated captain in the U.S. Marine Corps during World War II and the Korean War. Dr. Euler earned his BA and MA degrees in economics at Northern Arizona University, and his PhD in anthropology at the University of New Mexico. During his long career, he authored more than 150 publications, presenting his research to the Society for American Archaeology, Society for Applied Anthropology, American Anthropological Association, International Congress of Americanists, and International Conference on Climate and History at the University of East Anglia in Norwich, England.

Dr. Euler's work encompassed research, teaching, and consulting. He was chair of the Anthropology Department at Northern Arizona University and the University of Utah, founded the Center for Man and Environment at Prescott College, and later became president of Prescott College. He also taught at Wesleyan University in Connecticut, Arizona State University, and Fort Lewis College in Durango, Colorado. He was curator of anthropology at the Museum of Northern Arizona. For nearly two years early in his career, Dr. Euler lived with a Navajo family near the Little Colorado River to improve his understanding of Navajo economies, and he later studied the effects on Navajo families of large-scale coal mining at Black Mesa, Arizona. He also conducted research with the Hopis, Havasupais, Hualapais, and Southern Paiutes, advising the tribes concerning various land-claim cases; he was a scholar of Southwest and Great Basin tribes as well. In pursuit of his research, he enjoyed photography, camping, and numerous Colorado River boat trips.

Senator Barry Goldwater appointed Dr. Euler research anthropologist for Grand Canyon National Park in 1974, a position he held until 1984. However, his name was synonymous with Grand Canyon archaeology for more than twenty-five years. Best known for his research on split-twig figurines and Stantons Cave, Dr. Euler began interdisciplinary work on the archaeology, geology, biology, and paleontology of Stantons Cave in the mid-1960s prior to his employment with the National Park Service. He was known for his innovative techniques. While associated with Prescott College, he was contracted through the Arizona Power Commission to conduct a survey along the Colorado River corridor in preparation for the construction of Marble Canyon Dam. Dr. Euler's "helicopter" surveys became legend, and while the technique was not widely used after the Marble and Bridge Canyon surveys, it did provide a clue as to the number and extent of archaeological resources within the inner canyon. During his 1960s surveys for the Marble Canyon Dam site, for example, Dr. Euler recorded more than two hundred riverside archaeological sites, a surprising number considering the scant eight sites discovered by Walt Taylor in ground reconnaissance of the same area in the early 1950s.

While working as research anthropologist for Grand Canyon National Park, Dr. Euler was responsible for both archaeological research and tribal consultation. Of particular interest were the fortified archaeological sites found along the South Rim. His documentation of such sites led to theories of warfare among early Grand Canyon residents, a topic still researched today by others. Dr. Euler was also tribal liaison between the park and the canyon's affiliated

American Indian tribes. His most significant contribution in this role was the drafting of a Memorandum of Understanding (MOU) for the use of Havasupai Traditional Use Lands, established by Congress as part of the Grand Canyon National Park Enlargement Act of 1975. The MOU still guides National Park Service and Havasupai management of these lands.

Dr. Euler was a vital figure in the development of archaeological research, historical research, and tribal relations at the Grand Canyon. When considering the history of human uses of the canyon and National Park Service–tribal relations, his name appears constantly as a leader. His legacy is found in his publications, site records, and extensive photographic and documental archives at Grand Canyon National Park. His efforts will not be forgotten.

At the Grand Canyon History Symposium, which was dedicated in Dr. Euler's memory, Jan Balsom, Grand Canyon National Park's Chief of Cultural Resources, gave a superb presentation on his canyon career.

CONTENTS

PREFACE

Coordinating Grand Canyon's inaugural history symposium was quite a learning experience, as was the ensuing effort to convert the event's diverse audiovisual presentations into essays for this volume. At first, I thought conferences and proceedings should be straightforward. We arrive on an advertised date at a given place, say our piece, listen to others, and then go home enlightened by the experience. Afterward, I take what we brought, put a cover on it, and move on to other projects.

Today I wonder at this naïveté, but then, my family includes three dogs because people walk up to me with a puppy and I say, "How cute—I want it." The Grand Canyon History Symposium was conceived in a like manner with as much forethought. John Azar, an avid canyon hiker, called one night in late 2000 and offhandedly mentioned that we ought to have a history conference. I thought for several nanoseconds of everything I knew about organizing conferences then answered, "What a great idea—let's do it."

I can feed and otherwise maintain dogs by myself, although my wife Linda does it. I have even written several books, which are, despite considerable help, mostly solitary efforts that are personally gratifying. I do not feel *personal* gratification, however, as I write these words. I am instead sincerely thankful and downright relieved that nearly two hundred people and a half dozen organizations agreed that a conference and published proceedings were great ideas and that they made it all happen.

So thank you, John, and thanks to everyone else who pitched in. Among those in the forefront were the Grand Canyon Association (GCA), originally known as the Grand Canyon Natural History Association (GCNHA), and its teaching arm, the Grand Canyon Field Institute (GCFI). Since the founding of GCNHA in 1932, the association has been a strong ally in any effort to interpret Grand Canyon National Park for the public. Pam Frazier, deputy director of GCA, committed early on to the history symposium and jumped in with both feet. Ron Short, GCA's art director, proffered advice and designed our symposium brochure; Todd Berger, GCA's managing editor, edited the text and photographs; and Rudy Ramos designed this lovely volume from a challenging montage of text and illustrative materials. GCFI Director Mike Buchheit, as well as GCFI employees Rich Della Porta, Lois Henderson, and Jan Koons, worked tirelessly and enthusiastically (as usual) to register participants, prepare the facility, staff the four-day event, and clean up the aftermath. In fact, *everyone* at GCA and GCFI helped by contributing dollars, office space, supplies, and more than one thousand hours of time. *Gratis.*

Other organizations that made the history symposium possible include the National Park Service, Arizona Humanities Council, Xanterra Parks & Resorts, Grand Canyon Historical Society (formerly known as the Grand Canyon Pioneers Society), Grand Canyon Railway, and Northern Arizona University. I thank several individuals from these organizations who were of particular help with this project, including Judy Hellmich, John Sudar, and Mike Weaver of the park's interpretive staff; Bill Suran, Tom Carmony, and Fred and Jeanne Schick from the Grand Canyon Historical Society; Jan Balsom and Amy Horn from the park's Science Center; Bill Johnston and Henry Karpinski from Xanterra; and professors Val Avery, George Lubick, and Andy Wallace from Northern Arizona University. I know that these people called on others to help as well, and gratitude is owed these unnamed but appreciated history lovers.

Special thanks go to the Arizona Humanities Council, which supplied a $3,000 grant that covered many expenses and funded three wonderful speakers on Colorado River history. Bill Johnston, general manager of Xanterra at the Grand Canyon, actively participated as a member of our steering committee; opened El Tovar's Coronado Room to our keynote speaker, Hal Rothman, and his family; supplied rooms to participants at bargain rates; offered several field trips; and prepared luncheons and the closing banquet. Thank you, Bill, and all those who worked with you, for handling everything so well. National Park Service staff at the Albright Training Center opened the center's apartments to our speakers, and the Grand Canyon Railway offered good prices and a bonus, historian Al Richmond, to participants who chose to arrive by the iron horse. We could not have asked for better partners in this endeavor; their generosity is the reason we could present the conference at such a reasonable cost, and their diligence explains why the conference progressed with so few glitches along the way.

Don Lago, a true "canyon-phile" and symposium participant, remarked that our gathering in January 2002 seemed to embrace members from all of Grand Canyon's cultures: American Indians and pioneer descendents; park service administrators, archaeologists, rangers, interpreters, and naturalists; river runners and backpackers; concessioners and ecologists; writers and researchers; and avid readers. The common thread, of course, was a deep love for the Grand Canyon that many of us have trouble articulating, but the lodestone was human history. I thank Don for that insight, and thank the participants, presenters, speakers, and workers who spent four days together, learned from each other, and praised the effort despite some shortcomings.

MICHAEL F. ANDERSON
Director
Grand Canyon History Symposium

INTRODUCTION

by Michael F. Anderson

When I arrived at the Grand Canyon in 1990 to research the North and South Bass trails, I first looked for one good published source to establish a historical context. I discovered that the Grand Canyon Natural History Association (GCNHA), today known as the Grand Canyon Association (GCA), had published pocket-sized Grand Canyon trail guides containing good but narrowly focused histories of a few individual trails. The association had also published a series of monographs on selected topics that were helpful in my research. Will Barnes's *Arizona Place Names* (1935) and Byrd Granger's *Grand Canyon Place Names* (1960) offered a few insights on canyon history, and Al Richmond's *Cowboys, Miners, Presidents & Kings* (1985) was very informative and is still the best published account of the Grand Canyon Railway. Will Rusho and Greg Crampton's *Desert River Crossing* (1975) told the story of Lees Ferry and House Rock Valley on the canyon's fringes.

My search continued in that vein, uncovering works that nibbled at the edges, a few books and journal articles that touched on the Grand Canyon's past while telling other stories, brochures and handouts that used a little history to market the scenic wonder, and snippets offered in river and trail guides. Some early books, such as Miner Tillotson and Frank Taylor's *Grand Canyon Country* (1929) and George Wharton James's *In and Around the Grand Canyon* (1900), were helpful, especially James's, but they are more contemporary chronicles than histories written to organize and reveal the Grand Canyon's human past. The exception was J. Donald Hughes's *In the House of Stone and Light*, a summary history published by GCNHA in 1967 under the title *The Story of Man at Grand Canyon*. It was revised and retitled in 1978 (*In the House of Stone and Light*). The book is still in print, and it remains a valuable

source. Hughes served my immediate purpose, but as I scanned his bibliography I realized that he had traveled a similar road, finding published information here and there, but in the end, had to assemble much of his story from letters, memoranda, reports, diaries, and other dank documents in regional archives. Earle Spamer's *Bibliography of the Grand Canyon and the Lower Colorado River from 1540* (1981; 2nd ed., 1990), a fine history itself, only confirmed the paucity of comprehensive histories.

I sensed a promising niche in 1990 and have remained a researcher, writer, and teacher of the Grand Canyon's past ever since. I have not been alone. Since that year, early manuscripts and photographic collections have been edited for publication, among them Ronald Werhan's treatment of Margaret Verkamp's 1940 master's thesis, *History of Grand Canyon National Park* (1993), and Mona Lange McCroskey's *Summer Sojourn to the Grand Canyon* (1996). George Billingsley, Dove Menkes, and Earle Spamer borrowed on Billingsley's earlier unpublished research to produce *Quest for the Pillar of Gold* (1997), the first comprehensive history of Grand Canyon mining. Bill Suran turned out *The Kolb Brothers of Grand Canyon* (1991), and Richard and Sherry Mangum wrote the story of early transportation to the South Rim, *Grand Canyon-Flagstaff Stage Coach Line* (1999). Barbara Morehouse produced an intriguing historical analysis of canyon boundaries in *A Place Called Grand Canyon* (1996). Women's history also emerged with Virginia Grattan's *Mary Colter* (1992), Louise Teal's *Breaking into the Current* (1994), and Betty Leavengood's *Grand Canyon Women*, now in a second edition (2004) published by GCA.

Prior to the 1990s, histories of the Colorado River within the Grand Canyon consisted mostly of published journals or accounts based on journals, such as John Wesley Powell's conflated report of his first river expedition, Frederick Dellenbaugh's more accurate narrative of Powell's second expedition, Ellsworth Kolb's account of his and his brother Emery's adventure, and the Utah Historical Society's printing of journals from Powell's first expedition. There were exceptions, of course. Robert Brewster Stanton wrote *Colorado River Controversies* (1932), and Dwight L. Smith edited and the University of Oklahoma Press published a fraction of his 1890 railroad survey under the title *Down the Colorado* (1965). David Lavender's *River Runners of the Grand Canyon* (1985) is still the best summary of river trips through the 1950s, and, although he never got around to publishing much, Dock Marston was relentless from the 1950s to the 1970s, gathering a gush of river history that now resides in the Huntington Library in San Marino, California, awaiting interpretation.

The earlier river tales are good reads and supply information for today's historians, who have traveled well beyond sodden adventure stories. Louise Teal's book, aside from illustrating that the river is not all testosterone, offers sensitive biographies of early boatwomen. P. T. Reilly's massive *Lee's Ferry* (1999), edited by Robert H. Webb, covers broader ground than the title implies, including basic historical data on the river and the Arizona Strip. Brad Dimock, Cort Conley, and Vince Welch published *The Doing of the Thing* (1999), a biography of Buzz Holmstrom, and Dimock on his own wrote *Sunk Without a Sound* (2001), an award-winning biographical account of Glen and Bessie Hyde's tragic river trip in 1928. Eilean Adams published *Hell or High Water* (2001), a well-researched and comprehensive history of her grandfather, James White, and the controversy surrounding his float through the Grand Canyon in 1867.

Meanwhile, Gregory McNamee's *Grand Canyon Place Names*, now in a second edition (2004), and Nancy Brian's *River to Rim* (1992) have bettered our understanding of canyon nomenclature. *Fateful Journey: Injury and Death on Colorado River Trips in Grand Canyon* (1999) by Tom Myers, Christopher Becker, and Larry Stevens, and *Over the Edge: Death in Grand Canyon* (2001) by Michael Ghiglieri and Tom Myers, have convinced us that the Grand Canyon has always been a dangerous place. My own contributions to canyon historiography include *Living at the Edge* (1998), a summary of the Grand Canyon's pioneer era; *Polishing the Jewel* (2000), an economic, political, and developmental history of the park; and *Along the Rim* (2001), an anecdotal history told from viewpoints between Hermits Rest and Desert View. Historians with broader agendas—such as Hal Rothman in *Devil's Bargains* (1998), his analysis of twentieth-century park tourism—have also begun to include the Grand Canyon in their historical models.

The list of recent publications goes on and on, but there is another point to this brief bibliographical account. If John Azar had called in 1990 rather than in 2000, as he did, to suggest a Grand Canyon History Symposium, I would have chuckled and changed the subject. Of course, I was unaware then of the scholarly hum beneath the surface—researchers toiling in archives working on theses, dissertations, and pet projects—but I did have the impression, as I cast about in search of Bill Bass, that Grand Canyon history did not excite many people, and that few would gather to dwell on the subject. Ten years later that impression had changed.

I worked for Mike Buchheit and the Grand Canyon Field Institute in late 2000; our offices were in the historic Community Building at the South Rim. Because Mike has a keen sense for what will work and what will not, and because his entire staff would be knee deep in preparations if a history conference were launched, we talked about it at length. We knew that GCFI instructors were incorporating history into their backpacking trips. Park interpretive rangers were including more of the human story in their programs and many were digging for data. Park interpretive signs touched on the canyon's human past in a richer, more accurate way than I had noticed ten years ago. I had also learned that a whole lot of people floating 5,000 feet below the rim were fascinated with canyon history and that many guides knew more about river history than I ever would. We probed for opinions around the village, and although a few felt that a year was not enough time to prepare an inaugural conference, all agreed that the time *seemed* right and many were willing to help. Mike added his "let's do it" to mine.

Too much transpired between November 2000 and January 2002 to remember, much less recount, everything concerning preparations. We formed a steering committee that crafted a project plan and identified critical paths such as arranging for funding, *then* issuing a call for presentations, *then* developing, printing, and mailing a schedule, *then* taking reservations. We secured a $3,000 grant from the Arizona Humanities Council, in concert with the National Endowment for the Humanities Moving Waters program, and determined that we could pay for the rest with registration and event fees. Our call for presentations went out to more than seventy southwestern colleges and universities, as well as to Arizona museums and archives, and we personally appealed to local historians, prominent folks in other disciplines, and authors we knew. The call, distributed in April 2001, suggested a number of topics (the Civilian Conservation Corps [CCC], the pioneer era, roads and trails, the river, etc.), but solicited anything pertaining to the immediate Grand Canyon region. By September we had attracted forty-three speakers, field-trip leaders, and presenters, and had ironed out accommodations, luncheons, the banquet, field-trip logistics, railroad timetables, internal transportation, parking, meeting facilities, and a host of additional concerns.

The combination schedule and registration form went out in October 2001. Our mailing lists included Grand Canyon Association members, Grand Canyon Field Institute alumni, and members of the Grand Canyon Historical Society, but we also sent copies to everyone else we could think of who might be interested in attending, perhaps four thousand people in all. The front of our brochure read, "Please register now, since, because of meeting room limitations, participation is limited to the first 100 registrants." The statement implies anticipation of a rush, or a commercial appeal, as in, "The supply won't last, so buy now and receive a free set of steak knives; but wait, call in the next five minutes. . . ." The reality was that despite our calculations back in November 2000, and our bet that there was a pent-up demand for canyon history, none of us really had a clue how many people would rise to the bait then bite in the dead of winter. Our fears proved fleeting, however, as we garnered one hundred registrants within three weeks. Thereafter followed three months of regret about the necessity of turning away another two hundred people who wanted to sign up for a sold-out event.

The demand to attend this conference and the diversity of speakers and presenters who shared their research say more about the state of Grand Canyon historiography than my first few paragraphs, Spamer's *Bibliography*, or anyone's review of the published literature. As for diversity, the Arizona Humanities Council insists that events it helps to fund reach out to the general public, but this had always been our intention. Moreover, I wanted professionals as well as avid laypersons to present. Personally, I am familiar with historical models such as Donald Worster's hydraulic society, Patricia Limerick's legacy of conquest, and Immanuel Wallerstein's world system theory, but I am more likely to get excited about Bill Bass's copper mines and what really happened to the Howlands and Dunn.

Although academics with little patience for anecdotal history would be rubbing elbows with storytellers who could care less that the canyon may be characterized as a biological facade, I felt that each would complement the other. In my experience, there are indeed university professors who propose paradigms based on sparse research, as well as researchers who flounder with their favorite topics because they have not been exposed to larger contexts. If we could get some of both to attend and listen to each other, what might we achieve?

Well, we achieved a lot for a first go-around. As organizers, we accepted some criticism that the Community Building was a bit crowded, but there was nonetheless an electrical current running through the crowd that was something to experience. I noticed misty eyes in one pioneer descendent emerging from a talk that touched on his family, and there were lumpy throats aplenty for those who heard Roy Lemons's moving tribute to the CCC. Listeners beamed at Jim Ohlman's presentation of the 1919 trans-canyon tramway survey and seemed fascinated by Bill Bishop's slides of Grand Canyon postage stamps. Between sessions I listened to wide-eyed, animated participants chatting about what they had heard, seen, and *learned*. In fact, a consistent lament was that concurrent sessions allowed participants to attend only half of the presentations, a fact of life with most history conferences but a complaint I found flattering to all of our presenters.

It is impossible to convey in words the value of the interaction that took place, although more than one-third of the participants responded to the postconference questionnaire and all respondents rated their satisfaction level as "pleased" to "ecstatic." It is possible, however, to remark on the importance of the symposium and these proceedings to Grand Canyon historiography. In the preface to my administrative history of the park, *Polishing the Jewel*, I comment on a few historiographical gaps, most notably women's experiences and contributions, the environment, and roles of ethnic minorities, especially American Indians and their long, complex interaction with European Americans. I might add that comprehensive historical approaches to the political issues that plague the park today are also missing. Some of these subjects have been explored in a limited way, and symposium presenters made gains as well, although, upon reflection, they often did so by revealing how far we still have to go.

Polly Welts Kaufman published *National Parks and the Woman's Voice* in 1996, a study of women's roles in the parks from avid tourists of the late nineteenth century to emerging administrators of the 1970s. Two well-illustrated essays in these proceedings by Mary J. Straw Cook and Mona Lange McCroskey amply support Kaufman's portrait of exuberant, articulate female tourists visiting the national parks. Mary Cook's story of the Hollenback sisters at Hance Ranch led me to reflect on John Hance, one of very few bachelors to pioneer canyon tourism and who, along with another bachelor, Louis Boucher, ran the barest-boned operations. The Grand Canyon's earliest tourism businesses were nearly all family affairs—Bill and Ada Bass and their four children (three girls) at Bass Camp; Julius and Cecilia Farlee at Peach Springs and Diamond Creek; Pete and Martha Berry at Grand View; Thomas and Elizabeth McKee, as well as their son Robert, at Bright Angel Point; the Tolfree and Thurber families at Hance Ranch following

Hance's semi-retirement; the Buggelns and their children at Bright Angel Hotel; and several generations of the Church family at the Kaibab Plateau hunting camps. Moreover, wives and kids nearly always did the scheduling, inventory, billing, ordering, bill paying, clothes washing—ran the business, in other words—while husbands were etched in history because they had greater visibility as guides and storytellers. A comprehensive treatment of Grand Canyon tourism, especially its early years, would go a long way toward advancing the histories of canyon women, families, and communities.

Al Richmond contributes to community as well as ethnic history with his essay on regional railroad culture. Almost nothing has been written, much less published, concerning the presence of ethnic minorities at Grand Canyon National Park. Sources are scarce or deeply buried, but there are stories to be told of Japanese working at El Tovar before World War II, Mexicans and Mexican Americans throughout Grand Canyon Village, and Havasupais, Hopis, Navajos, and other American Indians in and around the park. A larger story of the "others," as non-whites and the poor are often called in academia, might include the segregated housing that existed here; the presence of the Ku Klux Klan in the 1920s; the racial, ethnic, and economic mix of construction workers who hefted the materials to develop the park, for better or worse; and the hundreds of desperate families who stopped to labor at the South Rim during the Great Depression rather than continue west on U.S. 66 to harvest the grapes of wrath.

Andrew Majeske addresses the cultural issue of Navajo and Hualapai reservation boundaries with the park in his review of law and legal opinions since the late nineteenth century. Without commenting on the difficult political issue of tribal tourism that lurks in the shadows of such disputes, I am reminded that relations with the federal government at the Grand Canyon must have seemed, and may still seem, bewildering to generations of American Indians. I once delivered a conference paper concerning the Havasupais' accommodations to capitalist economies once their traditional ways of life began to crumble in the face of European-American settlement. The small band of Havasupais shifted from limited farming, hunting, and gathering to ranching and larger scale farming, then to wage labor and finally to tourism as they were confined to a sixty-square-mile reservation, which was quickly reduced to 512 acres (less than 1/60th the size of the original reservation), then enlarged to some two hundred thousand acres in 1975. Along the way, they were alternately encouraged to pursue one economic avenue and discouraged to pursue others by the Departments of War, Agriculture, and the Interior, as these agencies altered their conservationist and preservationist ideas and agendas with nary a thought about

the effects on tribal neighbors. I suspect other tribes have similar histories, and although the government today does listen, I doubt its decision makers reflect on the past as much as neighboring tribal leaders do.

Grand Canyon administrators, tribal members, and special interests would benefit immensely from histories of their relationships and the "issues" that arise from conflicting views. As Park Superintendent Joe Alston noted at the beginning of the symposium, we need to at least think about and, if possible, understand the origins and historical byplay of issues that challenge fair use and biological preservation at the Grand Canyon, such as scenic overflights, river and backcountry use, traffic congestion, and hazardous waste. We tried to attract presenters on the history of issues (but *not* special-interest polemics), and we succeeded in some areas with Majeske's talk as well as Bill Swan's and Jack August's symposium presentations (August's is included in this volume), both reviewing historic river agreements. We also brought some ancillary data to the table. Al Richmond, Mary J. Straw Cook, Mona Lange McCroskey, Leland C. "Lee" Albertson Jr., and I offer essays in this volume that address historic transportation to the Grand Canyon, although a comprehensive study more helpful to modern traffic problems is still wanting. Gretchen Merten, Emma P. Benenati and Joseph P. Shannon, and Janet R. Balsom proffer histories of geomorphology, biological research, and archaeological research, reminding us that scientific surveys and studies supporting resource protection do exist and have increased in recent decades. Another contribution is J. Donald Hughes's overview of preservation versus use, which touches on important aspects of environmentalism within the National Park Service and at the Grand Canyon, but again reminds us that no one has written an environmental history of Grand Canyon National Park.

Our presenters also enriched the story of the CCC and historic river running at Grand Canyon National Park. In these proceedings, Peter MacMillan Booth does a wonderful job setting the CCC context with his essays on the "Civies," their accomplishments in Arizona, and how these young men were educated while they worked, while Louis Purvis and Roy Lemons, both stationed at Grand Canyon CCC camps in the mid-1930s, zero in on the corps' legacy. Members of the park interpretive staff—inspired, I think, by these presentations—have since prepared and presented programs for the seventieth anniversary of the creation of the CCC. Michael P. Ghiglieri and Richard D. Quartaroli share their considerable research on popular river topics, Ghiglieri revisiting and reinterpreting the journal of George Bradley, boatman on John Wesley Powell's first river exploration, and Quartaroli supplying a valuable bibliography of printed river guides as well as an analysis of Powell's navigational tools and knowledge in 1869.

I have neglected some of our presenters in the words above, but rest assured that the Grand Canyon Association has not. They recruited me to accept, organize, and edit every presentation submitted for publication, which, in closing, requires a few words of explanation. We received a wide range of materials, from reworked notes used by presenters in their visual presentations to long scholarly papers replete with exhaustive footnotes. I edited submissions for length, grammar, consistency, and clarity, but have not altered the authors' facts, conclusions, or arguments. I added brief introductions to most of the essays and the publisher included as many of the authors' illustrations as could be reproduced and accommodated. Therefore, the history herein belongs to the authors, the appearance to the Grand Canyon Association. Our hope is that these stories inspire the authors as well as readers to continue to research the Grand Canyon's past and to clamor for another history symposium in the not-too-distant future.

The 1919 Transcanyon Aerial Tramway Survey

by Jim Ohlman

Like many of the symposium's presenters, Jim Ohlman has explored the Grand Canyon for most of his life and has succumbed to the lure of its human history. In this presentation, he assembles all of the evidence for one of the little-known schemes surrounding canyon development. As with the plan to build an aqueduct from the San Francisco Peaks to the South Rim and attempts to build a road to Supai, the idea to string a transcanyon aerial tramway to "enrich" the tourism experience happily expired before getting far off the ground. But, as Ohlman illustrates, originators of this particular idea were serious, had all the backing required initially, and performed most of the preliminary survey before National Park Service Director Stephen T. Mather stepped in to quash the project.

It may be hard to imagine taking a "scenic ride" across the vast expanse of the Grand Canyon in a tiny gondola while suspended some two thousand or more feet above the landscape, but this is precisely what George K. Davol and his band of surveyors had in mind back in 1919. Their idea was simple—at least on paper. Connect the South Rim and the North Rim with a series of suspended cables, linked one to the other by massive steel towers; run a pulley-like device along the cables and attach a tram carriage, or gondola, beneath the pulley; and there you go: the perfect way to view the wonders of the Grand Canyon!

The principle is sound, evidenced by hundreds of alpine ski lifts around the world and by well-known aerial tramways such as those at Mount San Jacinto in southern California and at the Sandia Mountains near Albuquerque, New Mexico. Nevertheless, ideas on paper and principles effective elsewhere ran head-on into reality at the Grand Canyon. It was not some insurmountable engineering obstacle, lack of timely funding, or even lack of public interest that stalled this project; its demise hinged on the politics of conservation versus public use—an unending conflict waged throughout the administrative history of

Grand Canyon National Park. Today, it is obvious to even the most casual visitor that the canyon's rims remain unconnected by a tramway. More subtle are remnants of old camps and survey outposts littered with rusted cans, two-by-fours, and rotted rope—relics of a preliminary survey—and of several small-scale supply trams that were constructed.

Little in the way of written documentation for either the overall project or its preliminary survey has surfaced. What little we know about this survey comes almost entirely from four photographic albums and one letter written by a member of the survey party some fifty-eight years after the fact, but a few additional tidbits are recorded in two books. In 1951 Robert Shankland wrote an engaging biography of Stephen T. Mather, the first director of the National Park Service and one of the men directly responsible for bringing national park status to the Grand Canyon. According to Shankland, George K. Davol, a San Francisco engineer, approached the Santa Fe Railway as early as 1916 with his idea of spanning the canyon with a tramway and received their backing for a preliminary survey (Shankland 1951, 207). In that year the Santa Fe controlled not only passenger and freight service along the Grand Canyon

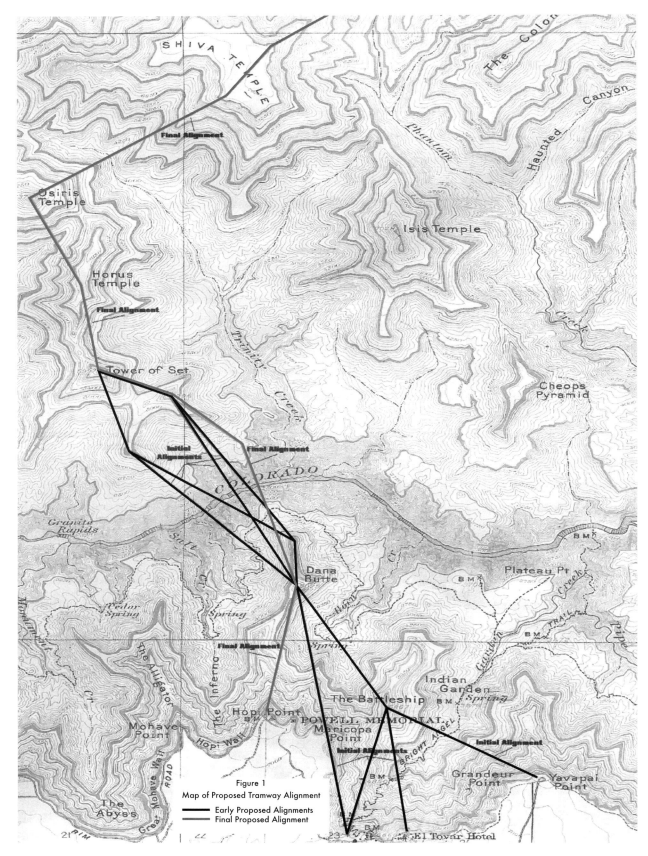

Figure 1
Map of Proposed Tramway Alignment
— Early Proposed Alignments
— Final Proposed Alignment

FIG. 1. *Various alignments considered for the tramway*

Railway, but also most of the utility and visitor services at the South Rim. In their thinking, linking the two rims would broaden their influence at the Grand Canyon by providing an additional "amusement" with which to attract tourists, and at the same time slap a glove in the face of the Union Pacific Railroad, which was trying to establish a presence in the budding tourist business at the North Rim (Anderson 1998, 152, 154).

With the Santa Fe on his side by 1919, Davol was ready to present his case to Stephen Mather (Shankland 1951, 207; Anderson 2000, 10). Mather, however, was busily engaged elsewhere, so his protégé at the Department of the Interior, Horace Albright, considered Davol's plan. Albright held a dim view of commercial "aero plane" activities at the Grand Canyon, but warmly embraced the idea of a trans-canyon tram and was able to elicit the support of Secretary of the Interior Franklin Lane; Francis Farquhar, the future president of the Sierra Club and influential friend of Mather and Albright; and notables at the National Museum (Shankland 1951, 207; Swain 1970, 107). Once Mather had time to study the proposal, however, he voiced strong opposition. To him the notion of tying up "the two rims of this sublime prodigy of nature with wire ropes would be nothing less than monstrous," but Davol did not receive an official refusal until October 1920, when John Barton Payne replaced Lane as secretary of the interior (Shankland 1951, 208).

Donald Swain's 1970 biography of Horace Albright relays a similar version of events, but Swain adds that this was one of the rare occasions when Albright's impulses as an administrator and conservationist ran counter to Mather's. Although Albright's early inclinations favored unrestricted public access to our national parks, under the tutelage of the elder Mather he came to view as more important the need to maintain our parks in near pristine condition (Swain 1970, 108). Nevertheless, between his first trip to Washington in early 1919, and the govern-ment's final "no" on the subject in late 1920, Davol was able to muster a survey team, assemble provisions and supplies, and complete more than half of a preliminary ground sur-vey—all in full sight of park service personnel (Shankland 1951, 208; Thoden 1977).

Information from a variety of sources indicates that the Santa Fe entertained several possible alignments for the transcanyon aerial tram (Santa Fe Railroad n.d.; Shankland 1951; Thoden 1977). One map shows proposed South Rim terminals at Yavapai Point, El Tovar Hotel, Bright Angel trailhead, and Maricopa Point (fig. 1). Three of these align-ments continue to a tower atop the Battleship, and from

there to another tower on Dana Butte. The fourth align-ment passes directly from the Bright Angel trailhead out to Dana Butte. At least four continuations were considered for the next tram segment, north of Dana Butte, but all ended at a tower atop Tower of Set, a spectacular, 6,012-foot-high, red-rock butte 1.5 miles north of the river. The final alignment shows the South Rim terminal at Hopi Point and the tramline extending north to Tower of Set, with three intermediate towers between those two endpoints (Thoden 1977; USDI 1961). Continuing north from Set, all of the proposed alignments cross the summits of Horus, Osiris, and Shiva temples before terminating at Tiyo Point, twelve miles west of Bright Angel Point. The total length of the shortest alignment would have been ten miles, based on Thoden's map.

George Davol and a team of twelve surveyors and pack-ers conducted a preliminary survey from August to November 1919 (Ryan n.d.). Whether Davol obtained local approval is unknown, but it appears park officials did not interfere. The Grand Canyon Railway brought in supplies, and Fred Harvey mules transported them to camps south of the river. The survey proceeded from the South Rim down to a point north of Dana Butte on the south side of the river (fig. 2). A cable-ferry was established about midway between Trinity Creek and Salt Creek, allowing direct, if not easy, access to points north of the river. The survey then continued northward to the top of the Redwall along the east side of Tower of Set (fig. 3). Camps were established at several places along this route, and lightweight "supply trams" were rigged at critical points to ease delivery of needed materials. As the survey neared the east side of Horus Temple, severe snowstorms forced curtailment of further work until the fol-lowing year. Before packing up, Davol and two of his men retraced the entire survey line to photo-document work com-pleted to that point (Thoden 1977).

Davol no doubt anticipated returning to the canyon in 1920 to complete his survey, but park officials had other plans and an aerial tramway was not among them. Mather's notion of a park free of "amusements" and "contraptions" held sway, so Davol moved on to other projects (Shankland 1951). It seems amazing that no subsequent attempts were made during the 1920s and 1930s, when shorter but similar aerial trams were built down to Hermit Camp and Indian Garden, or during the 1950s and 1960s, when much longer trams were constructed in Marble Canyon and far western Grand Canyon. Perhaps it is fortunate that Davol's plans for a transcanyon tram never materialized, as there is no telling how many of Albright's "aero planes" would have met untimely ends by plowing into unseen cables!

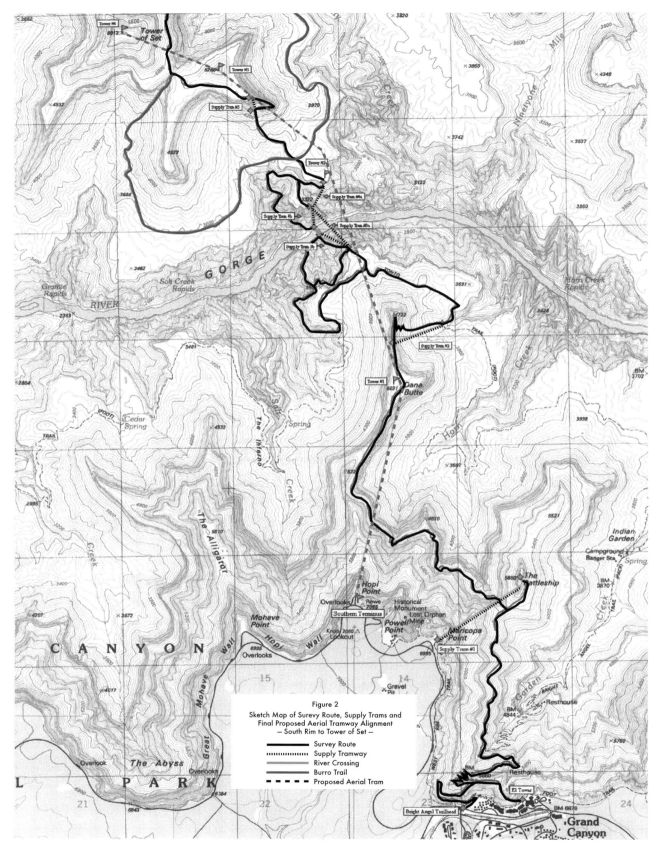

Fig. 2. *The survey route from the South Rim to Tower of Set*

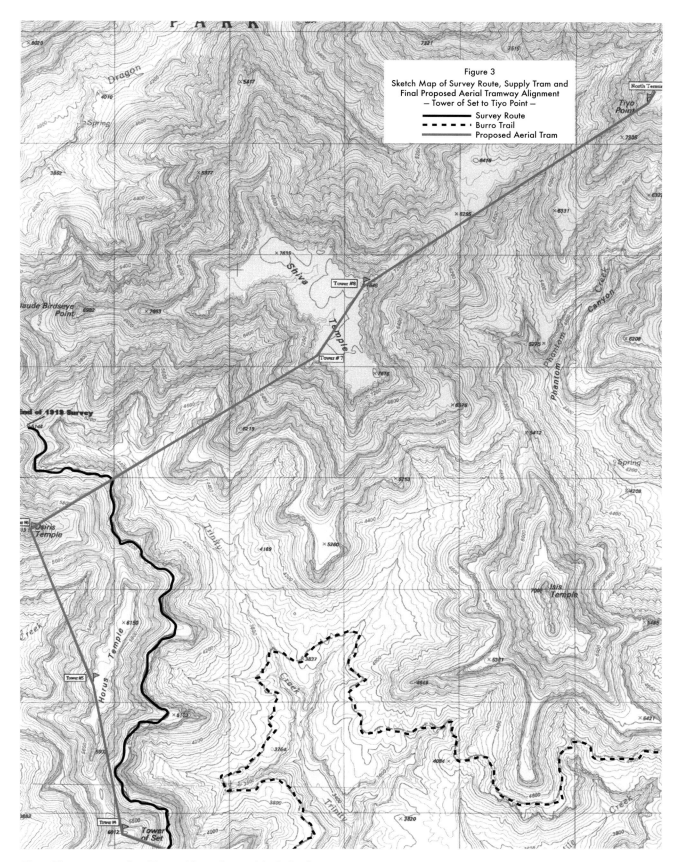

Fig. 3. The survey route from Tower of Set to the top of the Redwall

More Information on the Photographic Albums Featuring the Survey

Colter Album

Mary Colter, a Santa Fe Railway architect who worked at the Grand Canyon in the 1900s through the 1930s, donated the first of four known albums to the national park in April 1952. This album, now in the park's study collection, consists of fifty-four mounted photographs prepared for the Santa Fe to "show views that might be available to passengers if a tramway were built into Grand Canyon" (Colter n.d.). This information is found on the inside front cover of the album in a brief explanatory note written by then-Superintendent Harold C. Bryant. Bryant is correct, but he continues, "Most of these photos were taken from the tramway built and used during construction of the water supply from Indian Garden, completed in 1928." There are two obvious errors here: All of the photographs are from the 1919 survey, and the park service built the Indian Garden pipeline in 1931–32, not 1928. Perhaps Bryant was confusing the water pipeline built by the Union Pacific Railroad from the North Rim to Roaring Springs. That installation also required a supply tram, in use during 1927–28.

In the summer of 1995, Ranger Lon Ayers spent considerable time reviewing these photographs, discerning both their subject material and the possible location of each camera station (Ayers 1995). He had assistance from both Thoden's written account and copies of photographs obtained from the Ryan Album, discussed below, but at that time little field reconnaissance of the survey route had been done and the excellent sequential images of the Spamer Album, also discussed below, were not available. Several interesting features of the Colter Album are worth noting. First, all of the prints measure 6 3/4 by 11 1/4 inches, which is a rather large format for photographs placed in an album. Second, every image bears a number along its lower edge. These numbers are gap-sequential in ascending order from front to back of the album, starting from image #39 and ending with image #233 (image #90 is the only one out of order). These numbers indicate that a series of photographs was initially produced during the survey, and that this particular album contains only those images its compiler considered pertinent for its intended use. I refer to the entire series of numbered prints as the "Santa Fe" images because the following three albums contain additional photos of a different origin. Note that all of the images in this collection are represented in either the Ryan or Spamer albums.

Ryan Album

The Robert L. Ryan Album (Ryan n.d.) resides in Northern Arizona University's Cline Library, Special Collections, and was donated by Ryan's son, Bob Jr., in 1996. Ryan was a member of the 1919 survey team, and he was next in charge of the fieldwork after L. C. Willey and E. Schliewen. The album contains 323 images, 163 of which relate specifically to the tramway survey. Of these, ninety-three are of the type referred to previously as "Santa Fe" images, and another seventy are personal "snapshots" taken either by Ryan or by a designee. At least three duplicate prints are among the Santa Fe images. Whereas the Colter Album has images arranged in near-numerical order, the Ryan Album has them arranged every which way, starting with image #6 (NAU PH97.13.3) and ending with image #239 (NAU PH97.13.76). There are also four unmarked Santa Fe photos (NAU PH97.13.7, 9, and 14–15) that likely fit into the numbering sequence between photos #2 and #38 of the Spamer Album (see below). It is assumed that the numbers were cropped off these images during processing. One key feature of this album is the extensive captioning provided by Ryan. Nearly every page is annotated in some way, providing valuable insight into the survey effort.

Spamer Album

In 2000 Earle Spamer of the Academy of Natural Sciences discovered a third photo album (Spamer n.d.). Spamer retains the original album, but digital copies of the images have been graciously made available to the Cline Library and Grand Canyon's study collection. This album contains 145 images of the 1919 survey. All are presented in strict numerical sequence (using the Santa Fe numbering system), starting with #3 and ending with #240. Obviously, not every image in the set is represented in this album, but to date this is the most inclusive collection of photographs related to the survey that has been found. Seventy-two of the images in this collection differ from those included in either the Colter or Ryan albums, but together these three albums contain 162 out of an assumed total of at least 240 images.

Thoden Album

Along with several postcards, a clipped advertisement, and miscellaneous items, this scrapbook-like album contains sixty-one photos of the Grand Canyon, of which forty-eight are pertinent to the 1919 survey (Thoden n.d.). It was donated to the Grand Canyon study collection by one of Ed Thoden's relatives in December 1989 (Thoden was one of the packers or "camp rustlers" on the survey). While none of the photos appear to be part of the Santa Fe series, what the album lacks in style it makes up for in historicity, as many of the images include details of camp life that are lacking in the more formal collections discussed above.

Most of the photographs in the Thoden Album are personal snapshots of friends and scenes that Thoden wanted to keep alive through the wonder of film. He was less interested in grand scenery than in the people who were in it with him. Images in the Spamer Album are documentary in nature, serving to record progress of the survey and events, rather than daily life of the surveyors. The Ryan Album is a mixture of these two—a record of the survey and surveyors together. The Colter Album appears to be a carefully selected set of official Santa Fe photos, used to either draw attention to highlights of the survey, or perhaps just to convey a memento of the survey to Colter by her friends at the railroad.

Based on the style and content of photographs contained in these four albums, and on scant historical data found elsewhere, it is my opinion that all of the numbered photographs in these albums were commissioned by (and perhaps also produced by) the Santa Fe. Each album appears to have been individualized to suit a particular need, as no one album contains the entire series of images. Indeed, these albums collectively represent less than 70 percent of the known or suspected images. According to Thoden, a large number of images were made after the main survey had been completed and after all but two of the original crew had been discharged. It appears that only a handful of these later images were deemed suitable for inclusion in any of these albums, perhaps because of their overt documentary character. It would be most interesting if future researchers could locate these missing images, as well as the remaining numbered Santa Fe photographs.

THE THODEN LETTER

Prior to 1977 nearly all knowledge of the 1919 survey had been lost, save for one mislabeled set of photographs at the park library and two brief inserts in biographies of Mather and Albright. Physical artifacts connected with the survey were largely undiscovered due to their remote locations, and those that were found brought quizzical looks to passing explorers because their story was unknown. In early 1977 Ranger Tim Manns received a long, handwritten letter from Thoden. This letter contains eighteen pages outlining the work that was done, along with a transcribed map of the route surveyed and a three-part sketch of a typical supply tram (Thoden 1977).

In 1995 the Ryan Album surfaced. Researchers gathered around the new find and a flurry of literary activity followed, resulting in at least two articles or reprints thereof (Chesher 1996; Richmond 1996; Cook and Schafer 1994). Thoden's letter formed the core of the material in the albums, with Ryan's photographs providing the scenic backdrop. The Thoden Album, however, somehow escaped notice during this time, although according to park records it had become part of the study collection in December 1989. Ed Thoden died in April 1988, and with him the last flesh-and-blood connection with this fascinating saga of twentieth-century entrepreneurial activity vanished as well.

WORKS CITED

Anderson, Michael F. 1998. *Living at the edge: Explorers, exploiters and settlers of the Grand Canyon region.* Grand Canyon, Ariz.: Grand Canyon Association.

———. 2000. *Polishing the jewel: An administrative history of Grand Canyon National Park.* Grand Canyon, Ariz.: Grand Canyon Association.

Ayers, Lon. 1995. September 14 letter to Carolyn Richard. Grand Canyon National Park Study Collection, Grand Canyon, Ariz.

Chesher, Greer. 1996. Treasures of the Granite Gorge. *Canyon Journal* (Spring/Summer).

Colter, Mary E. J. n.d. Photo album containing 54 prints of the 1919 survey. Grand Canyon National Park Study Collection, Grand Canyon, Ariz.

Cook, James E., and Paul Schafer. 1994. Exploiters of the Grand Canyon. *Arizona Highways* (February):14–21.

Richmond, Al. 1996. Tram? What tram? *Nature Notes* (Summer):1–3.

Ryan, Robert L. n.d. Photo album with 323 prints of Grand Canyon, 163 relating to the 1919 survey. Cline Library Special Collections, Northern Arizona University, Flagstaff, Ariz.

Santa Fe Railroad. n.d. Map of possible routes from Santa Fe Railroad cross canyon survey. GRCA Image 17350, Grand Canyon National Park Study Collection, Grand Canyon, Ariz.

Shankland, Robert. 1951. *Steve Mather of the national parks.* New York: Alfred A. Knopf.

Spamer, Earle. n.d. Photo album with 145 prints of the 1919 survey. Original album in possession of Spamer; copies in Grand Canyon National Park Study Collection, Grand Canyon, Ariz., and Cline Library Special Collections, Northern Arizona University, Flagstaff, Ariz.

Swain, Donald C. 1970. *Wilderness defender: Horace M. Albright and conservation.* Chicago: University of Chicago Press.

Thoden, Ed K. 1977. Letter to NPS Ranger Tim Manns, received March 12. File Folder #4082. Grand Canyon National Park Study Collection, Grand Canyon, Ariz.

———. n.d. Scrapbook/photo album containing 61 prints of the Grand Canyon, 48 relating to the 1919 survey. GRCA #34654, Grand Canyon National Park Study Collection, Grand Canyon, Ariz.

USDI. 1903. *Bright Angel Quadrangle*. Repr., Washington, D.C.: U.S. Geological Survey, 1961.

RAILS AT BOTH RIMS

BY AL RICHMOND

Al Richmond has been intimately involved with the Grand Canyon Railway since the 1980s, when he walked its entire distance and worked with the present owners as they rebuilt the line to resume passenger service in 1989. Richmond's second presentation at the history symposium (the first, "Grand Canyon's Railroad Culture," appears later in this volume) concerns the contributions of the Santa Fe and Union Pacific railroads toward the development of Grand Canyon National Park. Moreover, he connects past rail service to the present and suggests that railroads may go a long way toward solving or mitigating traffic problems at the canyon's South Rim.

Grand Canyon National Park and its railroads are indelibly linked. The Atchison, Topeka and Santa Fe Railway arrived at the South Rim first, followed some years later by the Union Pacific (UP) Railroad, which served North Rim visitors with motor-coach service from the UP depot in Cedar City, Utah. Both companies brought their particular brand of tourism, architecture, advertising, art, and culture. Each in its own way left its stamp on the canyon through promotion and development of tourism. In 2001 the Santa Fe celebrated the one-hundredth anniversary of the start of passenger service to the canyon; the UP celebrated nothing. The former survives as a re-inaugurated tourist railroad; the latter's connection to the park has passed into dim memory. In the heyday of passenger service, however, both provided superlative transportation to the Grand Canyon. Only the Santa Fe brought the cream of world society, but both supplied the means for everyone to visit the "Titan of Chasms." Nature created a magnet like no other in North America; railroads offered the transport and amenities that made travelers feel welcome.

The Santa Fe's 1910 Titan of Chasms. *Booklets produced by the passenger service department educated travelers about the canyon and enticed them to come visit via the railroad. Author's collection*

In 1900 the short-lived Santa Fe & Grand Canyon Railroad began transporting passengers from Williams forty-five miles north to the end of the track at the mining community of Anita. Pioneer tourists then boarded stagecoaches for the remainder of the trip to the emerging community of Grand Canyon Village, which would have been named Lombard (for a principal's daughter) had the mines remained solvent and a bankrupt Santa Fe & Grand Canyon Railroad not relinquished its holdings to the Atchison, Topeka & Santa Fe Railway later that year. When the Santa Fe pushed the Grand Canyon Railway to the South Rim on September 17, 1901, the first train arrived at a small collection of ramshackle structures, one- and two-room log-and-canvas hovels that posed as hotels. The village offered little more than meals and shelter.

If the Santa Fe planned to attract visitors in large numbers to this community, their intimate gateway to the canyon's South Rim, circumstances had to be altered. They responded with facilities that rivaled the best accommodations found anywhere in the West. Before another decade passed, passengers not only had comfortable transportation to the grand chasm, but first-class hotels and restaurants with running water and electricity, all courtesy of the Santa Fe Railway in partnership with the Fred Harvey Company.

The Santa Fe eventually made the most of their position at the South Rim, but they could not claim the Grand Canyon as their sole realm. The UP gave them strong seasonal competition at the North Rim with a market that included not one but three national parks and one future national monument. The closest UP railway depot was more than 100 miles away at Cedar City, Utah, but passengers could visit the Grand Canyon, Bryce Canyon, Zion, and Cedar Breaks via multi-day, motor-coach tours. In the late 1920s, the railroad's subsidiary Utah Parks Company built lodges and cabins at all three parks and at Cedar City, along with dining facilities at Kanab and Cedar Breaks. Arguably, the most spectacular of these facilities is the Grand Canyon Lodge, located right on the rim of the abyss, its views rivaling those of El Tovar Hotel ten miles directly across the canyon. Unfortunately, like all main-line railroads in the United States, the UP ended passenger operations by the middle decades of the last century. Trains no longer reach Cedar City, and since 1972, Utah Parks Company lodges and other facilities have been transferred to new management or razed.

During its heyday in 1929, the UP offered a complete tour of the three parks and Cedar Breaks via motor coach, with meals and four nights' lodging, including two at the Grand Canyon, for $89.50. For this equitable sum, advertisements also promised to include the entire Kaibab National Forest. To illustrate their marketing literature, the UP's general passenger agent commissioned paintings and photographs (some color-tinted) that rivaled anything produced by their competition.

The Santa Fe also packaged multi-day tours to the South Rim, but relied primarily on booking individual travel to and from the canyon with advance reservations at El Tovar Hotel and Bright Angel cottages. Train fare in the 1920s and 1930s to and from the main line in Williams cost an additional $9.12. Lodging at El Tovar

The Union Pacific's 1926 "Red Book." By this time, the railroad was in competition with the Santa Fe for passengers to the canyon, and the UP produced this booklet that extols the many wonders of the great gorge and Utah's nearby national parks. Author's collection

averaged about $9.00 a day with meals included. Cottages and tents at Bright Angel cost $1.50 to $2.00 per day without meals. For those not staying at El Tovar who wished to dine at the restaurant, breakfast, lunch, and dinner cost from $1.25 to $1.75. All things considered, rates at the North and South rims were comparable. The major difference was the means of transportation: train and motor coach vs. train alone, respectively.

Today, North Rim visitors must arrive in a private motor vehicle or by motor coach. At the South Rim more than 90 percent of vacationers arrive by these means, but they continue to have the option of riding the Grand Canyon Railway from Williams, which deposits them within one hundred yards of the canyon rim. The railway closed its passenger service in the late 1960s, but reopened under new owners in 1989 to revive the convenient and romantic tradition of mass transit to an otherwise congested Grand Canyon Village. In 2004 some 180,000 passengers chose this option, more than twice the number that visited the park via the Santa Fe's tracks in its best year.

Part of the effort to revive the days of superior rail travel to the South Rim and to other parks of the lower Colorado Plateau includes a luxury train service begun in 1994. American Orient Express operates a Southwest Parks Tour from Denver to Albuquerque that mimics to some degree both the old UP and Santa Fe package tours. Using Amtrak power and UP tracks, the Express drops its passengers at Milford, Utah, for transfer to motor coaches that take them to Cedar Breaks, Bryce, and Zion. Passengers reboard at Caliente, Nevada, and make their way to Williams, Arizona, on Burlington Northern Santa Fe tracks. Here they again transfer to motor coaches for the trip to the South Rim, while the train is serviced at Williams in Grand Canyon Railway shops before following up to Grand Canyon Depot. After lunch and tours, passengers rejoin their train at the depot for the southbound journey. Routes are similar to UP and Santa Fe tours between the 1920s and the 1960s.

One may not picture railroad companies as being patrons of the arts, but prior to 1900 and for many years thereafter, all major western lines commissioned paintings of the West for advertising purposes. Although photographers covered many major attractions, their work consisted solely of black-and-white images. The Santa Fe and UP used several of the national parks as attractions to boost ticket sales. Scenic oil paintings and watercolors became mediums of choice. Stellar artists such as Louis Akin, Thomas Moran, and Gunnar Widforss contributed to what became outstanding collections of western paintings. Today these reside in museums around the country or in corporate collections such as the Santa Fe Railway Collection in Fort

In later years, both railroads produced less costly pamphlets that were no less persuasive than their forebears. This Grand Canyon Outings *from the Santa Fe dates to 1927. Author's collection*

Worth, Texas. The latter has been out on loan several times, and a recent tour included several months at the Northern Arizona University Art Museum. The Santa Fe's art revolved around the Grand Canyon, American Indians, the Southwest in general, California, and Yosemite National Park. The UP purchased art depicting the Grand Canyon's North Rim, as well as Bryce, Zion, and Yellowstone national parks.

Whatever their motivation, if not for the railroads, we would not have these priceless works, works which helped Congress decide to create our national parks in the first place.

The Santa Fe's passenger service department made good use of the Southwest's colorful scenery as a lure for travelers. In fact, the Grand Canyon became the emblem of the entire railroad, with all of their advertising throughout the nation carrying the trademark "Grand Canyon Line." This intimacy between the railway and the Grand Canyon derived from the fact that from 1901 through 1968, Santa Fe passengers, once on the Chicago to Los Angeles line, enjoyed a seamless ride to the very edge of the canyon, an experience unique to national park visitors. Trains detached their Pullman cars at Williams while customers slept. They awoke en route to the South Rim and arrived in time for breakfast at El Tovar Hotel.

To lure visitors to the grandest of canyons, both the Santa Fe and UP published dozens of tracts extolling the natural wonder, the comforts offered by their trains, and the luxury of their facilities. Most notable are the Santa Fe's books—*Grand Canyon of Arizona* and *Titan of Chasms*—and the UP's "red book," entitled *Zion, Bryce Canyon, Grand Canyon: 3 National Parks.* As printing costs soared, such high-quality publications went by the wayside, with the Santa Fe opting to produce its *Grand Canyon Outings* pamphlet folded to timetable size. To reduce its publication expenses, the UP cut pages, size, and quality from the books and turned out a similar pamphlet. Both railroads and their associated hospitality companies also published postcards promoting Grand Canyon sites.

Although the UP had its subsidiary Utah Parks Company, the relationship between railway and concessioner was not as intimate as that between the Santa Fe and its independent partner, the Fred Harvey Company. This partnership was forged on a handshake in 1876, and required Fred Harvey

to manage the chain of restaurants and hotels built by the Santa Fe alongside its tracks. Always operated to impeccable standards, Harvey facilities provided quality food and lodging at a level only dreamed of by other railroads of the nineteenth and early twentieth centuries. Passengers passed up trips on other lines for the chance to stay at first-class hotels with delicious, reasonably priced meals served by Fred Harvey's legendary waitresses, the "Harvey Girls."

The Utah Parks Company also provided top-notch service and hospitality at their facilities. Entire staffs at their fine hotels gathered to welcome guests when motor coaches arrived at the entryway. Dining rooms provided excellent meals served by well-trained and personable waiters and waitresses. When it came time to depart, the staff again lined up and sang as passengers boarded motor coaches and drove off to their next destination. This North Rim tradition became known as the "sing away," another nicety of early tourism now consigned to memory.

Many of the early tourism facilities are also only memories, although a few survive in different forms. Williams's Fray

Top: Postcards became a prime means of advertising. Here, Louis Akin's El Tovar Hotel, Grand Canyon *(1904) graces a Fred Harvey Company card dating to 1925. Author's collection*

Bottom: Not to be outdone, the Union Pacific built a superb lodge on the North Rim to rival El Tovar, and the Utah Parks Company also churned out postcards by the thousands, including this 1928 scene. Author's collection

Marcos Hotel has been partially restored and serves beside today's Grand Canyon Railway depot as both a hotel and temporary home of the Arizona State Railroad Museum. The Fred Harvey name is still remembered by longtime residents and occasionally used in advertising, but the family-run company has since passed into the hands of corporate concessioners. Amfac, recently renamed Xanterra, took over Fred Harvey operations at the South Rim in 1968, while Utah Parks left the North Rim in 1972, donating its facilities to the national park. In 1995 Amfac acquired the concession to manage former Utah Parks facilities at the North Rim.

The Santa Fe worked with the Fred Harvey Company for South Rim accommodations and dining, and the company developed a reputation for excellent service. To compete, the Utah Parks Company also provided excellent service. One of their appreciated touches was the "sing away." Here, the lodge staff sings farewells to guests departing from Grand Canyon Lodge. Author's collection

As for the Santa Fe heritage, one can still ride the Grand Canyon Railway and arrive within yards of the South Rim in a style not all that different from a century ago. Trains are steam- or diesel-powered with vintage cars that summon bygone days. But the railway serves another purpose beyond offering a nostalgic, scenic ride. Annual park visitation has neared five million people in recent years, and automotive congestion in the summer months, aggravated by inadequate parking, is an unpleasant introduction to the park experience. However, the train from Williams offers a relaxing ride without the hassles of waiting at entry stations, fighting traffic, and vying for parking space.

The historic rail concept may someday provide further solutions to traffic congestion. In the 1990s the Grand Canyon Railway entered into a design and bidding process to provide a light-rail system to the South Rim's new Visitor Center and to the village Historic District. When the park service changed the proposal and pushed projected costs beyond bidders' ability to compete, the railway proposed a study of a high-speed rail system that would transport passengers at motor-vehicle speeds between Williams and the South Rim. Under this proposal, visitors would use the alternative rail system if the park service closes the park to privately owned motor vehicles. This plan also allows motor coaches unrestricted access and privately owned motor vehicles access until a predetermined number is reached.

Studies conducted by Northern Arizona University's Center for Data Insight, Social Research Laboratory, and Arizona Hospitality Research and Resource Center indicate that many travelers are willing to park their vehicles in Williams rather than wait at the entrance station and then fight for parking space. The station in Williams would be co-located with the Arizona State Railroad Museum and provide adequate parking. This proposal creates a motor-vehicle destination at Williams that would improve the economies of Williams and Flagstaff with minimal impact on Grand Canyon and Tusayan businesses. Best of all, it is a user-friendly, environmentally sensible idea that will relieve congestion on Arizona Highway 64 and within the park. In 2001 members of the Arizona and Ohio congressional delegations directed the park service to revisit the light-rail proposal to determine if it is the best alternative for mass transit to the park.

Railroads opened Grand Canyon National Park's North and South rims to the world a century ago. They also created the tourism infrastructure that endures to this day. One can hope that with both federal and private-sector leadership, iron rails will one day again play a dominant role in transporting visitors to this scenic wonder in a less intrusive manner than offered by private motor vehicles.

Suggested Readings

Anderson, Michael F. 1998. *Living at the edge: Explorers, exploiters and settlers of the Grand Canyon region.* Grand Canyon, Ariz.: Grand Canyon Association.

Athearn, Robert G. 1977. *Denver & Rio Grande Western Railroad.* Lincoln: University of Nebraska Press.

Klein, Maury. 1987. *Union Pacific,* vols. 1 and 2. New Haven, Conn.: Yale University Press.

Myrick, David F. 2000. *Railroads of Arizona,* vols. 4 and 6. Wilton, Calif.: Signature Press.

Richmond, Al. 2002. *Cowboys, miners, presidents and kings: The story of the Grand Canyon Railway,* 5th ed. Flagstaff, Ariz.: Grand Canyon Railway.

Runte, Alfred. 1998. *Trains of discovery: Western railroads and the national parks.* Niwot, Colo.: Roberts Rinehart Publishers.

Chapter Three

KOLB AIRFIELD 1926

BY LELAND C. "LEE" ALBERTSON JR.

Brothers Emery and Ellsworth Kolb traveled west from Pennsylvania in the first years of the twentieth century to become two of the earliest residents of Grand Canyon Village. They built Kolb Studio in 1904, and although Ellsworth left for Los Angeles in the 1910s (returning frequently for visits thereafter), Emery stood fast to raise a family and run his photography business at the canyon's edge until his death in 1976. For more than half a century the two men made Grand Canyon history by taking the first motion pictures of the Colorado River through the Grand Canyon in 1911–12, exploring and photographing the inner canyon's nooks and crannies, and becoming guides and advisors for generations of river runners, hikers, and backpackers. In this presentation, Lee Albertson chronicles his extensive research into Emery's efforts to promote canyon aviation and tracks down the exact location of his elusive airfield.

Emery Kolb witnessed the earliest modes of transportation to the Grand Canyon of the Colorado. Horse-drawn stagecoaches brought passengers from Flagstaff and Williams to the South Rim in the 1890s and early 1900s. The Grand Canyon Railway replaced stages soon after 1901, and private automobiles in turn began to compete with the railway in the 1910s. Always the entrepreneur, Emery no doubt heard or read about "flying machines" by this time. Stories of people traveling coast-to-coast by air in just a few days would likely have stirred his interest. He certainly observed or learned of the first flights over the canyon in 1919, and he participated in others of the early 1920s. His fertile imagination went to work. Why not offer commercial sightseeing flights over the Grand Canyon? Why not land a plane within its depths? Why not pick up passengers at a siding along the railway, take them directly to a South Rim airfield, and then fly them over to the North Rim?

Today I will illustrate Emery Kolb's enthusiasm for the new mode of canyon transportation and his attempts to get in on the ground floor, but first I will acknowledge others who helped me to understand this story. I began my search by talking with Ron Warren and by reading his research of the early years of Grand Canyon aviation. Interviews with

Loren "Tiny" Lauzon, Bill Suran, and Gale Burak helped tremendously, as did regional history and photographs shared by canyon historian Mike Anderson and park photographer Mike Quinn. Al Richmond, researcher and author on the Grand Canyon Railway, supplied valuable background information. Ron Werhan, with his knowledge of early regional road systems, helped fit pieces into the puzzle. Harvey Butchart, as always, contributed his knowledge of inner-canyon events, and Edith Cole, Michael Harrison, Pat Lauzon, Bernice Meadows, Candace Owens, and Dan Tobin responded with informative letters. Larry Rallens and H. G. Frautschy provided information on the Lincoln Standard Biplane; Pete Eno accompanied me to the Kolb Airfield, once discovered, to help take pictures; and Jack Stanton supplied computer graphics to annotate and highlight map features. My wife Shirley checked my information and corrected many mistakes.

My interest in Emery Kolb's airfield was first aroused by a short paragraph in the *Bulletin* of the Grand Canyon Pioneers Society (today the Grand Canyon Historical Society) of October 1995, which mentioned Ron Warren's article in the summer 1995 edition of the *Journal of Arizona History* entitled "Aviation at Grand Canyon: A 75-Year

History." I read Ron's article about an airplane landing below Indian Garden at Plateau Point in 1922. Ellsworth Kolb photographed this event, which likely incited Emery to build his airfield. When the National Park Service rejected his request to build a landing strip inside park boundaries, Emery contacted the U.S. Forest Service and obtained permission to build on a mining claim near canyon pioneer Bill Bass's White House just outside the park boundary. A photograph sent to me by Bill Suran indicates that Emery cleared the airstrip in 1925 using a county or park service road grader.

A year passed and no one landed at Kolb Airfield. Was this poor marketing on Emery's part or poor sense on the part of commercial aviators who did not see a market for sightseeing flights over the Grand Canyon? Finally, Charley Mayse, who probably operated from an airfield at Williams, took the first paying passengers on a sightseeing flight over the Grand Canyon. Emery contacted Mayse after that flight and talked him into making the only documented landing at Kolb Airfield on June 16, 1926. Photographs taken by the Kolbs on that date include one of the passengers and the crew standing around the Lincoln Standard Biplane and the crew checking the plane prior to takeoff. In 1977 negatives of these photographs were found in a dusty box of junk stored in the Kolb Studio garage.

When I contacted Ron Warren to congratulate him on his fine article, I asked him where the Kolb Airfield had been located. He replied that it did not appear on any map of which he was aware. The concept of a lost canyon airfield caused me to embark on a personal quest to learn more about the airfield's operations and to find out where it had been located. I learned that one of my neighbors is a granddaughter of Bill Stout, an early aviator who designed and manufactured airplanes, including the Tri-Motor and

Aircoup. Warren's research indicated that Emery Kolb had tried to interest Stout in a joint venture to establish sightseeing tours and an air shuttle between the South and North rims. It would be Emery's job to furnish the airfield and business savvy while Stout supplied the airplanes and aviation expertise. Stout directed his chief pilot, Parker Van Zandt, to make inquiries with Fred Harvey Company officials, who disliked Emery Kolb and discouraged any form of business dealings with him. Van Zandt instead obtained landing permits at both rims from the forest service and built his own airfield at Red Butte.

So much for Emery's efforts to pioneer scenic flights, but where was his airfield? This was the more difficult search, but I picked up bits and pieces from people familiar with canyon history. Mike Anderson provided a photograph showing the Lincoln Standard Biplane on the ground at the Kolb Airfield, but knew nothing of its location. Harvey Butchart also knew nothing of the location, but was familiar with the landing at Plateau Point. Michael Harrison, who worked at the South Rim from 1922 to 1931, had not heard of the airfield, but personally recalled the inner-canyon landing. Ethel Cole, Ron Werhan, Dan Tobin, Lenora Bass, and Bernice Meadows responded to my inquiries, but could not provide a spot on the map.

Then I interviewed Loren "Tiny" Lauzon, who was born in a boxcar at Rowe Well and worked at the canyon until his retirement to Prescott Valley. His father was Hubert "Bert" Lauzon, who accompanied the Kolbs on the second leg of their famous river trip in 1911–12 and worked many years as a park service ranger at the South Rim. His mother was Edith Bass Lauzon, daughter of canyon pioneers William and Ada Bass. I visited Tiny twice, and he supplied a wealth of information about the Bass family hotel, stage stop, and area roads. He drew a

The Lincoln Standard bi-plane landing at Kolb Airfield, 1926. Grand Canyon National Park Museum Collection (#11040)

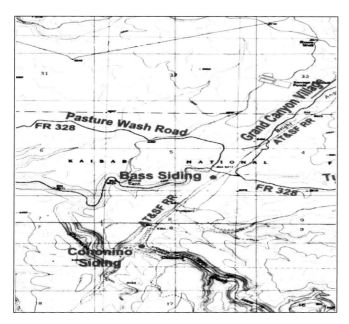

Map A. Modern identifying features have been added to the 1988 Bright Angel 15' quadrangle in the area where Kolb Airfield was likely located.

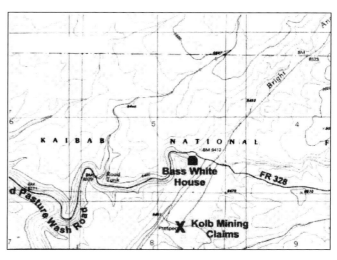

Map B. Features from the 1920s included in a close-up of a portion of the same area shown in Map A.

map identifying the location of Bass's White House, the old road to Tusayan and Pasture Wash, the path of the railway, and yes, the Kolb Airfield stretched out along the tracks. Both Ethel Cole and Bill Suran confirmed Tiny's knowledge of the area, Ethel having known him for a long time and Bill having interviewed Tiny on similar subjects while researching his history, *The Kolb Brothers of Grand Canyon*, published by the Grand Canyon Natural History Association in 1991.

I then interviewed Gale Burak and Bill Suran in August 1998. Gale had been Emery Kolb's personal secretary during the last years of his life in the early 1970s. She helped organize his papers and identify and organize his photographs. She remembered a day when Emery said, "Let's go out to the site of the airfield." He told her about the Lauzon homestead (Bass's White House) and the airfield across the road, and mentioned the name "White Fang" or "White Wolf."

I researched files in the Coconino County Recorder's Office in Flagstaff in December 2001 and found that Emery had filed two mining lode claims in the mid-1920s. The first was the Thunder Bird Lode, recorded November 25, 1925, in the Frances Mining District, about five miles south of Grand Canyon Village at Bass Siding on the east side of the tracks and adjacent to Donaldson's mining claim. The second was the White Hawk, recorded August 13, 1927, in the Frances Mining District and located about two miles in a northerly direction from Coconino Station on the railway. The White Hawk claim was probably the

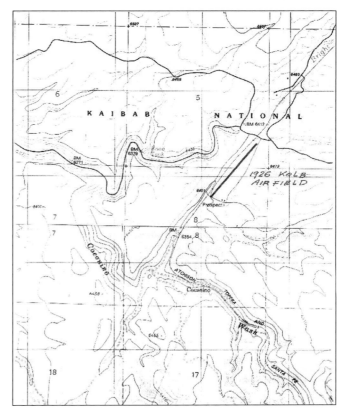

Map C. Kolb Airfield as it was positioned in 1926 on the two Kolb mining claims.

A panoramic photograph of the Kolb Airfield site, taken on December 7, 2001. The viewpoint is looking east from FDR 788 parallel to and to the west of the Grand Canyon Railway tracks. Photograph by the author

claim Gale Burak had recalled in 1998. Emery's two claims were contiguous, forming a 2,800-foot-long property on the east side of the tracks in the very location recalled by Tiny Lauzon.

Still trying to pin down the location on a map, I found a Kaibab National Forest Timber Atlas from the 1920s at the U.S. Forest Service Williams office that covered T30N R2E Sections 5 and 8. Map A identifies the location of Coconino Siding and the Bass Flag Stop, which was also known as Bass Siding, across the tracks from Bass's White House. Map B identifies the White House (built in 1906 and demolished in the 1950s, according to Steve Verkamp) and the Kolb mining claim, positioned as indicated in county records. Finally, Map C identifies the 1926 Kolb Airfield.

Thus ended my mission to place the Kolb Airfield on the map, but I was still interested in the only aircraft to land at this spot, the Lincoln Standard Biplane piloted by Charley Mayse. I do not know what happened to this particular craft, but according to Larry Rallens, a retired

commercial pilot living in Mesa, Arizona, it was manufactured by the Lincoln Aircraft Company of Lincoln, Nebraska, between the years 1923 and 1925. Models included two- and three-seat open cockpit "sport" types and a five-seat "cabin cruiser," each powered by a single 150-horsepower engine. In a letter received from H. G. Frautschy, director of the Vintage Aircraft Association, I learned that this type of plane "could very well have taken off from a relatively short strip, say 2,500 feet, in the early morning cool air. But later in the heat of the day, it may have been impossible at 6,400 feet elevation." The Kolb mining claims allowed for a 300-foot-wide, 2,800-foot-long airfield, and photographs seem to indicate that it was a cool morning when the plane landed and took off.

As a historical footnote, Charles A. Lindbergh was a student pilot at the Lincoln Aircraft Company. What a shame that in all his barnstorming across the nation, he did not choose to land at Emery's landing strip, providing the advertisement that may have placed Kolb Airfield on the map seventy-five years earlier.

LELAND C. "LEE" ALBERTSON JR.

GRAND CANYON NATIONAL PARK TOLL ROADS AND TRAILS

BY MICHAEL F. ANDERSON

My love for the Grand Canyon trails began in 1990 when the National Park Service hired me to write a history of the North Bass and South Bass trails. This assignment led to more research, and, with colleague Debra Sutphen, we later nominated ten of the canyon's more popular paths to the National Register of Historic Places. Today I work as the park's trails archeologist, a job that requires me to hike the trails, record their historic structures with an eye toward preservation, and write of their history. In this presentation, I argue that many of the canyon's early trails, not just the Bright Angel, were built as toll roads, and that their builders were betting on the boom promised by the arrival of the Grand Canyon Railway.

Arizona became a territory of the United States in 1863. Soon thereafter, its legislature assigned to the counties the responsibility to build and maintain roads, passing laws to provide guidelines for both public roads and privately constructed toll roads. Considering the importance of roads to commerce, alongside chronic impoverishment of county and territorial coffers, it is no surprise that legislators encouraged citizens to build and maintain their own roads. For these reasons, laws remained consistently generous and simplistic throughout the territorial period. They are, in fact, still on the books, and a glance at today's state statutes reveals that it is still possible to build your very own toll road.

My presentation at this symposium concerns toll roads and trails that were built or simply conjured by enterprising businessmen at the Grand Canyon in the years 1891 through 1903. These years coincide with the imminent promise of the Grand Canyon Railway's arrival in September 1901, years when astute local residents sensed an impending tourism boom at the South Rim. Research in the County Recorder's Office at Flagstaff uncovered no claims outside this date range. I therefore suggest that early prospectors and tourism operators were betting on the

canyon's potential in relation to a railway and not responding to needs of the 1890s when travel to the South Rim in horse-drawn conveyances remained light. Moreover, although savvy locals with canyon interests expected and promoted a railway to the South Rim throughout these years, and, to a lesser degree, a railway to the North Rim in the years that followed, the wide geographic distribution of claims suggests pioneer gamblers' uncertainty as to the exact terminus of a railroad and the manner in which inner-canyon travel patterns would develop.

To understand the importance of proprietary travel routes to early residents, and their willingness to build them, it is helpful to consider contemporary laws concerning their construction and operation. Laws passed in 1887 and 1901, which guided claimants in the canyon's early pioneer period, were nearly identical. Anyone could file a certificate with the county recorder that supplied the name of the road, its two termini, and a plat map that could be hand drawn and, as we will see in the following illustrations, not necessarily clear, to scale, or resembling geographic reality. Claimants usually included a general description of the route, although it was not required. The builder had to

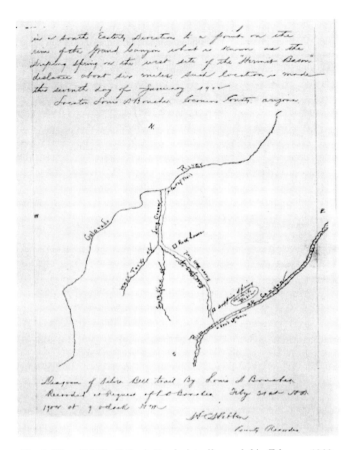

Fig. 1. Silver Bell Trail. Louis Boucher's trail, recorded in February 1902 as a "right-of-way." He more or less accurately depicted what are today called the Dripping Springs and Boucher trails. Boucher claimed nothing east of Dripping Springs, and I found no indication that anyone claimed the Waldron Trail or an earlier version of the Hermit Trail. Courtesy of Coconino County Recorder's Office

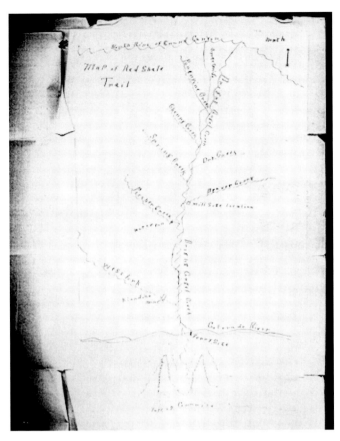

Fig. 2. Red Shale Toll Trail. Porter Guffy and Wash Henry, Flagstaff residents and canyon prospectors, filed this strategic claim in November 1901, less than two months after the arrival of the Grand Canyon Railway. Note the old names of tributaries to Bright Angel Creek. The trail south of the river is the path of David Rust's Cable Trail, today's South Kaibab through the schist. The trail north of the river is the oldest version of today's North Kaibab Trail. Rust may have negotiated with Henry to acquire his rights in 1906–07. Courtesy of Coconino County Recorder's Office

begin construction within thirty days of his claim and continue with "reasonable dispatch" until completed. He was assigned the power of eminent domain for a forty-five-foot right-of-way through private property. Once completed, the builder was allowed to set a reasonable charge (that could be challenged by any ten taxpayers if they thought it too high) and was required to post the fare on a billboard at each tollgate. He had to keep records, file quarterly reports, and pay the county 2 percent of receipts. After three years, if receipts in any one year exceeded 50 percent of the cost of construction, he was required to pay the entire excess to the state school fund.

The builder was responsible for keeping his road or trail in good (meaning safe) condition, and he was "liable" for any injuries to travelers if proved negligent in this responsibility. He was subject to prosecution if he charged more than the posted rates; likewise, travelers who tried to circumvent tollgates were subject to fifty-dollar fines. The

builder was allowed to operate the road or trail for ten years; however, the county could opt to buy it after the initial five years. At the end of the first ten years, the county at its discretion could extend the franchise for another five years. After that time—fifteen years in all—ownership passed to the county, which could continue to operate the road or trail, and could collect tolls or declare it a "free highway."

Most lovers of canyon history are familiar with the battle to control the Bright Angel Toll Road, recorded in 1891, and more commonly called the Bright Angel, or Cameron's, Trail. This divisive struggle permeated early South Rim history, and, among other issues relevant to public versus private rights, underscores the importance of proprietary roads and trails to their builders. Without recounting the various tactics and strategies of this twenty-year conflict, suffice it to say that Ralph Cameron, chairman of the Coconino County Board of Supervisors from 1905 to 1907, convinced the territorial legislature to pass a new toll road law, known at the time as the "Cameron Law." Cameron had good economic reasons to push for such a law, since he had spent money on the Bright Angel's construction in 1890–91, and again in 1897–1900, yet did not charge tolls until 1903, just three years prior to the legal expiration of the franchise. This had hardly been enough time to secure a reasonable return on his and his partners' investments.

The new legislation, effective as of March 1907, lengthened the franchise extension from five to ten years, and stipulated that if the county had taken control of the road at the time of the law's passage, the original builder(s) could regain control and retain authority over the route for the full ten-year extension. Cameron's partner, Pete Berry (official recorder of the trail) had surrendered the franchise to the county in early 1906, in accordance with the terms of the 1887 and 1901 laws. The new legislation succinctly allowed Berry and his partners, including Cameron, to regain the franchise. In addition, prior laws had not mentioned the legality of transferring toll road privileges from the builder to another party, but the courts, over the course of several decisions between 1904 and 1906, ruled that it had been illegal for Berry to transfer the Bright Angel franchise to Cameron in 1901. The new law reversed these court decisions and, retroactively, legalized Cameron's original sole acquisition in 1901.

The new law also stipulated that if original owners did not ask for an extension within thirty days of expiration, another party could acquire the franchise for five years and keep all receipts, paying only a "reasonable percentage" to the county. If the owners had lost the franchise for any reason prior to this act (which Berry and his friends did in early 1906), they were given thirty days after passage of this law to reapply for the additional five years. These new clauses in the toll road law allowed Berry to reapply or, if he chose not to, allowed Cameron as an original owner as well as a transferee to reapply. Cameron in fact did reapply, reacquiring the franchise in his own name in 1907 and subsequently holding it until 1912. Note that it was in 1907, no doubt in response to the new law's "reasonable percentage" clause, that the Santa Fe offered to pay the county 70 percent of receipts and provide liability insurance if they were awarded the franchise. The three-man county board, however, with Ralph Cameron as its chair, awarded it to Ralph Cameron, businessman, for only 12 percent of receipts.

Several additional changes in the 1907 law seem intended to protect Ralph Cameron's interests in the event his rights were ever again questioned. A new clause clarified toll "roads" to include "trails," which could be built in "mountains or precipitous places" where vehicular roads were not practicable. Former laws did not mention trails at all, although this seemed to be understood and common practice, as many claimants in the period between 1891 and 1903 identified their claims as a toll "trail," or "toll road or trail." This new provision, too, was made retroactive to the beginning of the toll road statutes. Another clause indicated that the road or trail did not have to follow its plat map exactly, but only the "general course" between two specified termini. Pete Berry's original 1891 Bright Angel plat is quite specific, delineating in fact the length of tangents between switchbacks to the nearest foot. The actual trail probably did not follow the plat exactly, and this provision covered that possibility.

Finally, and somewhat mysteriously, the 1907 law provided that any road on which tolls had been regularly collected for a year or more prior to January 1907, and which had been maintained as a toll road, was declared valid under this and previous laws. The only road or trail in the Grand Canyon region that fulfilled both requirements was the Bright Angel (and probably the Lees Ferry Toll Road).

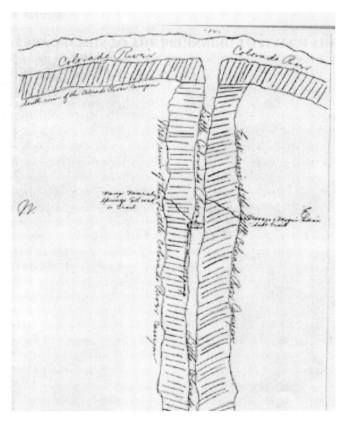

Fig. 3. Navajo Mineral Springs Trail. Recorded by Ralph and Niles Cameron in November 1902. Ralph Cameron is speculating outside his normal turf in the central Corridor. The certificate reads that the trail runs from the Little Colorado Rim at a point twelve miles upstream from the confluence with the Colorado River, about 3.5 miles south of the "Old Navajo and Moqui Indian Salt Trail," and down to Navajo Mineral Springs (Blue Springs)." A notice of the trail in a monument of stones is supposed to be at each end. Courtesy of Coconino County Recorder's Office

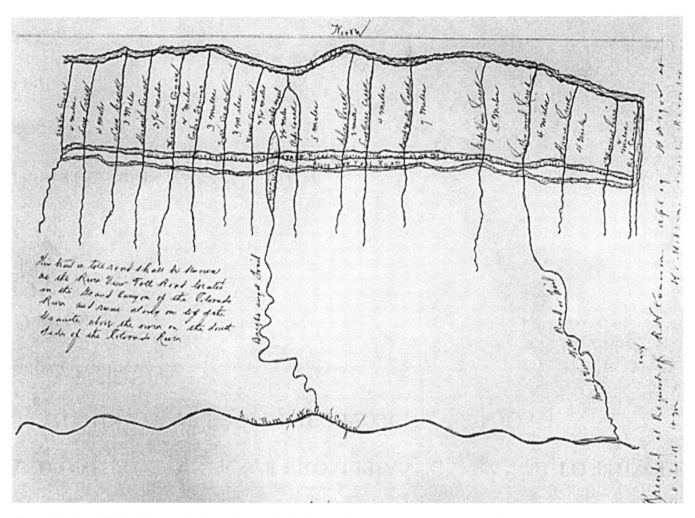

Fig. 4. River View Toll Road. Recorded by Ralph Cameron in March 1902. Cameron is claiming most of today's Tonto Trail, which was developed by many early pioneers, including Cameron, on an ad hoc basis. Note the pioneer names of side canyons and creeks from Red Canyon to Slate Creek. Courtesy of Coconino County Recorder's Office

Was the intent simply to clarify the Bright Angel Trail as a toll road, or was it to render all prior claims to canyon toll roads null and void by virtue of not meeting these requirements? If the latter, it would nullify any claims that Pete Berry might have to the Grand View Trail, or Bill Bass might have to the Mystic Spring Toll Trail (today's South Bass Trail as far as the Esplanade), among many others. Was this a Cameron compromise to territorial legislators, as in, "we will help you on this one, Ralph, but we don't want any more of these battles coming our way?" It seems uncharacteristic for Cameron, a popular man among territorial residents, to sell out contemporaries like Berry, Louis Boucher, and others who had built and claimed canyon toll trails. Then again, Cameron had laid claims to a trail through Hermit Basin to the river and to most of the Tonto Trail in 1902. He had built neither of these, at least not on his own, and did not seem concerned about his friends' interests.

In any event, the Cameron Law was written in extraordinary detail to benefit one and only one person. This fact did not escape the keen eye of the noted jurist and Arizona's federally appointed governor, Joseph Kibbey, who vetoed the bill faster than you can say "Ralph Cameron." The legislature, however, elected by territorial residents who favored individual enterprise and admired Cameron, mustered the two-thirds vote necessary to override the veto faster than you can say "we beg to differ." The bill became law on March 18, 1907. Within two years, the Santa Fe Railway and the federal government (for the time being) gave up their struggle for control of the Bright Angel Trail. Instead, in 1909 railroad managers allied themselves with the U.S. Forest Service, the administrator of the one-year-old Grand Canyon National Monument, and went to work building Hermit Rim Road (today's Hermit Road), Hermit Trail, and Hermit Camp to circumvent Cameron's lock on the central trail corridor.

Cameron's one-man war against anyone who would

interfere with his trail rights and his manipulation of territorial laws were a direct result of the Grand Canyon Railway's arrival near his trailhead in 1901. The railway passengers created demand for this inner-canyon trail, so it made economic sense for Cameron to erect a tollgate, hire gatekeepers, charge his one-dollar toll, and fight for his interests. We can speculate that had the railway arrived at Grandview Point or Bass Camp (alternative destinations considered in the late 1880s and 1890s), Pete Berry or William Wallace Bass—pretty hardheaded individualists themselves—would have reacted similarly. The fact that they and others lost the railway gamble and did not have the opportunity to capitalize on their claims in no way diminishes their investments, labors, and aspirations to make a decent living by building Grand Canyon's approach roads and inner-canyon trails.

I conclude my presentation with a few words on road and trail claims that I have documented in past years, and plat maps for other such claims. The number of claims and their geographic diversity supports several conclusions. Canyon pioneers were hopeful entrepreneurs, willing to risk their meager capital and physical labor in hopes of future rewards. In the process, they identified and in many cases built the first approach roads and inner-canyon trails that connected the canyon with the outside world, facilitating the canyon's only viable economic base: tourism. Some of these roads and trails, or at least their general routes, are familiar to us today, because they became strategic avenues of tourist travel in succeeding years. Others are puzzling in any context, but interesting. The following list includes the claimants and their routes:

- William Bass, today's South Bass Trail to the Esplanade, called Mystic Spring Toll Trail when recorded in August 1891
- William Bass, wagon road from Williams to Bass Camp, called Grand Cañon Toll Road (fig. 5), November 1891
- W. H. Ashurst, John Marshall, C. H. McClure, and T. C. Frier, all experienced canyon prospectors, recorded the Cottonwood Toll Road in December 1891. Its route, or proposed route, began at the rim about four miles west of the old Hance Trail, "above and opposite the head of Cottonwood Creek," thence down Cottonwood Creek, east across the Tonto Trail below Horseshoe Mesa to the Water Front Mine, a distance of about seven miles. If built, the upper segment may have been an earlier version of the Grandview Trail, improved by Berry and his partners for stock use a year later. The middle segment could be today's Cottonwood Creek Trail. The terminal segment description resembles the

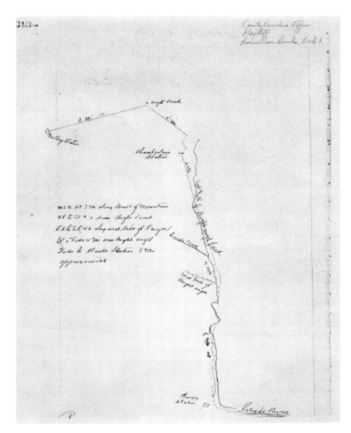

Fig. 5. Grand Canyon Toll Road. Recorded by E. D. Woolley, president of the Grand Canyon Transportation Company, in June 1903. This claim envisions a road from Harvey Meadow to "Hoyts Point" in Fuller Canyon, where Woolley and son-in-law David Rust maintained a cabin; then along today's E-2 fire road to the rim above Bright Angel Creek at "Chamberlain Station"; then along a trail that overlaid Guffy and Henry's Red Shale Toll Trail to the river. Rust built the trail and a cable across the river in 1906–07. Chamberlain was a prominent Arizona Strip resident and investor in the company. Rust used these proprietary roads and trails in summer seasons from 1909 through 1919. Courtesy of Coconino County Recorder's Office

current Tonto Trail and the long-abandoned and unnamed trail down into the schist at Hance Creek.
- Julius Farlee, stage road from Peach Springs to the Colorado River recorded ca. 1893 in Mohave County (all other claims in this presentation are from Coconino County)
- Ralph Cameron, stock trail to Horseshoe Mesa (Grandview Trail), called Grand View Toll Road when recorded in March 1893. Sole ownership later passed to Pete Berry in exchange for his Bright Angel Trail interests.
- John Marshall, C. H. McClure, T. C. Frier, John Hance, and William Ashurst, an unnamed trail down Red Canyon and across the river through Hance's asbestos claims and very likely to Clear and Bright Angel creeks—a total distance of twenty-seven miles,

per the claim. Recorded in January 1894, the first eight miles south of the river is today named the New Hance Trail, but it has also been called the Red Canyon Trail.

- Buckey O'Neill, trail from "O'Neill Camp" (today's O'Neill Cabin) to the river via Indian Garden. This overlays the Bright Angel Trail. Buckey called it Indian Gardens Toll Road when recorded in November 1897, and it is known that he worked on this trail in that year. Cameron and O'Neill probably had words over this, but they also had common interests and, in any event, O'Neill died in 1898. What a battle that would have been!

- James S. Emett, a wagon road from a point named North Gate one and one-half miles west of Lees Ferry north of the river, to a point named South Gate one and one-half miles west of the ferry south of the river, the entire road named the Lee's Ferry Toll Road when recorded in May 1898. Emett in fact did rebuild the old Mormon emigrant road near the river and charged tolls at the ferry.

- William F. Hull, P. C. Bicknell, W. F. McAdams, a two-and-one-half-mile unnamed trail from a point on Horn Creek straight down to the river, reportedly marked by stone monuments, recorded in July 1901

WHATEVER HAPPENED TO JAZZ?

BY GEORGE STECK

In 1979 the United Nations Educational, Scientific and Cultural Organization (UNESCO) named Grand Canyon National Park a world heritage site in recognition of its importance to humankind. George Steck, an inveterate canyon hiker, offers his perspective on how small the world really is in relation to the Grand Canyon. Yes, he had us wondering about the title of his presentation, but with a fair amount of ad lib, it turned out to be one of the most appreciated talks at the symposium. I am saddened to write that George passed away in the spring of 2004, but I am sure that his family and many friends will appreciate this reminder of his sense of humor.

What I have to offer in this presentation is a series of stories concerning people and circumstances I have encountered over my years of hiking in the Grand Canyon. It is not science in the sense of geology or archaeology, but rather history in the sense of exploring the network of people who have visited this remarkable place and how the canyon has a way of shrinking that network.

Those who experience the Grand Canyon are a rather small subset of all the people who *could* come here. There is a hypothesis that any two people in the world are connected through acquaintance by six or fewer other people—A knows B who knows C who knows . . . G who, in turn, knows A. I think six is too big a number for joining any two people in the Grand Canyon. I think here the number is more like three.

WHATEVER HAPPENED TO JAZZ?

One night at our camp on a lovely beach just downstream from Rider Canyon, I spotted a bottle circling in an eddy. Remembering the bottle of sherry Robert (Benson) found a few days before and realizing beer sometimes comes in bottles, I waited until this one floated about as close as it was going to, and I waded out and grabbed it. It was a wine bottle and it appeared empty—except for a piece of paper.

With some effort we extracted the paper. It was a short note and this is what it said:

> Today's date is Sept 6, 1982.
> We have been stranded on this beach
> For 48 days now and are running
> out of wine.
> Whoever finds this note—PLEASE—
> We are about 8 miles upriver
> from Lee's Ferry—you'll see are [*sic*] boat
> (or what's left of it by now). We may not
> Be strong enough to stand and atract [*sic*]
> Your attention (unless we eat the dog).
> So watch closely for the outhouse.
>
> (signed)
> Steve, Dixie, Jazz

> P.S. We ate the dog. (What next??)
> P.S.S. I'm afraid we won't last 3 more days.
> Please Hurry.

You can't tell from my printing of this note, but the name Jazz was crossed out on the original. I think the day I found the bottle was the ninth of September, so the "mail" was sent three days before I found it. Pretty quick delivery, don't you think? I have tried to locate Steve and Dixie, to no avail. However, I have reason to think that someone named Danny Mackleprang may have knowledge of them. So far I have been unable to reach Mr. Mackleprang.

WALKING EAGLE

A friend and I hiked down Jackass Wash on our way to the Tanner Trail, and we arrived at the big beach below Badger Rapid in the middle of the afternoon. We had company. There were two people splashing about in the water and another man standing on the shore watching. You no doubt know that the water is very cold this close to the dam, and I was surprised to see these people having such a good time. I went down to investigate. As I got closer I could tell they were American Indians, most likely Navajos. I went down to the man on the shore and said, "Hi." No response. I stayed a few moments longer and then went back to the place we had picked for a camp. After dinner, while I was writing up the events of the day, I spotted the three Navajos walking up the beach toward me. The beach was wide, and at first I was not sure whether they were just going up the beach or whether they were coming toward me. When they got to me, the bigger man, who was their spokesman in all things, started small talk.

After a suitable time he got down to the reason they were there. "Have you any cigarettes?" he asked. Unfortunately, neither my friend nor I smoked, and I told him so.

Out of curiosity I asked them if they thought the fact that their chairman, Peterson Zah, and the Hopi chairman, Ivan Sidney, had been childhood friends would lead to any sort of rapprochement between the two tribes. But their blank looks made me realize that "rapprochement" was not a good word to use, so I rephrased the question. But they did not take my question with the seriousness I had intended, and the conversation drifted away from that subject.

Then the big man said, "We call Zah 'Walking Eagle.'" Since this was not a question, I did not answer, but I remember thinking that an Eagle is a worthy bird, and that a flying eagle would be a more worthy bird than a walking one.

When I did not respond, the man asked, "Do you know why we call him Walking Eagle?"

I said "No."

He explained, "We call him that because he's too full of shit to fly." Actually, I had a high opinion of Zah so I was a little taken aback by the disrespect shown.

The spokesman then asked if we would like some fish or not. We both said, "Sure, fish would be nice."

He said, "Follow me." We did, and he led us to the water and pulled out a rope with about six trout strung on it.

"Here," he said, "take some."

My friend, with no regard for the possible fragility of the relationship being nurtured between our cultures said, "Well, I had in mind something cooked."

I need not have worried. The big man said, "No problem, we'll cook some for you."

I looked around and didn't see any camp and asked, "How are you going to do that?"

He said, "The same way the Anasazi did—in aluminum foil."

Behind a huge rock nearby was their fire with smoldering coals. They ended up cooking three fish for us. One was cooked in aluminum foil on the coals (like their ancestors did), one was cooked on a stick over the coals, and one was fried in cheese.

FIRE IN THE PARK?

This story concerns a trip my brother Allen and I made with his friends, who are quite iconoclastic. They don't take well to instruction and rules. I won't say where this story takes place, and I didn't put it in any of my books because I wanted to give the National Park Service a chance to comment or take action on the crux of the story. We spent most of the day on the first part of a long trip to the river and were camping on smooth Supai ledges. Shortly after we made camp, Allen's friend, Jim Wilson, started building a fire off to one side of the drainage. Well, I knew fires were forbidden in the park, and I told Jim that I would prefer that he not build the fire. But I might as well have been talking to a rock. All day he had been collecting bits of wood for this fire. In spite of this, I told Jim once more that no fire was permitted here.

Finally, after the third time I tried to stop him, he said, "George, if you knew half as much about your precious park as you think you do, you would know I am not in the park."

It is hard to take issue with an argument like that, so I did nothing further and decided to let things go. I resolved, however, to try to find out what the true boundaries of the park were when I got home. Sure enough, Jim was right. His fire was legal. The boundary of the park went right down the middle of the drainage we were camping in and the right-hand side of the drainage was therefore outside the park. Then as the fire went into the coal stage, and he put steaks on it, I was quite glad that, indeed, it was possible briefly to get out of the park.

These next few stories are of the "it's a small world" variety.

PETE AND REPETE

Sitting at the water's edge near Deer Creek, my brother and I were using up part of a rest day on our eighty-day hike through the length of the Grand Canyon. Soon we could see a kayak upriver in the distance, and eventually it came down to us. The paddler got out and sat down beside us. He said his name was Pete. As we chatted amiably about nothing, another kayaker pulled in and joined us. He also said his name was Pete, but the first Pete said the second Pete was Repete. We chatted some more, and the Petes told us about themselves. Finally, Pete #1 asked Allen about his story, and in the course of his recital Al mentioned he had quit working at the Ski Hut and helped start an outfit called Mountain Travel.

"That's interesting," said Pete, "I recently spent almost two weeks on a beach in Mexico with a girl and her boyfriend. Her name was Susan, and she said her father was one of the founders of Mountain Travel."

"That can't be," said Al, "I know all the founders and none of them have a daughter named Susan. But I have a daughter named Sara."

"That was it, her name was Sara," said Pete.

This has to be one of the smallest of "it's a small world" stories.

EMMITT, IS THAT YOU?

In April 2001 my son Stan had his Colorado River boating permit come up. I was invited to go along with fourteen others from all over the country. When I make such a trip I take a case of beer and a case of pop to give to hikers we spot along the river. Somewhere just below Soap Creek, we spotted five hikers resting on a Supai ledge near the river. Stan nosed his boat in, and we saw two men and three young boys. Actually, it was a father with three sons and a friend of the father's. We quickly disposed of three pops and two beers. The father explained they had come down Soap Creek Canyon that morning and were now on their way down to Rider Canyon. It was midmorning. The boys, ages 12, 10, and 8, or thereabouts, seemed tired, and there was still some hard hiking to be done. We had room for one person on our boat and chose to take the friend plus all their backpacks, leaving them with their lunch and water bottles. Emmitt got on our boat and off we went. As we passed one of the other boats, Charlia (from Santa Cruz, California) called out "Emmitt, is that you? What are you doing here?"

So that this will all seem natural, let me explain that Charlia is an MD and Emmitt is a nurse, and they had worked together years ago in some remote location like Tuba City.

SMALL WORLD TIMES TWO

This story takes place on our long trip in '82. There were five of us. We made our camp and then started up South Canyon to retrieve a cache hidden at the top of the Redwall. The inconvenience of having to go for the cache at the end of a long day leads me to one of my rules for successful caching—put your food where you will use it, not where it is convenient to stash it. After a few hours we returned with the cache and found the beach occupied by a boat party. Our packs had established this site as "ours" so there was no territorial dispute. We introduced ourselves and shared their wine. Adair Peterson, who was with us, recognized one of the boaters as someone she had met on several occasions while climbing in the mountains outside Albuquerque.

Another of the boat party came up to my brother and said, "Hi, Al, remember me?" When my brother said, "no," he added, "Hey, I used to work for you at the Ski Hut."

THE LOST IS FOUND

When we put out the caches for the long hike in '82, we put one in Nankoweap way up the creek near where the side canyon goes over to the falls. After returning to the rim, my brother found that he had left his walking stick at the cache site. He was not used to using one, so he just forgot it. We used old ski poles without the baskets, and our poles were identical. The next year after I had hiked down the Salt Trail and down the Little Colorado to meet Robert on his upstream hike at the confluence, a big baloney boat pulled in and someone got off with a walking stick just like mine.

"Hey, we are twins," I said.

"Just luck," he said, "I found this one up Nankoweap Creek yesterday."

I explained that my brother had left it there last year.

"Take it back," he said, "I don't want it. The boatmen say it can be bad for the boat."

So I took it back and put it with Robert's cache and got it home later. I still use it.

WOOLLY HAT

I use a woolly hat when I hike, even in warm weather. Mainly I wear it at night to keep my dirty hair from getting my pillow and sleeping bag dirty. In cold weather it has other uses like keeping my head warm. This day in early spring we were hiking from Phantom Ranch over to Clear Creek, and John Azar stopped midmorning to make us some soup. The soup made me warm, hot actually, and I took my woolly hat off and laid it on a rock. Later, when we left, it remained behind. There were some people at the Clear Creek campsite from Alaska, and others told me that someone from the Alaskan group had found my woolly hat. Somehow I got an address in Alaska, and I wrote the person who had my hat and asked for it back. He was happy to oblige, and I use it to this day.

CAMERA

On the first trip I made around Walhalla Plateau with Gary Ladd, Don Mattox, and his stepson, Kyle, I left my camera on a rock while we rested. Gary took some pictures, and when we started up again I left my camera behind. This took place in October, and a year from the following spring I heard from my son Stan, who lives in Alaska. Stan said that someone he knows there found a camera somewhere near Vishnu Creek. I was sure it was mine and asked Stan to ask his friend to communicate with me. The man, indeed, had found my camera, had it cleaned and was happy to have a nice new camera. He was reluctant to give it back, but he eventually returned it after I paid for the cleaning and shipping. I must admit I have not used that camera since. Perhaps I should just have said, "finders keepers."

Grand Canyon's Railroad Culture

by Al Richmond

In this, Al Richmond's first presentation at the history symposium (the second, "Rails at Both Rims" appears earlier in this volume), he reminded participants that railways were, and to a lesser degree still are, more than just transportation conduits. The Santa Fe and its subsidiary Grand Canyon Railway opened northern Arizona to settlement; directly aided the region's development; employed men, women, and families of diverse cultural backgrounds; and contributed to a strong connection and sense of community between Williams and Grand Canyon Village.

Railroads across America have a culture of their own. Those in northern Arizona are no exception. In our region, however, culture extends far beyond that of a main-line railroad such as the Santa Fe and is even more varied than in other locales. Although directly linked to the Santa Fe, we also have, or once had, cultures derived from logging, mining, ranching, and support services in the community of Williams. Mines in and around the canyon brought a diverse population to the region from the late 1800s to the present day. Ranching has existed all around the Grand Canyon in one form or another since people began to populate the Colorado Plateau. Just outside the park's southern boundary a logging enterprise thrived from 1929 to 1936. The people of Williams, "Gateway to the Grand Canyon," are representative of small-town USA. Their lifestyles and contributions are also part and parcel to the region's cultural heritage.

In 1882 something never seen by most southern Colorado Plateau inhabitants appeared on the horizon westbound out of the Rio Grande Valley. Black smoke billowing from coal- and wood-fired steam locomotives proclaimed the advent of mass transportation across New Mexico and Arizona territories. Riding on steel arteries that eventually stretched between Chicago and Los Angeles, Atlantic & Pacific Railroad freight and passenger trains opened up and pumped lifeblood into a land heretofore traveled only by horseback or wagon. New towns

appeared, young towns grew, and what eventually became Grand Canyon National Park acquired reasonable accessibility. Those who could afford it now traveled in passable comfort to Flagstaff, Williams, or Ash Fork, and then transferred to stagecoaches or other rattletrap conveyances for the spine-jolting journey to the South Rim. Nothing would ever be the same again.

Eighteen years later, a new enterprise, the Santa Fe & Grand Canyon Railroad, began working its way north from Williams. Originally constructed to access copper mines, it entered the passenger service business in 1900 by transporting travelers from the main-line Santa Fe Pacific (the new name of the Atlantic & Pacific) in Williams northward. Early passengers were transported speedily and comfortably forty-five miles to the railhead at Anita. Still twenty miles short of the canyon, passengers then boarded stagecoaches for the remainder of the trip. Later that year, the company went into receivership, and the line became part of the Atchison, Topeka & Santa Fe Railway.

The Santa Fe incorporated the Grand Canyon Railway and pushed it to the South Rim, arriving there on September 17, 1901. When the first trains pulled in, passengers looked out upon a ramshackle Grand Canyon Village. Nothing more than a collection of one- and two-room log and/or canvas hovels posing as hotels, the village offered barely edible meals and basic shelter from the elements. It

A Santa Fe railroad track gang in the early 1900s. Gandy brand tools and the rail workers' rhythmic chants to coordinate the alignment of rails gave them the name "Gandy Dancers." Author's collection

took another two years to bring about the first phase of a remarkable metamorphosis toward refinement that continued for the next fifty years.

RAILROAD DEVELOPMENT OF GRAND CANYON VILLAGE AND WILLIAMS

Santa Fe management envisioned Grand Canyon Village as their primary canyon destination. To attract ever-increasing numbers of visitors, the quality of accommodations had to be improved. In a classic example of railroad enterprise, the Santa Fe began construction of facilities designed to rival those found anywhere in the West. The railroad provided not only transportation to the very rim of the canyon, but it also built quality facilities in the form of first- and economy-class hotels, and restaurants complete with running water and electricity.

Fred Harvey was a name synonymous with excellent hotels and fine service. Harvey's partnership with the Santa Fe Railway has become legendary. At the South Rim, the Fred Harvey Company catered to the world's travelers and made

them comfortable in a rustic but luxurious style. This required a host of employees to provide every possible service. Mule wranglers, waitresses ("Harvey Girls"), chefs, laundry workers, vehicle operators, mechanics, shopkeepers, bartenders, bellhops, hostesses, desk clerks, guides, photographers, and housekeepers are but a few of many workers who made many a visitor's stay carefree and memorable. Most came from somewhere other than the Grand Canyon area and saw the great gorge for the first time upon reporting for work. They never forgot it or their stay at Grand Canyon Village.

With facilities and services, the Santa Fe created a major tourism destination at the South Rim, and their passenger service department made the most of it. Although trains ran throughout the Midwest, across the West, and throughout California, the Santa Fe became famous as the Grand Canyon Line. Most of their freight cars, bridges, and advertising carried this theme and logo. The railroad brought the Grand Canyon to the people figuratively and brought the people to the Grand Canyon literally.

Although a bit more community-oriented than some of their competitors, Santa Fe motives revolved around profit.

Passengers provided publicity and some profit from the accommodations, but as it has always been with railroads in this country, freight fed the bottom line. For the next sixty-eight years, Santa Fe trains hauled a plethora of ores such as copper, gold, silver, asbestos, and uranium from the canyon area. Other business interests included shipping livestock to and from the many ranches along the line and supporting logging railroads in and around Williams. Williams boasted the largest mill and box plant in the Southwest, and logs destined for its saws passed over the Santa Fe tracks from Bellemont, Challender, Apex, and areas south of Williams covered by the Saginaw Southern Railroad. In these same years, the Santa Fe mined another seemingly endless seam: the pockets of tourists.

From the very outset the Santa Fe also participated in the water business. An enterprise born of sheer necessity by the insatiable thirst of steam locomotives, the high-desert environment, and the ever-increasing number of tourists, it eventually extended to supplying Williams, ranches along the right-of-way, and especially Grand Canyon Village. The railroad accomplished this by erecting dams near Williams, building water systems at the South Rim, and hauling water in tanker cars from Santa Fe wells at Del Rio (Puro), north of Prescott. Santa Fe engineers also designed and built innovative water-reclamation systems at the South Rim that attracted engineers from around the world to study the technology.

The railroad improved the quality of life along the right-of-way. Williams and Grand Canyon Village enjoyed a standard of living equal to that of any midwestern or eastern town of comparable size. Businesses thrived, newspapers and schools sprouted, churches prospered with stable populations, and social life flourished. Both communities sported ball teams, bands, theaters, fire departments, and a diverse selection of fraternal organizations, leading to a year-round schedule of entertainment and social gatherings. Stores provided most of the food, hardware, clothing, furnishings, and appliances necessary for maintaining a good lifestyle. Without the railroad, few of these civilized refinements would have existed.

Primarily due to the jobs and higher wages that the Santa Fe engendered, residents of Williams and Grand Canyon Village in the early 1900s could afford more and better products available through railroad shipments. For example, if stores did not carry what a consumer required, they simply ordered it by mail. Customers carried an order form, complete with one-cent stamp, to the train station, where one of seven daily east-west trains on the main line picked it up. The order arrived in Los Angeles within half a day or in Chicago in a day and a half. Usually within three to four days they had their merchandise delivered by

Railway Express. Today, with all of our advanced technology, we cannot approach this level of cost effectiveness or convenience. Dozens of daily freight and Amtrak passenger trains still cross northern Arizona, but this level of railroad-community interaction remains only in the memories of fewer and fewer eyewitnesses.

In the early decades of the railroad's existence, Santa Fe officials learned to deal with a new set of administrators and bureaucrats. Until 1901 their experience had been with federal and state legislators, county supervisors, federal railroad regulators, and the Arizona Corporation Commission. From 1901 through 1919, the U.S. Forest Service had something to say about their passage to the rim and the location of various service and tourist facilities. In the latter year, the fledgling National Park Service took over the management of Grand Canyon National Park and added their brand of administration to the railroad's list of regulatory masters.

All things considered, relationships with these land management agencies proved symbiotic. The U.S. Forest Service and the park service needed certain utilities that the railroad provided. As the Santa Fe built tourist accommodations it also designed, constructed, and maintained electrical, water, and wastewater-treatment facilities for the park. Of course these utilities served the hotels, but without the railroad, the two federal agencies would have had to expend considerably more money than Congress allocated. In practice, the park superintendent became the "mayor" of Grand Canyon Village, but the Santa Fe agent served as "city manager."

This relationship lasted until 1956, when the Santa Fe decided to get out of the hotel business. They donated more than six hundred service-related structures and utilities to the park service and sold their tourism-related facilities to the Fred Harvey Company. All of a sudden, the park service found itself responsible for city services. Rangers who entered the service to protect the wilderness and educate visitors now found themselves with bureaucratic duties for which they had no training or experience. This has been the circumstance ever since, and since 1989, when the Grand Canyon Railway reopened as a tourism enterprise, park administrators have been forging a new railroad-park relationship.

THE RAILROAD AS DRIVER OF DEVELOPMENT

In many ways, railroaders, ranchers, and South Rim residents became one family. There is no arguing that the Santa Fe built most Grand Canyon facilities and established South Rim tourist patterns that persist today. In addition, there is no doubt that canyon residents had a close relationship over the years with the railroad.

However, the railroad also built many facilities along the line for ranchers and supported their businesses. Until 1974 the railroad served as primary transportation for the region's sheep and cattle interests. And certainly there is no doubt that people living along the Grand Canyon Line had a most personal and close association with the railroad and its people. Like family, they shared good times and bad.

Beginning in 1898, a community of about twenty families grew up at Anita, between Williams and the South Rim. The miners of the area used a ramp located at the small community to load their copper ore into cars for rail shipment. In short order the Santa Fe established a station with a section gang and bunkhouse, and built extensive stockyards as a livestock shipping point for ranchers. Teachers taught lessons in a one-room converted boxcar. In 1920 the town built a nice schoolhouse with a small bell tower, but it burned, and another boxcar replaced it in 1929. Students received a fine grade-school education well into the early 1940s. Residents built several nice houses on the rise to the west of the station, and a small store with a post office opened for business. Grace Lockridge served as postmaster from August 17, 1914 to August 31, 1918. The Anita-Moqui District Forest Service Station was also headquartered here until it was relocated to Tusayan in the 1950s. None of these buildings remains. As jobs dwindled and people began to leave in the 1950s, owners moved some of the houses to Williams and dismantled the rest.

In 1929 another group arrived on the canyon scene. The Saginaw & Manistee Lumber Company moved into the area immediately south of Grand Canyon National Park armed with a cutting lease for ponderosa pine issued by the Kaibab National Forest. This activity led to a community that lived, grew, worked, and moved with the job of cutting logs until 1936. The company built its headquarters camp in a small valley about one mile east of Apex (a former company town for railroad construction crews, located about ten miles south of Grand Canyon Village).

Virtually everything that became a part of this timber community arrived by rail from Bellemont and Garland Prairie. Housing for single men looked like wooden boxcars without wheels. Workers loaded two of these on flat cars or one on a log car for transportation to the end of track, where they established the logging camps. The company provided management and families with larger housing. Arvid Anderson, camp superintendent, had the largest house, consisting of a living room, kitchen, and two bedrooms. Family housing included a living room, kitchen, and one bedroom. These homes sat on temporary wood-and-stone foundations still visible today. One feature of these houses is that they came apart at the middle for transport and workers rejoined them in their original "L" or "T" configuration at their destination. These truly "mobile" homes provided reasonable comfort for their occupants.

The loggers had children and knew the value of a good education despite residing in the middle of a forest. Apex was home to these loggers, and home required an elementary school. In the fall of 1929, Apex School District Number 3 opened in two boxcars converted into

Teacher Rose B. Wilson with her class at Apex School in 1934. The Saginaw & Manistee Lumber Company hired her to live with and teach the children of the loggers working in the Kaibab National Forest. Photograph by Matson. Author's collection

Modern-day Grand Canyon Railway shop workers in the process of rebuilding Engines 29 and 18. Steam railroad shops and their workers have changed very little over the last 150 years. Author's collection

workers with families. All of these people wanted a better life for their children, and the two schools opened doors for them. Here a man earned his keep and maintained his self-respect while doing an honest day's work for a decent wage. In such an isolated area, the workers and their families interacted, learning something of each other's cultural backgrounds.

Residents of Apex and Anita did get to intermingle with residents of the South Rim and Williams on occasion. The Saginaw & Manistee commissary did not stock a complete line of groceries or merchandise, so most shopping had to be done elsewhere. Occasionally, community residents drove to Grand Canyon Village for their shopping and other needs, and less frequently, took the train or drove to Williams. Thanks to the park service and local political pressure, the state had built a nearby automotive road connecting the South Rim with Williams in 1930. But secondary roads to this paved artery remained dirt. In winter and during the summer monsoons, the secondary roads turned to mud, and people in the camps did not consider it unusual to get stuck and spend the night in some abandoned building or whatever shelter could be found.

THE RAILROAD THEN AND NOW

Few give thought to the diversity of people required to make the train trip to the Grand Canyon possible. Everyone knows about the engineer and conductor, but these figures are just the tip of the iceberg. A railroad does not run without firemen, brakemen, hostlers, track gangs, bridge and building gangs, signal maintainers, telegraphers, station agents, baggage handlers, porters, mechanics, dispatchers, boilermen, and an endless list of tradesmen and administrative personnel. In this respect, today's Grand Canyon Railway is little different from the Santa Fe of the early 1900s.

On a daily basis, the railroad delivered, and still delivers, visitors of many cultures to the very doorsteps of those who have lived and worked at the rim. Residents still rub shoulders with a cross section of America and walk along the rim with presidents, kings, queens, despots, movie stars, and other glamorous people. The Grand Canyon has always served as the magnet; the railroad as developer, maintainer, and delivery vehicle; and Williams and Grand Canyon Village as the caldron or melting pot. Local residents stir the heterogeneous brew. There are few places in this world that can boast of such regular and changing diversity in their population and visitation. Virtually all come away better for the experience.

a one-room schoolhouse. The company hired teachers from Arizona State Teachers College in Flagstaff for board and the generous sum of $130 per month. Classes never exceeded fifteen pupils, who rarely filled all eight grades. Situated on a hill, the school overlooked the camp on the western slope of the valley. Because of its small size, it provided a warm and friendly atmosphere where students made lasting friendships.

The Apex and Anita schools shared one unique aspect: they were the only racially integrated schools in Arizona. The Saginaw & Manistee had its roots in Swedish-American culture. Mexicans worked in the mill and box plant at Williams, but in the camps, most workers had been born either in Sweden or in the United States of Swedish heritage. Norwegians and Finns began to arrive in the camps, and during the 1930s, victims of the dust bowl and Great Depression—"okies," "arkies," "cajuns," and many others—joined them during their treks westward in search of work and a better life. Close neighbors of the camps, the railroad-section gangs at Apex and Anita were predominantly staffed by Mexican

Suggested Readings

Anderson, Michael F. 2001. *Along the rim: A guide to Grand Canyon's South Rim from Hermits Rest to Desert View.* Grand Canyon, Ariz.: Grand Canyon Association.

———. 1998. *Living at the edge: Explorers, exploiters and settlers of the Grand Canyon region.* Grand Canyon, Ariz.: Grand Canyon Association.

Myrick, David F. 2000. *Railroads of Arizona,* vols. 4 and 6. Wilton, Calif.: Signature Press.

Richmond, Al. 2002. *Cowboys, miners, presidents and kings: The story of the Grand Canyon Railway,* 5th ed. Flagstaff, Ariz.: Grand Canyon Railway.

Runte, Alfred. 1998. *Trains of discovery: Western railroads and the national parks.* Niwot, Colo.: Roberts Rinehart Publishers.

THE 1898 DIARY OF ZELLA DYSART

BY MONA LANGE MCCROSKEY

The following excerpts are from Mona Lange McCroskey's Summer Sojourn to the Grand Canyon: The 1898 Diary of Zella Dysart *(Prescott, Ariz.: HollyBear Press, 1996). We had asked McCroskey to speak on the Dysart photographs and diary in the event that another symposium presenter canceled at the last minute. No one canceled, but we included this presentation in these proceedings because the material fit so well with her presentation on Robert H. Kuhne and Mary J. Straw Cook's presentation on the Hollenbacks.*

In the late afternoon of July 23, 1898, four children of the Samuel Dysart family set out from their Phoenix home for a tour of the Grand Canyon, Flagstaff, and the Hopi Mesas. They spent seven weeks traveling in a wagon pulled by their horses, Nellie and Victoria, and accompanied by a dog, Trilby. The trip was made three years before the Grand Canyon Railway reached the canyon and twenty-one years before the establishment of Grand Canyon National Park. The travelers were Fred, age 25 (he had made the trip before and served as guide); Winifred, age 20; Zella, age 17; and Arthur, age 12. Zella kept a diary of the trip. She was intelligent, well read, and articulate, and editing of her diary was hardly necessary. Photographs depicting some of the places they visited accompany the following excerpts from the diary.

On August 5, the group toured the Saginaw & Manistee Lumber Company in Williams, then turned north toward the Grand Canyon.

AUGUST 7: ROWE'S POINT

This morning we breakfasted upon hotcakes, butter, and honey. Someone remarked this morning that next winter when we are busy teaching school, keeping books, and learning lessons we shall look back upon our summer outing with pleasant memories and long in vain to spend such another

morning as this. So we resolved to get all the enjoyment possible during our trip (a resolution scarcely necessary).

At two o'clock we reached Rain Tanks, where we watered the horses. From here we took our road to the Canyon, through pine, spruce, and cedar forests, and we "children" gathered some spruce gum.

The trees were so thick that had the Canyon been just in front of us we could not have seen it. But Fred had told us that we should approach it on level country and should not see it until we were on its brink, so we were expecting to be surprised in that way.

Zella, Fred, and Winifred Dysart, circa 1898. Photograph courtesy of John Vaughn

View of the Grand Canyon from Rowe's Point, circa 1900. Photograph by C. H. Shaw. Sharlot Hall Museum Library/Archives, Prescott, Ariz. (LA 206dd)

A glad shout from Arthur, who had disappeared through the trees, proclaimed that the Canyon was near us. Through the dense forest we could see a wide blue band resting upon the ground—the walls of the great Canyon. We girls scrambled out eagerly to behold the grand sight—and such a sight it was! Down, down we looked over great strata of rock looking like ancient temples of the gods, each a mountain in itself, so tall, so blue and so majestic. Down! Down 5,000 feet or more to where the muddy Colorado threads its course, so far away that we could neither see nor hear the rushing of its mighty waters.

Through the deep gorges of both walls numerous tributaries flowed, winding their ways among the rocky ledges. The view was quite extensive but very much of the same—great flat mountains forming an immense stairway that scaled the rugged walls of the great gorge. All was blue save for the golden tints left by the setting sun.

When we had given utterance to our first raptures, we drove back into the forest to find a camping place for the night. About a quarter of a mile from the rim of the Canyon the boys unhitched and tied the horses. Then we all walked back to take another look before going to bed.

AUGUST 8: ROWE'S WELL

We went back to Rowe's Well and there took a road leading to "The Indian Garden Trail," which we reached at noon. Winifred, Arthur, and I walked down about one-half mile just to see what a mountain trail was like. We soon satisfied our curiosity and didn't care to go farther. The path was so very winding that in traveling one-half mile we had gone perpendicularly only a very short distance.

Fred wished us to see the Canyon from the Hance trail, so we took a road going in that direction which Fred

thought would probably lead into the main road from Flagstaff to the Hance trail. We traveled through the most restful-looking and pleasant country we have yet seen.

Green, rolling hills, dense woods of tall pines and shaggy oaks; yellow, bright-eyed daisies; deep red "Indian paint" flowers; larkspur; and other varieties of wild blossoms—each added its peculiar beauty and helped to make a landscape faultless in beauty.

Rowe's Well near the Grand Canyon, circa 1900. Photograph by C. H. Shaw. Sharlot Hall Museum Library/Archives, Prescott, Ariz. (PO 555pb)

AUGUST 9: HANCE'S CAMP

About noon we arrived at the Hance trail. Now the Hance Hotel at this place is not so large or so grand as the Adams or Ford [hotels] of Phoenix. To be truthful, it is really only a neat little log cabin. Near it are about a dozen clean-looking tents, furnished for rent to tourists. Business is centered in a small cabin in which is [a] post office and store.

We climbed a little hill back of the hotel and viewed the Canyon once more from Lookout Rock. We each carried away a piece of the rock for a souvenir. Then we returned to the wagon and drove to the "camping grounds," which differ from the other land of the great Coconino Forest only in having pastures fenced in for stock, a pond of water, and four log houses. Of these conveniences we are making use of but one, i.e., the water. We preferred to camp in the open forest and let our horses run loose. The water here is nice and soft, but unfit to drink. Drinking water is hauled from Cedar Springs, forty miles away.

AUGUST 10: JOHN HANCE

But I must mention the fact that before we left camp we saw and talked with Mr. Hance, the owner and boss of the plantation [the Dysarts were originally from Missouri]. He is a queer old man, noted for his much talking, and is regarded by all tourists as one of the curiosities of the country. He spends part of his time escorting tourists down his trail to the bottom of the Canyon and keeps mules for that express purpose, charging five dollars for the trip.

We started toward Flagstaff, intending to reach Cedar Springs by night. At noon we stopped under some spruce trees and ate dinner. Fred watered the horses from the barrel and let them graze for about an hour. Then I read to him till he fell asleep upon a quilt on the ground.

After we first started we traveled over a few hills, and then came to an open prairie. San Francisco Peak reared its great blue head in the southwest, and just west of it we thought we saw Bill Williams Mountain.

About six o'clock we arrived at Cedar Springs. The spring and house are on the slope of a hill, luxuriant in malapai rock. The water comes through an iron pipe, in a cold pure stream, and empties into a series of troughs arranged each higher than the next below it.

We drove by the house and barn and are camped upon the side of the hill, east of them. The water and air is [*sic*] excellent, and if we can scrape enough rocks away to make our beds, we shall pass a very comfortable night.

John Hance with two mules on the Bright Angel Trail, circa 1910. Photo by the Kolb brothers. Grand Canyon National Park Museum Collection (#15003)

Hance's Camp, November 16, 1895. Photograph by C. H. Shaw. Sharlot Hall Museum Library/Archives, Prescott, Ariz. (PO 1703p)

The Grand Canyon-Flagstaff Stage Coach Line, 1902. Fred Clatworthy Collection, Museum of Northern Arizona, Flagstaff (74.1985)

AUGUST 11: EN ROUTE TO FLAGSTAFF

Soon we began to climb the hills—the low foothills of San Francisco Peak which lies southeast of us. Silvery quaken [*sic*] aspen trees made their appearance and arranged themselves in belts and groves around the green hills. The hills are covered with tall ripe grass so that the horses are bewildered and don't know where to begin grazing. Various kinds of pretty wildflowers grow thick in the long grass.

After a respite in Flagstaff the Dysarts traveled to the Hopi Mesas and back, then returned to Phoenix via Camp Verde and the Old Black Canyon Highway. They arrived home in September, ending what was for Zella Dysart "seven weeks full of the most unalloyed happiness for me that I have ever had."

Chapter Eight

Mary Elizabeth Jane Colter, Grand Canyon Architect: Stories in Stone

by David C. Frauman

Grand Canyon National Park is fortunate to possess buildings designed by some fine early-twentieth-century architects. Grand Canyon Lodge at Bright Angel Point by Gilbert Stanley Underwood, El Tovar Hotel by Charles Whittlesey, and Francis Wilson's Grand Canyon Depot are but a few. The most influential and celebrated of our architects, however, is Mary Colter, who worked here for more than thirty years and designed six major buildings and two building complexes, all of which still stand and inspire. Dr. Frauman traveled from Indiana to give this presentation, which combines his interest in the psychology of creativity, art, and artists with his interest in history in a review of Colter's tourism-related buildings, her vision, and her personality.

Mary Colter must be considered one of the grand ladies of the Southwest. She designed six major buildings at the Grand Canyon's South Rim, each a landmark and a hallmark, structures that complement the natural wonder and enhance a viewer's experience of the national park. When you design buildings that achieve harmony with the likes of the Grand Canyon, you have accomplished something remarkable.

Colter's forty-year career as an architect for the Fred Harvey Company and for the Santa Fe Railway coincides with the National Park Service era at the Grand Canyon. Although she designed other buildings along the Santa Fe main line, her South Rim buildings are the best preserved and remain her most inspired and creative designs. Uncelebrated in her lifetime, architectural historians have since credited Colter as an originator of an architectural style known as National Park Rustic. A 1935 National Park Service publication defines National Park Rustic as building design that results in a structure that appears to have been crafted with limited hand tools and "achieves sympathy

with natural surroundings and with the past" (Good 1935, 5). Colter's canyon creations typify this definition.

The purpose of my presentation is to explore the how and why of Colter's art. Would knowing something about her personality aid in understanding her unique vision as an architect? What in particular about her life fostered a style of architecture unlike any other? In contrast to other architects of the time whose buildings are modernistic, Colter seems to have taken a U-turn in her thinking, drawing her inspiration from the past, reworking American Indian or pioneer American ideas, and revitalizing designs a hundred or even a thousand years old. Hopi House at the Grand Canyon, for example, is her interpretation of the Hopi pueblo at Old Oraibi, Third Mesa, Arizona, which is at least eight hundred years old.

This was Colter's genius: an ability to use materials and designs of indigenous or pioneering peoples and place them in a contemporary setting for a contemporary purpose. This is also why her buildings have stood the test of time at the Grand Canyon. They do not appear out of place or simply plopped down arbitrarily even though they were meant to serve in everyday roles as sales rooms, tourist stops, and hotels. In this presentation, I explore the origins of that genius as well as her reputation as a perfectionist, a woman who was uncompromising, demanding, and pushy. I also examine the claim of one critic who labeled her designs "the most poorly illuminated buildings ever built" (quoted in Grattan 1992, 21).

EARLY LIFE

Mary Colter's father died when she was seventeen years old, and the young woman became the breadwinner for her mother and sister. Colter was born in Pittsburgh, but the family moved to Saint Paul, Minnesota, in 1880, when Mary was eleven years old. Her father left the family little money when he died. Her mother and sister worked some, but Colter provided the majority of the family's income.

It is not known if the young woman accepted this responsibility willingly, but she did convince her mother to let her go west to study so that she would have a vocation, namely art teaching, with which to support the family. She enrolled in the California School of Design in San Francisco, studying art and design at the school for three years and studying architecture as an apprentice in a local architect's office. It was unusual for a woman to aspire to be an architect at that time; California did not license architects until twenty years after her graduation, and even then only men could be licensed. Colter graduated in 1890, at age twenty-one, and returned to Saint Paul to support the family. She was hired by Saint Paul's Mechanic Arts High School, what today would be called a vocational high school, and began a fifteen-year career teaching freehand and mechanical drawing. For her own satisfaction, she studied archaeology.

Colter demonstrated an early love for American Indian arts and sciences. In the late nineteenth century, Saint Paul stood adjacent to the Sioux (Dakota) Indian Reservation, and Colter became fascinated with Sioux culture. A friend gave her some Sioux drawings of animals that she counted among her most cherished possessions. When a smallpox epidemic struck the Sioux and Saint Paul communities, and her mother gathered up and burned all of the American Indian objects in the house to protect the family from contamination, Mary hid her drawings under a mattress, saving them from destruction. She kept the drawings all her life and as an elderly adult, referred to them as "my most precious possession" (quoted in McQuaid and Bartlett 1996, 34).

EARLY LIFE AS AN ARCHITECT

Exactly how an obscure Minnesota high school teacher came to work for the Fred Harvey Company as designer and architect of some of the most noteworthy buildings in the Southwest is unknown. One theory holds that Colter came to the attention of Minnie Huckel, Fred Harvey's daughter (McQuaid and Bartlett 1996). Minnie may have convinced the Harvey Company to hire the unknown architect to oversee a decorating project at the Alvarado Hotel in Albuquerque. The Indian Building was a crafts sales area adjoining the Alvarado, a station on the Santa Fe's Southwest Chief route, and Colter was hired as a summer employee to design the interior and make it pleasant for tourists to browse and purchase American Indian crafts.

Although she had no previous experience designing sales rooms or expertise with American Indian crafts, Colter's ideas proved successful. After this initial project, she returned to Saint Paul to resume teaching for two years, but when the Santa Fe completed a spur line to the Grand Canyon's South Rim in 1901, they remembered her work. Railroad managers laid plans to build a hotel and adjacent sales building at the end of the track, and although they hired a more prominent Chicago architect, Charles F. Whittlesey, to design the hotel named El Tovar, they brought Colter back from Minnesota to design the sales building named Hopi House. Both opened for business in January 1905. They reflect the yin and yang of architecture, as Whittlesey's design is masculine in its Norwegian-hunting-lodge-inspired style, while the Hopi House is feminine with an emphasis on communal, cooperative living.

What a risk it must have been for Colter to propose this design. First, it looks like no other building in existence apart from a few pueblos along the Rio Grande in New Mexico and on the Hopi Reservation. She could have played it safe with a design more familiar to Caucasian Americans, who would comprise the majority of canyon tourists. Second, she was clearly inspired by American Indian architectural practice rather than the European influence prevalent at the time. Colter's design reveals much about her character. Here was an architect who took a stand to promote her vision, did not knuckle under to contemporary fashion, and demanded a design indigenous to the surrounding area. This required a forceful, determined, and visionary person. She did not promote herself; rather, she promoted the ideals of Puebloan peoples and the suitability of American Indian designs.

With this project completed, Colter returned to Saint Paul to resume teaching and supporting her family on a more secure income. In 1910, however, the Santa Fe and the Fred Harvey Company offered her full-time employment as architect and designer for Harvey buildings along the Santa Fe main line. Colter's change of careers at forty-one years of age reflected extraordinary confidence, courage, and love for her craft because it required sacrifice. Much of her time would hereafter be spent "out on the line," living in hotels near her projects, thereby limiting contact with her mother and sister and narrowing the possibility of a family of her own (she never married). Work became her primary interest and apparently served as a satisfactory substitute.

Colter's working arrangement was unusual in that half her salary was paid by the Fred Harvey Company and half by the Santa Fe Railway. This required her to serve two bosses and to have designs approved by separate companies. Because she was not a licensed architect, her designs were drawn in final form and signed by Santa Fe Railway engineers. A man would have had inordinate difficulties getting designs approved in this working environment; for a woman to work successfully under these conditions seems unimaginable. Her alleged demanding nature and pushiness might be better understood when viewed in this light. Her unusual and striking designs like Hopi House and later creations would require unparalleled persuasion and persistence to gain the approval of those who paid her salary.

At the Grand Canyon

As a full-time employee, Colter's first job at the Grand Canyon was to design a rest stop at the end of Hermit Rim Road (today known as Hermit Road). Horse-drawn carriages took sightseers along this road, and a terminal building was needed at the turnaround and head of the Hermit Trail. Various designs were considered. Some Harvey employees wanted a Swiss-chalet style with gingerbread trim, somewhat similar to El Tovar. Colter won over decision makers, however, with a primitive stone building christened Hermits Rest. It has a jagged, native-stone exterior that looks like a mountain man's cabin in the wilderness. This is the theme Colter wanted to express; it is the cabin Louis Boucher—an unimposing canyon pioneer some called the "hermit"—might have built had he chosen to build on the rim.

Hermits Rest reveals the manner in which Colter worked. For most of her important buildings she created a theme that she wanted to express, and the building's design flowed from this theme. The theme here is the story of a hermit and how he might have lived at the time when Louis Boucher really did live at the Grand Canyon. In this way Colter was a storyteller, a storyteller in stone. This

helps explain why her buildings look native to their surroundings; the story behind the building anchors it to the place where it stands.

An incident that occurred during construction of Hermits Rest reveals much about the architect's character. At one point during construction, she was high on a ladder in the arch of the fireplace rubbing soot on the stones so that the fireplace would look used. Some railroad men who were watching her teased her by saying, "Why don't you clean up this place?" Colter laughed and teased back saying, "You can't imagine what it cost to make it look this old" (quoted in Grattan 1992, 26). Her point was that no detail is insignificant when creating the desired atmosphere. The mood of a hermit's cabin would be ruined with shiny new stones in the fireplace. She was once quoted as saying, "We can't get the mellow effect until things have been used" (quoted in Grattan 1992, 52). Her perfectionism purposely realized her vision.

Colter's next building, completed the same year as Hermits Rest (1914), was Lookout Studio. Perched on the South Rim near the head of the Bright Angel Trail, Colter designed Lookout Studio as a sales area and observation point, and also as a competitive business to Emery and Ellsworth Kolb's studio just a few paces west. Colter came up with a design that was inspired by ancestral Puebloan dwellings. Like the stone ruins of these prehistoric residents, the building seems to disappear into the limestone of the rim; although there are three observation levels, the building is almost invisible from a distance. A chimney made of piled stones and vegetation planted between the stones of the roof add to the effect. All in all, it is a more interesting building than Kolb Studio.

When Congress designated the Grand Canyon a national park in 1919, the park service selected the Fred Harvey Company as the principal concessioner to operate South Rim hotels, restaurants, and curio shops. As today, mule trips took guests to the bottom of the canyon, and inner-canyon accommodations were needed for overnight stays. The park approved a guest ranch where Bright Angel Creek empties into the Colorado River, and Colter's plan for a rustic retreat that she named Phantom Ranch was adopted.

Colter designed Phantom Ranch to resemble a cattle ranch in the desert. When opened in 1922, it comprised several guest cabins, a dining hall, and a recreation hall. Buildings were constructed of rocks gathered from the area, but all other materials had to be packed in by mule. Because it is so remote—guests still arrive only by mule, in a raft, or on foot—the buildings could be seen as artificial or foreign, as inorganic elements imposed on natural surroundings. But Colter's vision has proven apt and enduring.

Even today, eighty years after it was built, the ranch remains comfortable, restful, and harmonious with the Inner Gorge environment.

Colter's next project was an ambitious one. Fred Harvey wanted to build a rest stop and gift shop at the east entrance to the park, and Colter responded with plans for a tower that would overlook not only the eastern section of the Grand Canyon but also the Painted Desert farther to the east. The Watchtower, as it was named, was modeled after ancestral Puebloan towers of the Southwest like those found at Hovenweep National Monument in the Four Corners area. Colter chartered a plane to spot ruins from the air, then went overland by automobile to sketch and photograph these examples. In her thorough fashion, she spent six months studying ancestral Puebloan construction techniques and then built a full-size wooden mockup to determine if the height was suitable for the panorama she envisioned. During construction, Colter was typically present and involved, early morning to late afternoon, selecting each exterior stone and making sure that if it had to be chipped to fit, the chipped surface was not visible. She wanted a weathered look. She also selected irregular rocks that created shadows along the walls and gave more vigor to the tower's exterior (Grattan 1992, 73).

Even at age sixty-three, Colter supervised all aspects of the Watchtower's construction, making sure that each detail fit her vision. Once, when she was away from the construction site for a few days and workers had gone ahead with some of the wall construction, she made them tear it down when she returned and begin again the way she wanted it done. Incidents like this illustrate why those subject to her supervision found her difficult. One coworker said that he did not enjoy working with her because she was so demanding; another recalled that everyone hated to see her arrive at the job site (Grattan 1992, 76). It did not help that she patronizingly called the workers "my boys." They retaliated by calling her "Old Lady Colter," although apparently never to her face. Crews completed construction of the Watchtower in 1932.

The Bright Angel Lodge followed in 1935. The lodge replaced Bright Angel Hotel, a disorganized collection of cabins and tents dating to the 1890s. By the 1930s more people were arriving by automobile seeking something better than a tent but more casual and economical than El Tovar. Colter responded with a pioneer-style village with a central services building of stone and logs surrounded by cabins of adobe, log, or stone. Following the pioneer theme, Colter insisted on preserving two older buildings that were slated to be torn down and on incorporating them into the design of outlying cabins. One was Buckey O'Neill's cabin, today the oldest extant building at the Grand Canyon; the other was the former Cameron Hotel, which later became the village post office. These buildings were restored and became guest cabins, once again reflecting Colter's sensitivity for regional history. Bright Angel Lodge today still feels appropriate to its surroundings.

MARY COLTER, THE PERSON

Much is revealed about Colter as a person by scrutinizing her buildings. Apparent are her respect and understanding for indigenous and pioneering peoples and her ability to honor them by bringing their cultural ideas forward to the present and adapting them effectively to contemporary needs. In particular, she displayed an appreciation for American Indian aesthetics, an appreciation that apparently stemmed from childhood. She identified with American Indian history and tradition, and she once said that she longed to design buildings with only American Indian, and not Anglo, motifs.

She must be credited with a unique vision that captured the history and culture of the surroundings and embedded each building within these surroundings. Again taking a cue from American Indians she wrote, "The primitive architect never intentionally copied anything but made every building suit its own conditions and each one differed from every other according to the character of the *site*, the *materials* that could be procured and the *purpose* for which the building was intended" (Colter 1933, 13). This could have been her motto.

Colter's demanding nature, as well as her obstinacy and perfectionism, seem understandable in light of childhood experience and the working environment in which she operated. Having full responsibility as a teenager for supporting her family meant that she had to lead, to tell others what to do, and to believe that her way was the best way. Being a woman in a male-dominated occupation, company, and society required her to fight with determination for her ideas to achieve fruition. One wonders if she had been born a man if she would have been called "bossy" or just "firm." As far as her dogged persistence to achieve a certain effect, one should note that recent changes to her buildings have diluted the themes she had intended, reinforcing her idea that all the details have to be correct for a building to stand as an accurate, pleasing re-creation.

And what about the criticism that she created the most poorly illuminated buildings ever built? Colter would laugh out loud at this comment. Leaving nothing to chance, she created exactly the type of lighting necessary to enhance the theme and mood of the building. Although not as well lit, perhaps, as modern interiors, Colter's designs in any light are enduring and precious gifts to all who visit the Grand Canyon.

WORKS CITED

Colter, Mary E. J. 1933. *Manual for drivers and guides descriptive of the Indian Watchtower at Desert View and its relations, architecturally, to the prehistoric ruins of the Southwest.* Grand Canyon, Ariz.: Fred Harvey.

Good, Albert H. 1935. *Park and recreation structures.* Repr., Washington, D.C.: National Park Service, 1990.

Grattan, Virginia L. 1992. *Mary Colter: Builder upon the red earth.* Grand Canyon, Ariz.: Grand Canyon Natural History Association.

McQuaid, Matilda, and Karen Bartlett. 1996. Building an image of the Southwest: Mary Colter, Fred Harvey Company architect. In *The Great Southwest of the Fred Harvey Company and the Santa Fe Railway,* eds. Marta Weigle and Barbara A. Babcock. Phoenix, Ariz.: Heard Museum.

New Mexico State Tribune. 1923. El Navajo Hotel reflects the Painted Desert. May 25.

BERT LAUZON'S GRAND CANYON

BY BRADFORD COLE

Many associated with Grand Canyon history have heard the name Hubert F. "Bert" Lauzon, aide to the Kolbs on their 1911–12 motion picture trip down the Colorado River, but nothing until now has been published on the man and his tenure at the Grand Canyon. Bradford Cole, former curator of manuscripts at Northern Arizona University's Cline Library, insists that his presentation is not a "full-blown" biography, but his narrative and photographs nonetheless add texture to a man who spent forty years at the South Rim, bridging its pioneer and modern eras.

On Christmas Eve 1911 twenty-five-year-old Hubert "Bert" Lauzon watched from shore as Emery and Ellsworth Kolb prepared to run their boats through the Colorado River's Walthenberg Rapid. Lauzon, an itinerant miner and horse wrangler from Colorado, had just signed on with the Kolbs as their assistant the week before. The Kolb brothers were on the last leg of their epic Colorado River float trip that began in Green River, Wyoming, earlier that year and would end at Needles, California, on January 18, 1912. Earlier in the day, as the group prepared to run Shinumo Rapid, Emery penned a note to his brother, Ernest, "I will now take Bert and give him the necessary baptism." (All quotations are presented as written by the Kolbs and the Lauzons.)

As Lauzon looked on from shore with rope in hand, Emery and Ellsworth endured the baptism. Ellsworth entered the rapid first and immediately was pitched from his boat. Emery followed and according to Lauzon became "hung up on a rock at the head of the rapid, got loose, went over big rock hit another rock just below and smashed the central compartment of his boat." Lauzon then wrote, "I had to swim for it got the boat—bailed it out with my hat and crossed to where Ed [Ellsworth] was. About this time Emery came in with the crippled boat. After we got a fire and dry clothes on and a good supper we felt good and lucky that we were all together. Camped on a big pile of boulders." As one might imagine, the Kolbs were a bit

more exuberant in their praise of Lauzon, "Though inexperienced our Nervy Bert rowed Ed's boat over to us. Ed could hardly speak but said I want to shake your hand."

As usual Lauzon's recollection of the disaster was understated. He was a man of small stature, about 5'6" in height, but had a reputation for being calm and steady. His son Loren "Tiny" Lauzon remembered his father as "ambitious [having] good reasoning power thought fast . . . no fear of anything, steady didn't drink, good sense of humor. Magnet for people. People couldn't stay away from him."

Bert Lauzon was born in Compton Village, Quebec, Canada, on January 25, 1886, to Francois and Mary Lauzon. Francois immigrated to Colorado in the 1880s, and on May 21, 1884, became a U.S. citizen in Delta County, Colorado. According to Lauzon, his father homesteaded a ranch in western Colorado along the Uncompahgre River while his family still resided in Compton Village, but by the 1890s, the entire family lived in Colorado. In the early 1880s, Francois mined near the towns of Leadville, Lake City, Ouray, and Silverton. In 1898 he was lured away to the Klondike Gold Rush, but returned to Colorado in 1900. When his wife died the following year, he began to move around to various mining towns throughout Arizona, Nevada, California, and Mexico.

Bert Lauzon dropped out of school in 1902, and for the next two years worked cattle and trained racehorses for

Bert Lauzon watches one of the Kolb brothers navigate a rapid on the Colorado River during their 1911–12 trip. Emery Kolb Collection, Cline Library, Northern Arizona University, Flagstaff (NAU.PH.568.2816)

Verdi L. Hotchkiss of Montrose, Colorado. His interest in horses became a lifelong pursuit. He stayed on the ranch until 1904, when he went to work as a trammer [a person who pushes the boxlike wagon carrying mined ore] at three dollars per day for the Barstowe Mining and Milling Company in Ironton, Colorado. After leaving Colorado in 1906, and before his arrival at the Grand Canyon in 1911, Lauzon spent about four years working in mines throughout the Southwest, primarily in southern Arizona and northern Mexico. He drew pay from at least four different mining operations. According to Lauzon his primary duties were "shaft sinking and general mining work." His pay averaged about four dollars per day.

Lauzon left southern Arizona in 1909, and ended up in California where, for a short while, he helped drill a tunnel to bring water from the Santa Inez Valley to Santa Barbara. He worked briefly near Keeler, California, before joining his family in Los Angeles in December 1909, to take part in a gold-mining venture in Baja, Mexico. More information about Lauzon's life prior to 1911 can be obtained from a 1944 National Park Service employment application and his handwritten memoir entitled "Recollections of Over 40 Years in the S West," written about the same time. There are date discrepancies between the two documents, but the chronology is the same in both.

Lauzon arrived at the Grand Canyon in June 1911, and was employed as a guide and laborer by tourism operator and miner William Wallace Bass. He worked for Bass until December and then quit to become the Kolbs' assistant for the lower portion of their Colorado River trip. He worked for the Kolbs until they arrived at Needles, California, where the river runners parted company. Lauzon returned to mining at Arizona's Gold Road Mine [near Oatman],

making five dollars a day sinking a shaft. In a letter to Ellsworth Kolb written February 7, 1912, he reminisced, "I guess those rapids are still howling, but we beat them out, didn't we. Well Ed I would like awful well to hear from you when you have time to write."

Lauzon spent the next year and a half working across the Southwest, from Gold Road to California, Nevada, and back to Arizona. In July 1913 he returned to the Grand Canyon and again went to work for Bill Bass. During the fall of 1913, his romantic interest in Bass's seventeen-year-old daughter, Edith, became all too obvious. According to the diary of Bass's wife, Ada, Bert was a frequent visitor and companion of their daughter, accompanying her on hayrides, concerts at El Tovar, and a New Year's Eve celebration at the Bass residence. Edith's parents knew something was up between the two and decided that Edith should go to school in California. On a train trip to Williams with her mother in January 1914, Edith learned that, "I was going to Oakland and the plans were made in December." Bill Bass even got his old friend George Wharton James to encourage Edith to work hard at school, and promised that if she did well he could secure her an art scholarship at a California university.

Distance apparently could not cool the flame between the young couple. Bass became more threatening when he wrote Edith on January 25 that he would take away her funding if she did not end the relationship. After Edith wrote Lauzon to tell him that she had left for school, Bass fired off another letter, warning her that, "Bert is all right where he is but never as my partner. . . . If I find out that you write him a word I write you I will discharge him at once and send for you to come home." He continued, "I sent you away to stop this foolishness."

By April 1914 Lauzon had left Bass's employ and moved to Wickenburg to work at his father's mine. In June 1914, when Edith returned to the canyon, the two were still corresponding, as Lauzon wrote to her from Wickenburg that "Yes! Looking after the saddle horse down there (Bass Camp) is much better than being up above where there is so much excitement all the time." He continued that, "If I had a stake big enough so we could live happy for ever after I would go up and get you tomorrow and we would get a ranch with some water and plenty of room on the outside for the cows and horses to roam over and have a fine time for ever and ever."

Lauzon again returned to the canyon to work for Bass in July 1914. Not only did Bass rehire Lauzon, but he promoted him to supervisor and raised his salary from $60 to $90 per month. Lauzon described his new duties as "guide, packer, and driver" and his responsibilities as "collecting fares, handling tourists, saddle horses, teams and pack animals." Also,

Hubert "Bert" Lauzon riding Flax on the Bright Angel Trail. Lauzon Family Photograph Collection, Cline Library, Northern Arizona University, Flagstaff (NAU.PH.96.3.19.1)

Clockwise from left: Edith, Bert, Loren, Muriel, and Hubert Lauzon at the Grand Canyon, circa 1922. Lauzon Family Photograph Collection, Cline Library, Northern Arizona University, Flagstaff (NAU.MS.96.3.9.4)

on at least one occasion in fall 1914, Bass sent Lauzon to a meeting authorizing him to "act in my behalf." In addition to guiding parties into the canyon, a large part of his job entailed greeting tourists as they arrived and taking them on tours along the canyon rim. Occasionally, when tourists left no tips, he would say that he had been "skunked," and once in a while he would make a comment such as "7 cheap skates."

In April 1916 Lauzon again left Bass's employ to establish a homestead near the canyon. On September 21 of that year he married Edith. With new familial responsibilities he needed a more secure job than that of hired hand. Although he continued to guide for Bass on occasion in 1917–18, he also did spot work on the Bright Angel Trail and continued to work on patenting his homestead. These jobs offered "not much cash, but lots of experience." In 1919 he became the official custodian for the Bright Angel Trail, a county toll trail, and he held this position until the trail became the property of the National Park Service in 1928. Lauzon entered the political arena in 1920, when he was elected Grand Canyon Constable for Coconino County. By 1922–23 he was earning $1,880 per year for his trail work and $360 per year as constable.

Life proved busy for the growing Lauzon family. By 1923 Bert and Edith had three children—Hubert, Loren "Tiny," and Muriel—but sadly, Edith passed away in Phoenix from surgical complications in September 1924. Lauzon had just returned to the canyon after visiting Edith in order to care for their children when he received the bad news. The nurse told him that Edith's last words were "do all you can for me and save me for my cute kiddies."

Despite this tragedy, Lauzon continued to lead an active life. As constable he mostly served warrants, arrested drunks, intervened in domestic violence cases, and helped locals with licensing issues, but on occasion he became involved in more exciting matters. In July 1925 he had to travel to Phantom Ranch to apprehend three thieves. His journal records the following:

At 9.30 PM Bob Fancy and I left Bright Angel in a rain storm for the North Rim to catch three thieves who had devastated the garden at Phantom ranch.
Arrived at Phantom at 1:20 AM slept until 4:30 Started for the North Rim at 5:30 arrived there at 10:30 Talked with Weiness ate lunch and started

back with Prisoners at 11 AM July 21st Arrived Phantom at 3 PM Left Phantom at 4:30 and arrived at head of Yaki trail at 7:30

22 hours for the round trip across the Grand Canyon a trip of 60 miles by trail is so far the record

Rode Canyonita [Bert's horse] to Phantom a Harvey Mule to N. R. and back to Phantom and Canyonita to S. R.

Had made a ride to Hance place and return on the same day that we had started to N. R. 100 mile ride in 36 hrs. 60 miles of trail.

The most notorious criminal Lauzon helped apprehend was Matt Kimes, a man wanted for murder in Oklahoma who had fled as far as the Grand Canyon. He was arrested after a considerable fight, and Lauzon was detailed to take him to the jail in Flagstaff (there was no jail at the South Rim). Although local lore relates that Lauzon held a gun to his head the whole way, he wrote that "Kimes from that time (after capture) until the cell door clanged behind him here this morning was a very peaceable hombre."

While enforcing the law and working on the Bright Angel Trail, Lauzon continued to care for his three children. In 1927 he married schoolteacher Rosa White and the two remained together until Lauzon's death. At his homestead, he also raised and trained horses with a passion, keeping detailed records of horses that he owned, sold, and trained. He talked about horses by name, entered rodeos, and of course, used them extensively for work. One of his favorites was a large palomino named for his friend, Governor George W. P. Hunt.

Lauzon's life changed dramatically in 1928, the year that Coconino County relinquished the Bright Angel Trail to the National Park Service. Lauzon's job as trail custodian ended, but he was hired as a park ranger, starting work on January 1, 1929. He worked as trails supervisor and as a law enforcement ranger, helped patrol park boundaries for poachers, assisted with fish plants on Clear Creek, and accompanied an expedition that investigated rumors about dwarf horses out toward Havasu Canyon. His long experience in the Grand Canyon's backcountry working for Bass and the Kolbs and time spent as constable made him especially suited to these types of responsibilities.

Hubert F. "Bert" Lauzon died of silicosis on November 3, 1951, shortly after his retirement from the park service. He was cited for meritorious service posthumously; the award was presented to his widow, Rosa Lauzon.

Bert and Rosa Lauzon on the rim of the Grand Canyon, circa 1950. Lauzon Family Photograph Collection, Cline Library, Northern Arizona University, Flagstaff (NAU.PH.96.3.15.16)

WORKS CITED

Bert Lauzon: Forty years at the Grand Canyon, 1911–1951. http://www.nau.edu/library/speccoll/exhibits/lauzon/. Northern Arizona University, Cline Library, Special Collections, Flagstaff.

Coconino County Collection. Collection #50. Arizona Historical Society/Northern Arizona Division, Flagstaff.

Emery Kolb Collection. Northern Arizona University, Cline Library, Flagstaff.

Lauzon Family Collection. Northern Arizona University, Cline Library, Flagstaff.

Lauzon Family Photograph Collection. Northern Arizona University, Cline Library, Flagstaff.

Lauzon, Loren. 1997. Oral History, November 14. Northern Arizona University, Cline Library, Flagstaff.

Suran, William C., ed. The papers and journals pertaining to the Kolb brothers 1911–1912 trip through the canyons of the Green and Colorado Rivers: including the journal of Hubert F. Lauzon by Ellsworth L. Kolb, Emery C. Kolb, and Hubert F. Lauzon. Northern Arizona University, Cline Library, Special Collections, Flagstaff.

BUCKSKIN MOUNTAIN

BY JOHN S. AZAR

*John S. Azar has spent many seasons on the Arizona Strip and Kaibab Plateau ("Buckskin Mountain"
to Mormon pioneers) volunteering his labor and expertise to the rehabilitation of historic cabins. In this
presentation, John reflects on the varied cultures and people to inhabit the plateau, and he also identifies some of the
historic buildings that still grace the forest and nearby canyons.*

Four thousand years ago, Desert Archaic peoples came to
the North Rim area. Archaeologists uncovered evidence of
their stone projectile points during a survey along Arizona
67 in 1984 and have found more since, but mystery still
surrounds these people. We know that they hunted with
spears and atlatls, fashioned split-twig figurines, snared
rodents, and lived nomadic lives, but we do not know much
more. They or their culture apparently vanished by 300 BC.

Nearly 2,000 years ago, Basketmaker peoples began to
use the mountain. They were followed by the ancestral
Pueblo, who grew corn and squash, hunted with bows, and
built clusters of stone-walled rooms beneath overhanging
cliffs and on the plateaus above for residences, religion, and
food storage. Petroglyphs and colorful pictographs imply
that there was time for creativity. They stayed for a thousand years, perhaps, then left. No one knows why for certain, although some believe that drought drove them out,
and others assert that Numan (Paiute) peoples displaced
them and their way of life. For whatever reason, the ancestral Puebloan people left the mountain by AD 1250.

For 600 years the Kaibab band of Southern Paiutes had
the mountain to themselves until European-American
trappers, traders, and hunters began to visit the area in the
early nineteenth century. In the 1850s Mormons arrived
and remained. To this day the majority of the inhabitants of
Buckskin Mountain and its surroundings are Latter-Day
Saints. Mormons fled from the Midwest to Utah to escape
persecution in Illinois. Led by Brigham Young, they arrived

in the Great Basin and spread south into Arizona. After the
original Fort Kanab was constructed, Jacob Hamblin and
John D. Lee crossed over Buckskin Mountain in their effort
to find a shorter route from Kanab to Lees Ferry. About
1860 they found their way up the mountain from the surrounding lowlands to a small sinkhole that today bears
Hamblin's name (Jacob Lake). Here the two men built a
multiroomed adobe "road house." This may have been the
first structure to be built on the mountain by white men.

Levi Stewart and his son John built the next log
dwellings. The founding of the town of Kanab in 1870 on
the site of the short-lived original fort created a demand for
lumber to build homes, barns, and all manner of outbuild-
ings. The Stewarts answered the call and hauled an old lumber mill purchased from John D. Lee up to a gushing spring
that emerges from a cliff face and cascades down a fern-
laden slope to a series of ponds below. Levi named it Big
Springs, and he built his lumber mill and cabins next to the
surging water. In 1871 John Wesley Powell's surveying party
wintered at Big Springs to set triangulation points for their
topographical survey. Frederick Dellenbaugh, a young member of the party, described coming into Stewart's camp:

> All day long we traveled through sandy hills gradu-
> ally rising toward the plateau, the foot-hills of which
> we reached late in the afternoon. We had followed a
> waggon [sic] road with our pack-train up to this
> point, but here we struck off on a trail that was said

to be a shorter way to the canyon we were aiming for, and a little before sunset we came to the brink of a steep slope, almost a cliff, where a picturesque, a romantic view opened before us. Below stretched away to the south a narrow, deep, and sharply defined valley or canyon one-eighth mile wide, the bottom of which seemed perfectly flat. . . . After four miles up the valley through beautiful pine trees of great height, we came to a deserted log cabin only half roofed over, and there we stopped to make our temporary headquarters. The Stewarts of Kanab had started a saw-mill at this place, but as yet the work had not gone very far.

The Stewarts had been suddenly summoned home after a fire at Kanab destroyed their main residence and killed Levi's wife and four sons. Somehow, Levi and John found the strength to carry on with the mill. They were successful with the lumbering enterprise for many years after Powell's men left the scene.

Cattle ranching on Buckskin Mountain began just after the Stewarts' lumber mill started cutting logs into usable beams and planks. The Stewarts, along with another Mormon family, the Naegels, ran cattle and sheep in the forests around Big Springs in the 1870s and 1880s. By 1890 the Stewarts had given their land and water rights to

Uncle Jim Owens on the front porch of his cabin, 1926. Grand Canyon National Park Museum Collection (#5499)

the church, which formed a cooperative with John W. Young as its leader. The best known of Brigham Young's sons, John Young was the "mover and shaker" of his day, jumping from one scheme to another. To his father's dismay, none of Young's enterprises were successful. P. T. Reilly, in his book, *Lee's Ferry*, describes Young's entry into the cattle-ranching business:

> He shifted to a large-scale operation in the cattle business, somehow acquiring the United Order range rights on Buckskin Mountain and House Rock Valley. . . . He formed corporations, using his ranch holdings as collateral, and dealt in high finance in Europe as well as the United States. Young lived on a high scale and always needed money.

While in England on a mission for the church, Young met Buffalo Bill Cody at one of his famous wild west shows. In Reilly's words:

> Young conceived the grandiose scheme of building a hunting lodge on the Kaibab (Buckskin Mountain) where wealthy sportsmen could experience a taste of the Old West. Evidently William F. Cody's Wild West Show, then playing in England, provided the motivation. Young got Cody's interest by emphasizing the number of horses in his herds and the opportunity whereby Buffalo Bill could replenish his stock. He painted such a glowing picture of the area that two well-heeled Englishmen, with Cody and his key personnel, decided to take a look.

The ensuing "party of exploration" detrained at Flagstaff on November 3, 1892, and quickly headed for Buckskin Mountain. After a few days spent organizing gear at Young's ranch in House Rock Valley, the dignitaries headed up onto the mountain. On November 26, a photograph was taken on a point along the North Rim. Cody named it "MacKinnon Point" after one of the Englishmen who had just shot his first buck. A piece of paper was signed by the members of the hunting party, stuffed in a tin can, and buried in a stone cairn on the point. The Englishmen apparently enjoyed themselves but decided to forego investing in Young's scheme.

After Theodore Roosevelt set aside Buckskin Mountain as part of Grand Canyon Game Preserve in 1906, the U.S. Forest Service hired James "Uncle Jim" Owens as game warden to kill cougars, wolves, and bobcats. Popular wisdom of the time held that a reduction in predators would protect the game animals. The unfortunate result was an irruption in the number of deer. Before the foresters could get approval from Washington to conduct hunts and issue hunting permits to private individuals, the deer population had denuded the mountain. The starving animals created a browse line eight feet high in the trees, suffered, and died in large numbers. To address the problem, ranger stations were built on Buckskin Mountain to accommodate and register hunters. During the early forest preserve period, ranger stations were built at Jump Up (1906), Ryan (1908), and Jacob Lake (1910). These cabins became beehives of activity as checking and information stations with the onset of deer hunting in 1924. In the off-season, the stations were used for overnight stops by timber counters, who marked the trees to be taken by local loggers. Although the Ryan station is gone, both the Jump Up and Jacob Lake stations remain as reminders of pioneer life on the mountain.

Cattle ranching on Buckskin Mountain crested about 1920. VT Ranch and the Bar Z outfit emerged by 1930 as major consumers of land and water both on the mountain and in House Rock Valley. A range war of sorts erupted between the Bar Z and a group composed of peripheral users of the Arizona Strip. The foreman for the Bar Z, Charles Dimmock, filed charges against Jim Emmet (the ferryman at Lees Ferry) for cattle rustling. Dimmock claimed to have an eyewitness who would testify against Emmet in court, while the western novelist Zane Grey took up the battle in Emmet's favor. It was through Grey's efforts that Emmet was exonerated, but violence erupted after the verdict was read. In an effort to calm the atmosphere, the forest service proposed a drift fence to separate the livestock of the opposing factions, after which the range war died down.

In the spring of 1911, Arizona historian Sharlot Hall left Prescott in a chuck wagon driven by regional guide Allen Doyle. Their route north from Flagstaff crossed the Little Colorado River near Cameron and the Colorado River at Lees Ferry. After a short stay with the ferryman

Jump Up Cabin, 1997. Photograph by the author

Bar Z Ranch buildings, with Kaibab Lodge in the background. Photograph courtesy North Kaibab Ranger District, Kaibab National Forest

and his family, Hall and Doyle made their way to Fredonia, where they remained a week or more as welcome guests of the small town. While the wagon was repaired, Hall interviewed residents and visited the Paiute Reservation. She was impressed with the agricultural progress made by the Mormons, and erroneously predicted that the vast Arizona Strip would some day bloom like a garden. Leaving Fredonia, the two tourists took the wagon up onto the mountain and visited Jim Owens at his station in Harvey Meadows. It was a short ride from there to the North Rim, where they viewed the Grand Canyon from Bright Angel Point. After saying goodbye to Owens, the pair rolled down the mountain and continued their loop around the canyon to the west, crossing at Pierce Ferry to reach the south bank of the Colorado River. After safely returning to Prescott, Hall went on to become Arizona's state historian and the namesake for today's Sharlot Hall Museum.

The Vaughn brothers, Bill and Bob, are unheralded characters who arrived on the mountain from the Texas panhandle in the early years of the twentieth century. They may have accompanied Jim Owens and Buffalo Jones from the Goodnight Ranch. Bill was killed in World War I, but Bob endured to become a popular cattleman on the Arizona Strip. He was not only adept at all cowboy tasks, but was an expert rodeo man and quite a colorful character. In his 1977 interview with Vaughn, Charles Niehuis remarked:

That afternoon at the House Rock Valley Store, the time John Schoppmann coffeed me and Bob, Bob talked about the first Buffalo hunt. "We was havin' a pretty good time that night. It was the beginning of World War II and meat rationing. Somehow a lot of likker dealers and saloon keepers got mighty lucky getting buffalo killing permits. But they was all good fellows. Each one of 'em brought along some whiskey. Everybody got a little of that tongue oil and everybody was real friendly and visiting until some mean feller got too much tiger's milk. We punchers damned near got into it with your boys from the game department . . . remember?"

Buckskin Mountain remains remote and rugged terrain. Mormon residents persist, as do the Southern Paiutes, who are still recovering from disruptions of their traditional culture and coping with new economies and ways of life. Tourists come in the summer months, motoring up to Jacob Lake then on to the North Rim for a short view of the canyon, and hunters arrive in droves for the autumn hunting seasons. Few hikers and backpackers make it to this side of the canyon, preferring the more accessible south side. So the mountain lives on relatively undisturbed.

Former president Theodore Roosevelt and his hunting party at Uncle Jim Owens's cabin on the North Rim, 1913. Grand Canyon National Park Museum Collection (#10455)

The Grand Canyon and Colorado River on Postage Stamps

by Bill Bishop

Bill Bishop's long experience as a river guide ignited an eclectic interest in canyon history, in pursuit of which he happened to attend the First Day of Issue Ceremony for the sixty-cent Grand Canyon postage stamp released in January 2000. Bishop donated a program obtained at the ceremony to Northern Arizona University's Cline Library Special Collections, and several Cline staff members asked him to assist in obtaining philatelic material relating to the Colorado River and the Grand Canyon. Subsequent research led to this fascinating, comprehensive, and well-received presentation.

Since the first postage stamps depicting the national parks were released in 1934, the Grand Canyon has been represented on more stamps than any other park (U.S. Postal Service 2000b). Before proceeding to discuss the individual stamps that the United States Postal Service has issued, certain terms that I will use throughout this presentation require definition.

The postal service issues many categories of stamps, including those used for regular mail, for postal stationary, for official government mail, and for duck stamps. Stamps presented here fall into four categories. *Definitive* or *regular issue* stamps are used for everyday postage; often depict famous people, flags, flowers, etc.; and are produced for several years or until rate changes make them obsolete. *Commemorative* stamps honor an individual or event. They are usually denominated with the current first-class rate, produced for a limited time, then recalled and any remaining stamps destroyed. *Airmail* stamps provide additional postage for air transport; however, most first-class intercity mail has been transported by airplane for many years. The current term for this class of stamps is *international rate*, since they meet international postage requirements. The final category, *postal cards*, have the rate imprinted on them and can only be purchased at postal service facilities. These cards are the same size as common postcards, but are usually blank except for the imprinted rate.

An *issue* or *series* results when the postal service issues, usually over an extended period, several stamps or sets of stamps having a similar purpose or theme. The postal service often releases commemorative stamps as part of an issue.

The Scott Publishing Company of Sidney, Ohio, assigns a unique identifying number to every stamp issued. Each country has its own set of *Scott Numbers*, which the company differentiates according to the category of stamp and then issues sequentially. Scott Numbers for definitive and commemorative stamps do not have a prefix; a typical definitive or commemorative stamp Scott Number would appear as Scott 1234, or simply 1234. Scott Numbers for airmail or international rate stamps use the prefix C; a typical airmail or international rate Scott Number appears as C123. Postal cards have the prefix UX, while airmail postal cards add a C to the prefix, i.e., UXC12. Scott uses numerous additional prefixes for other categories of stamps, but these are the only ones presented in the following discussion.

STAMPS PORTRAYING THE GRAND CANYON/COLORADO RIVER

Most of the stamps identified here are commemoratives, the majority released as part of an issue or series. The following paragraphs offer a brief history of the issue, if applicable, along with a few words on the individual stamp(s).

NATIONAL PARKS ISSUE OF 1934: A series of ten stamps, with denominations ranging from one to ten cents, in one-cent increments. The stamps were issued between July and October 1934 to stimulate interest in visiting the national parks, thereby helping to bring the country out of the Great Depression. The two-cent Grand Canyon stamp (Scott 741) depicts Bright Angel Canyon and the Temples of Deva, Brahma, and Zoroaster, as viewed from the North Rim. It was issued on July 24 at the Grand Canyon. The Great White Throne is portrayed on the eight-cent Zion stamp (Scott 747), which was issued at Zion National Park on September 18. These two commemoratives were also available at the Philatelic Agency in Washington, D.C., on the same dates.

The two-cent Grand Canyon stamps—both the perforated National Parks Issue Scott 741, released in 1934 at Grand Canyon and Washington, D.C., and the imperforate Farley Special Printing Scott 757, issued in 1935. Photograph by the author

FARLEY SPECIAL PRINTINGS OF 1935: The postal service issued this series of twenty stamps without perforations or gum. Postmaster General James A. Farley developed the dubious habit of taking sheets of stamps off the presses before they could be perforated or gummed, signing the back of the sheet, and presenting them to government officials as souvenirs. The imperforate sheets were easier to sign because the pen tip couldn't get stuck in perforations. Between 1933 and 1934, the postal service created ninety-eight of these special sheets. When a stamp dealer placed one of these rarities on sale and insured it for $20,000 just after their release, the public became outraged. To remedy the situation, the postal service reissued all twenty of the stamps as imperforate, ungummed, full-press sheets (usually two hundred stamps), and offered them for sale to the public on March 15, 1935, exclusively at the Philatelic Agency in Washington, D.C. The stamps were withdrawn from sale three months later and the unsold stamps destroyed. This issue came to be known as "Farley's Follies," the most notorious philatelic scandal this country has ever seen (Title 1966, 3). The scandal involved all ten of the National Parks Issue stamps of 1934; the postal service reissued the Grand Canyon stamp as Scott 757 and the Zion stamp as Scott 763.

BOULDER DAM STAMP: This stamp is one of only two stamps in this presentation that is not part of a larger series. The postal service issued the three-cent Boulder Dam stamp (Scott 774) to commemorate the dam's completion. The stamp depicts the dam as viewed from downstream, and the postal service scheduled it for release on September 28, 1935. But President Franklin Roosevelt had a last-minute schedule conflict and was unable to attend the dedication ceremony, so both the dedication and the first day of issue were postponed until September 30. The stamp was issued in Boulder City, Nevada, on that date, and at the Philatelic Agency in Washington, D.C., on October 1.

JOHN WESLEY POWELL STAMP: The postal service issued the six-cent John Wesley Powell stamp (Scott 1374) at the dedication of the John Wesley Powell Memorial Museum in Page, Arizona, on August 1, 1969. As with the Boulder Dam stamp, the Powell stamp was not part of a larger series. It commemorates the centennial of Powell's first expedition down the Green and Colorado rivers, and depicts three boats navigating the river with Major Powell at the tiller of the lead boat.

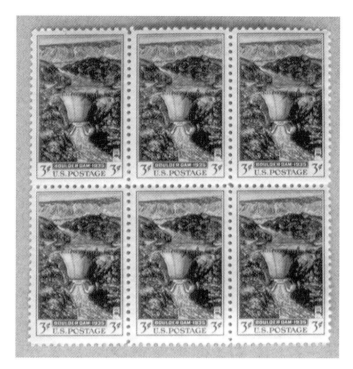

Three-cent Boulder Dam stamps (Scott 774) issued in 1935 at Boulder City, Nev. Photograph by the author

Six-cent John Wesley Powell stamp (Scott 1374), issued in 1969 at the dedication of the John Wesley Powell Memorial Museum in Page, Ariz. Photograph by the author

TOURISM YEAR OF THE AMERICAS, 1972 ISSUE: The postal service issued a set of five postal cards, three first class and two airmail, to promote the "Tourism Year of the Americas '72" campaign. Usually new issues have a "designated" first-day city where the stamp may be purchased on the first day of issue; it then becomes available nationwide the following day. However, all five of these postal cards could be purchased at any post office on the first day, June 29, 1972. The nine-cent Grand Canyon airmail postal card (Scott UXC12) portrays the canyon in the upper right corner, and the postal service printed four scenes depicting American tourist destinations on the reverse, as it did on all cards in the series.

UNITED NATIONS, WORLD HERITAGE–UNESCO ISSUE: The United Nations (UN) issues stamps at the post office in its headquarters in New York City and at UN post offices in Geneva and Vienna. In the United States, UN stamps can be used only at the post office within the UN Building. They are more a collectible than a functional stamp. Every few years a pair of stamps representing both a natural and a cultural feature is issued simultaneously at each of the three UN post offices as part of the World Heritage–UNESCO Series, to promote the protection of world cultural and natural sites. On April 18, 1984, the UN issued the twenty-cent Grand Canyon, United States of

The Tourism Year of the Americas Issue nine-cent Grand Canyon airmail postal card (Scott UXC12), released in 1972. Photograph by the author

The twenty-cent Grand Canyon, United States of America stamp (UN [NY] Scott 421), issued by the United Nations. Photograph by the author

America, stamp (UN(NY) Scott 421) depicting the canyon, and the fifty-cent Polonnaruwa, Sri Lanka, stamp (UN(NY) Scott 422), featuring an early Buddhist temple.

PUAS AMERICA ISSUE: The Postal Union of the Americas and Spain (PUAS), an organization consisting of Spain and countries in North and South America, proposed a series of stamps to commemorate the 500th anniversary of Christopher Columbus's arrival in America. The series was to commence in 1989, with each country issuing both a first-class and an airmail stamp on October 12 of each year through 1992. The United States issued both stamps in 1989 and 1990, but issued only the airmail in 1991 and neither in 1992. The theme for the 1990 stamps was "natural surroundings seen by explorers," with the twenty-five-cent PUAS America stamp (Scott 2512) depicting "the Grand Canyon as it may have appeared to the Coronado Expedition, the first European explorers believed to have seen the canyon." An "American Caribbean tropical isle coastline much like the shores of the outer islands first encountered by Columbus upon his arrival in America" is portrayed on the forty-five-cent PUAS America airmail stamp (Scott C127) (U.S. Postal Service, 1990). The postal service issued both stamps at El Tovar Hotel at the Grand Canyon on October 12, 1990.

CELEBRATE THE CENTURY SERIES: This was the most ambitious stamp project ever undertaken by the postal service. A total of ten sheets, one for each decade, each bearing fifteen different stamps commemorating significant trends, influential people, and memorable events of the decade, was issued from February 1998 through May 2000. The postal service issued both the 1900s and 1910s decade panes on February 3, 1998, in Washington, D.C.

Thereafter, the postal service issued a single-decade pane every few months. The postal service selected the thirty-two-cent Grand Canyon National Park stamp (Scott 3183h) for the 1910s pane to commemorate establishment of the park in 1919.

SCENIC AMERICAN LANDSCAPES ISSUE: This series, begun in 1999, presently consists of six international rate stamps and two international rate postal cards, all of which depict natural areas. These were the first stamps to use the new "international rate" designation. The postal service issued

The twenty-five-cent (Scott 2512) and the forty-five-cent (Scott C127) PUAS America stamps, both issued at Grand Canyon in 1990. Photograph by the author

A thirty-two-cent Grand Canyon National Park 1919 stamp (Scott 3183h) helped commemorate the 1910s in the Celebrate the Century Series. It was released in 1998. Photograph by the author

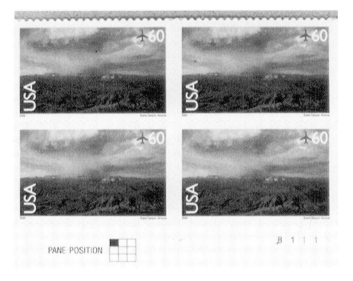

The reprinted sixty-cent Grand Canyon, Arizona, stamp (Scott C135), issued in 2000 at Grand Canyon. Photograph by the author

the sixty-cent Grand Canyon, Arizona, stamp (Scott C135) on January 20, 2000, at the Shrine of the Ages at the Grand Canyon. Originally scheduled for release in 1999, the initial stamps were printed with "Grand Canyon, Colorado," necessitating the destruction of 100 million stamps when the error was discovered. Two days after the stamp was finally released it was recognized that the image, based on a photograph of a sunrise taken from Lipan Point, had inadvertently been reversed during the printing. There was never any effort to recall these stamps (Trujillo 2000, A-1).

WORKS CITED

Information for this paper was obtained from two United States Postal Service publications unless otherwise cited: *The Postal Service Guide to U.S. Stamps,* a comprehensive catalog revised and published yearly, and *Souvenir Pages,* single-page sheets containing technical and historical information released for every stamp issued since early 1972.

Mellone, Michael A. 2000. *Scott 2001 U.S. first day cover catalogue and checklist.* Sidney, Ohio: FDC Publishing.

Title, Samuel H. 1966. The Farley reprint issues of 1935. *First Days,* May–June.

Trujillo, Laura. 2000. Stamp reverses canyon image. *Phoenix Arizona Republic.* February 3.

U.S. Postal Service. 1990. *25-cent and 45-cent America stamps.* U.S.P.S. Souvenir Page–90-21.

———. 1998. *1910s celebrate the century.* U.S.P.S. Souvenir Page–9803B.

———. 2000a. *Grand Canyon.* U.S.P.S. Souvenir Page–0003.

———. 2000b. *The Postal Service guide to U.S. stamps,* 27th ed. New York: Harper Resource.

GRAND CANYON SUMMER OF 1897

BY MARY J. STRAW COOK

This presentation was one of several to bring heretofore unknown or rarely seen historic photographs to the public eye. These images were special indeed, wrapped in the narrative of the young photographers, Amelia and Josephine Hollenback. The images and diary also reveal important historical details about John Hance's ranch, trails, and tourist services immediately before the arrival of the Grand Canyon Railway. Since the symposium in January 2002, Mary J. Straw Cook has edited the Hollenback letters and photographic collection into the book, Immortal Summer: A Victorian Woman's Travels in the Southwest *(Santa Fe: Museum of New Mexico Press, 2002).*

On June 21, 1897, twenty-year-old Amelia Hollenback wrote from the South Rim of Grand Canyon, Arizona Territory:

> Oh, if you could see us now. We are sitting in a most palatial canvas residence with a wooden floor and a Navajo blanket for a rug, two beds, three chairs, a Sibley stove in one corner, a washstand and what passes for a dressing table. Also three nails in the tent poles, at present decorated with the new cowboy hats which are the joy of our hearts. If that isn't a picture of luxury, I don't know where you will find one. (A. Hollenback 1897a)

Amelia and her older half-sister Josephine, of Brooklyn, New York, wrote their letters home from the log-cabin parlor of Thurber's Camp on the South Rim. During late June and early July the sisters, nicknamed Minna and Jo, rented a tent house for $2.50 a day (meals included) for $16\,2/3$ days totaling $41.67, according to Minna's arithmetic. When it came time to settle the bill, however, she paid only $37.50, the total of Mr. Thurber's arithmetic, noting in her expense diary "extra reductions must have been made." Mr. Thurber's statement was written in pencil on a sheet of 1897 Grand Canyon stationery—a piece of all-purpose tablet paper. The bill indicated that guide John Hance earned $60.34 for the

use of his animals and guide service. Apparently, there was no charge for his tall tales (Thurber; A. Hollenback 1897b).

Thurber's Camp, earlier known as Hance Ranch, was originally built by and named for the Grand Canyon's incomparable and lovable prevaricator, Captain John

Amelia Hollenback peering into the Grand Canyon with binoculars, 1897. Katrina Twyeffort Greene and Susan Twyeffort Spoor Collection, courtesy of the author

Hance. In 1895 Hance had sold the property and access trail for $1,500 to J. Wilbur Thurber, also owner of the Bright Angel Hotel and Grand Canyon-Flagstaff Stage Coach Line; Lyman H. Tolfree, owner of Flagstaff's Bank Hotel; and I. F. Wheeler, all three men of Coconino County. In the sales contract, Hance agreed thereafter not to "use or permit to be used my name as guide or in connection with the business of guiding tourists. . . ." If he did so, he would forfeit his quarter interest in the Red Canyon Trail, known today as the New Hance Trail. Nevertheless, by the summer of 1897, Hance was again leading tours because Thurber had rescinded the restrictive covenant a year earlier. Thurber's two partners, Tolfree and Wheeler, may have dropped out of the partnership by this time (Deed Book, 3:436; Promiscuous Records, 1:95; Mangum and Mangum 1999, 37, 68 n. 241).

One of the Grand Canyon's earliest tourist accommodations, the ranch encompassed 160 acres homesteaded by Hance in 1884. The site, near today's Buggeln picnic area, is nestled in a secluded spot approximately fifteen miles east of the Santa Fe Railroad's El Tovar Hotel, which opened in January 1905. The Fred Harvey Company built El Tovar following the 1901 arrival of the railroad to the South Rim at the nearby train depot, and the hotel and railroad terminus shifted most tourist business west to the central trail corridor, where it remains to this day (*Flagstaff Arizona Champion* 1886a).

Hance, who had retained possessory rights to the property in 1895, filed a new homestead notice and received a patent in early 1907, then sold the 160-acre parcel for $5,000 to Martin Buggeln, who earlier managed Bright Angel Hotel (Deed Book, 32:595, 599). In 1908 Buggeln built a two-story, seventeen-room hotel adjacent to Hance's

log cabin and Thurber's somewhat roomier tourist services building, intending to operate the whole as a stage stop. But the days of the stagecoach ended after the arrival of the railroad. All three of the buildings were still standing when the National Park Service purchased the property in 1947 for $50,000. The park service announced that they would preserve these structures as a historic site, but later tore them down, allegedly for safety reasons. Demolition took place in 1957, before Congress passed the 1966 National Historic Preservation Act (*Phoenix Arizona Republic* 1948; John Hance File; Deed Book, 32:598; Euler 1987; Mangum and Mangum 1999, 95).

In 1897, on their first trip to the Southwest, the Hollenback sisters traveled to the Grand Canyon by a rollicking all-day stage ride over a distance of seventy-five miles. The ride began at Flagstaff's red-sandstone Bank Hotel building, which still stands today across from the railroad tracks (belonging to the Santa Fe Pacific in 1897) that connected northern Arizona with the East and West coasts. The Grand Canyon stage began its journey promptly at 7:00 AM. J. Wilbur Thurber, a northern Arizona businessman and early canyon entrepreneur who owned the line, called himself the "gentlemanly" driver and held the reins. Thurber's family, including his wife, baby Grace, and Lotty, entertained tourists once the stage arrived at the South Rim camp.

As the stage climbed northward from Flagstaff, it crossed Fort Valley to Hart Prairie and wound through white-barked aspen trees, crossing the ferned flanks of the San Francisco Peaks. The stage stopped briefly for passengers to stretch at Little Spring, north of Fern Mountain Ranch (an earlier stage stop). By noon the bottom-sore, dusty, but eager passengers were greeted by

Thurber's Camp, Grand Canyon, 1897. Katrina Twyeffort Greene and Susan Twyeffort Spoor Collection, courtesy of the author

Hance's Cabin, 1897. Katrina Twyeffort Greene and Susan Twyeffort Spoor Collection, courtesy of the author

the lonesome folk at East Cedar Ranch for a fifty-cent lunch—which *usually* cost seventy-five cents, according to Minna Hollenback. Today, the ranch is owned by the Babbitt family. Between Fern Mountain and East Cedar Ranch the stage descended some two thousand feet in elevation to a cedar-covered plateau (Wahman 1975; Mangum and Mangum 1999). After the noonday meal, the stage driver with his precious cargo of money-bearing tourists again lunged northward. The last stop was Moqui Tanks.

Then, just at sunset, the stage arrive at the Grand Canyon's South Rim, more often than not in a cloud of dust, with the driver calling out to his passengers, "Keep a sharp lookout through the trees to the right and you'll see the glen." Minna wrote, "They have large ideas in the West!" The Hollenback sisters also noted in their letters that every path in Arizona no matter how small was called a trail, and the word "canyon" was often spelled "cañon," the Spanish variant. Minna described their stage arrival at Thurber's Camp:

The stage goes plunging down a hill and there in front of you is a little pine hollow and a settlement of about fourteen tents, log-house and a cabin with apparently a small crowd of people standing around watching for the stage. The sight of these people makes you suddenly remember the thick layer of dust with which you are decorated, and you wish you could get out on the other side; then you wonder if that "benevolent old Yankee" leaning over the fence is John Hance. In a few minutes you start to walk up the sandy slope back of the house. There are many-colored rock fragments strewed around, and wild flowers and cacti, sage brush and queer twisted cedars and piñons grow all about. Perhaps if

you stood on those rocks just ahead you might see better which way to go. You try it,—*and then you see IT!* As if half the world had fallen away before your feet, and after that you are no longer on the same old earth. (A. Hollenback 1897a)

Raconteur John Hance and his bar-nothing humor gained such popularity during the late nineteenth and early twentieth centuries that he was always in great demand as a Grand Canyon guide. As early as 1886 he advertised his accommodations and guide services in the *Flagstaff Arizona Champion* (1886b). Minna Hollenback wrote:

If there were no Cañon and no stage line, it would be worth anyone's while to come here and talk to John Hance. He is the greatest man in all this part of the country, owns the whole Cañon and everyone in it . . . and is a sort of grandfather or uncle to everyone around him. Years ago he was a scout and went through all the Indian wars, but took to lumbering . . . then a cowboy told him of the Grand Cañon, in days when people hardly knew of its existence, and he came out here in the middle of winter and was, I think, the first white man to climb down its awful walls and stand beside the Colorado River.[1]

Now he lives here, as he has for thirteen years, and spends his summer taking people over his trails; and I never saw a person whom I would rather trust

Tourists at Thurber's Camp stage stop, 1897. John Hance stands at the front of the stage coach by the fence. Katrina Twyeffort Greene and Susan Twyeffort Spoor Collection, courtesy of the author

[1] John Hance is generally thought to have arrived at Grand Canyon in 1883, although there is little known of his whereabouts after the early 1870s, when he left Camp Verde, Arizona, until leading his first canyon tours in 1883 or 1884.

with any number of children on a trail or my whole fortune if I had one to be left somewhere.

He is [as] patient, kind-hearted, thoughtful and unselfish a man as you can imagine, if he does have a peculiar and original way of pronouncing his English; but, oh my, what fish stories he can tell! (A. Hollenback 1897a)

Minna and Jo Hollenback sent for old John Hance early the morning after their arrival. When they asked if he could take them to the bottom of the canyon, he replied, "Sure Thing! [a favorite expression of his], but I can't promise to bring you back! And then in a very solemn and serious tone—there's many a *poor sole* has never come back from that river!"

"After our first gasp," wrote Jo, "we assured him that our shoe leather was of the strongest, and as it happened we used very little of it anyway on that trip."

Jo continued, "I mustn't forget to tell you that Minna was barely mounted on her mule, when she was somewhat startled to hear the other guide (who went part ways down the Cañon with us) calling out behind her—'Get up, Fatty! Get up, Fatty!!'—for that was the name of her mule!" (J. Hollenback 1897a)

It just so happened that Minna Hollenback's nickname at home also was Fatty. Jo revealed in 1897 that "Fatty" Hollenback *wasn't* brown like her mule when they got back that night, but the "loveliest shade of deep, rich crimson. . . ." Sunburn wasn't the only thing Minna sorely

recalled of the trip into the Grand Canyon, an experience, she wrote, that:

No one could forget five minutes of the day when he first did that. "A mile and a quarter you go into the solid earth, and if you put your ear to the ground by the river you can hear the Chinamen eating rice with their chop sticks." (Quotation from Captain Hance) The trail is very good, and there is only one place where people nearly always walk and lead their mules because, as Mr. Hance says, it "looks a leetle frightful." But it is an experience to make an innocent Easterner think that she has accomplished something quite wonderful, till she finds that John Hance and his men think nothing of going to the river and back twice a day. . . . (A. Hollenback 1897a)

Jo described more of the trip into the Grand Canyon:

Such a glorious ride as we had. . . . The trail is John Hance's second one, for the first (where one had to climb down rope ladders, over high precipices part of the way) has been abandoned on account of a bad wash-out in a heavy storm. . . .

We reached the river, a rushing muddy torrent, confined by high cliffs, except where the camp is, about one o'clock. The "camp" on its bank consists of one tent and a corral for the horses, but farther

Amelia and Josephine Hollenback on muleback in the inner canyon, 1897. Katrina Twyeffort Greene and Susan Twyeffort Spoor Collection, courtesy of the author

down the river John Hance has a little cabin, where he goes with his mules and horses when winter comes on, and it grows too cold to stay up here, on the rim, of the Cañon. . . .

John Hance has a little cabin up here on the rim, about half a mile away, where he goes after the log house here is closed in the fall, and it is yet too warm to go down into the Cañon and from the yard of his log cabin may be had a view of the Cañon nearly as grand as that from Moran Point. His way, however, of telling us that he enjoyed it was to say, that whenever he was hungry for breakfast he went to his cabin door and looked at the Cañon, and that when he wanted some dinner, he went and looked at the Cañon—and so on. (A. Hollenback 1897c)

John Hance and the Hollenback sisters took daily rides along the rim. Minna's horse was "graced" by the name of Sabine, while Jo's horse "gloried" in the name of Alexander. Minna's horse could "sing" such a lovely song that the sisters nicknamed her "Trilby." Jo's had "true general-like instincts and never wanted Sabine to get ahead of him." On Wednesday, June 29, Minna, Jo, and John Hance rode eastward along the rim for about twelve miles from Thurber's Camp, taking their lunch and cameras as they usually did each day. They discovered bighorn sheep tracks and cliff dwellings on pillars near to and beneath the rim. Jo wrote:

Sometimes near the rim we had every once in a while the grandest views of the Cañon, then having to leave it to find a better path, more inland, through the forests, for some three miles beyond Bissell [Zuni] Point. Then gradually the innocent looking clouds of the morning grew blacker and blacker and it began to rain in good earnest. . . . Just as we were leaving our horses Mr. Hance exclaimed, "It looks very much as if there were some cliff-dwellings over on that point." . . . On we hurried, the rain almost forgotten . . . Mr. Hance, as excited as we were, skipped from rock to rock like a most animated chamois, and we soon saw that the surroundings were as new to him as they were to us.

When we finally reached the top we discovered the ruins of what must have been a five or six roomed cliff-dwelling, the best preserved Captain Hance admitted, of any of the ruins which he knows anything about at the Cañon. One of its fort-like walls, right on the edge of the precipice, still stands as high as my head and even those which have tumbled have more the appearance of having

come to grief by means of erosion than by willful destruction by the hands of men. (J. Hollenback 1897b)

Upon reaching camp the evening of June 30, Hance described to Mrs. Thurber and others the new discovery they had made on the rim the previous day. Mr. J. S. Clayton, the general manager who assisted Minna in changing her photographic glass plates in the dining room of the log house and also passed the bread at the dinner table, suggested the new promontory be called "Fort Hollenback." Hance, who had named other Grand Canyon sites after his guests, agreed. So the name Hollenback Point (though misspelled Hollenbeck) remained on the South Rim promontory until 1906, when it was changed to Papago Point. Following discovery of the Hollenback letters and photographs in 1981, the original name of Hollenback Point was restored (in July 1985) by the U.S. Board on Domestic Geographic Names and the Arizona State Geographic Names Board (Orth 1985). In 1897 Minna commented:

What do you think of your distinguished daughters? The idea of leaving our name on a piece of the Grand Cañon makes me feel rather small, though the name is about long enough to reach half way round the particular rock to which they have fastened it. (A. Hollenback 1897d)

As the sun slowly sinks in the western sky, we see Minna and Jo's "every night view" near Thurber's Camp. Romantic Minna wrote:

We have fallen into the habit of taking all our letters up to the rocks to read, for we have not missed an evening on the rocks yet and the stage comes in just before sunset. Jo says she feels as if you must all have been there, you have talked to us so often in that same place.

On those rocks we have sat and talked, joked with other people, eaten chocolate, taken pictures, given yards of information to new arrivals, or more often only sat and thought and looked while night after night the colors changed to new beauty and the Cañon grew from an awful forbidding realm of another planet to a kind of protecting presence, grander and more beautiful but no longer oppressive. Sometimes I think that a person might feel safer here than in any other place on earth. It seems too calm, too great for any of the harms and bothers that vex the outside world to live near the shining of its walls.

And it is in such a place that we have laughed and grown warm and friendly toward all the world over the home news, and there we have shaken hands and congratulated each other because some day we may be able to lead the family up there and then just sit to one side and jubilate over their happiness. But we won't talk to you. On our first view of the Cañon, two kindly intentioned tourists went up with us and asked us what we thought of it and if it wasn't grand. You will excuse me if I keep a little wondering pity for those misguided individuals. (A. Hollenback [1897]e)

While Josephine Woodward Hollenback and Amelia Beard Hollenback of Brooklyn, New York, were by no means the first women to visit the Grand Canyon during the nineteenth century, their letters, diaries, and photographs of 1897 comprise a significant source of women's history of northern Arizona and northwest New Mexico. And to that, John Hance of the Grand Old Cañon would add, "Sure thing!"

Works Cited

Flagstaff Arizona Champion. 1886a. January 22.
———. 1886b. September 18.
Phoenix Arizona Republic. 1948. August 3.

Deed Book. Coconino County Recorders Office, Flagstaff, Ariz.
Euler, Robert C. 1987. Letter to author. December 27.
John Hance File. Arizona Historical Society, Tucson, Ariz.
Hollenback, Amelia. 1897a. Letter to Mabel Haddock. June 21. Hollenback Collection.
———. 1897b. Expense diary. Hollenback Collection.
———. 1897c. Letter to Juliette Hollenback. June 20. Hollenback Collection.
———. 1897d. Letter to mother. July 5. Hollenback Collection.
———. [1897]e. Letter to mother. Hollenback Collection.
Hollenback, Josephine. 1897a. Letter to Juliette Hollenback. June 20. Hollenback Collection.
———. 1897b. Letter to family. July 2. Hollenback Collection.
Mangum, Richard, and Sherry Mangum. 1999. *Grand Canyon-Flagstaff Stage Coach Line.* Flagstaff, Ariz.: Hexagon Press.
Orth, Donald J. (Exec. Sec. for Domestic Geographic Names, U.S. Board on Geographic Names). 1985. Letter to author. July 25.
Promiscuous Records. Coconino County Recorders Office, Flagstaff, Ariz.
Thurber's Grand Cañon bill. Hollenback Collection.
Wahman, Russell. 1975. Grand Canyon Stage Line. *Desert Magazine* (January): 33.

Chapter Thirteen

The Photographs of Robert H. Kuhne: Grand Canyon National Park in Its Infancy, 1920-23

by Mona Lange McCroskey

Many people are unaware that the Grand Canyon Museum Collection preserves approximately 20,000 images of canyon life dating to the late nineteenth century. Some of these photographs are grouped in collections or family albums; nonetheless, we rarely have sufficient background to place them in historical context. In her presentation, historian Mona Lange McCroskey does exactly that, combining the photographs of Robert H. Kuhne, taken at the Grand Canyon between 1920 and 1923, with a biographical sketch of the young photographer and the ambience of Grand Canyon Village in the years the images were taken.

Robert H. Kuhne, the youngest of five children, was born to German immigrants Frank Adolph and Marie Seidler Kuhne in Prescott, Arizona, on May 19, 1902. Frank Adolph, a miner, was frequently and mysteriously absent from the family home in Howell on Lynx Creek. When he died in 1903, the older brothers started a plumbing business in Prescott to support their mother and keep the family together. Their first service vehicle was a horse and wagon.

Too young to join the army during World War I, Robert misrepresented his age to obtain a job as an auto mechanic at Fort Whipple. He also worked for Yavapai County as a heavy-equipment operator in the building of Arizona 89A to Jerome. In 1920 Kuhne's love of automobiles led the eighteen-year-old to the Grand Canyon to work as a tour-bus mechanic for the Fred Harvey Company. Starting in 1901, the Santa Fe Railroad had made the canyon more accessible to visitors. The first automobile trip occurred the following year, when four intrepid travelers took five days—counting the time consumed by various mishaps—driving from Flagstaff to the Grand Canyon (Peterson 1988). Since 1904 the Fred Harvey

Robert H. Kuhne at the South Rim of the Grand Canyon, 1922. Courtesy of the Robert H. Kuhne Collection

Company (purchased by Amfac in 1968 and renamed Xanterra in 2001) has been the primary tourism operator at the South Rim, operating hotels, motels, restaurants, gift shops, a trailer camp, and sightseeing tours.

On February 19, 1919, Congress established Grand Canyon National Park. Immediately popular, the new park attracted 44,000 visitors in its first year. At the time, three unpaved roads led to the South Rim—one each from Williams, Ash Fork, and Flagstaff. The speed limit on Hermit Rim Road (today's Hermit Road), the only paved road in the park, was "20 miles per hour on straight stretches when no vehicle is nearer than 200 yards, otherwise 12 miles per hour but when passing animals only 8 miles per hour" (Hughes 1967).

It was the era of the open motor car. Robert Kuhne joined a crew of about a dozen mechanics in the repair shop. One of his co-workers was Bill Bass, son of early canyon entrepreneur William Wallace Bass. The mechanics maintained the Fred Harvey Company's fleet of cars and trucks, as well as limousines that shuttled tourists back and forth from Flagstaff.

Fortunately, Robert Kuhne carried a camera throughout his life. The photographs he took at the Grand Canyon between 1920 and 1923 show heavy sightseeing traffic early in the park's history. They also showcase canyon landmarks and depict the lives of American Indian artisans who were brought to Hopi House as tourist attractions. Early in Kuhne's career at the Grand Canyon, the photographer encountered one of these artisans—an elderly woman carrying a basket on her head. After he took her picture, she chased him with a stick until he offered to purchase the basket, which remains today

in his daughter's collection. Kuhne also took photographs of American Indian dwellings and horse races. American Indians added interest to long-distance foot races that were popular in the 1920s, and a picture of a Hopi runner appears in his daughter's collection. He formed friendships with Navajos and Hopis, as well as with Havasupais who lived within the Grand Canyon, in later years making innumerable trips to deliver food, clothing, and supplies to their reservations. He eventually joined with Barry Goldwater in efforts to secure land and water rights for the Havasupais.

In his free time away from the garage, Kuhne explored the Grand Canyon. He captured on film a former mining camp on Horseshoe Mesa, where he found his father's papers and belongings, undisturbed for more than twenty years. This discovery solved the mystery of Frank Kuhne's long absences from his family. On these hikes into the canyon and to the waterfalls below Supai, Robert became acquainted with the mule-train guides who worked for Fred Harvey. Armed with a camera, Kuhne returned to the canyon often and accumulated an enormous number of images through the years. He carefully organized them in albums and slide shows, and passed them on to his daughter.

Kuhne's doctor advised him to leave the Grand Canyon due to his high blood pressure. He purchased a house and property on Fair Street in Miller Valley in Prescott, and on December 6, 1923, married Helena Bolden. She was a descendent of pioneer families who had arrived in 1864, soon after the federal government created the Arizona Territory. In 1931 Bob and Helena were blessed with the arrival of their daughter, Joan, delivered by longtime Prescott

Mechanics in front of the Grand Canyon Garage, 1922. Kuhne is third from left. Courtesy of the Robert H. Kuhne Collection

American Indian village, 1922. Courtesy of the Robert H. Kuhne Collection

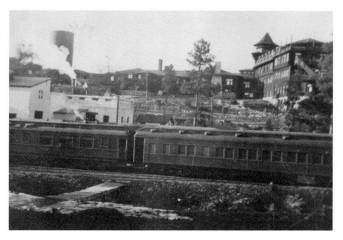

Kuhne recorded numerous early Grand Canyon scenes, including this 1922 view of El Tovar Hotel also picturing the rarely photographed original power station. Courtesy of the Robert H. Kuhne Collection

practitioner R. N. Looney at Grandmother [Laura] Bolden's maternity home. In 1933 the Kuhnes finished a new home on the Fair Street property, where Helena remained for forty-seven years before yielding to progress and a new Smith's grocery store. Two trees planted by the Kuhnes in 1931 remain as sentinels in the parking lot.

Kuhne continued to work as an auto mechanic, worked briefly for the county again, and operated his own garage on Miller Valley Road until 1932. In 1933 he built his first rig and became a full-time well driller. He ran the business from his home, where Helena took care of the books and answered calls. Kuhne drilled the first well at the Yavapai County Hospital, as well as most other wells in the Prescott area during the 1930s and 1940s. Although Kuhne maintained the home in Prescott, he spent much of his time drilling wells on ranches in outlying areas. His wife and daughter accompanied him on these excursions to Kingman, the Big Sandy, Wickenburg, Octave, and Chino Valley. Helena made many long trips into town for supplies and for repair parts when the well-drilling equipment broke down. Today, daughter Joan Kuhne Looney (she married a distant relative of the doctor) resides in Prescott and has happy memories of living in remote line shacks, camping out, home schooling, and exploring the countryside.

In spite of his busy working life, Robert Kuhne found time to present slide shows on various aspects of Havasupai life and the Grand Canyon to community organizations and to such prestigious institutions as the Heard Museum in Phoenix. In 1958 he was named Prescott's first "Man of the Year" for his involvement in civic affairs, including serving as a county supervisor, establishing the Miller Valley Fire District, building the first YMCA swimming pool, and especially for helping to build the Yavapai Community Youth Center (today enlarged to include a school for physically challenged children).

Hopi runner, 1922. Courtesy of the Robert H. Kuhne Collection

Robert Kuhne died in 1976, but he has not been forgotten. In December 1997 friends and family gathered to unveil a plaque honoring him at the Prescott Child Development Center, rededicated as the Kuhne Day School (*Prescott Courier* 1997). The photographs in this presentation commemorate his pioneering work with a camera in the first years of Grand Canyon National Park.

WORKS CITED

Hughes, J. Donald. 1967. *The story of man at Grand Canyon.* Bulletin 14. Grand Canyon, Ariz.: Grand Canyon Natural History Association.

Peterson, Tom. 1988. Flagstaff to Grandview in $3\frac{1}{2}$ hours! The first automobile trip to the Grand Canyon. Paper presented at the Arizona Historical Convention, Ephemera, Arizona Historical Society, Tucson, Ariz.

Prescott Courier. 1997. December 21.

The Civilian Conservation Corps' Role in Tourism: The CCC's Retooling of Arizona's Natural resources

by Peter MacMillan Booth

The year 2003 marked the seventieth anniversary of the inauguration of the Civilian Conservation Corps, a New Deal employment program that operated across the nation from March 1933 until June 1942—the long years of the Great Depression. In this presentation, Dr. Booth focuses on the CCC's role in Arizona, particularly its efforts to reclaim exhausted public lands and rebuild transportation infrastructure, in the process preparing the state for its fastest growing postwar economy—tourism. Dr. Booth illustrates that federal land managers were elated from the onset, but industry and many residents who first viewed the "socialist" program with skepticism had to be convinced as the Depression wore on.

One hot and dry evening in late May 1933, a trainload of young men left Phoenix. After rolling through Parker and crossing the Colorado River to Barstow (California), Las Vegas, and Lund (Utah), they detrained, then boarded Utah Parks Company busses bound for their final destination: Civilian Conservation Corps (CCC) Camp NP-1-A at Neil Springs on the North Rim of the Grand Canyon. They arrived at 1:00 AM, hungry—they hadn't eaten in forty-eight hours—and shivering in clothes more suited for the desert floor. Subfreezing temperatures and snow inspired the nickname "Icebox Canyon" (Purvis [1989], 27–31). By July 1933 twenty-one camps had opened throughout Arizona; over the program's nine-year history, the CCC became the New Deal's most popular and, arguably, most successful program.[1] The "Tree Lizards," as the Flagstaff *Coconino Sun* affectionately nicknamed them, or "Civies" as some Grand Canyon enrollees called themselves, became pivotal players in President Franklin Delano Roosevelt's Depression-era conservation policy (*Flagstaff Coconino Sun* 1933; Owen 1983, 3).

In the early 1930s Arizona found itself in the grip of an economic and environmental disaster. The local economy floundered as prices for Arizona's leading products—copper, cotton, and cattle—plummeted. Unemployment surged, average income plunged, and economic growth ground to a halt. Arizonans hoped that their vast natural resources would help them through the Great Depression, but decades of abuse had rendered the land unable to rescue her abusers (Lowitt 1989, 19–21; Sonnichsen 1982, 230–245; Levin 1979; Valentine 1968). Grass depletion, deforestation, and especially erosion caused by mismanagement had taken their toll. Southern Arizona's San Simon Valley, for example, had lost 19,000 acres to erosion, with one arroyo—measuring forty feet deep and one hundred to three hundred feet wide—enlarging a half mile per rainy season.

---

[1] For the CCC on a national level, see John A. Salmond, *The Civilian Conservation Corps, 1933-1942* (Durham, N.C.: Duke University Press, 1967). See also Leslie Alexander Lacy, *The Soil Soldiers: The Civilian Conservation Corps in the Great Depression* (Radnor, Pa.: Chilton Book Company, 1976). For a history of the CCC in Arizona, see Peter MacMillan Booth, "The Civilian Conservation Corps in Arizona, 1933-1942" (MA Thesis, University of Arizona, 1991), and William S. Collins, *The New Deal in Arizona* (Phoenix: Arizona State Parks Board, 1999).

Silt from unimpeded runoff clogged reservoirs and irrigation ditches (*Safford Graham County Guardian* 1934d; *Arizona Highways* 1935a; Owen 1983, 3). Henry Graves, head of the U.S. Forest Service, lamented the 50 to 90 percent decline in the land's "productive power" (Graves 1930) since the 1880s, when the railroad had brought hundreds of thousands of domesticated animals to a young territory.

Roosevelt, at the 1932 Democratic Party Convention, spoke of improving the productivity of "millions of acres of marginal and unused land" (Roosevelt 1932). His two-part conservation strategy required a concerted program to rejuvenate the nation's resources and make them sustainable through a federal land-management program. Technical management agencies implementing Roosevelt's environmental policy sensed opportunity in CCC men and money. In Arizona, offices of the U.S. Forest Service, Bureau of Reclamation, Office of Indian Affairs, National Park Service, and Southwestern National Monument Association undertook frenzied preparations for the CCC's arrival. Fred Winn of Coronado National Forest editorialized that his Tucson headquarters resembled a "Devil's Caldron" of CCC activity, but "at least we are getting somewhere and doing something" (*Coronado Bulletin* 1933b).[2]

These agencies rejoiced at the amount of work they could now accomplish with CCC assistance. Rex King of Crook National Forest (today part of the Coconino National Forest) credited the CCC for enabling his office to complete projects that had been on hold for years (King 1935). Likewise, at Grand Canyon National Park, superintendent M. R. Tillotson believed that "from a purely mercenary point of view the park [will] gain more in the form of physical improvements by the National Recovery Act than would have transpired for a number of years—in some instances not at all—under a normal trend of park affairs" (quoted in Anderson 2000, 25). After a year's operation, his experience with the CCC reinforced his belief that it had

enabled him to complete "projects which we had contemplated, but were unable to execute thru lack of funds" (Ranney 1934). While established agencies expanded their power, others such as the Soil Conservation Service, Division of Grazing (later consolidated with the General Land Office into the Bureau of Land Management), and Fish and Wildlife Service were born with CCC help (*Coronado Bulletin* 1933b).[3]

Although the emergency program operated under federal direction, Arizonans exerted significant influence. CCC Director Robert Fechner promoted the involvement of local groups in the establishment and maintenance of camps, and favored sites recommended by representatives, senators, governors, county boards of supervisors, and city councils.[4] He did this because the maintenance of camps required sustained local involvement. For example, overtaxed military and technical agencies needed help with transportation, supplies, water, and expertise.[5] In addition to practical reasons, Roosevelt wanted to promote a favorable atmosphere for his land-management polices, and nurturing grassroots support helped minimize local opposition (*Safford Graham County Guardian* 1934g).

In the early days of the CCC, however, considerable opposition to the program did materialize. Citizens feared militarization, the precedence of a dollar-a-day wage scale (the amount CCC recruits were paid), and the idea of "importing eastern unemployed undesirables."[6] Western residents believed that outsiders, both easterners and foreigners, would smuggle in seditious, radical, or immoral ideas to corrupt the hearts and minds of their youth. Others like wealthy Grand Canyon tourists and Fred Harvey employees looked down upon CCC enrollees as low-class recipients of the federal dole (Schroeder 1985).

In addition to these apprehensions, the state's powerful copper interests opposed the program; the industry did not stand to profit from the CCC and could suffer politically if

---

[2] See also *Coronado Bulletin* May 19, July 7, September 27, and October 20, 1933.

[3] The following examine CCC involvement with specific agencies: Alison T. Otis, et al., *The Forest Service and the Civilian Conservation Corps: 1933–1942* (Washington, D.C.: U.S. Department of Agriculture, U.S. Forest Service, 1986); John C. Paige, *The Civilian Conservation Corps and the National Park Service, 1933–1942: An Administrative History* (Washington, D.C.: Department of the Interior, National Park Service, 1985); Conrad L. Wirth, *Parks, Politics, and the People* (Norman: University of Oklahoma Press, 1980), 94-157; Hal Rothman, *Preserving Different Pasts* (Urbana: University of Illinois Press, 1989); Donald Parman, "Indians and the Civilian Conservation Corps," *Pacific Historical Quarterly* XL (1971); Phillip O. Foss, *Politics and Grass* (Seattle: University of Washington Press, 1960); Hugh Hammond Bennett, "Soil Erosion and its Preservation," in *Our National Resources and Their Conservation*, A. E. Parkins and J. R. Whitaker, eds., (New York: J. Wiley & Sons, 1936).

[4] Examples of camp requests fill these collections: Isabella Greenway Collection, Arizona Historical Society, Tucson; Carl Hayden Collection, Arizona Collection, Hayden Library, Arizona State University, Tempe; Governor Files, Gov. Mouer, Arizona State Archives, Phoenix.

[5] Local newspapers such as the *Flagstaff Coconino Sun* and the *Safford Graham County Guardian*, as well as CCC camp newsletters, commonly ran stories about the CCC's interactions with local communities.

[6] On fear of easterners, see *Phoenix Arizona Republic* April 9, 1933, April 11, 1933; *Salt Lake Tribune* April 9, 1933; Kenneth Wayne Baldridge, "Nine Years of Achievement: The Civilian Conservation Corps in Utah," (PhD diss., Brigham Young University, 1971), 11. On fear of a dollar-a-day wage, see *Southwest Labor Record* April 6, 1933; Salmond 1967, 16, 27, 28. On fear of militarization, see Lyon Strong, CCC Alumni, Tucson, personal interview, April 18, 1990; Fred Leake and Ray Carter, n.d., *Roosevelt's Tree Army: A Brief History of the Civilian Conservation Corps.* (Carmichael, Calif.: National Association of Civilian Conservation Corps Alumni, n.d.). Other examples of early opposition: *Phoenix Arizona Republic* May 19, 1933, June 25, 1933; *Flagstaff Coconino Sun* May 26, 1933.

other sectors of Arizona's economy grew more influential. One editorial claimed that if Roosevelt would help the copper mines reopen, "Arizona will never ask for a dollar from the CCC, the CWA, the ERA or any other government relief agency" (*Safford Graham County Guardian* 1934a, 1934b, 1934c, 1934e). The writer saw Roosevelt's program as a "pork barrel" project that helped only certain special-interest groups. Conservative elements attacked the CCC as an expensive and meaningless "hoax" that would do more harm than good to wildlife.[7] The *Holbrook Tribune* remarked that although the CCC "will probably save most of these men from becoming bums," the work accomplished would be of "slight" value (*Holbrook Tribune* 1933). The *Phoenix Arizona Republic* claimed that there "will never be an adequate return" on the money (1933a). The Kanab, Utah, newspaper made fun by suggesting a few ludicrous projects: widen and deepen the Grand Canyon; raise the summit of the San Francisco Peaks; build new approaches and reinforcement girders on the Natural Bridge; repaint the Painted Desert in more modern colors; and "build an indoor and outdoor auditorium with amplifying systems and speaker's platform for exclusive use of farmer Brown" (*Kanab Kane County Standard* 1933).

Once the CCC moved from dream to reality, Arizonans' sentiments changed as the benefits accrued. Arizona's highway commission, hoping to develop the state's scenic wonders as tourist attractions, became a leading promoter of public works (*Arizona Highways* 1934a, 1934b). Through its publication, *Arizona Highways*, commissioners argued that New Deal money was more "essential to the progress, welfare and development of all that vast territory lying in and between the Rocky Mountains and the West Coast than any other activity of the national government" (*Arizona Highways* 1933, 10; *Arizona Highways* 1935b, 10). Other economic interests also recognized potential gain. Lumber companies in northern Arizona went to great lengths to attract camps (Matheny 1977). Agricultural and livestock concerns in areas such as the erosion-devastated Gila River Valley fought hard for CCC activities. Tourist-oriented chambers of commerce in the communities of Phoenix, Tucson, Mesa, Kingman, and Flagstaff also expressed a sincere desire for CCC projects (*Phoenix*

Arizona Republic 1933b, 1933c, 1933d; *Mesa Tribune* 1934; Malach 1984; Summary of Arizona camps). *Arizona Highways*, in martial overtones, suggested that "War is Declared Against the Depression. . . . One major offensive in this war on [the] depression was the putting of men to work NOW . . . on civil projects in an effort to end the need of the dole" (*Arizona Highways* 1934b, 3).

Even groups opposed to most of the president's policies began to support the CCC. Newspapers serving the Arizona Strip looked on the concept of the New Deal unfavorably and characterized Roosevelt as an autocratic, left-wing dictator.[8] But at the same time, local citizens and ranchers lobbied to keep CCC camps in their area. With language reflecting their Mormon audience, one paper editorialized that they needed the CCC to save "The Groves [that] are God's first Temple . . . [that] tend to make man patriotic, religious, esthetic, meditative, romantic, heroic" (*Saint George [Utah] Washington County News* 1933). The editor rationalized his paradoxical support by commenting that "We have never seen a human project work out. But we have faith" (*Saint George [Utah] Washington County News* 1933).[9]

As state interests jumped on the New Deal bandwagon, local input swamped the technical management agencies responsible for implementation.[10] City and county governments and other concerned parties besieged CCC, military, federal, and state officials with camp and project requests.[11] Fred Winn of Coronado National Forest exclaimed that it "sure is remarkable how many different proposals for the use of the crews are submitted, from the construction of chicken coops to pulling out burro weed" (*Coronado Bulletin* 1933c, 1933d). Aside from requesting camps and projects, local communities influenced the program by providing assistance. Due to army shortages, furnishing supplies and transportation, for example, became a key factor for several camps, needs that local authorities could supply only some of the time. Most camps in Arizona had a continual problem securing water, but local help was sometimes available to fill the need (*Safford Graham County Guardian* 1934f).

Supportive communities also treated Roosevelt's "Tree Lizards" to dances, entertainment, sports competitions, and

---

[7] This viewpoint is expressed in C. Edgar Goyotte's Clipping File, Arizona Historical Society Library, Tucson. Fear of damage to the state's wildlife is in *Holbrook Tribune* July 3, 1933, *Springerville Round Valley Press* July 21, 1933, and *Globe Recorder* July 21, 1933.

[8] As late as 1940, one southern Utah paper printed a picture of Roosevelt doctored to look like Adolph Hitler. See *Kanab Kane County Standard* June 14, 1940 and November 8, 1940.

[9] See also *Arizona Cattle Growers* September 20, 1934; *Prescott Evening Courier*

September 20, 1934; Memorandum, Roak to (?) Richardson, March 12, 1940, Box 5, Region 9, Bureau of Land Management, Record Group 49, Pacific Southwest Regional Branch, Laguna Niguel, Calif.

[10] For example, see *Globe Recorder* July 11, 1933.

[11] For example, Western Loan and Building Co. to Isabella Greenway, October 8, 1934, Isabella Greenway Collection, Box 47, Folder 7, Arizona Historical Society, Tucson.

education. Even isolated camps such as the one below Grand Canyon's Phantom Ranch occasionally enjoyed the hospitality of surrounding communities. Enrollees deep in the canyon along Bright Angel Creek and on the North Rim attended dances at VT Ranch (today's Kaibab Lodge) and traveled into Kanab once a month. Enrollees even walked the twenty-one-mile one-way trip from the North Rim to the South Rim to enjoy a movie or a dance. The Community Club of Grand Canyon also supplied enrollees at Phantom Ranch with a pool table (for which they were very grateful even though they had to carry it down piece by piece) and a movie projector, from which the first movie at Phantom Ranch was shown—*The Terrible People* (Purvis [1989] 55–56, 81–86; Ranney 1934).

Public support often determined which CCC camps survived because some of the technical management agencies depended heavily on local interaction to accomplish their missions (Salmond 1967, 64–68; *Tucson Arizona Star* 1936). CCC enrollees working with the Soil Conservation Service, for example, operated on private land, requiring cooperative contracts in which private landholders agreed to provide supplies and maintain CCC improvements (Salmond 1967, 83; Civilian Conservation Corps 1938; Brown 1935).[12] The largest Soil Conservation Service operation during the New Deal encompassed five camps stationed in the erosion-ravaged Gila River Valley at Safford (*Happy Days* 1934; Collins 1999, 222–224). CCC camps working with the Division of Grazing were required to coordinate operations with newly established grazing boards made up of local ranchers who used the public domain. Cooperation between the groups achieved the goal of restoring and managing depleted public lands. It also placated ranchers' anxieties over losing unrestricted use of the public domain.[13]

The National Park Service assisted state park camps that depended on local input, although each camp worked directly with local governments. Because Arizona did not have a state park service, various government bodies were involved.[14] On October 17, 1933, the Pima County Board of Supervisors opened the first such camp at the county

fairgrounds (Hopps 1933; CCC camp occupation log SP-7-A; *Tucson Citizen* 1933). Pima County directed three more of these camps. Phoenix's Park Board supervised two camps at South Mountain Park (the enrollees here seasonally moved between the Salt River Valley and the Grand Canyon), and the Mohave County Park Board at Kingman maintained two camps at Hualapai Mountain Park. The Arizona Fish and Game Commission administered a camp at Papago Park, and the Tucson City Park Board directed another at Randolph Park. Even the University of Arizona took over a former forest service camp at Tanque Verde. Today, this land comprises Saguaro National Park (Summary of Arizona camps).

Logically, the CCC rarely worked where local support failed to evolve. Because the mining town of Clifton never fully supported the program, only two camps existed near this community and neither lasted more than a year (CCC camp occupation logs). CCC commander Louis Linxwiler pulled all contracts and patronage out of Holbrook due to continued animosity (Linxwiler 1990). In the fall of 1939, the CCC abandoned an Ajo camp after only a few months when "the promised cooperation from ranchers in the vicinity of this camp—on which promises the camp was established" failed to materialize.[15] In those areas where support did materialize, such as at the Grand Canyon, the CCC did participate in a wide range of projects from stringing fences to clearing undergrowth to constructing earthen dams (Civilian Conservation Corps [n.d.]a).

Within the broad notion of improving nature's economic value, CCC projects fell into four related categories: resource protection, resource development, rural infrastructure construction, and recreational-tourism development. For the first of these, resource protection, Arizona agricultural and lumber interests advocated defense of environmental capital against "wasteful destruction." In southern and lower elevation areas of northern Arizona, the prime objective was to protect ranch and agricultural lands from erosion, and CCC recruits responded with thousands of check dams, terraces, and water diversion dikes. In the northern forested part of the state where the primary con-

[12] *The Rillito Reveler* February 15, 1936, April 5, 1936. Arizona Historical Society, Tucson; "Tucson-CCC Educational Survey," 1936, Arizona Historical Society, Tucson; *Desert Digest* Thanksgiving Issue, 1936. Arizona Historical Society, Tucson.

[13] For rancher's anxieties over the 1934 Taylor Grazing Act, see Ernest Carleton to Isabella Greenway, February 14, 1936, Box 47, Greenway Collection, Arizona Historical Society; *Arizona Cattle Growers*, September 11, 1934, September 20, 1934, October 2, 1936; Prescott Evening Courier September 19 and 20, 1934; Lowitt, Richard, *New Deal and the West* (Bloomington: Indiana University Press, 1989), 64–72.

[14] For examples see *Phoenix Arizona Republic* September 1, 1933, September 28, 1933; *Tucson Citizen* September 1, 1933.

[15] Pima County Board of Safety to Governor Benjamin Mouer, October 2, 1933, Governor Files, Gov. Mouer, Box 5a, Arizona Archives, Department of Library, Archives and Public Records; E. W. Samuel, Phoenix Grazing Office, to New Cornelia Mine, Phelps-Dodge Corporation, April 17, 1940, Box 4, Arizona Archives, Department of Library, Archives and Public Records; and Regional Grazier, Phoenix, to Grazing Service Director, Washington, March 8, 1941, Bureau of Land Management, Region 9, Record Group 49, Pacific Southwest Branch, Laguna Niguel, Calif.

cern was to protect timber, recruits spent thousands of man-days battling forest fires, with camps competing with each other in how quickly they could respond to a fire. Despite an overall increase in the number of fires, the CCC cut the amount of acreage destroyed by one-half from the prior decade (Sawyer 1976, 6–7). Grand Canyon National Park especially benefited from the CCC's labor force in fighting and preventing destructive forest fires (Purvis [1989], 53–55, 119–121). Park staff as well as lumber interests around Prescott and Flagstaff also asked for CCC help in eradicating tree diseases (Ward 1933).

In the category of resource development, the idea was to improve Arizona's natural capital to a level where it could be productive again. Projects followed along similar regional lines. In northern Arizona, the CCC thinned existing tree stands, replanted seedlings in cutover areas, and provided assistance in improving second-growth ponderosa pine forests. The forest service had planned this activity for years, but lacked the manpower and money to get it done (Civilian Conservation Corps [n.d.]b; Pearson 1940). In southern Arizona, CCC project superintendents with the forest service and Division of Grazing tried to rejuvenate grazing land with range improvements, such as adding stock tanks and wells, and fencing and managing ranch leases (Brown 1935; Gatlin 1982; Willis 1982; CCC enrollees; ECW Progress Maps n.d.). Meanwhile, the Soil Conservation Service and Bureau of Reclamation developed agricultural areas by repairing erosion damage, improving water sources, and digging and improving irrigation canals. The newspaper in Safford expressed the hope that the CCC would bring back to these barren and rapidly eroding sedimentary valleys the "belly deep" wild hay the old timers talk about (*Safford Graham County Guardian* 1934d).

To improve resource management in northern and southern Arizona, the CCC helped management agencies develop rural infrastructure. Tree Lizards built dozens of government buildings on federal lands, including several at the Grand Canyon's South Rim: ranger stations, garages, storehouses, lookouts, and park staff houses. They also built less glamorous but equally important support structures such as parking lots, disposal tanks, sewage systems, and drainage ditches. This type of development was especially important on the South Rim where many tourist buildings existed but lacked support systems (*Grand Canyon Echoes* 1937; *Tucson Arizona Star* 1934; ECW Progress Maps n.d.; Coronado National Forest n.d.; Cameroon 1988). Enrollees also put up miles of telephone wire linking remote areas of the state, including the Grand Canyon's transcanyon telephone line (*Phoenix Arizona Republic* 1936; Purvis [1989], 88–95).

The construction of service roads was the most common and popular CCC project under the category of infra-structure development. For example, the Santa Rita Mountain camp, based south of Tucson, worked on the Box Canyon Road between Helvetia and Greaterville; the Tanque Verde camp completed the road over Redington Pass; and a camp north of Flagstaff completed a road through Shultz Pass. All over the state, new roads and truck trails connected outlying areas with the rest of Arizona.[16] While road construction and maintenance took place on both sides of the Grand Canyon, the North Rim's new automotive roads required constant maintenance, a crucial ongoing project for the Civies of NP-1-A throughout the 1930s (Purvis [1989], 118–119). Recognizing the importance of new roads for rural development, many Arizonans petitioned the managing agencies for a CCC road in their area. One forest service official in Arizona complained that the "favorite outdoor sport in these parts is to put 'the heat on the Forest Service' to improve every old wagon trail which followed its winding course through the hills" (*Coronado Bulletin* 1933a).[17]

Improving access to natural and wilderness areas contributed to the development of recreational areas. These activities received considerable support from chambers of commerce as a means to attract out-of-state visitors. Projects in this category included building trails, campsites, picnic areas, water facilities, outhouses, lodges, visitor centers, tennis courts, and one swimming pool (at Phantom Ranch). While the forest service directed some of these projects, such as those at Mingus Mountain and Madera Canyon, it focused more on improving natural resources. Camps run by the park service and local governments, however, concentrated on recreational development. The CCC established recreational infrastructure at Petrified Forest National Monument (now a national park), Chiricahua National Monument, Phoenix's South Mountain Park, and Pima County's Tucson Mountain Park, among others. At Grand Canyon National Park, recruits expanded visitor facilities, but the crews concentrated on the construction of the Colorado River, Clear Creek, and Ribbon Falls trails, as well as the maintenance of the Bright Angel, South Kaibab, and North Kaibab trails. Other Grand Canyon projects included landscaping along roadsides and in campgrounds to beautify some of the heavily used tourist areas. Even resource-protection projects such as fire fighting and erosion control were meant to preserve the aesthetic, not material, value of the parks. For example, NP-3-A at Phantom Ranch obliterated the old Kaibab Trail because it

---

16 Seven national forest and national park roads are listed in *Arizona Highways* X (September 1934):12. Most roads were truck trails into areas of high fire hazard. See *Coronado Bulletin* late 1935 or early 1936.

17 In addition, enrollees maintained miles of existing forest service roads.

was unsightly (*Phoenix Arizona Republic* 1936; Purvis [1989], 95–131; Ranney 1934; U.S. Department of the Interior 1938; CCC Office of Director 1938; *Tucson Citizen* 1937; *Tucson Arizona Star* 1979; *Colossal Cave Chronicle* 1936; *Caveman* 1937; CCC Camps Occupational Logs). The impacts of these efforts throughout the state were recognized as early as 1935, when *Arizona Highways* credited the CCC with the growth of the state's tourism industry (*Arizona Highways* 1934c and 1935c).

From 1933 until the CCC's demise in 1942, Roosevelt's Tree Lizards completed an impressive number of projects: in Arizona alone, the CCC built nearly 6,000 miles of roads, 85,000 check dams, 1,800 new buildings, 3,500 miles of telephone line, 2.25 million rods of fencing, and 32 acres of beach improvements, and the corps performed 50,000 man-days of forest fire fighting. This does not include additional effort expended on maintenance of existing structures (Civilian Conservation Corps [n.d.]a). These young men were far from lazy, but a qualitative assessment is more difficult to measure. Generally, projects were well done and, indeed, endure to this day. A trip down into Colossal Cave near Tucson or a hike along the Colorado River Trail in the Grand Canyon provide good examples of the quality work. Although the boys did their jobs well, some projects designed by the management agencies were questionable or wasteful. For example, after six years of cutting and trimming infected trees, CCC leaders began to wonder about the effectiveness of twig-blight eradication (Legder 1990). Some projects were even harmful to the environment, such as the eradication of over 180,000 predators (Civilian Conservation Corps [n.d.]a). Recruits at the Soil Conservation Service camp at Randolph Park helped Tucson authorities straighten Pantano Wash in order to limit flood damage and preserve the soil, but the project also reduced sediment deposits and increased runoff, thereby lowering the water table. In a larger sense, it might be acknowledged that helping extractive industries such as agriculture survive in an arid region perpetuated risks to the delicate environment (Park 1936; Civilian Conservation Corps 1938; *Rillito Reveler* 1936; Brown 1935).

It must be remembered, however, that the CCC was not intended to preserve wilderness. Instead, it pursued the more popular Progressive idea of improving nature's value for extractive industries and tourism. If returning the environment to a near-pristine state coincided with this goal, so much the better. The CCC enabled federal agencies to fulfill Gifford Pinchot's dream of Progressive land management. Increased labor backed with federal money helped restore, develop, improve, and manage Arizona's natural resources for multiple uses. In the process, CCC projects helped build a new Arizona. It was, in effect, a federal subsidy equal to the

railroad land grants of the nineteenth century. Although little was done to improve the mining industry, Arizona farmers and ranchers used the grants to retain their prominent position in Arizona's economy. Lumber industries also benefited: the thousands of man-days spent clearing and preparing Arizona forests for harvesting paid off when the demand for lumber grew during and after World War II.

The CCC's biggest impact, however, was on tourism and related service industries, which boomed following World War II. The corps improved Arizona's national parks, as well as the state's national forests and local recreational areas. It also expanded and improved communication and transportation infrastructure throughout the state, which, with its new tourist-friendly parks, was a factor in luring urban-based processing and electronics industries to Arizona in the 1940s and 1950s. Having recreational opportunities only a few minutes away from urban centers helped influence decisions by other corporations to move to Arizona as well (Kline 1990). By 1940, mining remained number one among the state's industries, and railroads still held the second position, but tourism had moved up to number three on the list of economic contributors. Since World War II, tourism and related services have continued to displace Arizona's extractive industries, helping the state escape its dependence on resource extraction. The CCC played no small part in making that happen.

WORKS CITED

Anderson, Michael F. 2000. *Polishing the jewel: An administrative history of Grand Canyon National Park.* Grand Canyon, Ariz.: Grand Canyon Association.

Arizona Highways. 1933. X (October).

———. 1934a. X (January).

———. 1934b. X (April).

———. 1934c. X (September).

———. 1935a. XI (July).

———. 1935b. XI (March).

———. 1935c. XI (February).

Brown, C. B. (Pima County Agricultural Agent). 1935. *1935 Agriculture Extension Annual Report, Pima County.* December.

Cameroon, Cathy. 1988. Building constructions by the Civilian Conservation Corps on the Coronado National Forest. Manuscript. Coronado National Forest Headquarters, Tucson.

Caveman (SP-10-A). 1937. April 31.

CCC camp occupation log. SP-7-A. Governor Files, Gov. Mouer. Arizona State Library, Archives and Public Records, Phoenix.

CCC camp occupation logs, Arizona camps. John Irish Collection. Flagstaff, Ariz.

CCC enrollees. 1982. Group interview with Alison Otis and Kim Lakin. November 9. Transcript at Coronado National Forest Headquarters, Tucson.

CCC Office of Director. 1938. Press release. May 15.

Civilian Conservation Corps. [n.d.]a. CCC-Arizona: Total work completed during the period April, 1933 to June 30, 1942. Entry 67, Record Group 35, CCC Collection. National Archives. Washington, D.C. Copy in Coronado National Forest Headquarters, Tucson.

———. [n.d.]b. Total work completed, Arizona. Entry 115, CCC Collection. National Archives. Washington, D.C.

———. 1938. *Annual report of the director of the Civilian Conservation Corps, 1938*. Washington, D.C.: Government Printing Office.

Collins, William S. 1999. *The New Deal in Arizona*. Phoenix: Arizona State Parks Board.

Colossal Cave Chronicle (SP-10-A). 1936. January 31.

Coronado Bulletin. 1933a. December 1.

———. 1933b. October 20.

———. 1933c. May 19.

———. 1933d. July 7.

Coronado National Forest. n.d. Cultural resources: CCC properties. Coronado National Forest Headquarters, Tucson.

ECW Progress Maps. n.d. Madera Canyon, F-30-A, Second Period, Book 2; Tanque Verde, F-42-A, Second Period; Tanque Verde, F-42-A, Third Period. Coronado National Forest Headquarters, Tucson.

Flagstaff Coconino Sun. 1933. Tree lizards. September 1.

Gatlin, Woody. 1982. Interview by Alison Otis. November 9. Transcript at Coronado National Forest Headquarters, Tucson.

Grand Canyon Echoes. 1937. Project news. April 1.

Graves, Henry. 1930. The public domain. *The Nation* 131 (August 6): 147–149.

Happy Days. 1934. CCC is large factor in great coordinated conservation job: Southwest outfits busy on biggest job in nation. October 27.

Holbrook Tribune. 1933. April 14.

Hopps, Capt C. W. 1933. Letter to Governor Mouer. November 26. Governor Files, Gov. Mouer. Arizona State Library, Archives and Public Records, Phoenix.

Kanab Kane County Standard. 1933. September 22.

King, Rex. 1935. They gave us the CCC. *Arizona Highways* XI (November):12.

Kline, Kerwin. 1990. The last resort: Tourism, growth, and values in twentieth-century Arizona. MA Thesis, University of Arizona.

Legder, Randell (CCC Commander). 1990. Interview by Peter Booth. February 19.

Levin, Rob. 1979. Work eased Tucson's crush. *Tucson Arizona Star*. October 28.

Linxwiler, Louis. 1990. Interview by Peter Booth. December 2. Arizona Historical Society.

Lowitt, Richard. 1989. *The New Deal and the West*. Bloomington: Indiana University Press.

Malach, Roman. 1984. *Home on the range: Civilian Conservation Corps in Kingman area*. Kingman, Ariz.

Matheny, Robert Lavesco. 1977. The history of lumbering in Arizona before World War II. PhD diss., University of Arizona.

Mesa Tribune. 1934. September 13.

Owen, A. L. Riesch. 1983. *Conservation under F.D.R.* New York: Praeger Publishers.

Park, Randolph. 1936. *Desert Digest*. Thanksgiving issue.

Pearson, G. A. 1940. *A guide to timber stand improvement in the Southwest*. Forestry Publication #6. Washington, D.C.: Government Printing Office.

Phoenix Arizona Republic. 1933a. March 29.

———. 1933b. September 23.

———. 1933c. September 25.

———. 1933d. September 29.

———. 1936. Work of CCC in Grand Canyon forms saga of accomplishment. August 9.

Purvis, Louis Lester. [1989]. *The ace in the hole: A brief history of Company 818 of the Civilian Conservation Corps*. Columbus, Ga.: Brentwood Christian Press.

Ranney, Frank. 1934. Land of the Hopi, the Havasupai and the Navajo now being given back to nature and to man by the work of the two C.C.C. companies. *Happy Days*. September 1.

Rillito Revealer. 1936. Rillito Park/Tucson. February 15.

Roosevelt, Franklin. 1932. Roosevelt's acceptance speech. Democratic National Convention at Chicago. July 2. In *Franklin D. Roosevelt and Conservation, 1911–1945*, vol. 1. Ed. Edger B. Nixon. Hyde Park, N.Y.: General Service Administration, National Archives and Records Service, Franklin D. Roosevelt Library, 1957. 112–113.

Safford Graham County Guardian. 1934a. June 15.

———. 1934b. June 22.

———. 1934c. October 5.

———. 1934d. October 12.

———. 1934e. October 19.

———. 1934f. October 26.

———. 1934g. Kelleygrams. November 2.

Saint George (Utah) Washington County News. 1933. May 25.

Salmond, John A. 1967. *The Civilian Conservation Corps, 1933–1942*. Durham, N.C.: Duke University Press.

Sawyer, Gregg. 1976. The history and effects of the New Deal on the Coconino history. Manuscript, National Association of Civilian Conservation Corps Alumni Collection. Arizona Collection, Hayden Library, Arizona State University, Tempe.

Schroeder, John. 1985. Forgotten men of iron: Conservation workers of long ago recall toil, joy of taming Arizona. *Phoenix Arizona Republic.* October 6.

Sonnichsen, C. L. 1982. *Tucson: The life and times of an American city.* Norman: University of Oklahoma Press.

Summary of Arizona camps. Governor Files. Gov. Mouer. Arizona State Archives. Arizona State Library, Archives and Public Records, Phoenix.

Tucson Arizona Star. 1934. CCC unit thanked for its work here. May 17.

———. 1936. Mrs. Greenway lauded by CCC camp leaders. May 3.

———. 1979. Catacombs gave him a needed break: CCC made cave accessible to public. March 8.

Tucson Citizen. 1933. Supervisors seek county CCC camps. September 1.

———. 1937. CCC unit to stay at Colossal Cave. June 30.

U.S. Department of the Interior. 1938. Press release. June 12.

Valentine, Richard. 1968. Arizona and the Great Depression: A study of state response to the crises. MA thesis. Northern Arizona University, Flagstaff.

Ward, H. R. (Secretary of Yavapai County Chamber of Commerce). 1933. Letter to Governor Moeur. September 1. Governor Papers, Gov. Moeur. Arizona State Library, Archives and Public Records, Phoenix.

Willis, Don. 1982. Interview with Alison Otis and Kim Lakin. November 9. Transcript at Coronado National Forest Headquarters, Tucson.

CIVILIAN CONSERVATION CORPS COMPANY 818: BUILDING THE COLORADO RIVER TRAIL

BY LOUIS PURVIS

Louis Purvis joined the CCC in 1934, and he was assigned to Company 818, Camp NP-3-A, situated along Bright Angel Creek below Phantom Ranch, on April 22. Company 818 was tasked with the construction of the Colorado River Trail (today commonly known as the River Trail). The CCC promoted him to assistant section leader on June 6 and section leader on July 1, a position he held until transferring to Camp BR-19-A near Tempe, Arizona, on February 2, 1937. He returned briefly to the Grand Canyon with Company 2833, Camp NP-1-A, in June 1937. Although Mr. Purvis could not attend the symposium, he submitted this history of his time spent at the Grand Canyon, which we presented for him. His book, The Ace in the Hole: A Brief History of Company 818 of the Civilian Conservation Corps *(Columbus, Ga.: Brentwood Christian Press, [1989]), is the most valuable single source available on the CCC at the Grand Canyon.*

INTRODUCTION TO COMPANY 818

CCC Company 818 was organized at Fort Huachuca, Arizona, in May 1933, under the command of Captain W. O. Poindexter, 25th Infantry. Captain Poindexter and his staff were regular army stationed at Fort Huachuca, assigned to our company on temporary duty. The company traveled by train from southern Arizona, through Barstow and Las Vegas to Lund Station in southern Utah—about as close as one could get to the Grand Canyon's North Rim by rail. The men then boarded buses supplied by the Utah Parks Company and rode to their first camp, Camp NP-1-A at Neil Springs, arriving at the end of May. Over the succeeding three years, Company 818 moved seasonally from one of several camps on the rim during the summer to Camp NP-3-A below Phantom Ranch (today's Bright Angel Campground) during the winter.

Company 818's projects were many and varied. Their work primarily entailed trail construction and maintenance,

building a park-boundary fence, insect control, road grading, and firefighting, but included visitor rescues, improvements to Phantom Ranch (including construction of the swimming pool, which has since been filled in), and construction of the transcanyon telephone line.

There was very little, in fact, that the young men did not do when asked, but the company's zest for recreation and education was comparable to that for its work. Pocket billiards was a popular game in the years of the Great Depression, and the good citizens of Grand Canyon Village donated a pool table to the company. When it proved too large to pack on a mule, it was dismantled and carried down the South Kaibab Trail by more than one hundred enrollees. It was the first, and probably the only, pool table to end up at the bottom of the Grand Canyon. The men were also known to hitch rides to VT Ranch (today's Kaibab Lodge) for dances, and to hike up to the South Rim for dances and movies. When not working or recreating, many took part in the educational programs offered by the camp's educational

The South Kaibab Trail in the Schist, intersecting with the River Trail at its eastern terminus, 1936. Photograph by the author

advisor, which included classes in writing, arithmetic, spelling, grammar, geography, and music.

It was a busy and full life for these young men, but probably one of their proudest achievements was the construction of the two-mile-long Colorado River Trail during the winter months of 1933–36. This strategic inner-canyon trail, blasted and carved from solid rock, connects the Bright Angel and South Kaibab trails at their base, and it is still one of the most frequently used trails at Grand Canyon National Park. The inexperienced youths, supervised by older, experienced, hard-rock miners, expended thousands of drill bits and 40,000 pounds of explosives to complete one of the most solid, but difficult to build, trails ever constructed in the canyon. In the process, they learned a great deal about construction and its hazards. In addition to building the Colorado River Trail, Company 818 maintained the South Kaibab Trail; the two assignments were known collectively as Project 14.

CONSTRUCTION OF THE COLORADO RIVER TRAIL

The Colorado River Trail and its location were first proposed in 1929 by Kyle Thomas and Paul Moritz under the direction of Park Superintendent M. R. Tillotson, Assistant Superintendent P. P. Patraw, and Park Engineer Clark

Carrel. Mr. Tillotson explored the possibilities, but the odds of getting the trail done seemed rather remote to many at the time. When the Emergency Conservation Works (ECW) Act became law in early 1933, Mr. Tillotson again called his group together, along with Emergency Conservation Works Engineer Mr. Montgomery, Project Superintendent J. H. Haines, and CCC Supervisor A. T. Sevey, to finalize plans for a camp to be located on the canyon floor. When the Colorado River Trail project and camp were approved, CCC Company 818 was assigned to newly designated Camp NP-3-A below Phantom Ranch, their base during construction of the trail.

Just how the Colorado River Trail got its name is uncertain, but the following story was told in Camp NP-3-A during the time Company 818 built the trail. Before the above-mentioned meeting ended, the question of a name was raised. All canyon trails had a name, and there was no reason for an exception in this case. This was not an extension or spur from another trail, but a new trail that would expose previously unseen vistas, as well as provide thrills and excitement to worldwide visitors for centuries to come. Such a trail should have an appropriate and meaningful name. Finally A. T. Sevey suggested that it be named for the first person to lose his life during the trail's construction. Until such a fatality occurred, it would simply be called the "Colorado River Trail." That seemed logical

Blasting away the rock wall while building the River Trail. Photograph by the author

enough to those present, and thus the trail got its working name. As it turned out, no one died during the construction of the Colorado River Trail, a fact that made all of the men involved in the project extremely proud; the name of the trail holds a special meaning to them.

The trail-planning group charged Company 818 with siting then building a new trail from the foot of the Bright Angel Trail at the mouth of Pipe Creek, along the south side of the Colorado River above historic high water, to a point on the South Kaibab Trail above the Kaibab Suspension Bridge, a total distance of about two miles. Although it is a safe path for hikers, it was probably the most hazardous trail to construct in the history of Grand Canyon National Park. The cliffs that form the south side of the Inner Gorge are 1,700 feet high, and the trail had to be carved into those cliffs along almost its entire length. The elevation above high-water mark would vary from forty to five hundred feet along the route. The only segment that did not have to be blasted was a break in the cliff—which had eroded much faster than the rest, forming a talus slope 0.4 mile long— about midway along the trail. Sand deposited on the nearby beach and blown up to the base of the cliffs by wind buried the slope, and the trail could be constructed in this area with somewhat less difficulty.

Indeed, carving a path through the cliffs was the primary difficulty. The rock type in the Inner Gorge is primarily Vishnu schist, a metamorphic rock that is the product of nature's reshuffling different kinds of rock formations, mountain-building pressures, and other massive land movements. From a practical perspective, we looked at the cliffs as being composed of four principal rock types: decomposed granite, schist, red granite, and black granite. Each type had to be worked according to a set of rules peculiar to it. Those supervising the construction had to know how to work each rock type, read the danger signs, and ensure that every person observed strict safety rules.

The decomposed granite was the most difficult to drill into with an air hammer. This type of granite would crumble and collapse, causing steel drill bits to stick in the hole. Retrieving the drill and removing the bits was hard to do, and it was often impossible. Danger signs were subtle: usually there would be some dust drifting up above the cliff before it came down in a heap of pea-size gravel. The powder man was very cautious about the amount of powder in his charges in this formation for fear of injuring the men working below. Luckily, the cliffs of decomposed granite were not all that high and were more sloping than vertical, which reduced risk of injury.

Schist is a stratified, crystalline formation that manifests in parallel layers, which split very easily. It is rather hard, but easy to work. There were many seams in the rock, but blasting seldom produced landslides. The dangerous places were near fault lines, fissures, or talc seams (fissures in the rock filled with powdery material from erosion). If a slide did occur, it was near one of those places, and usually there was some sign to the foreman that a slide was imminent. Sometimes, however, there was very little time to react to these signs before the cliff came down. For two slides there was no warning at all, and three men were injured. In many instances, the technician or leader watched the cracks in the rock. If they became wider or if sand began to trickle out of a crack or seam, the men were removed. If a stone fell off the side of the cliff or any unusual thing (however minor) happened, the men were moved out. Sometimes the men were moved out simply because the supervisor sensed that danger was near. He was often correct.

The red granite is an unstratified rock formation. This rock is harder than schist, difficult to drill, but easy to blast. We noticed that anytime the cliffs appeared vertical or overhanging to some degree the rock was likely to be red or black granite. Those cliffs were higher, steeper, and presented less danger from landslides.

Throughout the project, pack trains carried all equipment and supplies down the Bright Angel Trail. Tools were brought to our camp over "the Hump," a several-hundred-foot cliff forming the west wall of Pipe Creek, and down to the work site above the cliffs by the river. Pushing wheelbarrows over the Hump was quite a problem. It was also difficult to transport the air compressor from Indian Garden to the work site. Assistant Leader Jimmy Hays, who had been maintaining the trail at Indian Garden, brought it down to the top of the Devils Corkscrew and my crew brought it down to the foot of the Bright Angel Trail, the point where construction was to begin. Foreman Dee Frost triggered the first dynamite blast to signal the beginning of the project. The entire camp had been anticipating this event and was elated when the blast overpowered the rumbling sound of the river.

The crew considered Dee Frost the most knowledgeable, skillful, and experienced of the hard-rock miners in camp. He set the pattern for the other foremen as a leader. Mr. Frost was assigned the most difficult section of the trail, Section 1, which was at the highest point above the water, had the highest cliffs above trail level, and had the most difficult type of rock to drill. However, despite his knowledge of mining, safety rules, and skill in reading danger signs, Mr. Frost was supervising when the first accident that resulted in injury occurred on the rainy morning of February 20, 1934. That day, William Ashley, an enrollee, was working under a cliff clearing the debris from a large dynamite blast. The rain caused a landslide that struck him along the left side of his body, bruising his shoulder and

left leg and cutting his hand and foot. At the camp hospital, the company surgeon attended to his injuries, and he was evacuated the following day on a specially devised stretcher mounted on a mule. Mr. Ashley recovered and later returned to work.

Enrollee Nicholas Duncan, who operated a jackhammer for A. T. Sevey, told the following story of another landslide. The army catered lunches at the tram terminus on the south side of the river, and one day when lunchtime came, the men ambled down for their meal. The enrollee who was handling the dynamite and blasting powder (the "powder monkey") had prepared a charge, and when he fired it, they all moved off to eat lunch. After eating, they returned to their work and Mr. Sevey assumed his usual position about fifty to seventy-five feet from the cliff where he could observe the men and the cliffs above. The CCC leader was standing nearby when Mr. Sevey calmly asked him to remove all the gear, tools, and men to where he was sitting. He obeyed his foreman without question, and the men stood around waiting for further orders while Mr. Sevey stared at the cliff. He smiled and said, "Sit down boys and rest a few minutes." The enrollees, who didn't mind sitting down awhile, rested quietly for five or ten minutes when suddenly, a section of cliff turned to tons of rubble, crashing down and forming a talus slope in the drainage below. Mr. Sevey looked back at the cliff and the twenty feet of the trail bed that had disappeared beneath the landslide. He turned back to the crew and announced, "Okay boys, you may go back to work now."

Mr. Sevey supervised construction on Section 3 of the Colorado River Trail until April 15, 1934, when the CCC transferred J. H. Haines to another Arizona camp and promoted Mr. Sevey to project superintendent. With his promotion, Section 3 was without a supervisor. Eugene Mott, a former enrollee of Company 818, had advanced through the ranks and been promoted to junior foreman on January 16, 1934. He was assigned to supervise Section 3 until the company moved back to NP-1-A on the North Rim for the summer. On the company's return to the floor of the canyon in the fall of 1934, Section 3 again found itself without a foreman, and Donald Campbell subsequently received the job.

Mr. Campbell kept the project moving forward in the face of many difficulties and hazards. The cliff on which the enrollees were working was treacherous, and, unbeknownst to the workers, there was a talc seam that could not be seen from the trail. One afternoon while working on the trail, the crew removed support rocks, but there were none of the usual danger signs of an impending rockslide. Precautions had been taken, and the men worked using ropes, hard hats, goggles, and all, but that did not stop the slide that let loose without warning. Ropes that supported two of the boys were cut, and they were carried over the ledge into the drainage below along with tons of rock fragments. The first drop was about forty feet, followed by a steep slope for another twenty feet, then another drop of sixty feet onto the talus slope that was forty to fifty feet high. One of those who had fallen lay at the river's edge when help arrived; the other had stopped about ten feet above the river. The third man's rope had held, and he was spared the agony of the fall, suffering only minor injuries.

I was supervising the work on Section 2 when the accident occurred, and Mr. Campbell sent two runners for help. I sensed trouble as the runners labored through the deep sand and ran to meet them. After the exhausted men told their horror story, I ordered Assistant Leader Williams to take three men and get two litters to transport the injured, and for the remainder of the crew to follow him. Since it was impossible to reach the injured by trail, I scrambled to the river's edge, jumped from boulder to boulder, waded through knee-deep water and sand, and arrived at the scene before the foreman. Mr. Campbell fashioned a rope long enough to reach the top of the rockslide and descended the talus slope, reaching the men at about the time the litters arrived. In the meantime, I had secured clothes from other enrollees and covered the injured men, who were suffering badly from shock.

My crew and I put the men on the litters and arrived at the camp hospital less than an hour after the accident. I walked ahead of the litters to check for quicksand as they made progress toward the tram. The tram was ready when

The author during his later career as a teacher. Photograph courtesy Louis Purvis

the rescue party arrived, and they swung across the river and on to the camp in record time. When the two severely injured men were safely in the hospital and in the care of the camp surgeon, Dr. Aaron Burger, my crew and I returned to our station on the trail. This was the worst accident we experienced, but all three men survived.

Shortly after the accident, in the latter part of January 1935, my crew and I were told to discontinue work on Section 2 and move on to Section 4, which began at the foot of the Bright Angel Trail in Pipe Creek Canyon. The work would then proceed east to meet Mr. Campbell and his crew, who were still working on Section 3. Getting to and from the work site was a struggle. The men had to follow the completed section of the trail from the tram to the end of Section 3, then climb over the six hundred- to eight hundred-foot cliffs ("the Hump") and down into Pipe Creek Canyon, work all day, then climb the mountain again to return to camp.

Mr. Frost was accorded the honor of putting the finishing touches on the Colorado River Trail and was present when Shorty Yarberry appeared with a Fred Harvey pack train loaded with hay for Phantom Ranch. Shorty made the historic first trip along the Colorado River Trail on January 20, 1936. This marked the completion of the canyon's central trail corridor, and the beginning of a new era of flexibility for inner-canyon travelers who could now descend either the Bright Angel or South Kaibab trail to Phantom Ranch, reach the South Rim from Phantom by either trail, or take the full South Kaibab–Bright Angel Loop that is so popular today.

A Hard, Rocky Road to Nowhere

by Roy Lemons

Louis Purvis and Roy Lemons are ex–Civilian Conservation Corps enrollees and friends who planned to attend the symposium together until Mr. Purvis had to decline due to family illness. Mr. Lemons came with his wife and friends, however, even though he knew that he was terminally ill and that this might be his last "public appearance." All who attended his presentation—the room was full—were deeply moved by his words, his sentiment, and his appeal to secure national recognition for the CCC. Mr. Lemons passed away within months of the closing of the symposium, but we are all grateful that he chose to attend, and most of us, I believe, agree with his message.

On December 15, 1935, I celebrated my seventeenth birthday. Four months later I was inducted into the Civilian Conservation Corps (CCC) at Wichita Falls, Texas. Having passed our physical exams, we were sworn in and loaded onto a troop train the following afternoon. This train contained more than two hundred enrollees from Dallas alone (three hundred altogether), with U.S. Army personnel in charge. When we asked our destination, we were informed, "You will find out when we get there." I strongly suspect, at that point in time, the army violated our civil rights. However, we remained unaware that we *had* civil rights until thirty years later.

We traveled that afternoon and all night and arrived in Williams, Arizona, the next day. At dusk we were divided into truckload lots and dispersed across northern Arizona. I was very fortunate to have been placed in the group slated for Company 819, to be based southeast of the old water tower in Grand Canyon Village on the South Rim.

We were all dressed in light clothing and never dreamed we would end up at such high elevations as exist in northern Arizona. Needless to say, we were chilled to the bone when we arrived at camp about 1:00 AM. On the way, I was standing in the center of the truck cab, and I could see both the right and left sides of the road. The

scents of pine and juniper were completely foreign to me. Seeing the ponderosas outlined against the night sky as we approached the entrance to the park is something I will never forget. I will forever love this place. Time has in no way diminished this feeling.

The first few days in camp were devoted to another physical exam, inoculations, clothing distribution, and indoctrination. Afterward, we were assigned to various work projects. During the first year in camp, I worked near Cameron quarrying flagstone at the sewage disposal plant, as a barracks orderly and as an ambulance driver. The following one and one-half years, I was assigned to the naturalist department as assistant to Dr. Edwin D. McKee. My association with Dr. McKee forever affected my life; he inspired me to greater goals. Later in life, I achieved the rank of Directional Drilling Engineer, drilled oil wells, and traveled in more than sixty countries throughout the world over a thirty-five-year career. I shall forever be indebted to Dr. McKee.

I am adding a brief history of the corps since it touches on the roles we played during the most turbulent years of the twentieth century and brought us to middle age. It is entitled, "A Journey of One Hundred Years on a Hard Rocky Road to Nowhere."

March 31, 2002, marked the sixty-ninth anniversary of the founding of the Civilian Conservation Corps, which was made up of 225,000 World War I veterans plus more than 3.25 million youths between the ages of seventeen and twenty-eight. During the three and one-half years between the stock market crash and the creation of the corps, these men would pay a dear price that would forever affect their lives. In the case of the World War I veterans, many would march on Washington in 1932 in an attempt to get early payment of their promised war bonus. They organized a peaceful demonstration toward this end, erecting a shanty-town (a "Hooverville") on the Capitol grounds.

These men faced dire straights: they were hungry and in need. Instead of helping them, Army Chief of Staff Douglas MacArthur branded them "communist trouble-makers;" unleashed the army with bayonets, tanks, and cavalry in the wee hours of the night; drove them from the field; and burned their dwellings and belongings. I was about fourteen, selling newspapers on the streets, when this happened. I could not believe the headlines. I feel very strongly that the government owes these men an apology, even though there are only a few still living. I knew some of these men, many of whom had suffered injuries from mustard gas in the war. I can still hear their struggles to breathe.

For the young men who made up the corps, a great number had to drop out of school to provide for their families. As a result, enrollees averaged only an eighth-grade education. During the past three decades I have gathered stories from these men about how they and their families survived those first few years of the Depression. What I heard borders on the unbelievable. One fellow told me recently that his mother would get her seven children out of bed at 4:00 AM, and the entire family would go to some horse stables, break apart the pieces of manure, and glean out the whole grains of undigested oats or corn to feed themselves—this was their means of survival. Another man raised in the Dakotas told me his family survived by harvesting tumbleweeds in their early growth stage. They chopped them up like green beans, canned some for winter use, and ate the rest for as long as they lasted. As for myself, I still hear the sobbing of my siblings as they cried themselves to sleep because of the hunger in their bellies.

The 3.25 million young men of the corps were largely a part of the 25 percent of the nation's workforce that was unemployed. During the nine and one-third years of its existence, the corps got this nation back on its feet. The CCC men restored more than 360 Civil War battlefields and 4,000 historic structures. They planted four billion trees. They constructed 60,000 buildings, 38,500 bridges, and the infrastructure of Great Smoky Mountains National Park and Bandelier National Monument. They even built the presidential retreat, Camp David. The corps built or restored thousands of miles of roads, trails, fences, and telephone and electrical lines, as well as many dams, reservoirs, and lakes.

The corps' greatest project was restoration of the dust bowl of the Great Plains. Enrollees surveyed and staked out the contoured furrows for farmers to follow in order to limit erosion of our precious soil, planted windbreaks, hauled and spread limestone to sweeten the earth once more, sodded and reseeded thousands upon thousands of acres of land, repaired washed-out gullies, and built check dams. The plains are once again the breadbasket of America.

On January 8, 1937, President Franklin D. Roosevelt called on the U.S. Congress to increase the number of troops in the U.S. Army to 158,000 officers and men, a modest call that signaled preparation for the impending world war. By the end of that year, 2.5 million men were in or had already passed through the corps. They had learned vocations that would prove useful to the military at the outbreak of hostilities with the Axis powers four years later. They were a ready-made cadre absorbed into our armed forces during the first two years of conflict. In fact, they became the backbone of the armed forces in the early months of the conflict. It is estimated that 2.5 million former CCC men served in the armed forces, the equivalent of 166 divisions and one more of officers (reserves). These men were labor hardened, with vocations that helped from the very beginning.

The Civilian Conservation Corps was swallowed by the armed forces and made up about 15 percent of the overall force. CCC men made up 62 percent of all American forces that defended Bataan and Corregidor, as well as of the marines who invaded Guadalcanal. John Basilone, an ex-CCC enrollee, was awarded the Congressional Medal of Honor and the Navy Cross for his defense of his position. Another ex-enrollee, Tony Stein, won the Congressional Medal of Honor for his initial assault on Mount Surabachi on Iwo Jima. Two others, Michael Strank and Ira Hamilton Hays, helped raise the flag atop Mount Surabachi. Hays was the only one of the flag raisers to return alive to American soil. Sadly, he, too, became a casualty after returning to the States. Assigned to sell war bonds, he could not accept his portrayal as an American hero for simply raising a flag, took to drink, and died in a gutter in Chicago. He was a hero of the first order.

In October 1984 the CCC Alumni Association held its 50th Anniversary Convention at Eagle River, Wisconsin. We invited President Ronald Reagan, Vice President George H. W. Bush, and the secretary of the interior to address and honor the more than three million men of the CCC for their contributions to this nation and its freedom.

The government leaders all declined to attend, as has each president since our yearly conventions began. Shortly after President Reagan declined, he crossed the Atlantic to pay tribute to the German SS. At the very least, the presidents should have thanked the CCC for constructing Camp David, the retreat they all seem to have enjoyed for the past sixty-seven years. High-ranking government officials pay tribute to show-business personalities and sports teams. For all the men who labored to rebuild this nation, who suffered and died to preserve it, there has never been even a thank you for a job well done. In his campaign for the presidency, all Ronald Reagan could talk about were American values. Something is wrong, for in no way can I correlate his sense of values to those we, the CCCers, have lived our lives by.

Our nation's historians, elected leaders, heads of our educational systems, and other influential citizens should hang their heads in shame for the treatment accorded these men and the trashing of our history. Case in point: Tom Brokaw, in his recently published book, *The Greatest Generation*, omits any mention of the more than three million men who made up the CCC. In all probability he has walked the trails, camped in some of the eight hundred state parks, or fished in the thousands of lakes we created and did not know from where these things came. It appears he simply did not know anything about us, but it is hard to single him out because he seems to share his ignorance with most of those born following World War II.

I close with a poem I composed while driving across southern Kansas on U.S. 54, the approximate center of the former dust bowl, on my return from our 50th Anniversary Convention. It tells the story of these CCC men together with what happened to many of them. Following the poem is my epitaph to our legacy, both written in 1983. America, we were your true and faithful sons. We served you in hunger and hopelessness, yet never faltered or lost our faith. The bodies of our comrades abide in the depths of the seven seas, on a thousand faraway battlefields, and in graveyards all across America. All we ever asked is to be recognized.

I gaze across vast fields of grain
That spread far beyond these western plains
Where contoured furrows weave and flow
To yonder hills you knew of yore

Where in your youth you labored so
To plant the trees, reclaim the land
You did so many things that stand

And as you labored there
"Oh did you hear that distant thunder in the air?"
It called for you "Oh silent ones"
From far off shores you never knew

You would know the sound
Of shot and shell
Screams of death, the fiery hell

For four long years, you struggled there
You dreamed of home and things to be
But dreams are never as they seem
And now you sleep on far off shores

And in the place you called your home
Those trees you planted now reach the sky
They spread to yonder mountains high
Where even eagles dare to fly

Hear their screams
"Remember Me, Remember Me"

To the future generations of Americans: We men of the CCC, who labored to restore this great mother land, pass it into your hands. Her productivity fuels the torch of freedom. Neglect and weaken her and the flame will die, and you shall surely perish. Keep her production of natural resources strong, and she will reward you and keep you free forever. If you future generations see fit to raise voices in song of praise for us, we will consider this our reward.

—From "A Proposed Plaque for
a CCC Memorial"

Like the great Martin Luther King Jr., I too have a dream, that one day a president of these United States of America will, while delivering the State of the Union address, call before him an ex-CCC enrollee or the president of our alumni association and bestow upon that person, as a unit citation, the Presidential Medal of Freedom. Perhaps this would help preserve our history. The century is ended, we are out of time. If our ears are ever to hear the singing of our song, the time is now.

BLUE DENIM UNIVERSITY:
THE CIVILIAN CONSERVATION CORPS' RETOOLING OF ARIZONA YOUTH

BY PETER MACMILLAN BOOTH

A complete history has never been written of the CCC's many contributions to Grand Canyon National Park, but we were fortunate to have the recollections of two ex-CCCers—Louis Purvis and Roy Lemons—presented at our gathering. Equally rewarding were Dr. Peter Booth's essays on the CCC's role in Arizona. This essay concerns the practical and academic programs offered to enrollees, designed to teach work skills and to provide a modicum of science and social studies information, but also to reinforce democracy, patriotism, moral values, and in some regards, character traits of the mid-twentieth-century "American man."

Less than a month after Franklin D. Roosevelt's inauguration as president, Congress passed the Unemployment Relief Act, officially establishing the Civilian Conservation Corps (CCC). Roosevelt designed the CCC to save the human and natural resources of the nation. The Department of Labor mobilized the nation's unemployed youths into a peacetime army that lived in camps run by the Department of War and undertook various projects directed by the departments of Agriculture and the Interior. More than 120 camps were established in Arizona throughout the corps' nine-year history from 1933 to 1942, six within Grand Canyon National Park: two on the North Rim, two at Grand Canyon Village, one at Desert View, and one just south of Phantom Ranch.

Through the corps, Roosevelt hoped to conserve the environment for future use and, in the process, mold idle young males into productive citizens. To accomplish the latter goal, the CCC invented what enrollees affectionately nicknamed the Blue Denim University, a "training ground for youths who need and should have a foundation in work experience in order to build their future lives as self-reliant

citizens." The "Civies," a nickname used by the enrollees themselves, received lessons in life, skills, and traditional American values as defined by the federal government. In the process, the CCC and its Blue Denim University tended to standardize and entrench white-male, blue-collar, Protestant biases in American society (Federal Security Agency n.d.).[1]

When the emergency work program first began, the CCC focused on conservation while slighting the human mission, although the editor of the *Holbrook Tribune* reflected the opinion of many when he remarked that the CCC "will probably save most of these men from becoming bums." Due to public apathy concerning education, designing and implementing an educational program was

---

[1] For a national perspective on the CCC see John A. Salmond, *The Civilian Conservation Corps, 1933–1942* (Durham, N.C.: Duke University Press, 1967), and Leslie Alexander Lacy, *The Soil Soldiers: The Civilian Conservation Corps in the Great Depression* (Radnor, Pa.: Chilton Book Company, 1976). For the CCC in Arizona, see Peter MacMillan Booth, "The Civilian Conservation Corps in Arizona, 1933–1942" (MA Thesis, University of Arizona, 1991), and William S. Collins, *The New Deal in Arizona* (Phoenix: Arizona State Parks Board, 1999).

left to CCC leaders (*Holbrook Tribune* 1933; *Arizona Highways* 1935).[2] The question facing CCC Director Robert Fechner was how to interpret the objective of saving America's youth. He and other CCC leaders believed that simply bringing the boys together in a disciplined environment with clear rules and hard work provided enough education. The camps did strengthen impoverished young men physically and mentally. Good food, medical attention, physical exercise, and athletic competition left many in the best physical shape of their young lives. Athletic contests were especially valued, and organized sports were common. For example, the baseball team from one of the three camps on the South Rim, NP-2-A, dominated all other teams in the Flagstaff area. Boxing was very popular, and occasionally, enrollees traveled to other camps and communities for volleyball matches (Robles 1984; Keller 1984; *Happy Days* 1934a; *Ace in the Hole* 1936a; *Echo of the Peak* 1934a, 1934b; *Lakeside Mirror* 1935).

Although the corps placed emphasis on the physical, Fechner also hoped to teach marketable skills. In the CCC's first year, enrollees were taught within their various work projects rather than in independent classes. Supervisors and foremen doubled as instructors, providing "forestry lectures" pertaining to whatever project was at hand, be it road building, tree trimming, fire suppression, digging Phantom Ranch's swimming pool, or leading tours at Casa Grande Ruins National Monument. For example, Grand Canyon trail work was lauded for the educational experience of using jackhammers and dynamite. Overall, leaders felt that enrollees' experience alone would strengthen the men's physical condition, pride, and self-confidence within an organized "American" community (Stone n.d.; *Ace in the Hole* 1936b; *Tucson Arizona Star* 1933; Legder 1990; Pugh 1984). This kind of education, however, had its mishaps, as illustrated in the *Camp News* newsletter concerning the Phantom Ranch camp: "The first jackhammer lesson: Well the boys didn't do too bad—broke one bit, stuck one bit, tore up two jackhammers" (*Ace in the Hole* 1936c).

More conservative elements of government, especially the army, resisted the idea of establishing a set curriculum to supplement informal education. They questioned the value of educating young men in specific tasks when businesses would simply retrain them. They argued that it was enough to teach them to be good, dependable workers. Many also held a fear of "long-haired men and short-haired women," that is, classroom educators spreading

fringe ideas such as communism. At the heart of the resistance to formal education, however, was the concern that education would diminish the amount of work accomplished (Lacy 1976, 42–46; Major 1933).

By the second year of operation, after the CCC's popularity ensured its survival, national pressure for an organized educational system grew. Fechner and the army realized such a program was needed, for safety training if for nothing else. As a compromise, General Douglas MacArthur insisted that the army control the program and that the system parallel army command structure. An "educational advisor" was appointed to each level of command—national, corps, district, subdistrict, and camp. Although advisors came from the Office of Education, they answered directly to the commander, who had the final say in all matters (Salmond 1967, 49–50; Lacy 1976, 36–46).

In December 1933 Fechner formally launched the Blue Denim University. He appointed Clarence Marsh of the University of Buffalo as director. Marsh, in turn, named L. W. Rogers the educational advisor for the Eighth Corps, which included Arizona, and Rockwall A. Davis for the Arizona-New Mexico District. Rogers and Davis recruited camp advisors for Arizona from among the state's unemployed teachers, principals, and graduating college students. In addition to directing the camp's educational programs, these individuals also coordinated each company's recreation and entertainment. By the fall of 1934, the five-state area of the Eighth Corps had advisors in 120 of 159 camps (Salmond 1967, 51; *Tucson Arizona Star* 1934; Marsh 1934).

Because Fechner insisted that participation be voluntary and not interfere with the eight-hour workday, the Blue Denim University's success hinged on advisors' ability to attract enrollees with programs that fit their needs and wants. This proved a challenge considering the wide range of educational levels among the incoming Civies, and the program's quality varied dramatically. For instance, a former CCC commander recalled that the training program in the Tucson Mountains and Cottonwood camps excelled while his Groom Creek camp near Prescott suffered due to a poor educational advisor (Lacy 1976, 46–48; Legder 1990; *Tucson Arizona Star* 1934; *Tucson Citizen* 1933; *Alibi* 1936a; Hanson 1973, 184–188; Civilian Conservation Corps 1934a; *Desert Digest* 1936).

Fechner and Rogers agreed with the army's insistence that courses be practical, not filled with "useless" academics. L. S. Tabor of the American Vocational Association summarized CCC desires when he said, "we must lift manual toil, successfully and well performed, to the nobility and dignity of the highest place in the life of the race." Primarily, instruction had to complement projects, and secondarily, had

---

[2] See also *Mesa Tribune*, September 13, 1934, concerning requests for CCC projects in the Valley of the Sun. See also Richard Lowitt, *The New Deal and the West* (Bloomington: Indiana University Press, 1989), 218–219.

to prepare the boys for employment after they left the corps. Advisors supplied the training while projects provided valuable on-the-job experience in a company-like atmosphere. Therefore, skills learned largely depended on a particular camp's projects. Enrollees at the Grand Canyon's South Rim assisted in landscaping and building projects at Grand Canyon Village, where enrollees gained carpentry, masonry, and landscaping skills. Other camps gave instruction in truck driving, welding, machine operation, surveying, cooking, typing, and blacksmithing, among other blue-collar crafts. The value of combining formal training with projects proved itself in the high quality of work accomplished (Lacy 1976, 48–50; *Tucson Citizen* 1934; *Rillito Reveler* 1936a; *Tucson Arizona Star* 1934; *Flagstaff Coconino Sun* 1933, 1937; *Arizona Nightingale* 1936a).[3]

Advisors sometimes expanded the curriculum by recruiting businesses and schools to provide vocational classes. The local Safeway grocery store offered meat cutting to interested boys from Camp BR-13-A in Yuma. Flagstaff's Northern Arizona Teachers College sponsored mechanics classes for Camp F-6-A at Mormon Lake. This local cooperation also helped build community support for the camps (*Safford Graham County Guardian* 1934a; *Broadcaster* 1936; *Desert Digest* 1937).

In Arizona, providing vocational education filled an important gap created by Governor Benjamin Moeur's efforts to balance the state budget. He refused to make provisions for a state vocational education program. Because of high unemployment, Arizona's youth needed training to compete for the few jobs available. The CCC offered one of the only vocational programs available to Arizona's young men looking for training in a skilled profession (Valentine 1968, 32, 33).

Due to strong antischolarly viewpoints among CCC leaders, academics held a secondary position to vocational education. Rogers commented that the purpose of the CCC's academic classes was "to instill and inspire in each man a desire to further his education." When academics were employed, they emphasized the basics. Reading and writing alone proved a godsend for the many illiterate enrollees. Arithmetic was taught in the contexts of business, taxes, and insurance. Occasionally camps offered algebra, geography, or trigonometry. Educational Advisor Ellis Johnson at Phantom Ranch offered writing, spelling, grammar, arithmetic, geography, citizenship, algebra, and music, the latter due to the camp blacksmith, a talented musician who taught choral and instrumental classes and organized musical groups such as "The Seems Funny Orchestra." In the early years, however, an expanded in-camp curriculum

was the exception. For instruction beyond the basics, Rogers commented, "better, more effective [academic] educational work can be done under such a system of correlation [with existing educational institutions] than if we conduct our camp education as isolated groups." CCC officials in Arizona did cooperate with area high schools and colleges. If located close to a school, enrollees could attend night classes and, in more isolated camps, participate in correspondence courses offered by schools such as Phoenix Union High (Purvis [1989], 78–81; *Tucson Arizona Star* 1934; *Big Tree Breeze* 1934a; *Desert Digest* 1937; *Arizona Nightingale* 1936a; *Broadcaster* 1936; *Tucson Citizen* 1934).

Advisors also tapped camp libraries, lectures, movies, recreational activities, and field trips to complement the Blue Denim University, often setting aside one night per week for lectures. Depending on the ingenuity of the advisor, an entertaining program might accompany the talk. One advisor at Camp SES-2-A near Pima led the evening off with a joke-filled monologue, followed by music and a lecture by an honored guest, and topped off by a boxing match between an enrollee and a visiting athlete. Two of the most popular circulating lectures were "Prospector's Mineralogy" and "G-Men Operations." Movies also became an educational tool. In addition to feature films such as *Romance in Manhattan*, educational films included *Voice of Business*, *Revolution of X-Rays*, *Mountains of Copper*, *Construction that Endures*, and *Automotive Lubrication*, along with army classics on venereal disease. Sports proved useful for lessons in teamwork, cooperation, fair play, and sportsmanship. To broaden enrollees' worldly experiences, advisors also arranged field trips to nearby points of interest such as the Grand Canyon (*Broadcaster* 1936; *Safford Graham County Guardian* 1934a, 1934b, 1934c, 1934d; *Rillito Reveler* 1936b, 1936c; *Cactizonian* 1936a; *Alibi* 1936b; *CCC Camp Talk* 1936). One enrollee from a Payson, Arizona, camp wrote about his experience in a poem that was reprinted nationally:

> *We stood on the rim of the canyon, Where the Colorado flows,*
> *And gazed at the grandeur of nature, Myself, Jim, John, and Mose.*
>
> *Ten miles across as the crow flies, Five thousand feet straight down,*
> *Six miles, by trails, to the river, Mose said, "What a hole in the groun'."*
>
> *The colors were red, gray and orange, Then changed to purple and white,*

[3] L. S. Tabor's speeches were printed and distributed among the camps.

The clouds descended and covered, A large part of the wonderful sight.

There were towers, castles and spires, That caught the rays of the sun,
There were shadows, darkness and dungeons, That showed where the river had run.

And, I thought, as I gazed entranced, of the gigantic force and power,
That the mighty river exerted, to hue out its rocky bower.

The colors were not painted by humans, The carvings not done by man.
The presence of God showed everywhere, As far as the eye could span (*Happy Days* 1934b).

After its first year, Rogers proudly announced the rising popularity of the educational program among Eighth Corps enrollees. One of every three in Arizona had enrolled in classes. Nevertheless, problems such as material shortages, overworked advisors, resistant army commanders, too little time devoted to education, and uncertainty among educators about proper teaching methods hampered the program (Salmond 1967, 50–52; *Tucson Arizona Star* 1934, 1937; *Tucson Citizen* 1934; *Rillito Reveler* 1936c; State Conference 1936). In 1935 the Blue Denim University enjoyed a big boost when the CCC doubled in size, and Arizona was divided into two districts—southern Arizona, commanded from Tucson, and northern Arizona (including the Grand Canyon), commanded from Phoenix. But in the debate over expansion, Congress started questioning the corps' educational quality and the army became the scapegoat for perceived failures. In response, CCC commanders set out to enlarge the program, but they did not alter the framework (Tucson-CCC and Byrd 1936; Salmond 1967, 53, 57–58, 163).

District advisors called on company advisors to increase the number of courses in order to attract more enrollees. Vocational training continued to lead the way. New classes included photography, stenography, journalism, drama, leatherworking, and copper crafts. The Beaver Creek camp near Rim Rock offered twenty-six classes and the men received 6,400 hours in formal instruction. Districts also started trade schools that taught mechanics, cooking, radio operation, lifesaving, and a special course in junior leadership. One former camp clerk recalled a cooking school graduate as "a big red headed young man who perhaps had never been near a kitchen. Before the summer was half over, he was lauded by the dining room manager as the best baker he had ever developed. We had fresh bread daily . . . and his cakes were second to none" (Ingram 1990).[4]

Nonvocational subjects experienced more modest expansion, although a few camps did offer English, Spanish, general science, astronomy, and library science. Firmly opposed to a compulsory curriculum, Arizona CCC officials nonetheless now required all illiterate men to study until they could read at a third-grade level. District commanders also worked to improve collaboration with local businesses and educational institutions. Arizona high schools and colleges agreed to accept CCC-earned credits. Districts also transferred interested boys to camps close to state colleges to pursue college degrees, and a few even worked on graduate degrees. By the end of 1936, Arizona's CCC leaders proudly pointed to their 75 percent participation rate in camp vocational and academic educational programs (Tucson-CCC and Byrd 1936; *Desert Digest* 1937; *Oasis* 1937; *Camp News* 1936; *Cactizonian* 1936b; *Flux Canyon Recorder* 1935; *Rillito Reveler* 1936a, 1936b, 1936c; *Big Tree Breeze* 1934a; *Arizona Nightingale* 1936a; *Ingram* 1990; *Alibi* 1936b).

As part of a larger morale-boosting campaign that paralleled educational expansion, districts encouraged journalism classes to put out camp newsletters. These ranged widely in size and quality, from the one-page *Camp News* of Camp SCS-15-A on the Rillito River, to the twenty-page *Alibi* of Camp F-30-A at Madera Canyon. Imaginative titles included *The Desert Tattler*, *The Big Tree Breeze*, *The Colossal Cave Chronicle*, *The Graham Kracker*, *Turkey Creek Gobbler*, and the *Cactizonian*. At the Grand Canyon, newsletters included *Ace in the Hole* from the Phantom Ranch camp and *Grand Canyon Echoes* from the South Rim, filled with miscellaneous activities, sports, community events, special interest stories, and a forum for opinions, complaints, and humor (Tucson-CCC and Byrd 1936). One example of camp humor included this "Psalm of the C.C.C.":

The CCC is my restoration; I shall not want,
But it maketh me arise early in the morning: it giveth me baths with hard water.

It restoreth my appetite: it leadest me in the paths of work for my bankroll's sake.

Yea, tho I oft do K.P. duty from morn to night, I will fear no evil, for the Infirmary is near me; the oils and pills they discomfort me.

Tables are prepared for me in the presence of my buddies; my plate is heaped up; my stomach all but runneth over.

---

4 See also Bob Robles (CCC alumnus, F-6-A, Mormon Lake, Arizona), Interview with Joe Stocker, 1984; Beaver Creek, *Lone Beaver*, [n.d.].

Surely goldbricking and tree nursing shall not follow me all the days of my life; but I shall probably remain in the CCC forever (Preslar 1934).

Because commanders viewed newsletters as educational tools, they serve today as valuable sources for understanding messages being taught to the Civies. Besides schedules of educational services, they were sprinkled with articles, editorials, stories, and tips on ways each individual could improve his situation and how the corps could help. Proverbs such as "laziness feeds on empty deeds" filled pages. An editorial in *Grand Canyon Echoes* advised readers to "make wise use of your time," while a second editorial in the same issue advised that "the men that put through what they start out to do, are the men who win out in the fight." The same issue contained a long article on how to get a job. Likewise, *The Caveman*, published by camp SP-10-A at Colossal Cave, ran an in-depth article on job seeking that included advice such as beware of commissions, keep trying, do not use slang, gather references, and shave because "whiskers have degenerated into one of America's most unprofitable crops" (*Desert Sun* 1940; *Grand Canyon Echoes* 1937; *Caveman* 1936).

An expanded Blue Denim University improved the CCC's ability to press its version of traditional American standards and values. As the commander of the camp developing Colossal Cave phrased it, "the officers and technical personnel strive day and night to rid the enrollee of his false notions and conducts." In their place, the corps installed values "harmonious" to society. In building the self-respect of the enrollee, educators emphasized virtues such as pride, honesty, loyalty, discipline, and responsibility. Educational advisors usually reinforced these lessons in how to live an honorable life with a reminder to have a "healthy" competitive attitude (*Caveman* 1937; Federal Security Agency 1941, n.d.; Gaston 1984; Enriquiz 1984; *Big Tree Breeze* 1934c; *Arizona Nightingale* 1936b; DeLost 1984; *Alibi* 1936a). Along with lessons on how to be productive citizens, the corps fostered respect for employers, work without complaint, and doing a good job regardless of personal feelings about the work. The advisor at the Colossal Cave camp told his students not to "argue about wages. Be content with a modest start and be willing to work at any job that offers advancement to a better one" (*Big Tree Breeze* 1934b; Maddox 1979; *Caveman* 1936; *Timberwolf* 1935).

Additionally, CCC education concentrated heavily on how to be an "American man." This included instruction on manners and how to conduct oneself. One advisor told his enrollees "the only portions of a fellow's anatomy or features that he can pick himself are his teeth." In the spirit

of training boys to be men, the CCC indirectly taught them how to drink beer, cuss properly, have sex safely, and even how to smoke, as in when "you smoke the stump of a cigarette or the familiar 'short' from another's mouth you are liable to get one of several different diseases." "My God, it built *men*," declared enrollee Henry Keller of Camp F-23-A at Indian Gardens near Payson. "It made *men* out of *boys*" (*Caveman* 1936; *Broadcaster* 1937; Lundquist 1990; Keller 1984).

The corps also reinforced traditional roles of women as both supportive mothers and wives, and sexual objects. The very nature of the CCC strengthened traditional roles that had waned somewhat since the flapper phenomenon of the 1920s. Enrollees went off to work in the woods, earning money to be sent home to their mothers, girlfriends, and wives who waited at home. Newsletters and cartoons were filled with images of the strong mom and wife. A common joke that circulated in camps: "What is a Lieutenant Commander?" answered by "A Lieutenant's wife." Unattached females, however, were commonly portrayed as conniving, husband-starved, sexual objects. Several newsletters joked that the CCC was "A New Deal for the County Girls." One popular cartoon character was "Smart Cora," an unattached, slightly dippy, but manipulative woman who spent her time juggling CCC boyfriends (*Date Creek Rattler* 1935; Civilian Conservation Corps 1934b).

To complete the picture of ideal American values, the corps also emphasized the importance of conformity to American society and the need to protect the nation from subversive ideas. One pro-isolationist editorial in the Madera Canyon camp newsletter warned enrollees that immigrant peoples and ideas worked against American values and goals. This article argued that the Allies the United States had helped in World War I were now assaulting the country with treacherous anti-American attitudes. The fear of fringe ideologies spurred the fear of outsiders. CCC leaders such as Rogers felt that purging the boys of "communistic ideas about our government" was a primary goal of the corps (*Alibi* 1936a; *Tucson Arizona Star* 1934).

The CCC also reinforced stereotypes of minorities, who were thought to hold subversive ideas. Even if it was not meant maliciously, nearly every ethnic and racial group found itself the victim of this treatment. Jokes concerning Jews and blacks commonly appeared in newsletters. One cartoon about blacks added a racial twist to traditional female roles: "Well Mose, I heard yo'all is injoyin' a *blessed event*." Mose answered, "Boy, an is! My ol' 'oman got her se'f a *JOB!*" Even Scots found themselves stereotyped: "Then there was a Scotchman who married a half-wit because he got 50% off." A poem describing the CCC read, "We are the boys of the three 'C' camp you've heard so much about. . . . We're farmers, laborers, and artisans too, Polacks, Wops, and some are Jews, Ukranian, Spiks, and darkies galore, Stand up in mess and shout for more." Again, although malice seemed absent, the CCC had no intention of breaking down old stereotypes. On the contrary, leaders were more concerned about getting the enrollees to conform to the status quo, vices and all. These lessons in social attitudes and values persisted in the Blue Denim University until the end (*Broadcaster* 1936; Civilian Conservation Corps 1934b; *Big Tree Breeze* 1934a; Lacy 1976).

Although content changed little, attempts to improve the educational structure continued through the 1930s. In the Civilian Conservation Corps Act of 1937, officials finally sacrificed some project time for the sake of education by requiring ten hours of instruction and five hours of study in each forty-hour workweek. The corps expanded the vocational trade school system and made Arizona's literacy program mandatory nationwide. CCC textbooks in math and reading began to proliferate (Goodwin 1990; Legder 1990; Federal Security Agency and Civilian Conservation Corps n.d.). These reforms came at an auspicious time for Arizona's minorities. Earlier in its history, CCC enrollees had arrived mainly from rural farms and urban blue-collar neighborhoods, and most were poor to middle-class European Americans. As the economy improved in Arizona, CCC companies recruited a greater number of blacks, urban American Indians, and Hispanics. Because of language difficulties, several Arizona camps were forced to provide English classes to Hispanic enrollees. Perhaps more important than learning English, Hispanics acquired skills useful to compete for jobs. For rural Hispanics and other immigrants, CCC life also served as an important, if sobering, introduction to mainstream American society (Anderson 1984; Molner 1984).

Unfortunately, other factors worked against the CCC providing a truly beneficial experience to Arizona's minorities. Although it increased emphasis on education, the 1937 act also cut the number of enrollees by half. This was accompanied by reduced funds, and since projects took priority, education suffered. Additionally, local support that had bolstered the Blue Denim University diminished due to an improved economy as well as animosity for heavily ethnic companies. In 1937 Yaqui Indian refugees from Mexico and other undocumented immigrants were banned from enrollment, and recruitment practices continued to discriminate against blacks. Minority enrollment had gotten off to a good start, but in the end, CCC leaders missed their chance to effect real social reform.

Before Congress discontinued the CCC in the summer of 1942, the Blue Denim University placed a new emphasis on military training. Antimilitary sentiment had made this unthinkable earlier, but by the late 1930s, the public accepted the necessity for some war preparation, if not actual combat training. A compromise called for instruction in specialized, supportive roles such as signal communications and bridge construction. By late 1940, enrollees were receiving twenty hours of instruction in high-priority vocational skills needed to produce the labor infrastructure essential for defense (*Tucson Arizona Star* 1940; Condon 1982, 72; Paige 1985, 29–30; Federal Security Agency 1941; Salmond 1967, 116–120, 194–198). After Pearl Harbor, leaders tried to save the corps by demonstrating their willingness to contribute to the war effort. The CCC director ordered military drills for the camps and sent crews to help build new airfields and expand others. Nevertheless, Congress let the program die in the summer of 1942 and inducted enrollees directly into the military.

In its nine-year history, the CCC and its Blue Denim University surpassed stated objectives for the Depression-era relief agency. It gave distraught young men paying jobs; taught them discipline, work ethics, and skills; and returned them to society better prepared to deal with the depressed employment market of Arizona and the nation. One ex-Civie, and no doubt many others, proclaimed that the program "saved my life." Another who served at the Grand Canyon's South Rim wrote a moving testimonial on how his life had changed: "At last I could lift my eyes and square my shoulders and meet my fellow friends, man to man. I was earning unsoiled money, for it was honest and willing toil. I am a better man because of the months in the service in the CCC" (Strong 1990; Hernandez 1934).[5]

But what kind of men did it build? The Blue Denim University trained blue-collar workers loyal to American values and traditions. CCC projects and education helped millions of enrollees survive the Great Depression and provided the United States with trained labor and military forces. In the process, however, it continued conformist traditions in Arizona and the rest of the United States. For minorities, it prepared some to be a part of that growing urban labor force in Arizona, but did not improve their social standing. Critics claimed that the "make-work" agency missed an opportunity to bring about real social reform. Instead of reinforcing mainstream American proclivities, the Blue Denim University could have introduced lessons of social equality. Contrary to local prejudice, the federal program could have been more persistent with its initial attempts at camp integration and could have made the program still more accessible and relevant for minorities.

---

5 See also Julian Hayden (CCC supervisor, Tucson), 1990, Interview with Peter Booth; *Alibi* (F-30-A, Madera Canyon), November 11, 1936.

These criticisms are legitimate, but Franklin Roosevelt did not intend the CCC or the New Deal to effect social reform; rather, he designed it to reinforce the status quo. The CCC fulfilled Roosevelt's objective to help the United States in its economic recovery—and in the process save the boys themselves. More than fifty thousand young men went through the Arizona camps; at least four thousand of these served their enlistments at the Grand Canyon. A significant percentage came from Arizona, and former enrollees with their new skills, education, and values helped speed the state's development in directions that would have been unlikely without federal intervention and leadership. During World War II, many enrollees became integral cogs in the military, while others formed the nucleus of trained technicians who constructed the mighty American fighting machine. As a postwar labor force, CCC-trained workers fueled Arizona's growing industrial sector. Although far from a perfect program, the CCC not only surpassed its goals, it also had an enduring influence on the United States, especially western states such as Arizona, long after it disbanded.

Works Cited

Ace in the Hole (NP-3-A, Phantom Ranch). 1936a. Sports. January. Arizona Historical Society, Tucson.

———. 1936b. River trail. January. Arizona Historical Society, Tucson.

———. 1936c. Camp news. January. Arizona Historical Society, Tucson.

Alibi (F-30-A, Madera Canyon). 1936a. November 11. Arizona Historical Society, Tucson.

———. 1936b. September 30. Arizona Historical Society, Tucson.

Anderson, Cleo J. (CCC Project Supervisor). 1984. Interview with Joe Stocker. Transcript. NACCCA Collection, Arizona State University, Tempe.

Arizona Highways. 1935. 11 (November):18.

Arizona Nightingale (SCS-14-A, San Simon). 1936a. June 1. Arizona Historical Society, Tucson.

———. 1936b. July 7. Arizona Historical Society, Tucson.

Big Tree Breeze (F-6-A, Double Springs/Mormon Lake). 1934a. July 14. Arizona Historical Society, Tucson.

———. 1934b. 27 July. Arizona Historical Society, Tucson.

———. 1934c. 11 August. Arizona Historical Society, Tucson.

Broadcaster (BR-13-A, Yuma). 1936. February 22. Arizona Historical Society, Tucson.

———. 1937. March 25. Arizona Historical Society, Tucson.

Cactizonian (SP-6-A, Tucson Mountain). 1936a. November 24. Arizona Historical Society, Tucson.

———. 1936b. November 26. Arizona Historical Society, Tucson.

Camp News (SCS-15-A, Rillito River/Tucson). 1936. December 5. Arizona Historical Society, Tucson.

Caveman (SP-10-A, Vail). 1936. August 15. Arizona Historical Society, Tucson.

———. 1937. April 31. Arizona Historical Society, Tucson.

CCC Camp Talk (NM-2-A, Bonito Canyon). 1936. July 27. Arizona Historical Society, Tucson.

Civilian Conservation Corps. 1934a. Camp inspection report, F-14-A, July 14. Record Group 35, Entry 115, National Archives, Washington, D.C. Copy in author's collection.

———. 1934b. *Company Hysterical History.* Little Rock, Ark.: Peerless Engraving Company.

Condon, Jim. 1982. Growing up in the CCC. *Modern Maturity* (October/November):72.

Date Creek Rattler (DG-47-A, Congress Junction). 1935. February 3. Arizona Historical Society, Tucson.

DeLost, Frank (CCC alumnus, F-78-A, Chevelon Canyon). 1984. Interview with Joe Stocker. Transcript. NACCCA Collection, Arizona State University, Tempe.

Desert Digest (SCS-21-A, Reed Park, Tucson). 1936. Mr. Ogan. August. Arizona Historical Society, Tucson.

———. 1937. May. Arizona Historical Society, Tucson.

Desert Sun (SCS-25-A, Safford/Solomanville). 1940. March. NACCCA Collection, Arizona State University, Tempe.

Echo of the Peak (Flagstaff). 1934a. July 11. Arizona Historical Society, Tucson.

———. 1934b. July 25. Arizona Historical Society, Tucson.

Enriquiz, Manual (CCC alumnus, SP-3-A, South Mountain Park). 1984. Interview with Joe Stocker. Transcript. NACCCA Collection, Arizona State University, Tempe.

Federal Security Agency. n.d. *Work experience that counts.* Washington, D.C.: Government Printing Office.

———. 1941. *Civilian Conservation Corps: Contributing to the defense of the nation.* Washington, D.C.: Government Printing Office.

Federal Security Agency and the Civilian Conservation Corps. n.d. *Camplife arithmetic workbook,* 5 vols. Washington, D.C.: Government Printing Office.

Flagstaff Coconino Sun. 1933. July 21.

———. 1937. July 9.

Flux Canyon Recorder (F-63-A, Patagonia). 1935. December 3. Arizona Historical Society, Tucson.

Gaston, Frederick (CCC alumnus, SP-5-A, Papago Park). 1984. Interview with Joe Stocker. Transcript. NACCCA Collection, Arizona State University, Tempe.

Goodwin, Felix (CCC alumnus, Kansas). 1990. Interview with Peter Booth.

Grand Canyon Echoes (NP-2-A, Grand Canyon). 1937. April 1. Arizona Historical Society, Tucson.

Hanson, James Austin. 1973. The Civilian Conservation Corps in the northern Rockies. PhD diss., University of Wyoming.

Happy Days. 1934a. August 11. Arizona Historical Society, Tucson.

———. 1934b. Sing you sinners: Poems of the CCC. October 25. Arizona Historical Society, Tucson.

Hernandez, Peter. 1934. Meditations amid the pines. *Happy Days.* September 1. Arizona Historical Society, Tucson.

Holbrook Tribune. 1933. April 28.

Ingram, Jerry (CCC alumnus, Grand Canyon and Papago Park). 1990. Interview with Peter Booth. May.

Keller, Henry (CCC alumnus, F-23-A, Indian Garden). 1984. Interview with Joe Stocker. Transcript. NACCCA Collection, Arizona State University, Tempe.

Lacy, Leslie Alexander. 1976. *The soil soldiers: The Civilian Conservation Corps in the Great Depression.* Radnor, Pa.: Chilton Book Company.

Lakeside Mirror (F-6-A, Double Springs/Mormon Lake). 1935. June 14. Arizona Historical Society, Tucson.

Legder, Randall (CCC Commander, Arizona). 1990. Interview with Peter Booth. February 19.

Lundquist, George (CCC alumnus, SP-6-A, Tucson Mountains). 1990. Interview with Peter Booth. February.

Maddox, Danny. 1979. Catacombs gave him a needed break. *Tucson Arizona Star.* March 8. Based on interviews with Jesus "Jesse" Miranda, CCC alumnus of SP-10-A.

Major, Colonel Duncan. 1933. To Howe. August 11. Quoted in Salmond 1967, 48–49.

Marsh, C. 1934. Letter to Isabella Greenway. June 28. Greenway Collection, Arizona Historical Society, Tucson.

Molner, Steve (contracted CCC engineer). 1984. Interview with Joe Stocker. Transcript. NACCCA Collection, Arizona State University, Tempe.

Oasis (SCS-19-A, St. David). 1937. March 31. Arizona Historical Society, Tucson.

Paige, John C. 1985. *The Civilian Conservation Corps and the National Park Service, 1933–1942: An administrative history.* Washington, D.C.: Government Printing Office.

Preslar, S. D. 1934. *Happy Days.* October 13. Arizona Historical Society, Tucson.

Pugh, Jack (CCC alumnus, F-78-A, Chevelon Canyon). 1984. Interview with Joe Stocker. Transcript. NACCCA Collection, Arizona State University, Tempe.

Purvis, Louis Lester. [1989]. *The ace in the hole: A brief history of Company 818 of the Civilian Conservation Corps.* Columbus, Ga.: Brentwood Christian Press.

Rillito Reveler (SCS-15-A, Tucson). 1936a. February 22. Arizona Historical Society, Tucson.

———. 1936b. April 5. Arizona Historical Society, Tucson.

———. 1936c. May 25. Arizona Historical Society, Tucson.

Robles, Bob (CCC alumnus, F-6-A, Double Springs/Mormon Lake). 1984. Interview with Joe Stocker. Transcript. NACCCA Collection, Arizona State University, Tempe.

Safford Graham County Guardian. 1934a. October 26. Arizona Historical Society, Tucson.

———. 1934b. 17 August. Arizona Historical Society, Tucson.

———. 1934c. 19 October. Arizona Historical Society, Tucson.

———. 1934d. 13 July. Arizona Historical Society, Tucson.

Salmond, John A. 1967. *The Civilian Conservation Corps, 1933–1942.* Durham, N.C.: Duke University Press.

State Conference of Arizona Educational Advancement and Cooperative Agencies. 1936. Report on proceedings. May 14–16. RG-75, Box 245. National Archives, Washington, D.C.

Stone, Joseph (CCC alumnus, NP-1-A Grand Canyon, North Rim). n.d. Interview with Peter Booth.

Strong, Lyon (CCC alumnus, SP-6-A, Tucson Mountains). 1990. Interview with Peter Booth. April 18.

Timberwolf (F-74-A, Columbine). 1935. August 7. Arizona Historical Society, Tucson.

Tucson Arizona Star. 1933. June 1.

———. 1934. November 24.

———. 1937. September 24.

———. 1940. July 19.

Tucson Citizen. 1933. November 24.

———. 1934. November 23.

Tucson-CCC and Major Carl Byrd. 1936. *Tucson Educational Survey.* Tucson.

Valentine, Richard. 1968. Arizona and the Great Depression. MA thesis, Northern Arizona University.

Chapter Eighteen

GEOLOGY IN THE AMERICAN SOUTHWEST: NEW PROCESSES, NEW THEORIES

BY GRETCHEN MERTEN

Great innovations, whether in art or literature, in science or in nature, seldom take the world by storm. They must be understood before they can be estimated, and must be cultivated before they can be understood.

—*Clarence E. Dutton,* Tertiary History of the Grand Cañon District, with Atlas

In the late nineteenth century, the American Southwest emerged as one of the most important regions for geological study in the world. When geologists first encountered the canyon country of the Colorado Plateau, and the Grand Canyon in particular, they lacked vocabulary, methodology, and theory to describe and analyze the myriad stratigraphic and structural features and geomorphological processes that confronted them. Consequently, in numerous publications on the canyons and mountains of the Southwest, the region's initial explorers articulated theories that would come to inform a distinct "American school" of geology. John Wesley Powell, Clarence Edward Dutton, and Grove Karl Gilbert revolutionized the science of geology by revealing the primacy of streams in shaping the landscape (fluvialism) and by relating large-scale structures to motions in the earth's crust. At the heart of Powell's and Gilbert's geomorphological theory and Dutton's principle of isostasy is the concept of dynamic equilibrium. For these scientists, as for Darwin, natural processes inherent to our dynamic planet continuously work to correlate physical or biological structure with environmental conditions; for geologists, this process also works in reverse. Just as natural selection guides the evolution of life, processes of sedimentation and erosion, as well as crustal loading and rebound, perpetuate a tenuous, fleeting balance between the forces of creation and destruction. The crowning achievement of geology in the West was

and remains the organization of time according to basic principles of geomorphology and structure revealed in the stunning geography of the American Southwest.

The first great geologist to describe the canyon was John Wesley Powell. Powell, a one-armed Civil War veteran and self-taught, home-schooled naturalist, developed the idea of exploring the canyons of the Colorado River when he was studying the headwaters of the Grand and Green rivers in Colorado and Wyoming during his Rocky Mountain Scientific Exploring Expedition of 1868. Through his research, he came to believe "the Grand Canyon of the Colorado will give the best geological section on the continent" (Hughes 1967, 44). Powell's first exploration of the Colorado commenced on May 24, 1869. He and his small party successfully negotiated the river from Green River, Utah, to the mouth of the Virgin River, today under Lake Mead. Because his first journey involved more survival than science, Powell led another expedition in 1871–72 with the explicit purpose of scientific exploration. The product of these expeditions is Powell's *Exploration of the Colorado River of the West and Its Tributaries* (1875). It is the first major description of the Grand Canyon and contains the first generalized stratigraphic column of the entire canyon section and the first physiographic diagram illustrating the cross-sectional nature of the region (Spamer 1989, 3).

Powell's most important contribution to geology is his system of stream classification; these divisions are basic principles in modern geomorphology. Streams and their drainages are categorized as *antecedent*, *consequent*, or *superimposed*. In the case of antecedence, the drainage is established prior to the elevation of the strata by folding or faulting, that is, streams predate structural deformation. Streams and their concomitant valleys that depend upon the structural features of a region are termed consequent, that is, structural deformation precedes the carving of the drainage. Superimposed waterways are not determined by the structural features of the rock through which they are carved but were in existence when the region last appeared above sea level. As a corollary, Powell also pioneered the concept of *base-level erosion*, defined as an imaginary surface inclining slightly in all parts toward the end of the principal stream draining the area through which the level is supposed to extend (Merrill 1964, 365). This is a vital insight, as all streams, regardless of their type of drainage system, work to achieve base level; the greater the deviation from base level, the greater the cutting power of the stream.

Powell characterized the Colorado as an antecedent stream. He noticed that the Colorado flowed across and incised Mesozoic strata upon entering the canyon. Then, as the region was uplifted, the Colorado stripped away the Mesozoic veneer, and cut down into the Paleozoic strata and metamorphic basement of the Colorado Plateau (Spamer 1989, 40). Powell likened the process to a buzz saw slicing through a log rising into the blade from below. As flexures on the Colorado Plateau rose, the river sought its level by cutting a canyon into the rising mountains (Merrill 1964, 479). Clarence Dutton would later agree with Powell's antecedence paradigm, while Grove Karl Gilbert would argue for cases of consequence and superimposition in addition to antecedence.

In addition to his work on streams and drainages, Powell was the first geologist to describe the rocks that unconformably underlie the Paleozoic strata of the canyon. Powell's "non-conformable rocks" included the metamorphic basement and the Grand Canyon Supergroup: a tilted, down-faulted series of Proterozoic sedimentary and metamorphic rock (Spamer 1989, 15). The beveled nature of the basement and Grand Canyon Supergroup, coupled with his own concept of base-level erosion, prompted Powell to realize the transitory nature of earth's mightiest features and the vastness of geologic time: "Mountains cannot long remain mountains [as] they are ephemeral topographic forms. Geologically all existing mountains are recent; the ancient mountains [implied by the canyon's beveled Precambrian rocks] are gone" (Moore 1956, 237).

Powell's other major geological publication is his *Report*

on the *Geology of the Eastern Portion of the Uinta Mountains* (1876). In the *Report*, Powell divided the region west of the Great Plains, east of the Sierra Nevada, and south of the North Platte, Shoshone, and Sweetwater rivers into three physiographic provinces. The *Park Province* is characterized by massive ranges and great parks that serve as the watersheds and drainages of the Colorado and Rio Grande rivers. The *Plateau Province* is denoted by tablelands bordered by canyons and cliffs, is marked with occasional lone mountains and short ranges, and drains into the Colorado. The *Basin Province* consists of short north-south trending mountains and valleys, and it is remarkable for its internal drainage into salt lakes and sinks (Merrill 1964, 543–544).

As for Utah's Uinta Mountains, Powell correctly describes them as a fault-block mountain range with its longer axis oriented in a west-east direction. Faulting began in the late Mesozoic and ended in the late Cenozoic era, producing 30,000 feet of uplift. The erosion that accompanied the uplift removed more than 7,000 cubic miles of material from a 2,000-square-mile area (Merrill 1964, 543–544). Gilbert and Dutton would later use Powell's physiographic classifications, and Gilbert would be the first to articulate fully the structure of the Basin and Range (Basin) Province. Taken together, Powell's *Colorado River* and *Uinta Mountains* reports of 1875 and 1876 initiated the modern science of physical geology (Stegner 1954, 155).

While Powell provides the definitive view of the Grand Canyon from the river's edge, Captain Clarence E. Dutton, U.S. Army Ordnance, articulated the view from the rim. Dutton's first report on the region concerns the geology of Utah's plateaus (Dutton 1880). In the realm of structural geology, Dutton concurred with Powell's idea that the great flexures that are the dominant features of the high plateau country are due to faults and subsequent monoclinal flexure. Because unbroken anticlinals are underlain by faults, one form of displacement passes continuously into the other (Merrill 1964, 545). Most importantly, Dutton's *Report on the Geology of the High Plateaus of Utah* (1890) contains his first ruminations on isostasy. Dutton realized that the erosion of 6,000 to 10,000 vertical feet of rock from a 10,000-square-mile area precipitates regional uplift (Merrill 1964, 545).

Dutton's greatest work, however, remains *The Tertiary History of the Grand Cañon District, with Atlas* (1882). The volume itself is a monumental production and quickly and deservedly became the definitive geological description of the canyon region. The atlas, a folio-sized volume of twenty-three sheets, contains the first geological (time-stratigraphic units in color, structure) and topographic maps of the Grand Canyon (Spamer 1989, 5, 50). In addition, the sublime, atmospheric works of Thomas Moran and the photographically precise panoramas of William Henry Holmes provide visuals to accompany Dutton's poetic, richly descriptive narrative. Indeed, Dutton's stirring analysis of the Grand Canyon region, coupled with his ability to fuse aesthetic appreciation and scientific insight, launched southwestern North America as a premier field for geological study and marks the founding of the American school of geology (Spamer 1989, 5, 50).

In *Tertiary History*, Dutton studies the canyon's geomorphology by relating the structure of the region to the development of the chasm's drainage systems and consequent landforms. His main conclusion is that a geologically short time is all that is necessary for a river to cut through a great thickness of rock rising isostatically as a result of large-scale denudation (Faul and Faul 1983, 204). According to Dutton, "Erosion depends for its efficiency principally upon the progressive elevation of a region, and upon its climatical conditions. . . . The present Grand Canyon is the work of late Tertiary and Quaternary time" (Dutton 1882, 1, 7–8).

Dutton thus fuses the insights of Powell about geomorphology and the primacy of fluvial action with his own work on geomorphology and isostasy. Dutton's analysis of the dynamics of cliff recession is an example of a basic geomorphological tenet established in his canyon studies. Differential rates of erosion, controlled by strata of varying lithologic competence, "explain how [the canyon's] abnormal architectural forms so abundantly displayed in the chasm and the region round-about have been formed" (Dutton 1882, 8).

Finally, Dutton also introduces the concept of the Great Denudation, an elaboration on Powell's sense of deep time and the transformative power of fluvial systems. Powell realized that the Great Unconformity—the boundary between the crystalline basement and lowermost Paleozoic strata—marks two orogenies and their associated mountains' obliteration to a nearly level plain by erosion. The Great Denudation, the wearing-away of the Mesozoic and Cenozoic strata in the region, illustrates the principle of "dynamic equilibrium," as it is the consequence of isostatic rebound and the river's relentless quest to reestablish base level (Pyne 1982, 35). Dutton's genius lay in his ability to render the Grand Canyon as a comprehensible whole, as the product of evolutionary physical laws that are best revealed through scientific and aesthetic insight.

In 1883 Dutton wrote a positive review of Osmond Fisher's *Physics of the Earth's Crust* (1881). In his volume, Fisher reviews the secular-contraction hypothesis, the dominant paradigm of his day on crustal deformation and on the earth's inner structure (Greene 1982, 244). At the time, the earth's crust was thought to move vertically, not laterally.

In short, continents were elevated when contractions (the result of heat loss) under ocean basins relieved the crust of its stress. Ocean basins were uplifted when the base of uplifted continents solidified, cooled, and sank. Fisher believed that such a "contraction" mechanism could not account for the amount of compression seen in sedimentary sequences or the inequalities in relief that existed on the earth's surface (Greene 1982, 244). Accordingly, Fisher suggested that the earth consists of a series of concentric shells of increasing density and is composed of a solid outermost crust, a semi-solid layer made "mobile" by heat and pressure, and a highly pressurized, solid nucleus (Greene 1982, 245).

Dutton's positive evaluation stemmed from his own geophysical model of the earth, as he also envisioned an inhomogeneous planet with regional differences in density that could cause bulges and depressions on the earth's surface. The heterogeneity of the earth's composition is necessary, Dutton reasoned, because a spinning earth of homogenous density would be utterly featureless. In 1889 Dutton finally defined isostasy as the tendency of the rotating earth to seek "dynamic equilibrium" with regard to the distribution of materials of different densities (Greene 1982, 248–249). However, a dynamic equilibrium is never reached because of the ceaseless processes of erosion and deposition. In practical terms, erosion along continental margins causes a gradual crustal subsidence in the area of greatest accumulation while the bordering upland that is shedding sediment rises as it is divested of its sediment load by way of erosion. For Dutton, then, the earth's crust and the earth itself are dynamic structures that continuously seek a Darwinian-like state of balance between internal structure and external process.

Also in 1889, Dutton addressed the Philosophical Society of Washington. In his speech on "some of the greater problems of physical geology," Dutton fully articulated the paradoxical nature of isostasy. Erosion creates uplift, as the "flanks of platforms with the upturned edges of strata reposing against them, or with giant faults measuring their immense uplifts, plainly declare to us that they have been pushed upward as fast as they were degraded . . . by erosion" (Moore 1956, 251). Furthermore, Dutton correctly reasons that such "rebound" necessitates the existence of a "viscous" or "plastic" under crust. While geology would have to await the theory of plate tectonics to explain large-scale regional uplift, Dutton's modern law of isostasy remains valid on a smaller scale. In short, mountains are raised in unstable areas by the earth's maintenance of its crustal balance (Moore 1956, 255); this corresponds to his own as well as Powell's and Gilbert's concept of dynamic equilibrium.

The final member of early American Southwest geology's triumvirate is Grove Karl Gilbert, perhaps the most talented of the three. Upon Gilbert's death in 1918, T. C. Chamberlain, an important American geologist, stated that it "is doubtful whether the products of any geologist of our day will escape revision at the hands of future research to a degree equal to the writings of Grove Karl Gilbert" (Wallace 1980, 42). Indeed, Gilbert's analyses of the Basin and Range Province, the Henry Mountains of Utah, and Lake Bonneville remain valid for the most part, and they are the sources for several principles basic to structural geology and geomorphology today.

Gilbert first realized that faulting—not folding, as in the Appalachians—is the force behind mountain-building in the intermountain West during his explorations as chief geologist with G. M. Wheeler's survey of the lands west of the one-hundredth meridian in 1871 and 1872. In 1875 Gilbert, in "Report on the Geology of Portions of Nevada, Utah, California, and Arizona," first applies the terms "Basin Range System" and "Basin Ranges" to "all that system of short ridges separated by trough-like valleys which lies west of the Plateau System" (Gilbert 1875, 22). Gilbert correctly surmised that blocks of mountains were raised along nearly vertical, deep-seated faults (Wallace 1980, 36). Furthermore, the valleys between the upthrusted blocks are not erosional features but are intervals existing between planes of maximum uplift (Merrill 1964, 541). This analysis is the contemporary understanding of the Basin and Range physiographic province.

Gilbert's work in the Southwest next found expression in his *Report on the Geology of the Henry Mountains* (1877). He suggested that the Henrys were created by the intrusion from below of igneous material through Paleozoic and lower Mesozoic strata, causing the overlying Cretaceous and Tertiary beds to bulge outward (Merrill 1964, 546). Gilbert was the first to show that intrusive igneous masses can deform rocks into which they are extruded (Hunt 1980, 25). These intrusions were termed *laccolites* (later laccoliths). His analysis is even more remarkable when placed in its historical context. As late as the 1830s, geologists were still skeptical about the igneous origin of rocks and were even more reluctant to accept Gilbert's idea that igneous masses may intrude and be younger than their host rocks (Hunt 1980, 29). Indeed, he showed that rock that is brittle and rigid on the scale of a hand specimen will bend and deform plastically on a regional scale (Faul and Faul 1983, 204).

Gilbert employs Powell's drainage schematic in his discussion of the drainage patterns of the Henry Mountains. The streams are, he asserted, generally consequent. It is here that Gilbert relates dynamic equilibrium to geomorphology and fully articulates the concept that landforms are the manifestation of process, the central theme of contemporary geomorphology (Yochelson 1980, 140). In brief, drainage systems are the manifestation of a self-regulating process, driven by the force of gravity, whereby topographic form is adjusted to correspond to changes in mass and energy flow (Yochelson 1980, 130). In addition, Gilbert formulated the *law of uniform slopes* ("The tendency [of streams] is to abolish all difference of slope and produce uniformity"), the *law of structure* ("Erosion is most rapid where resistance is least"), and the *law of divides* ("The nearer the water-shed or divide the steeper the slope; the farther away the less the slope") (Gilbert 1877, 115–116). Just as Dutton's crust seeks dynamic equilibrium, so do Gilbert's streams.

In his *Lake Bonneville* report of 1890, Gilbert expands on Powell's isostatic studies of Utah by establishing geomorphology as a quantitative science. His meticulous mapping and correlation of petrified beaches proved that the level of Lake Bonneville, a great inland lake of Pleistocene age, varied by approximately one thousand feet over time, resulting in differential loading of the crust (Faul and Faul 1983, 207). The phenomenon of "non-horizontal" beaches led Gilbert to propose a model of the earth similar to that of Dutton's. He concluded that major deformations of the crust reflect "horizontal movements of the upper rocks (the lithosphere) without corresponding movements in the nucleus, thereby [implying] mobility in an intervening layer." Furthermore, the driving forces of such movements result from "a primal heterogeneity of the earth which gives diversity to the flow of heat energy" (Yochelson 1980, 61). These two ideas clearly predict the modern geophysical picture of the earth and the motive force (convection) behind contemporary tectonic theory.

In 1875 Gilbert succinctly articulated the value of the canyon lands and mountains of the American Southwest for geological study: "It is impossible to overestimate the advantages of this field for the study . . . of mountain building (and other processes). [Here] can be found differentiated the simplest initiatory phenomenon, not obscured, but rather exposed, by denudation, and the process can be followed from step to step, until the complicated results of successive dislocations and erosions baffle analysis" (Wallace 1980, 36). Thus, the Grand Canyon in particular and the American Southwest in general stimulated new geological theories because the region reveals stratigraphic relations, three-dimensional structural features, and geomorphological processes with textbook clarity.

The work of Powell, Dutton, and Gilbert produced a series of fundamental principles in the areas of geomorphology and structural geology that have come to define a distinct branch of American geology. This is geology on an appropriately monumental scale, as Powell, Dutton, and

Gilbert sought to relate the origin of the Grand Canyon to the genesis of the modern Colorado River, and to the regional uplift of the Colorado Plateau and its associated structures. In addition, these pioneering geologists strove to associate structure with historical geology, thereby revealing the causation of major depositional and erosional events and their spatial and temporal extent. At the core of their analyses and theories lay an unabashed faith in the timelessness of geological process, of nature's relentless quest to establish a "dynamic equilibrium" between structure and the environment. Most notably, the early geologists of the Southwest believed in the power of scientific insight and aesthetic awareness to reveal the fundamental processes of physical geology. Their legacy lives in introductory geology textbooks and profoundly shapes the minds of all who peer into the mysterious, beautiful depths of the Grand Canyon.

WORKS CITED

Dutton, Clarence E. 1880. *Report on the geology of the high plateaus of Utah, with atlas.* Washington, D.C.: Government Printing Office.

———. 1882. *Tertiary history of the Grand Cañon district, with atlas.* U.S. Geological Survey Monograph 2. Washington, D.C.: Government Printing Office.

Faul, Henry, and Carol Faul. 1983. *It began with a stone: A history of geology from the Stone Age to the age of plate tectonics.* New York: John Wiley and Sons.

Fisher, Osmond. 1881. *Physics of the Earth's Crust.* London: Macmillan.

Gilbert, G. K. 1875. Report on the geology of portions of Nevada, Utah, California, and Arizona. In *Report upon the geographical and geological surveys of the one hundredth meridian*, vol. 3 (Geology). G. M. Wheeler, Washington, D.C.: Government Printing Office.

———. 1877. *Report on the geology of the Henry Mountains.* U.S. Geographical and Geological Survey of the Rocky Mountain Region. Washington, D.C.: Government Printing Office.

———. 1890. *Lake Bonneville.* U.S. Geological Survey Monograph 1. Washington, D.C.: Government Printing Office.

Greene, Mott T. 1982. *Geology in the nineteenth century: Changing views of a changing world.* Ithaca, N.Y.: Cornell University Press.

Hughes, Donald J. 1967. *The story of man at Grand Canyon.* Bulletin 14. Grand Canyon, Ariz.: Grand Canyon Natural History Association.

Hunt, Charles B. 1980. *G. K. Gilbert, on laccoliths and intrusive structures.* In *The Scientific Ideas of G. K. Gilbert*, ed. Ellis Yochelson, 25–34. Boulder, Colo.: The Geological Society of America.

Merrill, George P. 1964. *The first one hundred years of American geology.* New York: Hafner Publishing Company.

Moore, Ruth. 1956. *The earth we live on: The story of geological discovery.* New York: Alfred A. Knopf.

Powell, John Wesley. 1875. *Exploration of the Colorado River of the West, and its tributaries. Explored in 1869, 1870, 1871, and 1872, under the direction of the Secretary of the Smithsonian Institution.* Washington, D.C.: Government Printing Office.

———. 1876. *Report on the geology of the eastern portion of the Uinta Mountains and a region of country adjacent thereto, with atlas.* U.S. Geological and Geographical Survey of the Territories. Washington, D.C.: Government Printing Office.

Pyne, Stephen J. 1982. *Dutton's Point: An intellectual history of the Grand Canyon.* Monograph 5. Grand Canyon, Ariz.: Grand Canyon Natural History Association.

Spamer, Earle E. 1989. *The development of geological studies in the Grand Canyon.* Tryonia No. 17. Philadelphia: Academy of Natural Sciences of Philadelphia.

Stegner, Wallace. 1954. *Beyond the hundredth meridian: John Wesley Powell and the second opening of the West.* Repr., New York: Penguin Books, 1992.

Wallace, Robert E. 1980. G. K. Gilbert's studies of faults, scarps, and earthquakes. In *The Scientific Ideas of G. K. Gilbert*, ed. Ellis Yochelson, 35–44. Boulder, Colo.: The Geological Society of America.

Yochelson, Ellis L., ed. 1980. *The scientific ideas of G. K. Gilbert: An assessment on the occasion of the centennial of the United States Geological Survey (1879–1979).* Special Paper 183. Boulder, Colo.: The Geological Society of America.

SCENERY VERSUS HABITAT AT THE GRAND CANYON

BY J. DONALD HUGHES

It was a great pleasure to have Dr. Hughes and his wife return to the Grand Canyon for the symposium. They met at the park, left, then returned in the 1960s after their wedding to spend four summers at the South Rim where Don worked as a seasonal ranger/naturalist. It was in these years that he wrote The Story of Man at Grand Canyon *(1967), the first comprehensive human history of the Grand Canyon, revised and retitled* In the House of Stone and Light *in 1978. In his presentation, Dr. Hughes reviews the reasons for the creation of the national parks, the National Park Service's (NPS) dual mission of preservation and use, and ecological threats that have confronted the Grand Canyon since the early years of the twentieth century.*

Stephen J. Pyne's perceptive book *How the Canyon Became Grand* (1998) explores some of the meanings that people of different origins have given to the Grand Canyon. He argues that it was human expectation, bound up in the cultures of those who visited it, or lived there, that determined what aspects of that part of the world would impress them, and thereby suggested names they gave it. Members of Coronado's expedition saw the canyon in 1540 and, like many visitors since, greatly underestimated its size. They gave it no name other than to call it a "*barranca*," a ravine. "Grand Canyon" became the accepted name of the erosional feature only after the mid-nineteenth century. Its status as a national park, bestowed by the U.S. Congress in 1919, is in large part the result of the meaning connoted by the word "Grand."

The impact of the canyon's form, color, monumentality, and unusual beauty is so overwhelming that only after a while do visitors begin to notice the life that is all around them. The air is full of birds. White-throated swifts zoom after insects, red-tailed hawks soar near its cliffs looking for small mammals, and ravens play, squawking and doing midair somersaults. In the rocks at the edge of the chasm, ground squirrels "beg" to become known. A low forest of twisted pines

and junipers frames the rim. One can often see mule deer, or more seldom come across a bobcat crossing the road with a rabbit in its jaws, or spot a mountain lion at dusk.

Topography on a grand scale and wildlife are two aspects of the national park experience, and are among the reasons why national parks were created in the United States. The purpose of national parks, according to the Organic Act of 1916, which created the NPS, is to "conserve the scenery and the natural and historic objects and the wild life therein and to provide for the enjoyment of the same in such manner and by such means as will leave them unimpaired for the enjoyment of future generations." Many historians and commentators on the national parks have noted that this sentence contains two purposes, "to conserve" and "to provide for enjoyment" by the public, that were likely to come into conflict with each other, and have indeed done so (Runte 1983, 464–467). Few, however, have noted that "scenery" and "wild life" imply two distinct attitudes of visitors: "sightseeing," the enjoyment of spectacular landscapes, and "biophilia," the appreciation of life within natural ecosystems.

The first part of the statement of purpose for the national parks directs that four characteristics be conserved:

scenery, natural objects, historic objects, and wildlife. In the early days of the designation of parks, the first two received the greatest emphasis. There were thirteen national parks in 1916. All were places primarily noted for monumental scenery, except Mesa Verde, where "historic objects," the ancient cliff dwellings, were the primary interest.

It is notable, however, that the first proposal for a national park advocated the preservation of animals, vegetation, and native people. In 1832 the artist George Catlin recommended that an area on the Great Plains be set aside as "a nation's park, containing man and beast, in all the wild and freshness of their nature's beauty. . . . What a beautiful and thrilling specimen for America to hold up to the view of her refined citizens and the world, in future ages!" (Catlin 1841, 261–262). Catlin's suggestion was ignored, however, and creation of a national park on the Great Plains awaited another century, after the land had been plowed and the bison had almost disappeared.

It is striking that Catlin, many of whose paintings were of American Indians, considered American Indians appropriate dwellers in a national park. The Grand Canyon was the home of several tribes, and is still to the Havasupais, but relations between these people and park administrators have often been painful. Tribal ancestors traditionally hunted and gathered in a large area of the canyon, but officials sometimes treated the Havasupais as interlopers and tried to limit them to their tiny reservation tucked away in a tributary canyon (Hirst 1976).

The first national park, Yellowstone, had its own Grand Canyon as well as waterfalls and geysers. Its herds of megafauna were something to see, but by themselves perhaps could not have generated the tourism desired by its promoters and the congressional delegation that visited in 1872. The primary purpose of parks then was to save the crown jewels of America's natural scenery. Yosemite was designated a park for its waterfalls and granite domes, and Sequoia and General Grant (today part of Kings Canyon) for trees—biological phenomena indeed, so large and old that they were awe-inspiring features of the landscape. These early parks were created before the science of ecology had received wide recognition, so backers of the parks in those days had only a general desire to protect nature, along with a wish to encourage people to visit the areas. At Mount Rainier, Crater Lake, Rocky Mountain, and Lassen Volcanic, the principal theme was great scenery, and no feature of the American earth fit that theme better than the Grand Canyon.

John Wesley Powell, who led expeditions by boat down the Colorado River in 1869 and 1871–72, urged Congress to make the Grand Canyon a national park because of its grandeur and geological interest. When John Muir saw the canyon in 1896, he repeated the call for park status because of its superlative scenery (Muir 1898, 28). President Theodore Roosevelt visited seven years later and voiced similar thoughts: "Leave it as it is. You cannot improve on it. The ages have been at work on it, and man can only mar it. What you can do is to keep it for your children, your children's children, and for all who come after you, as the one great sight which every American . . . should see" (*New York Sun* 1903). Congress, however, was favorable to mining companies that sought bonanzas, ranchers who feared curtailment of grazing rights, and timber concerns that wanted access to forests. Since chances of passage for a national park bill seemed slight, Roosevelt took unprecedented action by invoking the 1906 Antiquities Act to proclaim Grand Canyon National Monument in 1908. The area included was the section regarded as most scenic, with narrow strips of land along the rims that avoided impinging too far on commercial timber and grazing interests. There was opposition, however, and a suit challenging the proclamation on the grounds that the Antiquities Act did not authorize making national monuments of large natural features went to the Supreme Court, which ruled in the president's favor (Strong 1969, 36).

Arizona became a state in 1912, and local pride and hope for a robust tourist industry strengthened the movement to create a national park. The first director of the NPS, Stephen T. Mather, supported the idea, and his close associate and successor, Horace M. Albright, worked with Arizona's Representative Carl Hayden and Senator Henry F. Ashurst to get a bill through Congress, which was signed by President Woodrow Wilson on February 26, 1919 (Crampton 1972, 206). The area included was somewhat smaller than the monument; the intent was clearly to protect the scenic and geological features of an easily accessible portion of the canyon itself, with only a small slice of neighboring forests for administrative purposes.

Another purpose of national parks, however—protection of wildlife, and assurance that ecosystems would continue to function as whole systems—was beginning to be recognized. John C. Merriam, head of the Carnegie Institution of Washington, urged that national parks be regarded as laboratories where natural processes could be observed and studied (Morehouse 1996, 66). Scientists, envisioning the Grand Canyon as a treasure trove of evidence for the evolution of life as well as its present ecological interactions, offered a reason for preservation for the sake of understanding the origin and nature of the living community. Vernon Bailey, chief naturalist of the U.S. Biological Survey, argued that the boundaries of national parks, including the Grand Canyon, had been drawn without sufficient attention to the need to provide wildlife with habitat during all seasons of the year (Morehouse 1996, 55–62). The area included, he maintained, should be large enough to sustain a viable population of animals under natural conditions. In 1929 he recommended an expansion of Grand Canyon National Park, a suggestion that was lost in interagency disputes.

The national park in that year embraced only 105 miles of the canyon's total length of 277 miles. The idea of an expanded park did not die, but the argument in favor of it that eventually prevailed was the old idea of monumental scenery. A bill to enlarge the park to embrace the entire canyon, except for portions within American Indian reservations, gained the support of Senator Barry Goldwater of Arizona, the NPS, and environmentalists, and was signed into law in 1975. The act almost doubled the size of the park, to 1,892 square miles. But the idea that the national park was intended to protect scenery was implicit in the fact that the new boundaries primarily ran along the rims, putting the interior of the canyon within the national park and leaving most areas back from the rims, with their wildlife habitats, in other jurisdictions. A new national monument to include some of these areas was proposed by Secretary of the Interior Bruce Babbitt, former governor of Arizona, and proclaimed by President Bill Clinton in 2000.

The Grand Canyon has indeed supplied a great amount of evidence for the understanding of living communities. Even without the scenic monumentality of the canyon, there would be enough biological interest to justify designation as a national park. In 1889 C. Hart Merriam, chief of the U.S. Biological Survey, studied the distribution of plants and animals in the Grand Canyon region. Within a range of 10,000 feet in elevation from the Colorado River at canyon bottom to the top of the San Francisco Peaks he distinguished seven "life zones," that is, "areas inhabited by definite assemblages of animals and plants" (Sterling 1974, 294). Merriam's ideas represented a step toward the concept of ecosystems (Merriam and Stejneger 1890). When he wrote, "The Grand Canyon of the Colorado is a world in itself, and a great fund of knowledge is in store for the philosophic biologist whose privilege it is to study exhaustively the problems there presented," he aptly explained his reasoning (Krutch 1962, 12).

The purpose of national parks was to some extent redefined as a result of a crisis of wildlife management that occurred in the Kaibab National Forest north of the Grand Canyon in the 1920s. The theory of game management in those years maintained that "good" species such as deer should be protected from "bad" predators such as wolves and mountain lions. James T. "Uncle Jim" Owens was appointed Kaibab National Forest game warden by the forest service in 1907, and in the twelve years preceding the establishment of the national park, reportedly killed 532 mountain lions, among many other predators. Those using his services as guide included Zane Grey, Buffalo Jones, and Theodore Roosevelt, who came to

hunt lions in the game reserve he, as president, had created. The policy of destroying predators on sight continued until 1931 (Wallace 1972, 56). As a result, mountain lions and bobcats were greatly reduced in number, wolves were extirpated, but coyotes continued to flourish. The Kaibab herd of mule deer, spared from most predation, increased from 4,000 in 1906 to an extreme estimate of 100,000 in 1924. They ate every green thing they could reach, and the forest took on the appearance of a clipped city park. The forest service inaugurated limited hunting, fawns were captured and transplanted, and there was a bumbling attempt to drive deer across the canyon by trail to the South Rim, all to little avail (Hughes 1978, 90). During the severe winter of 1924–25, tens of thousands of deer died of starvation.

Game managers such as Aldo Leopold, who had worked at the Grand Canyon, were convinced by the tragedy on the Kaibab that "predators are members of the community" (Leopold 1949, 211), and that overpopulation was more dangerous to deer, and to the land, than any predator. Subsequently, park service policy aimed at the restoration of a functioning ecosystem by protecting all native species, including predators, herbivores, and plants, and by allowing their natural interactions. Some later parks, such as Everglades and the rainforest sections of Olympic National Park, were designated parks because of their biological interest. Unfortunately, most parks, even the expanded Grand Canyon National Park after 1975, are too small to protect all members of the ecosystem, especially larger animals.

The NPS in 1963 changed its wildlife management policies to protect interactive complexes of species when it adopted the "Leopold Report," named for Aldo's son, A. Starker Leopold, chairman of the National Park Service Advisory Board on Wildlife Management. The plan advocated that large national parks be managed as "original ecosystems" (Sessions 1992, 93). Where parks were not large enough to encompass entire ecosystems, the report recommended that surrounding areas be managed as peripheral zones with the parks as core areas, similar to a plan for biosphere reserves then being discussed by United Nations agencies.

Certain species in the Grand Canyon area have received study and protection. For example, the Kaibab squirrel is limited to the ponderosa pine forest on the Kaibab Plateau north of the canyon. It is a tassel-eared squirrel related to the widespread Abert squirrel. The Abert is gray, with white underparts; the Kaibab is dark gray or black, including the underparts, and has a conspicuous white tail. Both species depend on pines for food and shelter, and could not exist outside an ecosystem dominated by ponderosa pine. But the two populations do not overlap. The Kaibab squirrel has been isolated by the canyon and surrounding deserts for thousands of years, and its evolution has taken a separate path. Its white tail may help it hide from predators during snowy winters at 8,000 feet above sea level. Due to its narrow range and small population, it is listed as an endangered subspecies.

Restoration of species formerly present in the Grand Canyon region has been tried with varying degrees of success. The California condor, with the largest wingspan in North America, once flourished in the canyon, but the last known individual there was shot in 1881. By 1982, only twenty-two condors existed in the wild, all in California. They were captured and placed in zoos, along with birds previously captured, for breeding purposes. The program raised the captive population to seventy-one birds. Some were released in California's Coast Range, but the condors encountered power lines, chemicals, and bullets. In 1996 a few were released north of the Grand Canyon, and with added releases, condors are today observed soaring above or resting at the rims, particularly at Grand Canyon Village (Snyder and Snyder 2000, 345).

Aggressive nonnative species have damaged natural ecosystems in the Grand Canyon. Prospectors' burros escaped or were abandoned following the prospecting years of the late nineteenth century. Lovers of desert vegetation, they proliferated, particularly on the Tonto Platform, where they destroyed native plants, fouled springs, and competed with indigenous wildlife such as desert bighorn sheep. The NPS tried to eliminate the invaders beginning in the 1920s, and in later years used helicopters to fly in rangers with rifles. But a children's book, *Brighty of the Grand Canyon* (Henry 1953), romanticized the burros, helping to gain popular support against shooting feral burros, and Congress passed legislation banning such practices. The park service arranged for The Fund for Animals to round up and airlift out the burros in 1981. Private citizens adopted many of them. At the moment they are absent from the park except for a few that wander in from the Lake Mead area from time to time.

Another introduced species is the tamarisk, a bushy tree that, like the burro, is native to the Mediterranean. It has spread beside the river margins and tributary streams along with other introduced plants, replacing native vegetation and offering less diverse habitats to native birds and animals. There are no surefire means of eradicating tamarisk.

Ideas about ecological interpretation and management of national parks have gained popularity in recent years along with a popular recognition of the biological value of places such as the Grand Canyon. The parks have been spared from more extreme pressures that would surely have overwhelmed them before now if they had not been set aside, in view of development in the Southwest and the crushing numbers of visitors who besiege them every year.

Annually, nearly five million people visit Grand Canyon National Park alone. But it is unclear whether ecosystems can maintain integrity in the face of an increase in human activity that seems certain to continue. The park's 1995 General Management Plan intends to reduce congestion along the South Rim by locating new facilities outside park boundaries and by building a light-rail system for transit from Tusayan, seven miles to the south, to viewpoints and trails beside the rim. If implemented, these actions would be more in the way of technological fixes to allow still more people to visit the park than attempts at ecological protection. In the decades-long competition between the two stated purposes of our national parks—to conserve the scenery (or ecological integrity) and to provide for the public enjoyment thereof—enjoyment still holds the upper hand.

WORKS CITED

Catlin, George. 1841. *Letters and notes on the manners, customs, and condition of the American Indians*, 2 vols. Repr., Minneapolis: Ross and Haines, 1965.

Crampton, C. Gregory. 1972. *Land of living rock: The Grand Canyon and the high plateaus of Arizona, Utah, and Nevada.* New York: Alfred A. Knopf.

Henry, Marguerite. 1953. *Brighty of the Grand Canyon.* New York: Rand McNally.

Hirst, Stephen. 1976. *Life in a narrow place.* New York: David McKay.

Hughes, J. Donald. 1978. *In the house of stone and light: Introduction to the human history of Grand Canyon.* Grand Canyon, Ariz.: Grand Canyon Natural History Association.

Krutch, Joseph Wood. 1962. *Grand Canyon: Today and all its yesterdays.* New York: Doubleday and the American Museum of Natural History.

Leopold, Aldo. 1949. *A Sand County almanac and sketches here and there.* London: Oxford University Press.

Merriam, Clinton Hart, and Leonhard Stejneger. 1890. Results of a biological survey of the San Francisco Mountain: Region and desert of the Little Colorado, Arizona. In *North American fauna*, vol. 3. U.S. Department of Agriculture, Division of Ornithology and Mammalogy. Washington, D.C.: Government Printing Office.

Morehouse, Barbara J. 1996. *A place called Grand Canyon: Contested geographies.* Tucson: University of Arizona Press.

Muir, John. 1898. The wild parks and forest reservations of the West. *Atlantic Monthly* 81 (January):28.

New York Sun. 1903. May 27.

Pyne, Stephen J. 1998. *How the canyon became grand: A short history*. New York: Viking.

Runte, Alfred. 1983. National parks and the National Park Service. In *Encyclopedia of American forest and conservation history*, 2 vols., ed. Richard C. Davis, New York: Macmillan.

Sessions, George. 1992. Ecocentrism, wilderness, and global ecosystem protection. In *The wilderness condition: Essays on environment and civilization*, ed. Max Oelschlager, San Francisco: Sierra Club Books.

Snyder, Noel, and Helen Snyder. 2000. *The California condor: A saga of natural history and conservation*. San Diego: Academic Press.

Sterling, Keir Brooks. 1974. *Last of the naturalists: The career of C. Hart Merriam*. New York: Arno Press.

Strong, Douglas Hillman. 1969. The man who "owned" Grand Canyon. *American West* 6 (September):33–40.

Wallace, Robert. 1972. *The Grand Canyon*. New York: Time-Life Books.

A Little Knowledge Goes a Long Way: A History of Archaeological Research at the Grand Canyon

by Janet R. Balsom

Like Emma P. Benenati and Joseph P. Shannon's essay on Colorado River biological research later in this volume, Janet R. Balsom's presentation affirms that every discipline benefits from an understanding of its past. Since the days of John Wesley Powell, explorers, surveyors, ephemeral professionals, and park archaeologists have accumulated evidence of human occupation at the Grand Canyon. Most has been collected in the past few decades, however, driven by compliance with archaeological and historical protective legislation. The story of the canyon's human presence that emerges today is far richer than the information available just twenty years ago.

The Grand Canyon evokes an image that is nearly universal: a grand spectacle of earth's geology extending back two billion years. In 1979 the United Nations Educational, Scientific and Cultural Organization (UNESCO) designated Grand Canyon Nations Park a World Heritage Site in recognition of this worldwide image. But the park was also famous for its cultural resources, which, in 1979, had been known if not well understood for more than one hundred years. What did we know then, and just how far have we come since?

Archaeologists have been observing the nature and extent of prehistoric occupation at the Grand Canyon since the mid-nineteenth century. Until twenty years ago, a relatively uncomplicated picture of four thousand years of human history had emerged. This picture developed from considerable research undertaken between 1940 and 1980, but what about all the information we have collected over the past twenty years? Data have been gathered, and continue to be gathered, that are changing the story of human use of the canyon and surrounding areas, beginning with a single artifact made nearly ten thousand years ago.

Let us review what we know about archaeological research in the Grand Canyon.

The first documentation of archaeological remains is found in the journal of Major John Wesley Powell, who noted "moqui" ruins along the Colorado River during his

Bright Angel Pueblo, an ancestral Puebloan site that today lies between the Kaibab and Silver bridges along the Colorado River, was first documented by John Wesley Powell in 1869. NPS photograph

first expedition in 1869. He wrote, "Late in the afternoon I return and go up a little gulch just above this creek [Bright Angel Creek], about 200 yards from camp, and discover the ruins of two or three old houses, which were originally of stone laid in mortar. Only the foundations are left, but irregular blocks, of which the houses were constructed, lie scattered about. In one room I find an old mealing stone, deeply worn, as if it had been much used. A great deal of pottery is strewn around, and old trails, which in some places are deeply worn into the rocks, are seen" (Powell 1875, 259). It would be nearly forty years before anyone else wrote of the thousands of archaeological sites that comprise the Grand Canyon's archaeological heritage.

Although exploring and recording the canyon's archaeological resources did not begin in earnest until the early twentieth century, there were a few notable exceptions, namely, the 1869 and 1872 Powell expeditions and the 1889–90 Stanton expedition. Powell observed eight archaeological sites during his two river trips, one of which was excavated nearly a century later by Douglas Schwartz and the University of Kentucky field school near the mouth of Bright Angel Creek. Powell's influence on scientific investigations in the Grand Canyon is not restricted to his river explorations. He established the Bureau of American Ethnology, and much of its early work occurred in the canyon region. Robert Brewster Stanton noted at least four prehistoric sites along the Colorado River, including the granaries at Nankoweap and the "fort" above Cardenas Creek, two of the most documented and photographed archaeological sites in the Grand Canyon. It is rare for an archaeologist to have the good fortune of site photographs at the time of European-American contact, but the Cardenas fort is one of the few for which we have photographs.

Moving into the twentieth century, we find Neil Judd undertaking *Archeological Observations North of the Rio Colorado* (1926), which marks the beginning of professional archaeological documentation in the Grand Canyon; Judd

Top: Hilltop Fort in Cardenas Canyon as it appeared during the 1889–90 Stanton expedition. NPS photograph. Bottom: Modern-day image of the same site. Photograph by Tom Brownold, courtesy of the Desert Laboratory Repeat Photograph Collection, U.S.G.S. (Stake 1439)

undertook his initial fieldwork in 1918. At times, archaeology may have been secondary to the scenery, as Judd extolled the "wondrous panoramas disclosed from the north rim of the Grand Canyon. . . . Nature was never so lavish as when she created the fairyland below the Walhalla Plateau." Judd did notice the archaeology, however, stating, "Prehistoric ruins were seen throughout much [of] the region traversed. Their walls were rough, unworked blocks of limestone, sandstone, or chert, depending upon the material most accessible to the site occupied. Most of them had so completely collapsed as scarcely to be recognized as one-time human homes. No two of them were exactly alike. Each was distinct within itself, and yet each possessed certain characteristics common to the others" (Judd 1926, 76). Judd spent time on Walhalla Plateau, Saddle Mountain, Nankoweap, North and South canyons, and Bright Angel Creek, recording everything from granaries and cliff dwellings to agricultural gardens.

Judd's early observations form the cornerstone for those who followed, and many followed in the same locations. In the summer of 1923, the Public Museum of Milwaukee undertook the Barrett, or West, expedition. In addition to reconnaissance in Bright Angel Creek, they surveyed around Lipan Point on the East Rim, along the Bright Angel Trail, and atop the Tonto Platform. Seventeen sites were recorded in their report (West 1925).

As the science of archaeology was in its developmental phase, early professionals began exploring the canyon and describing its archaeological remains. Judd, West, and archaeologists associated with the Gila Pueblo consortium, most importantly Emil Haury, conducted reconnaissance surveys from the late 1910s through the 1930s, providing a picture of how canyon prehistory may have appeared. Gila Pueblo and Emil Haury, under the direction of Harold Gladwin, conducted the first significant excavation at Tusayan Ruin that would aid in the definition of the western boundary of ancestral Puebloan cultures. For the relatively young National Park

Service, the excavation was intended to provide a focal point of archaeological interpretation for the visiting public at Grand Canyon National Park. Completed in 1930, the ruins and the Wayside Museum still serve that purpose.

The year 1930 brought the age of classification to archaeology (Willey and Sabloff 1974), and the work of Gila Pueblo fit right in. In a 1930 letter from Haury to Gladwin, Haury described the sites he saw in Bright Angel and Clear Creek canyons, noting that, "the pottery is very much like that of the north rim as one would expect it to be on that side of the river. None of it could be classed as III; some of it might be late II." The III and II Haury discusses coincide with archaeological classifications for prehistoric remains found in the American Southwest. The Roman numeral III refers to the Pueblo III period (AD 1150 to 1300), or the third period of ancestral Puebloan occupation, and II to the Pueblo II period (AD 1000 to 1150). There is also a Pueblo I period (AD 800 to 1000) and two Basketmaker classifications: Basketmaker II (500 BC to AD 500) and Basketmaker III (AD 500 to 800). As early as 1930, the canyon's archaeological remains were being summarily described and classified with very little evaluation aside from surface descriptions.

The course had been set for what would become the popular notion of what Grand Canyon archaeology was all about; however, how "true" was the explanation? Was anything else going on, or was the canyon simply a Pueblo II–III outpost? By 1940 there had been three surveys in Bright Angel and Clear creeks (Judd, West, and Haury), three surveys of the Walhalla Glades area of the North Rim (Judd, Haury, and Hall), and two surveys of the East Rim area (West and Haury). The picture was fairly clear: possibly a little Basketmaker, then Pueblo I–III. As a profession, we were into classification, and at the Grand Canyon, that classification and description entailed small pueblos with clear evidence of agriculture. These generalizations became

A mano (handstone) and a metate (millstone with the concave surface), used for grinding corn, at a site along Clear Creek. NPS photograph

entrenched over more than fifty years, but work over the last twenty years by park archaeologists has painted a more dynamic, robust picture of prehistoric occupation.

Systematic surveys have been conducted for specific projects as part of cultural-resource management compliance beginning in the early 1960s. Anthropologist Robert Clark Euler undertook surveys related to the proposed construction of Marble Canyon Dam under the auspices of the Arizona Power Company (a forerunner of today's Arizona Public Service) and Prescott College. Although much of his work was done by helicopter, Euler added more than two hundred archaeological sites to a growing list. Douglas Schwartz, working under contract for the National Park Service, began intensive work at Unkar Delta, Walhalla Glades, and Bright Angel in the late 1960s. Both men added to our understanding of Grand Canyon prehistory, working in archaic split-twig figurine caves as well as ancestral Puebloan sites.

Schwartz completed the majority of his fieldwork in 1970; his reports followed through the early 1980s. Euler served as park anthropologist until 1984, authoring many reports along the way. Park archaeologists have continued the work, following up with intensive surveys of selected areas on both rims and along the Colorado River. Thereby, with more recorded sites and a richer collection of artifacts, the story of the people who lived at the Grand Canyon continues to unfold in finer detail.

Examples of our increased information base are found everywhere in our files, but a few are representative. Staff of the Museum of Northern Arizona surveyed in the vicinity of Grand Canyon Village in the early 1970s, and found about twenty sites. Since then, park archaeologists have resurveyed the same area and documented nearly one hundred sites. What at first appeared to be mainly a middle Pueblo II occupation now appears to have a significant Archaic component, expanding our understanding of prehistoric land use on the rim. This pattern of resurvey has been repeated in many locations. For example, Judd initially surveyed Walhalla Glades in 1918, recording four sites. In 1923 the Barrett/West expedition wandered onto Walhalla, adding another site. In 1936–37, park naturalist Louis Schellbach added six more sites, while in 1937, E. T. Hall recorded 273 sites (Hall 1942). Schwartz added another ninety-four during his research in the late 1960s, and NPS archaeologists identified eighty-four more in the early 1980s.

Exploration and explanation of the cultural history of the Colorado River is an even more dramatic example of uncovering previously unknown cultural remains. In 1869 Powell noted eight sites along the Colorado River; twenty years later, Robert Brewster Stanton mentioned four; sixty-four years later, Walter Taylor found eight sites, concluding "that there was very little aboriginal occupation of the near reaches of the Colorado River in the stretch between Lees Ferry and Lake Mead. . . . And in any event, even had they lived there, their remains would long since have been washed down river" (Taylor 1958, 29). As noted above, Euler recorded more than two hundred sites along the Colorado River between 1960 and 1966. During an intensive survey in 1990–91, NPS archaeologists recorded more than 475 sites along the river corridor, nearly three hundred of them in the "near reaches" referred to by Taylor as having little evidence of aboriginal occupation. Although most past researchers identified small Pueblo-period remains, our recent research suggests considerable Archaic (6000 to 2000 BC) occupation, with a site in Marble Canyon dating to more than 4,500 years ago. Archaic, Basketmaker, Puebloan, Kayenta, Cohonina, Pai, Ute, Hopi, Zuni, and Navajo have all left their mark, but the popular literature has yet to reflect all that we have learned in the past decade or two.

Archaeological evidence from the eastern section of the South Rim has also been accumulating. Tusayan Ruin, GC1 (the first site to be excavated in Grand Canyon National Park), was thought to be the largest and the latest Pueblo occupation. A recent survey near Tusayan Ruin uncovered a pueblo at least twice as large, however, with surface ceramics indicating a later occupation, likely early Pueblo III. A single partial Folsom projectile point dating to nearly ten thousand years ago represents the earliest evidence of human use of the Grand Canyon. With the discovery of a single artifact, human history at Grand Canyon expanded by six thousand years. Recently, another partial point was found, which may expand human history at the Grand Canyon by another one thousand years, taking us back to the earliest of the Paleo-Indian hunters. Each new piece of information adds to the human story of Grand Canyon. Additional radiocarbon dating and site placement of split-twig figurines have added new discussions to the interpretation of the people who left them. While the popular literature suggests that Pinto Points and figurines represented the only Archaic period remains, we now know that these canyon inhabitants also left vibrant rock art to reinforce the message that they were here.

How do we view the big picture today? We know that we still have a very small inventory of the Grand Canyon—at last count, about 3 percent of the park's 1.2 million acres had been covered by intensive survey. We have now recorded

The first site form created at Grand Canyon for the GC1 site at Tusayan Pueblo, 1934. NPS photograph

more than 4,300 sites, many of them incidental recordings and visitor reports. We are certain that we did have an intensive ancestral Puebloan occupation during the Pueblo II period, as has long been known, but we also know that we had Archaic populations that did more than leave figurines in caves. These earlier people lived in the canyon, and they left pictographs and petroglyphs; campsite remains along the canyon bottom, side canyons, and both rims; and offerings in caves documenting their presence. We know that people have continued to occupy the canyon into protohistoric times (the period immediately preceding recorded history), with radiocarbon dating of roasting pits suggesting their presence into the 1300s and beyond without interruption.

The Grand Canyon was home to thousands of people of varied cultures for thousands of years. As archaeologists and anthropologists, the more we discover about this place, the better we can translate the human story. I do not know if we will ever know the full extent of human use and occupation, but with each new site and the information found within, we get closer to what the "true" picture may have been.

Works Cited

Hall E. T. 1942. *Archaeological survey of Walhalla Glades.* Bulletin 20. Flagstaff, Ariz.: Museum of Northern Arizona.

Judd, Neil H. 1926. *Archaeological observations north of the Rio Colorado.* Bulletin 82. Bureau of American Ethnology. Washington D.C.: Government Printing Office.

Powell, John Wesley. 1875. *The exploration of the Colorado River and its canyons.* Repr., New York: Dover Publications, 1961.

Taylor, Walter W. 1958. *Two archeological studies in northern Arizona. The Pueblo ecology study: Hail and farewell and a brief survey through the Grand Canyon of the Colorado River.* Bulletin 30. Flagstaff, Ariz.: Museum of Northern Arizona.

West, George A. 1925. Cliff dwellings and pueblos in the Grand Canyon, Arizona. In *Yearbook of the Public Museum of Milwaukee* 3 (1925):74–96.

Willey, Gordon R., and Jeremy Sabloff. 1974. *A history of American archaeology.* London: Thames and Hudson.

Chapter Twenty-One

Environmental History of the Colorado River: The Changing Focus of Science

BY EMMA P. BENENATI AND JOSEPH P. SHANNON

To quote the authors, the "Colorado River has a plethora of national and local agencies and organizations firmly shackled to it for reasons ranging from preservation to profits." Rather than propose specific actions to protect the river's biological integrity, a task far too complex for a single presentation, Emma Benenati and Joseph Shannon help unravel the issues by outlining the history and changing focus of scientific investigations of the pre-dam (before 1964) and post-dam era in relation to the evolution of human values and our views of the natural world. Along the way, they identify some of the problems of modern river management by stakeholders with conflicting agendas.

Although long appreciated for phenomenal beauty and natural attributes, in recent decades the Grand Canyon and the Colorado River flowing within have become the center of political, economic, and environmental controversy. The heart of this controversy stems from differing views on the best use, or nonuse, of the resource. Factors contributing to controversy include:

- Grand Canyon National Park (GCNP) visitation now approaches five million people annually.
- The number of Colorado River rafters below Lake Powell and in the Grand Canyon exceeds 50,000 annually.
- The river corridor is critical habitat for endangered species, including the humpback chub, razorback sucker, Kanab ambersnail, and southwestern willow flycatcher (Schmidt et al. 1998).
- Rainbow and brown trout, introduced fish that thrive in the cold waters below Glen Canyon Dam, provide a sport-fishing industry for nearby communities, yet are responsible for the decline of native fish through predation and competition for food and habitat.

- The river lies between two of the largest dams and reservoirs in the United States and is part of a regulated system that exports more water out of its basin than any other river basin on earth (Hirsch et al. 1990).

Because of conflicting interests and uses, the Colorado River has a plethora of national and local agencies and organizations firmly shackled to it for reasons ranging from preservation to profits. Examples of the wide range of Grand Canyon "stakeholder" groups include the Bureau of Reclamation (BOR), Western Area Power Administration, Colorado River Energy Distributor Association, Arizona Game and Fish, Grand Canyon Trust, Bureau of Indian Affairs, commercial fishing and rafting companies, boaters' and river runners' organizations, states, and several American Indian tribes.

The nature of scientific investigations on the Colorado River has evolved over time, reflecting prevailing human values in much the same way as changes in management policies and laws. Relationships and influence among scientists, managers, legislators, and the public are convoluted and dynamic, and as population and resource demands have exploded, "final authority" has fluctuated between these sectors. This is primarily because managing agencies are confused about their mission or have not been allowed to follow it. Years of vague and conflicting legislation combined with political influence within and outside management agencies have made it dangerous to voice an opinion, much less make decisions that benefit the resource.

For example, during the Bridge Canyon Dam controversy in the early 1950s, all Grand Canyon National Park personnel were prohibited from voicing personal opinions after Acting Superintendent Lemuel Garrison expressed anti-dam sentiments in written correspondence. National Park Service (NPS) Region Three Director M. R. Tillotson immediately ordered park personnel to limit comments to "factual data and known Service policies or decisions." A decade later, during hearings on Marble Canyon Dam, NPS Director Conrad Wirth spoke against reclamation projects that involved park lands after having been warned by Secretary of the Interior Stewart Udall not to express his personal opinions (Pearson 1992). Within a year Udall removed Wirth as NPS director.

All too often, responsible government agencies rely on the most powerful voice of the time, a dubious way to manage natural resources. In this paper we will describe the changing focus of scientific investigations of the Colorado River over the past four centuries since Europeans realized its existence. This change in focus is presented in relation to the evolution of human values and our view of the natural world relative to ourselves.

PRE-DAM INVESTIGATIONS

The Grand Canyon and the Colorado River have a long history of human investigations. Recorded history over the past few hundred years shows the slow progression of investigative themes shifting from exploration to exploitation to restoration. Science has been a part of all these themes and has grown in importance, especially in the last few decades. Biological investigations on the river had a rather slow start, largely because the objectives and priorities of early researchers were more physical-based. The most striking features of the Colorado River and the Grand Canyon to most observers are their physical components: rocks, colors, depth, danger, rapids, etc. Moreover, surface appearances did not reveal much "biology" in pre-dam days, with the river corridor generally appearing as a scoured, muddy waterway with little riparian vegetation. Biological features were subtle and required time to be noticed and understood, which is still the case, even after

post-dam increases in ecological systems. Today, however, due to the effects of Glen Canyon Dam, the corridor appears to be a biological wonderland with both positive and negative aspects.

One element that has not changed is that the Grand Canyon is both a spectacular and challenging place to conduct scientific investigations. The challenge of travel on the Colorado River often impedes science, and it can be a struggle to keep the research in perspective. Scientists have always had to deal with conditions that confront expeditions in remote settings, such as a lack of outside assistance in the event of illness or equipment loss. Other common problems include collecting data in or beside the river regardless of season or weather conditions. Living in cramped or awkward conditions tests a person's resolve, as does constant packing and unpacking of gear. One hundred and fifty rapids must be negotiated while preventing loss or damage to equipment and workers. Despite these challenges, however, most of us gladly accept the inconveniences and danger just to work in the Grand Canyon.

Explorations in the canyon region from the 1500s through the early 1800s were primarily land based and not "scientific" as we define the term today. During these years, Spaniards dominated the investigative landscape, searching for gold, silver, and other immediate economic opportunities (Spicer 1962). Science became a part of exploration in the mid-1800s, when a series of government surveys scoured the Colorado Plateau; at that time, scientific objectives changed to more in-depth examination of land resources, mapping, and wagon-road and railroad surveys. Natural-history observations of plants and animals were also documented, usually by physicians who served as the collectors and naturalists in addition to their medical duties. Professional geologists such as John Newberry and Grove Karl Gilbert were often employed to study rock strata and construct geologic cross sections of explored areas. These expeditions were led by military officers, including John C. Frémont, Lorenzo Sitgreaves, John Gunnison, and Amiel Whipple, and usually assisted by civilian specialists such as the trapper-guide Antoine Leroux and artist-cartographer Richard Kern (Wallace and Lubick 1991). Two of the first Colorado River surveys were accomplished by Lieutenant Joseph Ives in 1857–58, and by Lieutenant George Wheeler in 1871–72, both of whom concentrated on the lower river. Ives determined the lower river's navigability by steaming upstream from the Gulf of California as far as Black Canyon, the present site of Hoover Dam. Wheeler undertook the more difficult task of exploring the river within the Grand Canyon itself, rowing, towing, and portaging rowboats upriver from Camp Mohave near today's Needles, California, to Diamond Creek.

The earliest systematic research was a geographical and geological survey conducted by John Wesley Powell during two river trips in 1869 and 1871–72 (Powell 1895). Although Powell's research comprised a predominantly physical examination of the largely unknown river drainage, he also documented some plant species. He later proved instrumental in ushering in the age of reclamation, a decade before the 1902 Reclamation Act. As head of the U.S. Geological Survey in 1889, entrusted with management of the new Irrigation Survey project, Powell directed numerous survey trips on western rivers to map potential dam sites (Aton 1988). Based on his research, Powell developed a democratic and science-based reclamation plan for the West that logically organized water districts based on watershed boundaries and available water. His plan explicitly excluded government interference, and instead proposed that the support, labor, and control of western water development remain with local cooperative associations after initial government surveys for dam sites. His ideas were never implemented, however, due to opposition by members of Congress who stood to gain personally through governmental development of western water (Worster 1994). Powell appreciated the beauty of the rivers and canyons, as his romantic descriptions attest; however, he supported the control and damming of western waters, in particular, large rivers such as the Colorado and Rio Grande (Aton 1988). One can only speculate what his opinion would be of monopolistic policies practiced by today's BOR and Western Area Power Administration.

Coincident with Powell's years of governmental service, a national environmental movement began to flourish. The 1890 census revealed an end to the American "frontier," and concerns regarding land use continued to grow in two directions. One view held that there was an increasing and justified need for use of land and resources for national progress and growth. The opposite view held that land and natural-resource consumption was occurring too quickly and carelessly, requiring immediate conservation. While Americans struggled with these ideas from the middle 1800s to the early 1900s (Merchant 1993), a national conservation movement began, a movement split between those who would preserve the land and those who would conserve it. Preservationists, ideologically associated with Henry David Thoreau and John Muir, believed that the best in life could be found in nature and that land development did not necessarily lead to progress. Conservationists, led by Theodore Roosevelt, defined their policy as the "use of natural resources for the greatest good of the greatest number for the longest time." Many citizens were caught between these opposing ideologies, wanting to preserve the qualities of wilderness

yet desiring the advantages and conveniences afforded by development of wild lands. While preservationists were often viewed as radicals and romantics, conservationists considered their position to be based in science.

The roots of conflict between the use and preservation of the Colorado River date to the early-twentieth-century conservation movement and its scientific base. More than two decades of controversy preceded the passage of legislation creating Grand Canyon National Park in 1919; unfortunately, thanks to Arizona Senator Carl Hayden, the same law allowed for reclamation projects within park boundaries. When questioned on his position, Hayden responded that reservoirs for water storage and irrigation would be built only when "consistent with the primary purposes of the park" (Pearson 1992). Since the primary purpose of national parks, to paraphrase the National Park Service Organic Act of 1916, is to conserve the scenery, the natural and historic objects, and the wildlife therein, and to provide for the enjoyment of the same in such manner and by such means as will leave them unimpaired for the enjoyment of future generations, it is clear that human-induced additions or "impairment" of the Grand Canyon and its wildlife are inconsistent with the "primary purposes of the park." The problem that scientists as well as managers, politicians, and environmentalists grapple with today, however, is that although nearly two thousand miles of the river and its tributaries are legally protected as national parklands or are designated critical habitat, water has become the lifeblood of the Southwest (Carothers and Brown 1991).

Theodore Roosevelt illustrated early on the conflict and political contradiction between conservation and preservation. In 1903 he spoke at the canyon's South Rim and asked its residents and, by implication, the nation, "to keep this great wonder of nature as it is now . . . Leave it as it is. You cannot improve on it" (quoted in Hughes 1978). Five years later, in his White House speech formally inaugurating the conservation movement, Roosevelt proclaimed the virtue of using our national resources in such a manner not only as to leave them undiminished, but to "actually be improved by wise use." He added that "men can improve on nature by compelling the resources to renew and even reconstruct themselves to serve increasingly beneficial uses—while the living waters can be so controlled as to multiply their benefits" (Merchant 1993). He must have forgotten his visit to the Grand Canyon.

Back on the Colorado River, the general theme of investigation changed from exploratory-based expeditions to exploitation using the physical sciences but still very little biology. In 1889–90, Frank Brown, president of the Denver, Colorado Cañon, and Pacific Railroad Company, and his engineer Robert Brewster Stanton surveyed the river through the Grand Canyon for a water-level railway that would run from Grand Junction, Colorado, to San Diego, California (Smith and Crampton 1987). The expedition incidentally gathered information on plant life. In August 1923 Claude Birdseye led a U.S. Geological Survey trip that produced a topographical map of the canyon bottom and, more importantly, twenty-one potential dam sites within the Grand Canyon. They called this survey the "conquest of the Colorado," an excellent reflection of the sentiment of contemporary citizens and government.

By the 1930s biological research was on the rise. Between 1933 and 1938 a series of trips sponsored by the Museum of Northern Arizona floated the San Juan and Colorado rivers as far as Lees Ferry. Although archaeology was their main purpose, researchers also pursued biological studies of mammals, birds, reptiles, insects, and plants. In 1938 Norm Nevills guided the first biological research trip through the canyon. Professor Elzada Clover and her graduate student, Lois Jotter, of the University of Michigan— the first women to float all the way through the Grand Canyon—studied botany on this trip. Nevills himself used the publicity to launch a commercial river-running business. Angus Woodbury of the University of Utah conducted biological studies on the river in the late 1950s (Woodbury 1959), although he worked above the later site of Glen Canyon Dam.

Despite the rise in scientific interest, very little information was obtained on the Colorado River prior to the completion of Glen Canyon Dam in 1963. Immediately thereafter, the physical and biological condition of the river corridor began to change dramatically (Carothers and Brown 1991; Webb et al. 1999). It took years for managers to realize the dam's effects. Some were immediate and obvious, but many developed over time and are still developing today. Although the river and corridor appears to be "improved" to many people, with its clear water, lucrative trout fishery, abundance of riparian life, and absence of scouring floods, a tremendous part of the natural ecosystem has been lost.

Research conducted since the gates of Glen Canyon Dam closed has revealed that the ecosystem today is completely altered above and below the dam (Stanford and Ward 1986; Blinn and Cole 1991). One of the changes is river water temperature, which remains in a narrow range between forty-six and fifty degrees Fahrenheit. Therefore, the macroinvertebrate community is dominated by alien cold-adapted species that also have a narrow range of temperature tolerance (Oberlin et al. 1999; Blinn and Cole 1991). The dam as barrier has reduced the former carbon source of "externally produced" upland woody vegetation that used to wash in and serve as the base of the food web

(Haden et al. 1999, 2003). The loss of sediment, at least 80 percent less today, results in greater water clarity and exposed cobble substrate on the river bottom, which allows sunlight to penetrate the water column and promotes photosynthesis and growth of aquatic plants such as algae and macrophytes that now serve as an "internally produced" base of the food web (Blinn et al. 1998; Benenati et al. 2000). Finally, due to the lack of seasonal floods, discharge has changed to a narrow range of flows on an annual basis; however, due to the production of hydropower, there is now a daily tide that influences physical and biological aspects of the river channel (Benenati et al. 1998).

POST-DAM INVESTIGATIONS

The 1970s ushered in an era of long-term research on the Colorado River. The 1960s wave of national environmental awareness gained momentum due to proposed dams within the Grand Canyon. Congress passed environmental legislation, such as the Endangered Species Act in 1973 and the National Environmental Policy Act in 1969, which mandated improved management of national resources (Carothers and Brown 1991). Science commissions under the Department of the Interior called for the NPS to manage in accordance with the original intent of the NPS Organic Act of 1916 and to use scientific research as a basis for NPS policies (National Research Council 1992).

Meanwhile, greater numbers of people were rafting through the Grand Canyon, both creating and publicizing problems on the river. Campsites were trashed, vegetation was trampled, and human feces and toilet paper permeated beaches. As many as 5,000 unregulated potty dumps occurred every season along the corridor; favorite beaches could receive more than 150 potty dumps per year (Phillips and Lynch 1977). Waterfalls, side canyons, and other scenic spots were polluted with urine, feces, and garbage. These problems of overuse prompted the Colorado River Research Program in the early 1970s, combining the efforts of Grand Canyon National Park, the BOR, and the Museum of Northern Arizona (Grand Canyon National Park 1979). The Colorado River Research Program was "reactive science" that addressed well-established recreational use problems from the previous decade. Participants studied conditions and assisted in the development of the 1979 Colorado River Management Plan to mitigate recreational impacts, but little thought was given to the effects of dam operations. Implementation of the river plan did result in better camping and cooking procedures and portable toilets, however, and studies did include the effects of feral burros and how to remove them, as well as the issue of motor use. Research in the later 1970s also produced a flora and fauna survey, documentation on native and non-native fishes, and some attention to the effects of dam operations on riverine resources.

A research program known as the Glen Canyon Environmental Studies (GCES) followed the Colorado River Research Program from 1982 through 1996. GCES was envisioned as a multiagency, multibureau effort to study the dam's effects on downstream aquatic and terrestrial resources. The scope was wider than previous projects of the 1970s, although still something less than a total ecosystem approach due to program restrictions and lack of direction from responsible agencies; the underlying assumption of some scientists outside the GCES was that no useful information would be obtained (Wegner 1991). Initially, the main areas of study included sediment, biology, and recreation, with additional studies in river temperature modification and hydrology. The BOR established this program in response to public pressure regarding concerns for the overall effects of Glen Canyon Dam on the river. Listing of the humpback chub as an endangered species in 1978 and concern for other native species served as catalysts. Two primary triggers for the GCES were concerns regarding the "peaking power program," which resulted in large, erratic fluctuations in daily water discharge (for the purpose of instantaneous electricity production and revenues), and the BOR's proposed "uprate and rewind project" on dam generators to increase hydropower production.

Although resigned to an environmental study mandated by the National Environmental Policy Act, the BOR wanted to avoid an Environmental Impact Statement (EIS) that would have entailed a full-scope examination of dam operations (National Research Council 1996). The Department of the Interior decided that the bureau would instead proceed with an Environmental Assessment, a scaled down version of an EIS requiring no new data collection, and at the same time proceed with the generator upgrade. The GCES, originally envisioned to be a two-year project, was intended to provide data that would support the BOR's decision not to conduct an EIS (National Research Council 1996). This was essentially the root of most problems that would plague research for years. Because GCES was created and funded by the BOR essentially to minimize environmental compliance and support their water-development mission, the program and program manager would remain subject to BOR control and authority for the duration of the program.

Aside from limited direction, the GCES research scope was constrained both geographically and conceptually. Studies were initially limited to only the Glen Canyon reach of the Colorado River, hence the name, Glen Canyon

Environmental Studies. Any analysis that might result in reduced hydropower revenues was prohibited, as were investigations of cultural and aesthetic values, referred to as "non-use values," a term still used today. The BOR also limited research to agency scientists, precluding more objective academic and outside scientists. Even before these constraints became known, BOR administrators had been criticized for conflict of interest because of their close association with the Western Area Power Administration, which marketed power, and because both agencies provided the funds and management of the research program and both stood to benefit from the status quo of dam operations (National Research Council 1996).

In 1986, to maintain credibility for conducting its own environmental studies, the BOR asked the National Research Council to review the science of the GCES. The National Research Council reviewers, who are outside professionals and scientists charged with ensuring quality and objectivity in federal research, addressed many of the problems hampering the research program. Research scope and scientific expertise were expanded, economic (power) and cultural aspects were added, and an ecosystem emphasis was incorporated into the program. By 1989, GCES had gathered considerable evidence of the dam's negative environmental impacts that enabled Secretary of the Interior Manuel Lujan to order an EIS to be completed by 1994. Under the direction of program manager Dave Wegner, the GCES project became the database for analysis of potential management alternatives for the EIS process (Wegner 1991).

Although conflicts with the BOR continued through the GCES years, the program contributed significant environmental knowledge regarding the Colorado's ecosystem and management specifically as well as large regulated rivers in general. The EIS supplied a wide range of dam management options to Secretary of the Interior Bruce Babbitt's Record of Decision announced in 1996. The secretary's decision authorized a "Modified Low Fluctuating Flow Alternative" that would somewhat reduce the daily change in discharge volume and ramping rates (speed of increasing or decreasing water discharge). In addition, GCES devised a long-term research and monitoring plan to be implemented following the EIS called the Glen Canyon Dam Adaptive Management Program (GCD-AMP). Another benefit of the GCES program was an informed and involved general public, and the growth of numerous environmental watchdog organizations.

In 1997 GCES was reorganized into the Grand Canyon Monitoring and Research Center (GCMRC) under the GCD-AMP. The GCMRC's purpose is to coordinate scientific studies suggested by designated work groups of the AMP that address requirements of the Grand Canyon Protection Act of 1992. The purpose of the GCD-AMP is to use data from ongoing, long-term monitoring and experiments as a basis for change or "adaptation" in management policy in order to better manage the ecosystem and ensure compliance with the Grand Canyon Protection Act (National Research Council 1999). In the AMP hierarchy, GCMRC is on the bottom tier along with a technical advising work group (TWG) and an independent review panel. These three groups report to the second tier, the Adaptive Management Work Group (AMWG), which has the authority to vote for or against science studies and experiments as well as recommend implementation of certain operational policies to the secretary of the interior's designee. The secretary's designee sits on the third tier, and after receiving the recommendations of the AMWG, reports them to the secretary for a decision.

The science advisory groups TWG and AMWG are composed of representatives of "stakeholders" who have an interest related to the Grand Canyon or the Colorado River. Stakeholders include the BOR, Western Area Power Association, Colorado River Energy Distributor Association, each of the seven basin states that receive water or electricity benefits of the Colorado River, commercial recreation groups, Arizona Game and Fish, U.S. Fish and Wildlife Service, Grand Canyon National Park, seven southwestern American Indian tribes, and two environmental organizations: Grand Canyon Trust and Southwest Rivers. The large number of stakeholders with their own interests and infrequent meetings often result in stalemates and a lack of measurable progress for months or years at a time; such delays benefit the agendas of water and power interests.

The organizational structure of the GCD-AMP appears well-planned, but a critical problem that hampers environmental successes is a lack of scientific expertise at all levels. Representatives of TWG and AMWG are largely administrators who are far removed from science. The National Research Council has made several unheeded recommendations to GCMRC for an outside senior scientist to serve as an advisory and interpretive liaison between the science work groups and the secretary of the interior (National Research Council 1999). In addition, GCMRC administrators do not recruit outside objective researchers, but instead use their own agency technicians for research projects—a continuing problem from the GCES era. The National Research Council has also identified conflicts within GCMRC in executing its role of science coordination versus expending considerable effort performing administrative tasks requested by AMP stakeholders.

The GCD-AMP has not attained an integrated ecosystem approach to Colorado River scientific research. In reality, the program appears to be following the historical pattern, with physical resources, especially sediment retention, continuing to dominate research funding and effort over biological and cultural studies (Fritzinger et al. 2001). Sediment loss, movement, and retention remain primary investigation objectives, despite the fact that no data exist to show a positive relationship between biological resources and the amount of sediment in or along the river. The impacts of Glen Canyon Dam encompass a wide range of interconnected biological and ecological effects, yet biological research since the inception of this program in 1997 remains unfocused and single-species directed.

To its credit the AMP has taken on a complex, controversial task and at least posits the need for a worldwide river-resource-management plan. Although the concept of adaptive management is good, adaptive-management programs of the past have been criticized for being all talk and no action and for failing to change management policies (Moir and Block 2001). A major drawback is the anticipation of quick environmental fixes, an unrealistic hope that leads to a loss of commitment, effort, and funding to continue long-term studies to truly understand the ecosystem (Hardin 1985).

Recent events indicate that the public is once again awakening to the issues. A missing link in the GCD-AMP identified by the National Research Council was public outreach and education (National Research Council 1999). The AMP finally added public outreach to its 2002 Monitoring and Research Plan (Fritzinger et al. 2001). In addition, since 1997, environmental organizations have been informing the public of their views of GCD-AMP progress toward compliance with the Grand Canyon Protection Act. Several prominent environmental groups, including the Center for Biological Diversity, Living Rivers, Sierra Club, and Audubon Society, joined in an early 2002 effort to pressure the AMP to show progress in their charge to protect the Grand Canyon ecosystem (Living Rivers 2002). Although the AMWG voted not to acknowledge receipt of the written challenge (per David Orr, Living Rivers), a revised AMP operational plan complete with a series of experimental flows and nonnative fish eradication efforts was announced to the public several months later. Perhaps through the combined efforts of long-term science and an involved society, future management decisions and legislation will reflect human values as well as protect our natural treasures great and small while they still exist.

WORKS CITED

Aton, J. M. 1988. *Inventing John Wesley Powell: The major, his admirers and cash register dams in the Colorado River basin.* Cedar City: Southern Utah State College.

Benenati, E. P., J. P. Shannon, D. W. Blinn, K. P. Wilson, and S. J. Hueftle. 2000. Reservoir-river linkages: Lake Powell and the Colorado River, Arizona. In *North American Benthological Society* 19:742–755.

Benenati, P. L., J. P. Shannon, and D. W. Blinn. 1998. Desiccation and recolonization of phytobenthos in a regulated desert river: Colorado River at Lees Ferry, Arizona, USA. In *Regulated rivers: Research and management* 14:519–532.

Blinn, D. W., and G. A. Cole. 1991. Algal and invertebrate biota in the Colorado River: Comparison of pre- and post-dam conditions. In *Colorado River ecology and dam management*, ed. Committee to Review the Glen Canyon Environmental Studies. Washington, D.C.: National Academy Press, 85–104.

Blinn, D. W., J. P Shannon, P. L. Benenati, and K. P. Wilson. 1998. Algal ecology in tailwater stream communities: The Colorado River below Glen Canyon Dam, Arizona. In *Journal of Phycology* 34:734–740.

Carothers, S. W., and B. T. Brown. 1991. *The Colorado River through Grand Canyon.* Tucson: University of Arizona Press.

Fritzinger, C., B. D. Gold, F. M. Gonzales, V. Kieffer, R. Lambert, M. Liszewski, S. Mankiller, T. S. Melis, S. Mietz, and B. Ralston. 2001. *The Grand Canyon Monitoring and Research Center fiscal year 2002 monitoring and research plan.* Flagstaff, Ariz.: Grand Canyon Monitoring and Research Center.

Grand Canyon National Park. 1979. *Proposed Colorado River management plan, Grand Canyon National Park, Arizona: Final environmental impact statement.* San Francisco, Calif.: Grand Canyon National Park, National Park Service, Department of the Interior, Western Region.

Haden, G. A., D. W. Blinn, J. P. Shannon, and K. P. Wilson. 1999. Driftwood: An alternative habitat for macroinvertebrates in a large southwestern desert river. *Hydrobiologia* 397:179–186.

Haden, G. A., J. P. Shannon, K. P. Wilson, and D. W. Blinn. 2003. Benthic community structure of the Green and Colorado Rivers through Canyonlands National Park, Utah, USA. *Southwestern Naturalist* 48:23–35.

Hardin, G. 1985. *Filters against folly: How to survive despite economists, ecologists, and the merely eloquent.* New York: Viking Press.

Hirsch, R. M., J. F. Walker, J. C. Day, and R. Kollio. 1990. The influence of man on hydrologic systems. In *Surface water hydrology*, vol. 1, ed. M. F. Wolman and H. C. Riggs. Boulder, Colo.: Geologic Society of America Decade of North American Geology.

Hughes, J. D. 1978. *In the house of stone and light: A human history of the Grand Canyon.* Grand Canyon, Ariz.: Grand Canyon Natural History Association.

Living Rivers. 2002. Grand Canyon in crisis. *Living Rivers Currents* 1 (2).

Merchant, C. 1993. *Major problems in American environmental history: Resource conservation in an industrializing society.* Lexington, Mass.: D. C. Heath.

Moir, W. H., and W. M. Block. 2001. Adaptive management on public lands in the United States: Commitment or rhetoric? *Environmental Management* 28:141–148.

National Research Council. 1992. *Science and the national parks.* Washington, D.C.: National Academy Press.

———. 1996. *River resource management in the Grand Canyon.* Washington, D.C.: National Academy Press.

———. 1999. *Downstream: Adaptive management of Glen Canyon Dam and the Colorado River ecosystem.* Washington, D.C.: National Academy Press.

Oberlin, G. E., J. P. Shannon, and D. W. Blinn. 1999. Watershed influence on the macroinvertebrate fauna of ten major tributaries of the Colorado River through Grand Canyon, Arizona. *Southwestern Naturalist* 44:17–30.

Pearson, B. E. 1992. The plan to dam Grand Canyon: A study in utilitarianism. MA thesis. Northern Arizona University, Flagstaff.

Phillips, R. A., and C. S. Lynch. 1977. Human waste disposal on beaches of the Colorado River in Grand Canyon: Final report. Colorado River Research Program Report Series No. 17. Grand Canyon, Ariz.: Grand Canyon National Park.

Powell, J. W. 1895. *The exploration of the Colorado River and its canyons.* Repr., New York: Penguin Books, 1997.

Schmidt, J. C., R. H. Webb, R. A. Valdez, G. R. Marzolf, and L. E. Stevens. 1998. Science and values in river restoration in the Grand Canyon. *BioScience* 48:735–747.

Smith, D. W., and C. G. Crampton, eds. 1987. *The Colorado River survey: Robert B. Stanton and the Denver, Colorado Canyon and Pacific Railroad.* Salt Lake City: Howe Brothers.

Spicer, E. H. 1962. *Cycles of conquest: The impact of Spain,*

Mexico, and the United States on the Indians of the Southwest, 1533–1960. Tucson: University of Arizona Press.

Stanford, J. A., and J. V. Ward. 1986. The Colorado River system. In *The ecology of river systems*, eds. B. R. Davies and K. F. Walker. Dordrecht, The Netherlands: Junk Publishers.

Wallace, A., and D. C. Lubick. 1991. Exploring scientists of the Colorado Plateau. *Plateau* 62 (3):17–30.

Webb, R. H., J. C. Schmidt, G. R. Marzolf, and R. A. Valdez, eds. 1999. *The controlled flood in Grand Canyon.* Geophysical Monograph No. 110. Washington, D.C.: American Geophysical Union.

Wegner, D. L. 1991. A brief history of the Glen Canyon environmental studies. In *Colorado River Ecology and Dam Management,* ed. Committee on Glen Canyon Environmental Studies. Washington, D.C.: Academy Press.

Woodbury, A. M., ed. 1959. *Ecological studies of flora and fauna in Glen Canyon.* University of Utah Anthropology Papers. Salt Lake City: University of Utah Press.

Worster, D. 1994. *An unsettled country: Changing landscapes of the American West.* Albuquerque: University of New Mexico Press.

Chapter Twenty-Two

Historic River Running

by Bonnie Brune

As a seasonal associate naturalist at Grand Canyon National Park, Bonnie Brune is no stranger to speaking before rapt audiences. For our symposium she put together a summary of successful river trips through the Grand Canyon before completion of Glen Canyon Dam, from James White to early commercial boaters. Brune plans to refine her symposium presentation as an interpretive program for park visitors.

My presentation is an overview of known trips down the Colorado River from Lees Ferry to the Grand Wash Cliffs completed prior to the surge of commercial river running in the 1960s. River runners have always sought each other's knowledge and advice and shared a common bond, appreciating each other's achievements, rather like a river-running brotherhood or sisterhood. In their own accounts, including the authors and river runners noted in this presentation, you will often find names revered and repeated—Powell, Stanton, Galloway, Stone, Kolb, and Loper, as well as river runners of the present. River-running history has been rich in mystery, controversy, and alternative points of view from the very beginning.

FIRST TO RUN THE RIVER: STANTON'S VIEW

Did the nineteenth-century prospector James White float the Colorado through the Grand Canyon in 1867, two years before John Wesley Powell? This controversy might be considered the "origin story" of rafting history, a debate that persists around riverside campfires even today. Robert Brewster Stanton, acknowledged as the second man to lead a river party through the Grand Canyon, interviewed James White in later years and analyzed his adventure following Stanton's own trips in 1889–90. He concluded that White had not rafted through the canyon but instead floated "from a point near the Grand Wash to Callville, Nevada,

where he was stopped and taken off his raft. To Major John Wesley Powell . . . belongs the honor and distinction of having been the first to conquer the Colorado River" (Stanton 1932, 93).

Stanton's examination of James White's river trip appeared in his 1932 book, *Colorado River Controversies*, and John Wesley Powell was accorded (and still is accorded, by nearly all experts) the honor of the first river trip. Powell's trips in 1869 and 1871–72 are well documented and not repeated in this presentation, but it is worthwhile

River historians refer to this unnamed boat as the "Stone-Galloway." Nathaniel T. Galloway designed the boat and used it to guide a 1909 trip down the Colorado. Julius F. Stone, who went along on the trip, paid for Galloway's services, making him the first river runner to hire a guide. Photograph by the author

to note that Stanton, in his book, was the first to publicize many distortions and exaggerations in Powell's account of his own trips. In 1874 Powell went before the U.S. House of Representatives Appropriations Committee to obtain funds to continue his western surveys. He was told that he would get his money only if he wrote an account of his explorations, to be published by the Government Printing Office. Powell then proceeded to conflate four years' work encompassing both river trips, side trips, and all related materials he could gather to create a story that was part fiction, part fact, all romanticized—a common writing practice of the late nineteenth century. Congress, impressed but unaware of the manipulation of records and facts, appropriated the funds that launched Powell on his illustrious career as a federal bureaucrat (Anderson 1982, 255–256).

A RAILROAD SURVEY

In the 1880s, S. S. Harper, a prospector with some knowledge of the Grand Canyon area, encouraged his Denver acquaintances to build a water-level railroad through the Southwest. Convinced of the potential and eager to build along the Colorado River through the Grand Canyon, businessman Frank Mason Brown secured funds and in 1889 assumed leadership of a survey of the Green and Colorado rivers. Brown hired Robert Brewster Stanton to serve as the railroad's chief engineer. Stanton consulted with John Wesley Powell concerning logistics, but failed to acquire respect for the rivers he planned to run. As a result, the ensuing expedition unfolded as "the Great American Dream turned to nightmare" (Ghiglieri 1992, 156–157). With virtually no river experience, Brown bought light boats of thin red cedar. He carried no life preservers. His boats were too small to store adequate provisions, so he improvised a clumsy driftwood supply raft. These mistakes and others led to the exploration's fatal conclusion in Marble Canyon when Brown drowned near Soap Creek Rapid, and two members of the crew, Peter Hansbrough and Henry Richards, drowned several days later near Twentyfive Mile Rapid. Near Vaseys Paradise, the survivors stored their remaining supplies in a cave, known today as Stantons Cave, and left the river.

Robert Brewster Stanton returned to lead a second attempt at a railroad survey through the Grand Canyon. Outfitted in boats much like those used by John Wesley Powell on his second expedition and, equipped with life jackets, Stanton's group launched within Glen Canyon on December 10, 1889, and arrived safely at the Gulf of California on April 26, 1890.

TRAPPING, PROSPECTING, AND ADVENTURE

James White ran the river, or some portion thereof, because he was desperately trying to escape a small band of American Indians anxious to steal his goods. Powell followed to advance exploration of and scientific research on the Southwest, while Brown and Stanton sought economic gain through the commerce a railroad would foster. Others followed into what was still the great unknown for a variety of reasons—to trap beaver, prospect for precious minerals, or simply to seek adventure.

George Flavell and Ramon Montez were the first to successfully follow Robert Brewster Stanton. They left Green River, Wyoming, on April 27, 1896, in the *Panthon*, a craft designed by Flavell, and required a mere thirteen days to negotiate the Grand Canyon proper from the mouth of the Little Colorado River to the Grand Wash Cliffs. Flavell and Montez were followed by Nathaniel T. "Than" Galloway and William C. Richmond, who started from Lodore Canyon, Utah, and reached Needles, California, on February 10, 1897. While Flavell and his partner seemed more intent on adventure than anything else, Galloway and Richmond took the time to prospect, pan for gold, and trap along the river and its feeder streams. Galloway was the first person to run rapids stern first, and his boats, which he designed and built himself, became models for river runners who followed.

Elias Benjamin "Hum" Woolley, John King, and Arthur Sanger embarked from Lees Ferry on a little-known prospecting trip in August 1903, using a boat assembled by Woolley at the launch site. Very little is known of the trip itself, other than that the men intended to reach "salt water" before quitting, but they did make it beyond the Grand Wash Cliffs in September. According to river historian David Lavender, Sanger, who was interviewed much later, thought Woolley had been through the Grand Canyon before this 1903 trip, but there is no record of such a run (Lavender 1985, 40).

Charles S. Russell, Edwin R. Monett, and Albert "Bert" Loper started a run from Green River, Utah, on September 20, 1907. Loper dallied upriver of Lees Ferry and was left behind, while Russell and Monett reached Needles on February 8, 1908. Charlie Russell's subsequent river trips ended in various disasters long before reaching the Grand Wash Cliffs, requiring the participants to hike out to the Grand Canyon's South Rim. When Russell abandoned his 1914 expedition he left his steel-skinned boat, the *Ross Wheeler*, beside the river. Nearly a century later the boat still rests above high water near the base of the South Bass Trail.

Robert Brewster Stanton hired Than Galloway to help dredge for gold upstream of Lees Ferry. The job gave

Galloway an opportunity to become acquainted with Julius F. Stone, a wealthy industrialist who was financing and observing Stanton's operation. The gold dredging failed, but the Galloway-Stone friendship persisted. Stone financed a Galloway-guided river trip that left Green River, Wyoming, on September 12 and ended on November 19, 1909, at Needles, California. This trip marks the first time a "tourist" hired a guide to run the river.

BOATS, MOVIES, AND A HONEYMOON

A fragment of the *Nellie Powell* from John Wesley Powell's 1871 river trip is in the park's museum collection, but a 1909 Stone-Galloway boat—currently being restored at the Grand Canyon's South Rim—is the oldest extant craft to have run the Colorado through the Grand Canyon. For the next successful run, brothers Ellsworth and Emery Kolb had Galloway-style boats made from plans supplied by Stone. They named their crafts the *Defiance* and the *Edith*, the latter for Emery's daughter. The Grand Canyon photographers took both still and motion pictures of their trip, which launched at Green River, Wyoming, on September 8, 1911, and took out at Needles, California, on January 18, 1912. Emery's *Edith* is now on display with the Stone-Galloway boat at the South Rim, and Ellsworth's *Defiance* is displayed at the Powell River History Museum in Green River, Utah.

The Kolb brothers incorporated their motion pictures into a thrilling tourist presentation at Kolb Studio's auditorium, a presentation that ran daily from 1914 until Emery's death in 1976. They added to the film footage while assisting the U.S. Geological Survey (USGS) on a river trip within Cataract

Emery Kolb's Edith *was first used on the river during the Kolb brothers' 1911–12 river trip down the Green and Colorado. The brothers shot a movie of their adventure, and the resulting film was shown at Kolb Studio on the canyon's rim until Emery's death in 1976. Photograph by the author*

Brad Dimock's replica of Glen and Bessie Hyde's 1928 sweepscow. Although the original Hyde scow was not suitable for Colorado River rapids, the Hydes managed to reach Diamond Creek before their disappearance. Photograph by the author

Canyon in 1921 and while Emery served as lead boatman for the USGS trip in 1923. The *Glen*, another Galloway-style boat undergoing restoration at the South Rim, was used for both USGS trips.

In 1927 two river parties tried to duplicate the Kolbs' success with motion pictures of the Colorado through the Grand Canyon. Clyde Eddy's party successfully made it through the canyon, but didn't shoot much usable film. Eddy, among many others, then assisted the Pathe-Bray party of six boats and thirteen men, including professional filmmakers, who failed in their missions to complete a full canyon run as well as produce a motion picture.

A honeymoon trip filled with mystery followed in 1928. Glen and Bessie Hyde attempted to celebrate their marriage in a stubby scow Glen had built based on a design long used on Idaho rivers. The young couple launched at Green River, Utah, and arrived at the foot of the Bright Angel Trail in record time. While relaxing a bit and obtaining supplies at the South Rim, Glen refused to accept life jackets offered by Emery Kolb. When the pair missed their expected arrival date at Needles, California, Glen's father asked Kolb and others to search for the newlyweds. Their scow was recovered in good condition near River Mile 237 below Diamond Creek Rapid, but the Hydes were never found. Although they never made it to the Grand Wash Cliffs (at least, not in a boat), when one considers that nearly all canyon river runners today take out at Diamond Creek, Bessie deserves consideration as the first woman to run the Colorado River through the Grand Canyon.

Parley Galloway, Nathaniel Galloway's son, guided the successful Clyde Eddy river expedition in 1927. Not long thereafter, Bus Hatch met Parley and "listened eagerly to his tales of the deep canyons of the Green and the Colorado" (Webb

1989, 24). Family and friends began building boats and running the Green in 1931, with Hatch as the self-appointed head boatman.

On July 19, 1934, Hatch, Eddy, and others launched at Lees Ferry. They arrived at Separation Rapid on August 3. Here they installed a plaque honoring brothers Oramel and Seneca Howland and William Dunn, the three men who had walked away from the Powell expedition of 1869 and were subsequently killed on the Arizona Strip. These men had been considered deserters by many, especially by river historian Frederick Dellenbaugh who had accompanied Powell's second expedition and played a major role in having their names banished from the South Rim's Powell Memorial. Robert Brewster Stanton's *Colorado River Controversies* (1932) revealed another side of the story, and of Powell's leadership, which apparently inspired Hatch and Eddy to place their own memorial.

GOING SOLO

In 1936 Haldane "Buzz" Holmstrom, a gas station attendant from Oregon, wrote to Emery Kolb explaining that he wanted to serve as a boatman on the Green or Colorado rivers. Emery referred Buzz to geologists from Carnegie and Cal Tech who planned to run the river through the Grand Canyon, but the trip was already fully booked. Unneeded on this scientific expedition, Holmstrom instead built himself a boat, consulted with Bert Loper while en route to Green River, Wyoming, and started a solo run on October 4, 1937. The Carnegie–Cal Tech river trip left Lees Ferry on October 11, 1937, traveling slowly. Buzz had the satisfaction of catching up with them at Diamond Creek, then continued alone to Hoover Dam, where he arrived on November 25. Buzz ran the river again in 1938 using the boat from his 1937 trip, but he painted it red and named it the *Julius F.* in honor of Julius F. Stone.

TRIBUTES

Norman Nevills, using boats he designed and built, was the first to run commercial trips on the Colorado River through the Grand Canyon. His first trip, launched at Green River, Utah, on June 20, 1938, included the first two women to run the entire canyon—Elzada U. Clover and Lois Jotter. Emery Kolb joined Nevills's party from Bright Angel Creek to Lake Mead, where they met up with a tour boat piloted by Buzz Holmstrom. Nevills completed seven commercial canyon runs in the *WEN*, which is presently undergoing conservation at the Grand Canyon's South

Rim, and the *Mexican Hat*, which is on display at the Powell River History Museum in Green River, Utah. Alexander "Zee" Grant's foldboat kayak, the *Escalante*, became the first kayak to run through the Grand Canyon, with support from the Nevills trip of 1941; the kayak is stored at the Grand Canyon's South Rim. Barry Goldwater ran the Green and Colorado rivers with Norm and Doris Nevills in 1940. In 1949 Norm and Dor's small plane crashed due to an engine malfunction, and both were killed. In 1952 a plaque commemorating the Nevills was placed at Navajo Bridge, and Goldwater spoke at the dedication.

Bert Loper, known as the "Grand Old Man of the Colorado," primarily for the time he spent on the river above Lees Ferry, finally made a run through the Grand Canyon when he was nearly seventy years old. His small party ran from Hite, Utah, to Hoover Dam in 1939. Loper launched at Lees Ferry with another river trip on June 7, 1949, in his boat, *Grand Canyon*. While running 24.5-Mile Rapid, Loper probably suffered a heart attack or stroke, fell overboard, and drowned. His disintegrating boat now lies in the rocks above high water in Marble Canyon with an adjacent memorial plaque.

The *Esmeralda II*, built for Ed Hudson to power upriver through the Grand Canyon, instead became the first powerboat to run all of the Grand Canyon's rapids during a down-canyon run in 1949. The next year the craft was abandoned below Crystal Creek Rapid. Jim Rigg, who had taken over Mexican Hat Expeditions with J. Frank Wright following Norm Nevills's death, found and repaired the *Esmeralda II* and ran it down to Lake Mead. It is now at the Grand Canyon's South Rim.

The only historic river raft at the Grand Canyon's South Rim belonged to Georgie White, "The Woman of

The WEN *(the initials of Norm Nevills' dad) is one of the first three "cataract boats" designed and built by the younger Nevills. Nevills used these three boats in 1938, a trip that pioneered commercial river running through the Grand Canyon. Photograph by the author*

The motorized Esmeralda II *was built to power upriver in the Grand Canyon, but in 1949, it became the first motorized boat to travel down the Colorado River through the canyon. Photograph by the author*

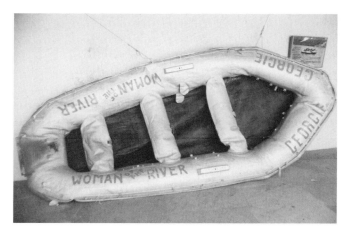

In 1952 Georgie White, the "Woman of the River," rowed her first trip through the Grand Canyon in this Army surplus raft. The next year she lead a "share-the-expense" river trip; she would go on to run the river commercially in the canyon for nearly forty years. Photograph by the author

the River." Georgie began her long love affair with the canyon on extended hikes and daring Colorado River swims. Using a ten-person, war-surplus raft, she led her first river trip through the Grand Canyon in July 1952. The following summer she guided her first "share-the-expense" party. Georgie continued to lead commercial trips, promote river running, and add innovations to canyon rafting until her death in 1992.

SWIMMING AND KAYAKING

Bill Beer and John Daggett swam the full length of the Colorado River through the Grand Canyon in 1955. The 26- and 27-year-old men stepped into the river at Lees Ferry on Easter Sunday, April 10. They spent about five hours a day in the water, filmed their trip, and swam every rapid until reaching Pierce Ferry on May 5.

Walter Kirshbaum started kayaking at the age of fourteen. He continued to pursue the sport and search for new challenges into adulthood, when a friend encouraged him to kayak the Colorado River with the aid of support boats. In 1960 he built a nineteen-inch-wide, fourteen-foot-long fiberglass craft and launched at Lees Ferry to become the first person to run the river's rapids in a modern-style kayak. Kirshbaum's historic kayak is stored at Grand Canyon Village.

DAM CHANGES

Two watercraft at the Grand Canyon's South Rim floated the river as Glen Canyon Dam's reservoir began to fill.

Otis "Dock" Marston, foremost river historian of the mid-twentieth century, piloted *The Dock*—a sportyak, or 7'4" pressure-formed polyethylene dinghy—when it started its run from Lees Ferry in August 1963. Accompanying Marston in sportyaks were Bill Belknap and Bill's son Buzz. The elder Belknap, under contract with the National Park Service, took frequent photographs of the exposed river bottom during the twenty-seven-day run to Lake Mead.

When Glen Canyon Dam was completed in 1963, the Bureau of Reclamation restricted water releases to the river below to give the new reservoir, Lake Powell, a jump start. This caused Lake Mead's pool to drop precipitously, threatening Hoover Dam's hydroelectric production. The bureau began to release more water for a time and subsequently encouraged the departure of a May 1964 Sierra Club trip, pushing off from Lees Ferry in dories (an adaptation of small wooden boats used on the McKenzie River in Oregon). Days later a National Park Service airplane dropped a message to the party suggesting they leave the river at Whitmore Wash because Glen Canyon Dam's gates had again closed and the river level would soon drop. Rather than leave the river early, the group rowed hard nearly a hundred miles ahead of the diminishing flow to Lake Mead. One of their dories was the *Suzie Too*, later renamed the *Music Temple* for a Glen Canyon site named by John Wesley Powell. The *Suzie Too/Music Temple* is the youngest craft in the park's historic boat collection.

SUGGESTED READING

For an excellent if vicarious Colorado River trip and additional river history, see Michael P. Ghiglieri's *Canyon*, noted below. There are also many books by and about river runners and their histories in print. An excellent overview is David Lavender's *River Runners of the Grand Canyon*, also noted below. Also recommended are John Wesley Powell's *Canyons of the Colorado* (Meadville, Pa.: Flood and Vincent, 1895), reprinted in recent years and generally available as *The Exploration of the Colorado River and Its Canyons*; Frederick S. Dellenbaugh's *A Canyon Voyage* (New York: Putnam, 1908), reprinted by Yale University Press and the University of Arizona Press in the 1960s and 1980s, respectively; Vince Welsh, Cort Conley, and Brad Dimock's *The Doing of the Thing* (Flagstaff, Ariz: Fretwater Press, 1998); Dimock's *Sunk Without A Sound* (Flagstaff, Ariz.: Fretwater Press, 2001); and P. T. Reilly's *Lee's Ferry* (Logan: Utah State University Press, 1999). For a fresh look at the James White controversy, see *Hell or High Water: James White's Disputed Passage through Grand Canyon, 1867* (Logan: Utah State University Press, 2001), by White's granddaughter, Eilean Adams.

WORKS CITED

Anderson, Martin J. 1982. Commentary on part two: The affair at Separation Rapids. In *Colorado River controversies,* Robert Brewster Stanton, Repr., Boulder City, Nev.: Westwater.

Ghiglieri, Michael P. 1992. *Canyon.* Tucson: University of Arizona Press.

Lavender, David. 1985. River runners of the Grand Canyon. Grand Canyon, Ariz.: Grand Canyon Natural History Association.

Stanton, Robert Brewster. 1932. Colorado River controversies. Repr., Boulder City, Nev.: Westwater, 1982.

Webb, Roy. 1989. *Riverman: The story of Bus Hatch.* Rock Springs, Wy.: Labyrinth.

Chapter Twenty-Three

GPS in 1869:
The Geographical Powell Survey

by Richard D. Quartaroli

Richard D. Quartaroli first boated the Colorado River through the Grand Canyon in 1973, and he credits river running for his fascination with the history of the Southwest in general and the Grand Canyon in particular. Regional explorers since the late nineteenth century have carried accurate maps, and since the 1990s backcountry hikers have been aided by the Global Positioning System (GPS), but just how much did John Wesley Powell know of his location along the Colorado River in 1869? Which maps were available to him and which did he carry? What navigational aids did he have on board? In this presentation, Quartaroli starts with a puzzling notation in Powell's journal that launched a cross-country archival search for the answers.

To quote John Wesley Powell from his 1875 government report, *Exploration of the Colorado River of the West and Its Tributaries,* "Ah, well! we may conjecture many things." Even in the centennial of Powell's death, much about his explorations remains speculative. The fate of William Dunn and half brothers Oramel G. and Seneca B. Howland, three men who left Powell's Colorado River trip on August 28, 1869, at Separation Rapid, for example, is not clearly known.

While researching the plaques commemorating the Howlands and Dunn, I reread Powell's original journal. Other than dates and camp numbers, Powell's *Notebook #1* contained only one set of figures. As August 28 became an important date, Powell, or more likely one of his men, wrote on the 27th what appeared to be a longitude for Separation: 119° – 42' – 40" (J. Powell 1869a). This number has never occurred in publication (J. Powell 1875, 96; J. Powell 1895, 277; J. Powell 1947, 131) and only once in transcription (Anderson n.d.).

The longitude for Separation Rapid is actually 113° – 34' – 19", or about six degrees of separation from the longitude noted by the Powell expedition. Powell's figure is

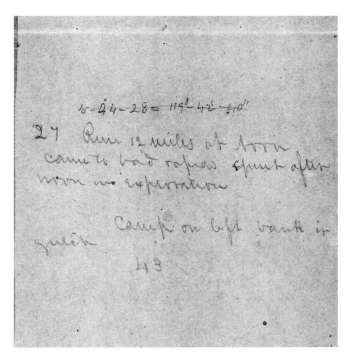

Powell's Notebook #1 *entries for August 27 and 28, 1869. Courtesy of Cline Library, Northern Arizona University, Flagstaff*

almost exactly that for Fresno, California. Why the apparent discrepancy? Was it really 119 and not 114? By comparing the other numbers, it is definitely a closed, not an open, 4. It could have been intended to be 114° and incorrectly written. The number to the left of the equal sign, 5 – 24 – 28, might lend a clue. Subtracting from 119°, 114° – 18' – 12" is within one degree of Separation's location. If it is not longitude, what could it otherwise be?

When William Culp Darrah transcribed the party's journals for *Utah Historical Quarterly*, he included a portion of Powell's "Geological Observations" from *Notebook #2* but not his "Astronomical Observations" (Darrah 1947, 132). To verify the Separation number, I requested copies from the National Anthropological Archives of the Smithsonian Institution. Meanwhile, I decided to find out what I could about what Powell and his men might have known about where they were as they traveled through "the great unknown" of southern Utah and northern Arizona.

What maps might Powell have had either prior to, or on, his 1869 expedition? According to Darrah, "a half dozen maps of equal quality were available in 1868. The Major does not remember any particular map." However, on May 5, 1947, E. Wright Allen, brother of Rhodes Allen, Illinois Wesleyan freshman ornithologist (Watson 1950, 90), wrote Darrah: "For many years I had my brother's map that he had with him [in 1868] in Colorado. Maj. Powell bought them for several of the students who went

with him. As I recall the map was printed by . . . the General Land Office and was drawn by Gurlinsky [Gorlinski]. It was a big wall map" (Darrah 1951, 108). The 1867 map measured $2\frac{1}{2}$ by $4\frac{1}{2}$ feet and was the first General Land Office map Joseph Gorlinski drafted, issued October 18 of that year (Wilson and Gorlinski 1867; Darrah [1950]). He was also draftsman of the General Land Office's 1868 map, not issued until November 1, 1869, after Powell's trip had ended (Wilson 1868; Rumsey 2000).

The 1867 Gorlinski map may have been what George Bradley called "the official map from Washington" and what Oramel Howland referred to as "a Government map we have with us." In charge of mapping, Howland tried to determine their location about fourteen miles below the Bear River with regard to two tributaries, "Brush Creek" and "Ashley's Fork." However, Jack Sumner indicated a John C. Frémont map when he mentioned "Red Fork" coming in from the east off the "Bitter Creek Desert" and a small trout stream, also from the east below "Brown's Hole," "named on Fremont's map, 'Tom Big Creek'" (Bradley 1947, 57; Howland 1947, 102; Sumner 1969, 179; Dimock 2002, 26; Ghiglieri 2003). None of the Frémont maps I have examined contains all these names and neither does the 1867 Gorlinski map.

In 1861 the government issued a seminal, twelve-volume report of the Pacific Railroad surveys (United States War Department 1855–60). William H. Goetzmann

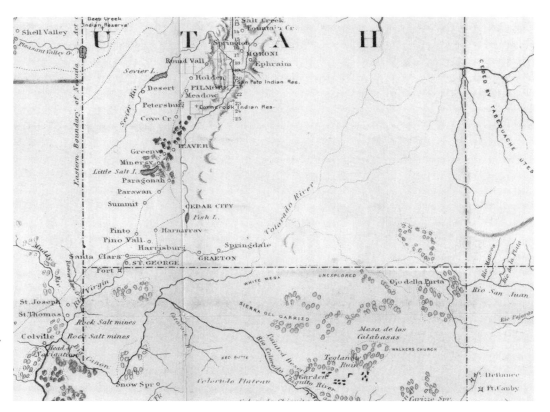

Detail from the 1867 Joseph Gorlinski map issued by the General Land Office showing southern Utah Territory and northern Arizona Territory. Courtesy of the David Rumsey Historical Map Collection, http://www.david rumsey.com

and Donald Worster agreed that "the most important achievement of the Pacific Railroad Surveys" was the publication of the 1850s maps of the Army Corps of Engineers under Lt. Gouverneur Kemble Warren (Goetzmann 1959, 313; Worster 2001, 578), "the culminating achievement of the Great Reconnaissance period" (Goetzmann 1967, 314). In 1861 Warren, "as much historian as cartographer," studied all existing maps and records to select the best data in order "to represent only such portions as have been actually explored, and of which our information may be considered reliable." Warren continued, "In some large sections, we possess no information, except from uncertain sources. In these parts the rule was adopted to leave the map blank, or to faintly indicate such information as is probably correct" (Warren 1861; Schubert 1980, 123). Thus, by "1858, the basic contours of the enormous region [of the trans-Mississippi West] were at last understood and [by 1861] a general map was readily available" (Schubert 1988, 69). Both Goetzmann and Worster failed to acknowledge Warren's continually updated maps of the 1860s, particularly what Carl I. Wheat described as the "1868 Freyhold" (Warren 1861):

> Edward Freyhold having been especially responsible for drafting it[,] . . . [he] displays the western reaches of the continent within virtually the same framework as Warren. . . . In the recompilation of this map the geographical positions of the first edition have to the greater extent been preserved, with the exception, where recent and more extensive explorations and surveys have caused changes. . . . Freyhold had been credited by Warren for his labors upon the original map of 1857, so a family resemblance is to be expected. But we have here a tremendously advanced map, detailed beyond any possibility of descriptions, and reflecting almost incredible change in the aspect of the United States within a mere eleven-year period. Freyhold's is the first recognizably modern map of the West. (Wheat 1963, 243–244; Buttery 1990, 20)

Powell could be very thorough in some regards, as he was with obtaining the latest maps. The 1868 Warren/Freyhold is the only map I have found that contains all the geographic locations listed in the journals. Some of the names are no longer applicable on contemporary maps and two of Sumner's names need further explanation. Bitter Creek is on the map, but not the Bitter Creek Desert; instead we find the notation "Barrens with some pasture on the Water Courses." Sumner called it "Fremont's map," referring to the fact that Freyhold plotted and named Frémont's 1845 exploration in this particular area (Warren

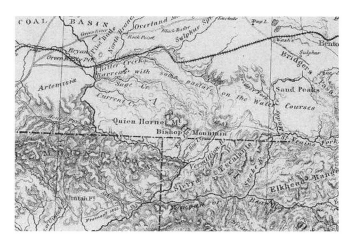

Detail from the 1868 Warren/Freyhold map showing the first portion of the route the Powell expedition followed. Courtesy of the David Rumsey Historical Map Collection, http://www.davidrumsey.com

[1868]; Wheat 1960, 33; Rumsey 2000). It is ironic that Powell should be carrying a Warren map as Goetzmann philosophized that "[i]n the post-Civil War jurisdictional conflicts between the Army and John Wesley Powell, the Warren map was often attacked as being either inaccurate or too large in scale to be of value" (Goetzmann 1959, 315).

The Utah State Historical Society in Salt Lake City holds the Darrah Collection. In notes concerning *Notebook #2* Darrah wrote, "The journal proper starts with 2 pages of figures and 29 pages of geological notes, followed by what appear to be . . . astronomical/barometric readings . . . we find a total of 32 pages of notes of daily entries. . . . They consist entirely of lengthy series of tabulated figures, and appear to record astronomical data. . . . We question the possible value of this material to you" (Darrah [1945]).

After reading Darrah's comments, I planned a visit to the Huntington Library in San Marino, California, home of the Otis R. "Dock" Marston Collection. If Powell's astronomical notes are anywhere other than the Smithsonian, they would be in Dock's 431-box accumulation of Colorado River history. There, I found Dock's 1951 request for microfilm of exactly what I need (Marston 1951a). Scrolling forward to August 27, 1869, I found that the figures from *Notebook #1* and *Notebook #2* do not match: 125° 13' 00" (J. Powell 1869a, 1869b). I then noticed a small, orange slip of paper, folded and slipped inside the microfilm box. On it, Dock had written,

Sep 113-34-30 35-48-45

which is the longitude and latitude of Separation Rapid (Marston 1951b). Fifty years ago, Dock was not only on a quest for the very same astronomical observations, but was also double-checking the Powell notebooks for the accuracy of the figures for Separation.

As Powell was no favorite of Dock's, I consulted his unpublished manuscript (Frank 2001), my rationale being that if Powell was really that far off in his longitude, Dock would not have missed the opportunity to note it at least. Although Dock often summed the number of observations and even gave some readings, he made no mention of their accuracy (Marston [1977]). When I returned from the Huntington, I found a message from my Smithsonian contact that copies of the astronomical notes were forthcoming. With the much clearer second set of copies, I transcribed the handwritten notes. Those in hand, ninety-one-year-old Lowell Observatory Astronomer Emeritus Henry Giclas explained the use of a sextant—that the 119° reading I originally supposed was a longitude was actually a double-angle star sighting, that Powell obtained it using an artificial horizon, and that the number should be halved for a true star angle. I asked how accurate Powell's data collection was; Giclas replied that it seemed adequate considering the time and conditions on the river (Giclas 2001).

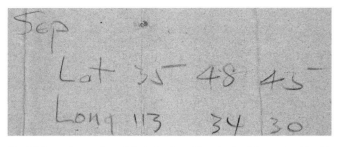

Dock Marston's notation of the latitude and longitude of Separation Rapid. Courtesy of the Huntington Library, San Marino, Calif.

About one hundred years before Powell, John Hadley's double-reflecting octant evolved into the sextant and, in solving the "problem of longitude," John Harrison constructed accurate chronometers. As Isaac Newton knew, the former would be used to find the longitude astronomically, the latter as a timekeeper to keep the longitude (Randall 1998, 224–225). Supposition as to the type, quantity, and source of instruments Powell carried with him is based on very brief mentions in letters, journals, and Powell's report: "We are provided with instruments for determining latitude, longitude and altitude, and for making observations of the climate" (J. Powell 1947, 74; Holland 2001). Powell identified no brand names, but indicated some amounts: "For scientific work, we have two sextants, four chronometers, a number of barometers, thermometers, compasses, and other instruments" (J. Powell 1875, 8; J. Powell 1895, 119). Regarding the retrieval of some of the equipment from the wreck of the boat *No Name*, the journal entries for June 8th and 9th make it appear that they had saved the three original barometers (J. Powell 1947, 82; Sumner 1969, 181; Bradley 1947, 36; Howland 1947, 97). They lost one barometer on July 11 when the lead boat, *Emma Dean*, filled with water; according to Jack Sumner, that same event also "ruined $800 worth of watches" (Sumner 1947, 114).

Even though Powell does not mention them, it was necessary for him to have navigational texts and tables to reduce his observations and to do his calculations in the field. In 1868 the U.S. Naval Hydrographic Office assumed publication of the "Bowditch," a title initially proposed by Giclas as a possibility for Powell (Giclas 2001). Originating in 1802, Nathaniel Bowditch's *The New American Practical Navigator* was an outstanding book that enabled the mariner of little formal education to grasp the essentials of his profession. Bowditch vowed "to put down in the book nothing I can't teach the crew, . . . including the ship's cook (Bowditch 1939, 3). In April 1874, Almon Harris Thompson's order for field supplies listed "Nautical Almanac and Ephemeris," a reference perhaps to *The American Ephemeris and Nautical Almanac*, which first appeared in 1855 under the Bureau of Navigation (United States Naval Observatory 1867, [i]). Thompson also listed "Loomis Star Catalogue" and "Loomis Tables" (Loomis 1869a, 1869b, 1873a, 1873b), items perhaps more suited for overland field surveying off the river, and "Chanrimts Tables" (Thompson 1939, 126; Kinsley 2002). Viewing a photocopy of Thompson's original diary reveals that "Chanrimts" is an incorrect transcription of "Chauvenet's," referring to William Chauvenet's *Manual of Spherical and Practical Astronomy* (Chauvenet 1874; Thompson 1939).

Although Powell's astronomical notes mentioned "observation for latitude" several times, it contained just one calculation for same, an approximation for the mouth of the San Juan River, which was very accurate (J. Powell 1869b). At the confluence with the Little Colorado River, George Bradley correctly noted that the "Major got Latitude . . . by which we find ourselves as far south as Callville" (J. Powell 1869b; Bradley 1947, 63). No calculations for longitude are listed. A viewing of the original *Notebook #2* is necessary, as some pages of illegible numbers appear to be the working calculations (J. Powell 1869b; Darrah [1945]). However, it does appear that Powell knew his location and thus his map did not need the marginal notation *hic sunt dracones*, "here are dragons" (Blake 1999, 3).

Observations of celestial features included those for the sun, moon, Saturn, Spica, Altair, Aquila, Ophiucus, Ceti, and Polaris. Wording such as "rate of Elgin" and "time Elgin" (J. Powell 1869b) at first led me to believe Elgin was a star or that Powell set his timekeepers to Elgin, Illinois, time. Determining that Powell referred to a watch, I reconfirmed that the Grand Canyon National Park Museum Collection holds his key-wind, key-set Elgin railroad watch from the National Watch Company in Elgin, Illinois (Colcord 1969; Alft 1984, 54; Alft 2001). It is a B. W. Raymond movement, serial #4056, manufactured in 1867 to 1870, the company's first years (Smith 1948). In 1867 18,000 movements came off the line (Alft 1984, 56). The first Raymond movement, #101, on April 1, 1867, cost $117 at a time when pork chops sold for three cents a pound (Smith 1948; Hanewacker). In addition, casings could cost from $3.50 to $30 for silver and $50 to $150 for gold (Richardson 1869, 182). When the widow of Powell's nephew donated it to the park in 1948, the family believed Powell took the Elgin #4056 down the river (Davis 1948).

Powell's Elgin watch. Courtesy of the Grand Canyon National Park Museum Collection (#20836)

In a letter in the *1871 Illustrated Almanac*, Powell sang the Elgin's praises (National Watch Company 1871, 19; see illustration). Powell's letter confirms the number of chronometers at four and, for the first time, identifies them as pocket chronometers. Although Sumner on the 1869 trip noted that they ruined $800 worth of watches, in 1907 he told Robert Brewster Stanton that Powell had "an especially valuable chronometer for which he had paid six hundred and fifty dollars" (Sumner 1932, 209), a price that may have become inflated over the thirty-eight year interim. On Powell's second river trip in 1871–72, the second *Emma Dean* also filled with water. On September 3, crewmember Walter "Clem" Powell explained: "The Maj. had his $500 chronometer about ruined. Soaked it with glycerine to prevent it from rusting" (W. Powell 1872, 38; W. Powell 1948–49, 446). Frederick Dellenbaugh added, "The Major's Jurgenssen [*sic*] chronometer had stopped at 8:26:30 from the wetting" (Dellenbaugh 1908, 237). In 1874 Almon Thompson listed instruments to buy for fieldwork, including chronometers, but did not identify brand names (Thompson 1939, 126). An 1883 *Elgin Advocate* article (Taylor 1883) praised the Elgin watch and stated "four other chronometers, of well known make, which Major Powell took with him failed," but did not specify the make.

Although both are timekeepers, interchangeable use of the terms *watch* and chronometer causes confusion. The *Oxford English Dictionary* defines chronometer as "an instrument for measuring time, specifically applied to timekeepers adjusted to keep accurate time

in all variations of temperature. They differ from watches in having a more perfect escapement and a compensation balance." Powell may have also had a pocket chronometer made by Jules Jurgensen of Le Locle, Switzerland, on his first trip, but at a price of $500, this is doubtful. Perhaps the four pocket chronometers that failed on that trip, which Sumner called watches and averaged $200 each, influenced Powell to obtain a higher-quality Jurgensen for the second trip. Prices of a Jurgensen watch at $500 and an Elgin at $150 are mentioned in a *Chicago Republican* article in the 1871 Elgin *Illustrated Almanac* (National Watch Company 1871, 29).

So, what new information do we have concerning the 1869 Geographical Powell Survey's knowledge of their locations along the river and their ability to obtain that knowledge? There were four pocket chronometers, brands unknown but possibly one made by Jurgensen. Powell carried one Elgin watch, which was more dependable than the chronometers. The men relied on an 1868 Warren/ Freyhold map, printed by the U.S. government. Their observations for latitude were accurate. Ongoing research is necessary to determine further names and types of instruments as well as methods. Since the 1869 river map is not extant (Rusho 1969, 208), reduction and recalculation of Powell's and his men's observations could lead to replication of their mapping effort.

In a display of humor, rare for him on his river trips, Powell wrote, "Soon I see [the cook, Billy 'Missouri Rhodes'] Hawkins down by the boat, taking up the sextant, rather a strange proceeding for him, and I question him concerning it. He replies that he is trying to find the latitude and longitude of the nearest pie" (J. Powell 1875, 59; 1895, 213).

ILLINOIS STATE NATURAL HISTORY SOCIETY,
BLOOMINGTON, ILL., June 20, 1870.

T. M. AVERY, President of the National Watch Company:

DEAR SIR,—Last year, in the explorations of the canons of the Colorado River, I had unusual opportunities to test the accuracy of one of your watches. I was provided with four pocket chronometers for use in astronomical observations. I also had with me an "Elgin" watch, which I rated from time to time together with the chronometers by observations with the sextant. Of the five instruments its rate was second best. With the ordinary disturbance due to transportation, its rate was the least variable, while, with the extraordinary disturbance incident to such an expedition, it was the only instrument on which I could rely, the chronometers at last becoming useless.

I am, with great respect, yours cordially,   J. W POWELL.

Powell's 1871 Illustrated Almanac *testament about his Elgin watch. Courtesy of Bernard J. Edwards*

WORKS CITED

Alft, E. C. 1984. *Elgin: An American history*. [Elgin, Ill.?]: Crossroads Communications.

———. 2001. Personal communication.

Anderson, Martin J. Manuscript Collection 77, box 1, ser. 1, fol. 4; and J. W. Powell journal 1869: Transcript and photocopy of original, box 1, ser. 1, fol. 12. Cline Library, Northern Arizona University, Flagstaff.

Blake, Erin C. 1999. *Where be "Here be dragons"?* http://www.maphist.nl/extra/herebedragons.html.

Bowditch, Nathaniel. 1939. *American practical navigator: An epitome of navigation and nautical astronomy*. Washington, D.C.: Government Printing Office.

Bradley, George Y. 1947. George Y. Bradley's journal, May 24–August 30, 1869. Ed. William Culp Darrah. *Utah Historical Quarterly* 15.

Buttery, Lewis M. 1990. Warren map of 1867. *Old maps of the Southwest* 9 (Spring).

Chauvenet, William. 1874. *A manual of spherical and practical astronomy: Embracing the general problems of spherical astronomy, the special applications to nautical astronomy, and the theory and use of fixed and portable astronomical instruments, with an appendix on the method of least squares*, 5th ed. Philadelphia: J. B. Lippincott.

Colcord, Edwin H. 1969. Old Elgin watch was explorer's guide. *Elgin Daily Courier-News*. January 8.

Darrah, William Culp. [1945]. William Culp Darrah Manuscript Collection. Book 2: Geological notes and sections—1869. MSS B-361, Box 4 [misfiled in], Folder: Friends and associates of JWP. Utah State Historical Society, Salt Lake City.

———. 1947. Geological notes by Major Powell. *Utah Historical Quarterly* 15.

———. [1950]. William Culp Darrah Manuscript Collection. *Map of the United States and territories, National Archives map #8, 1867*. MSS B-361, Box 4, Folder: Maps. Utah State Historical Society, Salt Lake City.

———. 1951. *Powell of the Colorado*. Princeton, N.J.: Princeton University Press.

Davis, Fanny Waugh (Mrs. K. C.). 1948. GRCA-820, Catalog #20836. Grand Canyon National Park Museum Collection, Grand Canyon, Ariz.

Dellenbaugh, Frederick Samuel. 1908. *A canyon voyage*. New York: G. P. Putnam's Sons, 1908.

Dimock, Brad. 2002. White lies, major distortions, and several new stabs at the truth: 8 recent publications on James White and Major John Wesley Powell. *Boatman's Quarterly Review* 5 (1).

Frank, Bill. 2001. Personal communication.

Ghiglieri, Michael P. 2003. *First through Grand Canyon: The secret journals and letters of the 1869 crew who explored the Green and Colorado rivers*. Flagstaff, Ariz.: Puma Press.

Giclas, Henry. 2001. Personal communication.

Goetzmann, William H. 1959. *Army exploration in the American West, 1803–1863*. New Haven, Conn.: Yale University Press.

———. 1967. *Exploration and empire: The explorer and the scientist in the winning of the American West*. Repr., Austin: Texas State Historical Association, 1993.

Hanewacker, Hans W. *Mini-history: Elgin National Watch Company*. http://rustyrobin.com/ElginHistory/ElginHistory.htm.

Holland, Al. 2001. CLIO, an online river-history Listserv, communication.

Howland, Oramel G. 1947. Letters of O. G. Howland to the *Rocky Mountain News*. Transcribed by William Culp Darrah. *Utah Historical Quarterly* 15.

Kinsley, Shaw. 2002. Personal communication.

Loomis, Elias. 1869a. *Elements of plane and spherical trigonometry, with their applications to mensuration, surveying, and navigation*, 25th ed. New York: Harper & Brothers.

———. 1869b. *Tables of logarithms of numbers and of sines and tangents for every ten seconds of the quadrant, with other useful tables*, 25th ed. New York: Harper & Brothers.

———. 1873a. *Elements of plane and spherical trigonometry, with their applications to mensuration, surveying, and navigation*, 36th ed. New York: Harper & Brothers.

———. 1873b. *Tables of logarithms of numbers and of sines and tangents for every ten seconds of the quadrant, with other useful tables*, 36th ed. New York: Harper & Brothers.

Marston, Otis. 1951a. Otis R. Marston Manuscript Collection. Powell, J. W.: Chronological 1838–1874. Box 187, fol. 18. Huntington Library, San Marino, Calif.

———. 1951b. Otis R. Marston Manuscript Collection. Microfilm 18. MS Film 754. Huntington Library, San Marino, Calif.

———. [1977]. Otis R. Marston Manuscript Collection. The professor opens a text: Beginning the boat trip of 1869. Box 422, Folder 1. Huntington Library, San Marino, Calif.

National Watch Company. 1871. *The National Watch Company Elgin illustrated almanac 1871*. Elgin, Ill.: National Watch Company. Repr., Bernard J. Edwards, 1977.

Powell, John Wesley. 1869a. Notebook 1. MS 1795a, No. 1.

National Anthropological Archives, Smithsonian Institution, Washington, D.C. Photocopy and transcript of original by Martin J. Anderson in Martin J. Anderson Manuscript Collection 77, Box 1, Ser. 1, Folder 12. Cline Library, Northern Arizona University, Flagstaff.

———. 1869b. Notebook 2: Geological and Astronomical Observations. MS 1795a, No. 2. National Anthropological Archives, Smithsonian Institution, Washington, D.C.

———. 1875. *Exploration of the Colorado River of the West and its tributaries. Explored in 1869, 1870, 1871, and 1872, under the direction of the Secretary of the Smithsonian Institution.* Washington, D.C.: Government Printing Office.

———. 1895. *Canyons of the Colorado.* Meadville, Pa.: Flood & Vincent.

———. 1947. Major Powell's journal, July 2–August 28, 1869, ed. William Culp Darrah. *Utah Historical Quarterly* 15.

Powell, Walter Clement. 1872. Journal of W. C. Powell, April 21, 1871–December 7, 1872. GRCA 20821. Grand Canyon National Park Museum Collection, Grand Canyon, Ariz.

———. 1948–1949. Journal of W. C. Powell, April 21, 1871–December 7, 1872, ed. by Charles Kelly. *Utah Historical Quarterly* 16–17.

Randall, Anthony G. 1998. The timekeeper that won the longitude prize. In *The quest for longitude: The proceedings of the longitude symposium,* ed. by William J. H. Andrews. Cambridge, Mass.: Collection of Historical Scientific Instruments, Harvard University.

Richardson, Albert D. 1869. Making watches by machinery. *Harper's New Monthly Magazine* 39 (July).

Rumsey, David. 2000. David Rumsey Historical Map Collection. http://www.davidrumsey.com. Cartography Associates.

Rusho, W. L. 1969. Francis Bishop's 1871 river maps. *Utah Historical Quarterly* 37 (2).

Schubert, Frank N. 1980. *Vanguard of expansion: Army engineers in the trans-Mississippi West, 1819–1879.* Washington, D.C.: Historical Divisions, Office of Administrative Services, Office of the Chief of Engineers.

———. 1988. *The nation builders: A sesquicentennial history of the Corps of Topographical Engineers, 1838–1863.* Repr., Washington, D.C.: Office of History, U.S. Army Corps of Engineers, 1989.

Smith, Roscoe R. 1948. GRCA-820, Catalog #20836. Grand Canyon National Park Museum Collection, Grand Canyon, Ariz.

Sumner, John C. 1932. Jack Sumner's [1907] account. In *Colorado River Controversies* by Robert Brewster Stanton. New York: Dodd, Mead & Company.

———. 1947. J. C. Sumner's journal, July 6–August 31, 1869, edited by William Culp Darrah. *Utah Historical Quarterly* 15.

———. 1969. A daily journal of the Colorado River exploring expedition (Jack Sumner's diary of the first Powell expedition from Green River, Wyoming, to the Uinta Basin). In The lost journal of John Colton Sumner, by O. Dock Marston. *Utah Historical Quarterly* 37 (2).

Taylor, S. L. 1883. *Elgin Advocate.* December 20.

Thompson, Almon Harris. 1939. Diary of Almon Harris Thompson, geographer, explorations of the Colorado River of the West and its tributaries, 1871–1875. *Utah Historical Quarterly* 7.

United States Naval Observatory, Nautical Almanac Office. 1867. *The American ephemeris and nautical almanac, for the year 1869.* Washington, D.C.: Bureau of Navigation.

United States War Department. 1855–60. *Reports of explorations and surveys to ascertain the most practicable and economical route for a railroad from the Mississippi River to the Pacific Ocean.* Washington, D.C.: Beverley Tucker, printer.

Warren, Gouverneur Kemble. 1861. Memoir to accompany the map of the territory of the United States from the Mississippi River to the Pacific Ocean, giving a brief account of each of the exploring expeditions since AD 1800, with a detailed description of the method adopted in compiling the general map. In *Reports of explorations and surveys, to ascertain the most practicable and economical route for a railroad from the Mississippi River to the Pacific Ocean,* vol. 11. George W. Bowman, printer.

Warren, Gouverneur Kemble, and Edward Freyhold. [1868]. Territory of the United States from the Mississippi River to the Pacific Ocean. Map. Washington, D.C.: Office of Pacific Railroad Surveys, War Department. Copy in David Rumsey Historical Map Collection, 2919000, http://www.davidrumsey.com.

Watson, Elmo Scott. 1950. *The Illinois Wesleyan story, 1850-1950.* Bloomington, Ill.: Illinois Wesleyan Press.

Wheat, Carl I. 1960. *Mapping the trans-Mississippi West, 1540-1861: From the Pacific railroad surveys to the onset of the Civil War, 1855-1860,* vol. 4. San Francisco: Institute of Historical Cartography.

———. 1963. *Mapping the trans-Mississippi West, 1540-1861: From the Civil War to the Geological Survey,* vol. 5, part 2. San Francisco: Institute of Historical Cartography.

Wilson, Joseph S. 1868. *Map of the United States and territories*. General Land Office. Copy in Texas A&M Collection, Map G3701.B5 1868 .U5.

Wilson, Joseph S., and Joseph Gorlinski, Draughtsman. 1867. *Map of the United States and territories*. General Land Office. Copy in David Rumsey Historical Map Collection, 1882001, http://www.davidrumsey.com; University of Nevada, Las Vegas Special Collections, Map G3701.B5 1867 .U54.

Worster, Donald. 2001. *A river running west: The life of John Wesley Powell*. New York: Oxford University Press.

George Young Bradley: Chronicler of the 1869 John Wesley Powell Expedition down the Green and Colorado Rivers

by Michael P. Ghiglieri

Like others in this volume, Michael P. Ghiglieri's long experience on the Colorado River has nurtured his fascination with the river's history, including the controversial aspects. In this presentation, he reexamines the journal of the most experienced boatman to run the river with John Wesley Powell in 1869. He concludes that errors in transcription and omissions have led to faulty conclusions about the man, his character, and his role in the ill-fated expedition. Ghiglieri's larger project to revisit the original diaries of members of the first Powell expedition resulted in the book First through Grand Canyon: The Secret Journals and Letters of the 1869 Crew Who Explored the Green and Colorado Rivers *(Flagstaff, Ariz.: Puma Press, 2003).*

Introduction

The Major as usual has chosen the worst camping-ground possible. If I had a dog that would lie where my bed is made tonight I would kill him and burn his collar and swear I never owned him. —George Young Bradley, June 11, 1869

In May 1869, eleven men stood beside four boats moored on the Green River where, weeks earlier, the Union Pacific Railroad had completed a bridge to facilitate the nation's first transcontinental railroad. The mission of these men was to navigate the unexplored canyons of the Green and Colorado rivers some one thousand miles to, through, and beyond the Grand Canyon. Ninety-eight days later, only six men and two boats would land at the mouth of the Virgin River. Their story and harrowing accomplishments form one of the most astonishing epics in the history of North American exploration.

This saga of adventure, optimism, courage, fear, heroism, humor, triumph, treachery, and tragedy was told by the men

themselves in journals and letters written while on the river, but, until now, accurate transcriptions have been unavailable. In my effort to reconsider original writings concerning the Powell expedition, I retranscribed Sergeant George Young Bradley's journal (Bradley 1869), which has been housed since 1915 in the U.S. Library of Congress, Manuscript Division. Bradley was the only man to write a coherent, detailed, and candid account of the expedition. Throughout, he reveals a vexing array of dangers while burdened with inappropriate equipment and naive leadership, blithely challenging a landscape so inhospitable that even American Indians avoided it. This document—the Rosetta Stone for the 1869 expedition—came to light in September 1915, a gift of Bradley's nephew, Charles Morss, to the Library of Congress (Sibussat 1947). Although additional material written by the crew has since been uncovered, nothing more written at the time of the expedition has added to our understanding of Powell's tragic expedition. Bradley's chronicle doubled what we know, yet, ironically, Powell himself never knew that his most experienced boatman had kept a journal.

What sort of man was Bradley? Powell biographer William Culp Darrah wrote, "Bradley is harshest when he speaks of the Major. He appears to have been somewhat sentimental, somewhat lonely, something of a scholar. Largely self-taught, he was nonetheless an intelligent observer, an expressive diarist, and an honest critic" (Darrah 1947b, 30). Bradley was the best person for the job of expedition chronicler since he knew boats and water better than the rest of the crew. Whether describing the painful labor of lining a boat around a bad rapid or revealing the adrenaline-soaked joy of running big whitewater; recounting how to choose a camp, escape a raging inferno, catch a three-foot fish on a thin silk line, track a bighorn ram up a cliff, collect fossils, or repair a battered boat; or depicting the aridity and expanse of a southwestern landscape while trapped in the middle of it with diminishing rations, Bradley offers an insider's insight into the ultimate western adventure. His journal is self-revealing and self-effacing, sensitive, humorous, evocative, critical, optimistic, determined, inspiring, descriptive, and true to the essentials of what every boatman faces: the terror of nasty rapids, a terror that paradoxically metamorphoses into an addiction to run the great rivers. For example, while in Desolation Canyon on July 9, he wrote:

[A] terrible gale of dry hot wind swept over our camp and roared through the cañon mingling its sound with the mellow roar of the cataract making music fit for the infernal regions. We needed only a few flashes of lightning to meet Milton's most vivid conceptions of Hell. The sand from the beach buried our beds while that from an island below filled the air until the cañon was no comfortable place for repose, for one had to cover his head to get his breath. The barometer fell over 290° [sic]. It moderated to an ordinary gale this morning, and we started on the wildest day's run of the trip thus far. [July 9, 1869]

Fellow boatman William Hawkins wrote that Bradley was "a man of nerve and staying qualities, as he proved later on." He added after they had launched that "we were all green at the business [of rowing]. Bradley was the only one that had any experience" (Hawkins, in Bass 1920, 19, 20).

In 1947 Bradley's journal and other manuscripts of the 1869 expedition were published in the *Utah Historical Quarterly*. Unfortunately, this volume contains nearly a thousand errors of research and transcription from Powell's, Bradley's, Sumner's, and Howland's original missives. Some errors are understandable. Powell wrote his 2,922-word *Notebook #1* and his 2,714-word geology *Notebook #2* with his left hand; he was right-handed prior to losing his favored arm in the Battle of Shiloh and his penmanship

thereafter was atrocious. Bradley's writing was nearly microscopic. This explains many transcriptive errors made by the *Quarterly's* editor, William Culp Darrah, but some are simply ludicrous. For example, after blasting through Sockdolager Rapid, Bradley writes, "we are a lucky set." Darrah deciphered this as "we are a lusty set." Darrah's other errors range from simple misreading of single words to losing entire paragraphs that were present, for example, in Powell's original *Chicago Tribune* letter from the river but absent from Darrah's transcription of that letter.

Ironically, many people interested in the history of the Colorado know nothing of this valuable if flawed volume of the *Utah Historical Quarterly*. They know only that Major Powell wrote a book in 1895 containing his journals of the 1869 expedition and later journeys to the West—the standard history. Yet the 1895 book is far less accurate than the 1947 *Quarterly*. In 1875 Powell simply recycled the series of adventure-oriented articles he had written for *Scribner's Magazine* and combined them into a self-serving account presented to the U.S. Congress as his official report, entitled *Exploration of the Colorado River of the West and its Tributaries*. In 1895 Powell expanded this report for publication, retitled *Canyons of the Colorado*. This version is still reprinted as an accurate history, but it is a facile if colorful document, leaving much of the truth marooned and forgotten on the banks of the Colorado.

Powell's report and book not only failed to resemble his journal entries, they also failed to recount what actually happened on the 1869 expedition. He added episodes and accomplishments that occurred later, on his second expedition of 1871–72, attributing them to the earlier trip and crew. He also changed dates, locations, and adventures of the first expedition to enhance, one supposes, their dramatic impacts. Add his manipulation of geography and history and we are left with documents that are blatantly inaccurate. Powell, from the onset, was also a shoddy note taker with a poor memory for detail (Anderson n.d., 10–11), and he ignored important accomplishments of his crew. Overall, his accounts are inexcusable when one recalls that he submitted his 1875 report as an accurate story of exploration to Congress, to be printed with federal funds by the Government Printing Office.

Powell added more fiction by grossly exaggerating dangers. In the now famous first run of Sockdolager Rapid, for example, Powell wrote in his report that there is "a descent of, perhaps, seventy-five or eighty feet in a third of a mile, and the rushing waters break into great waves on the rocks, and lash themselves to a mad, white foam . . . and we must run the rapid or abandon the river. There is no hesitation." But in his brief journal that day (August 14), Powell wrote: "Must run it or abandon the enterprise. Good Luck! Little boat fills with water twice. Chute $^1/_2$ mile long, fall 30 ft., probably. Huge waves." Sockdolager drops roughly nineteen feet; his exaggeration for public consumption nearly tripled his own estimate of its descent.

Indeed Powell's fictions have made fools of dozens of history writers. His excesses were so glaring that the head boatman of the 1869 expedition, John Sumner, spilled the beans to the second man to run the river through the Grand Canyon, Robert Brewster Stanton, some twenty years later. Stanton's river diary for Friday, December 13, 1889, reads:

> At about 2 PM was hailed by a man on shore asking us for tobacco . . . found it was old Jack Sumner, Major Powell's right hand man in 1869. I had a half hour's talk with him and he gave us encouragement & good cheer and advice. Simply to go slow & carefully & we would be alright. . . .
>
> I asked Jack many questions about the river below, particularly about the Catarect [*sic*] where the three men left the party and had gone out and were killed by the Indians, telling him that was the one rapid & one place on the whole river from Maj. Powell's acct. that I was afraid of. He assured me there was [*sic*] no such awful difficulties at that point and encouraged us in every way. But I said, "Jack, Major gives a long detailed account of your experiences at that rapid," & read it to him from the copy we had. Sumner turned away with an air of resentment and said, "There's lots in that book besides the truth."
>
> I don't understand this, but Sumner wouldn't tell anymore about it. (Stanton 1932, 104)

After Stanton's 1889–90 expedition, he became obsessed with the Grand Canyon and with Powell. Stanton originally idolized Powell and his report. "To John Wesley Powell belongs all the glory and renown possible for his first trip through the unknown canyons of the wonderful river," he wrote, adding that "Major Powell's work and that of his companions in 1869, to my mind, stands out as one of the bravest exploits ever known anywhere. . . . When I first became acquainted with Major Powell's *Report* giving his account of that first exploration, it was to me the most fascinating story I had ever read. . . . I first read the document as I would the Gospel of St. John, with an almost worshipful reverence" (Stanton 1932, 97, 100, 102, 107, 111, 122, 137).

After Sumner led Stanton to question Powell's 1875 report, Stanton, in his apostasy, ripped apart one after another of its gratuitous distortions and fictionalizations. His ferocity was triggered in part by Powell's having told Stanton, in person, that the 1875 report was indeed his "diary written on the spot." Stanton's assiduous research revealed Powell's claim to be a mendacity. The original journals, believed lost until located by

a *very* determined Stanton after Powell's death, are fairly accurate despite some sloppy errors. Through comparison, Stanton found that the later report and book were "in many instances distorted and exaggerated . . . demonstrably inaccurate and, it would seem, deliberately misleading on a number of counts . . . [showing] that the Major was undoubtedly guilty of suppression of the truth and unblushing exaggeration." Biographer William Culp Darrah also grudgingly admitted of Powell's *Canyons* that the "Major was not blameless when it comes to deliberate inaccuracy" (Darrah 1947a, 16).

Powell's crew of 1869 worked hard and worked smart to overcome the lethal risks of running whitewater with inadequate boats and no life jackets. Moreover, they toiled week after week on starvation rations. They did this faithfully and in good humor. And, as we will see, Bradley chronicled it accurately.

WHO WAS GEORGE YOUNG BRADLEY?

Born in October, most likely in the year 1836, in Newbury, Massachusetts, Bradley at age thirty-two was one of the oldest men on the 1869 expedition. At five feet, nine inches (and 150 pounds at the onset), he was also one of the tallest. John Colton Sumner, Powell's next in command, described Bradley as "something of a geologist and, in my eyes far more important, he had been raised in the Maine codfishery school, and was a good boatman, and a brave man, not very strong but tough as a badger" (Stanton 1932, 174).

Before the Civil War, Bradley worked as a shoemaker in West Newbury, and it was apparent that he had been at sea as well. Like 80 percent of Powell's 1869 crew, he was a Union Civil War veteran. He enlisted in the army on August 12, 1862, reported to Company A, 19th Regiment, Massachusetts Volunteer Infantry Battalion, and eventually attained the rank of lieutenant. During the bloody river crossing at Fredericksburg on December 13, 1862, Bradley was wounded in the thigh. His wound proved slow to heal, so he was transferred to Company H, 12th Regiment, 2nd Battalion Veteran Reserve Corps. He retired from active duty on July 28, 1864.

On January 16, 1867, Bradley reenlisted in the army as a private, giving his profession as "druggist." The military assigned the dark-complected, hazel-eyed, mustached, brown-haired recruit to Company B, 36th Infantry Regiment, Fort Kearney, Nebraska Territory. As the Union Pacific laid track to span the continent following the Civil War, the U.S. Army trotted ahead to defend workers from Plains Indians who viewed the iron horse as public enemy number one. The army transferred Bradley from Fort Kearney to Fort Sedgwick, and then on (in succession) to Lodge Pole Creek, Fort Sanders, and Fort Bridger near

Green River City, Wyoming. By November 1868 he was promoted to First Sergeant, but found fossil-hunting more engaging than skirmishing with the Dakota (Sioux) and Cheyenne. John Wesley Powell arrived at Fort Bridger in 1868 to make arrangements to explore the Green and Colorado rivers the following spring, and his arrival changed the course of Bradley's life.

Once Powell learned of George Bradley's talents in geology, running boats, and surviving western rigors, he invited him to join his expedition as boatman and geologist. The sergeant agreed, if Powell could secure his discharge from the army. As he would write eighty days downriver on August 11, "Thank God the trip is nearly ended for it is no place for a man in my circumstances, but it will let me out of the Army and for that I would almost agree to explore the River Styx." The secretary of war issued a special order facilitating First Sergeant Bradley's honorable discharge on May 14, 1869. Almost immediately he was put to work instructing the rest of Powell's crew—mostly mountain men except for Powell's brother, Walter—on how to caulk and paint their four Whitehall boats so they would not sink or deteriorate prematurely. The expedition launched ten days later, and Bradley then had to teach the men how to row.

Bradley found beauty and joy in the great canyons; saw irony and sometimes incompetence in the antics of his fellow expeditionaries; and perceived an enigmatic self-absorption in his leader, Major John Wesley Powell. His formal education ended with the sixth grade, but his writing indicates that he had since progressed well beyond that level. Bradley retained his sense of humor throughout the expedition, as the following journal entry illustrates:

> I fell to day while trying to save my boat from a rock and have a bad cut over the left eye which I fear will make an ugly scar. But what odds, it can't disfigure my ugly mug and it may improve it, who knows? [June 14, 1869]

Powell wrote that Bradley was "scrupulously careful, and a little mishap works him into a passion, but when labor is needed he has a ready hand and powerful arm, and in danger, rapid judgement [*sic*] and unerring skill. A great difficulty or peril changes the petulant spirit into a brave, generous soul" (Stanton n.d., 441). Given Powell's overall assessment, it is difficult to understand how many historians have since characterized Bradley as a complainer or "inveterate worrier" and, aping Powell, as a "petulant" man (Worster 2001, 159). Such characterizations are inaccurate, perhaps due to ignorance of river running. Most of these historians, such as William Culp Darrah, Wallace Stegner, Donald Worster, and Ed Dolnick, are akin to virgins writing authoritatively about sex. Powell historians have not been men of action or professional whitewater boatmen with first-descent expeditions on uncharted rivers under their belts. Hence they could not understand the true nature of the 1869 expedition. I can assert that Bradley's writing captures the joys and pains of a first descent with clarity, accuracy, exuberance, optimism, wry humor, and self-effacing modesty, without undo "worry" or "petulance."

SELECTED JOURNAL ENTRIES

The following entries are a small fraction of Bradley's ninety-nine-day, 22,200-word journal. Daily entries are abbreviated here due to space limitations, but misspellings and questionable grammar are presented as Bradley wrote them. Although the full journal provides a vastly more comprehensive view of the 1869 experience, these vignettes offer insights into the expedition and the expeditionaries themselves, especially George Bradley.

June 3rd. 69. After eating a hearty breakfast of fried grouce and hot biscuit went out to hunt for game and foccils. Found neither but found the country just as I expected, too much covered with trees and earth to be an interesting place to study geology. Think it will not be many years before these green hills will be covered with cattle and dotted here and there with the homes of ranchmen, for the hillsides are green and watered with little mountain torrents that seem to leap and laugh down the hillsides in wild delight. Can stand on almost any eminence and overlook thousands and thousands of acres of most excellent grazing land, and we have lowered our altitude and latitude until it is warm enough to raise almost any kind of vegetables that will grow in northern New England. Think it would pay well to buy cattle in Texas and bring them here to fatten and then send them to market, but it would not pay to raise horses for the Indians (Utes) would steal too many of them to make it profitable. Have not yet seen any Indians on our journey and if we do they will be Utes, and they are friendly and we are prepared to trade with them.

June 8. 69. Started quite early this morning and find that what seemed comparatively easy rapids from the top of the mountains are quite bad ones, and as we advanced they grew worse until we came to the wildest rapid yet seen. I succeeded in making a landing in an eddy just above where the dangerous part begins. So did one of the other heavy boats.

But one (the "*No Name*") with three men in it [Oramel Howland, Seneca Howland, and Frank Goodman] with one third of our provisions, half our mess-kitt, and all three of the barometers went over the rapid, and though the men escaped with their lives yet they lost all of their clothing, bedding, &c., everything except shirt and drawers, the uniform in which we all pass rapids. It is a serious loss to us and we are rather low spirrited tonight for we must camp right at the head of a roaring rapid more than a mile in length and in which we have already lost one of our boats and nearly lost three of our number. Yet I trust the sun of another day will bring better cheer. "All's well that ends well," but the end is not yet.

June 17. 69. We camped for this night on a little point where the mountain pine and sage-brush was very thick, and the cook built his fire and had supper on the way when the fire spread to the pines. At first we took little notice of it but soon a whirlwind swept through the cañon and in a moment the whole point was one sheet of flames. We seized whatever we could and rushed for the boats and amid the rush of wind and flames we pushed out and dropped down the river a few rods. My handkerchief was burned that I had tied around my neck, and my *ears* and face badly scorched. We had hardly landed before the fire was again upon us and we were forced to run a bad rapid to escape it. We got through safely however and are alright tonight except that we lost most of our mess kit.

July 8. 69. Have made a run of 12 miles. Didn't start until 1 o'clock PM. Climbed the mountain this morning, found it a very hard one to ascend, but we succeeded at last. In one place Major, having but one arm, could not get up; so I took off my drawers and they made an excellent substitute for rope, and with that assistance he got up safe.

Found the mountain 1,500 ft. above the river. The scenery from its summit is wild and dessolate. A succession of craggy peaks like the one we were on was all we could see near us. We seemed to be in about the center of the range as we could look backwards or forwards and they looked about the same in extent, so judge we have got half way through the cañon—but not the worst half for since we started today we have had a succession of bad rappids but have run them all through. One, I think, was the worst we ever ran. Every boat was half full of water when we got through. It is a wild and exciting game,

and aside from the danger of losing our provisions and having to walk out to civilization, I should like to run them all, for the danger to life is only trifling. We could almost sure get to land on one side or the other for the river generally narrows up considerably where the rapids are, so that we are near the shore.

July 11. 69. Sunday again and Major has got his match, for in attempting to run a rapid his boat swamped [capsized], lost all of his bedding, one barometer, and two valuable rifles which we can ill afford to loose as it leaves but 7 rifles in the outfit and we may meet Indians who will think our rations worth a fight, though if they try it they will find them dear rations. The rapid is not so bad as some we have run but they shipped a heavy sea at the start which made their boat unmanageable and she rowled over and over turning everything out. Major had to leave the boat and swim to land as he has lost one arm and her constant turning over made it impossible for him to hold onto her with one hand. But the other two (Jack & Dunn) brought the boat in below safe with the losses stated and the loss of the oars [the only two that remained on the boat]. We will have to make some oars so Major is compelled to keep Sunday, though against his will. Weather windy. Run $^1/_2$ mile.

July 23. 69. Another day of hard labor. Have made $5^1/_2$ miles with three good long portages and all the way rappids. Much of the last three miles we have let down with ropes. Rappids get worse as we advance and the walls get higher and nearly perpendicular. We camp tonight above a succession of furious cataracts. There are at least five in the next mile around which we shall have to make portages. Let it come. We know that we have got about 2,500 ft. to fall yet before we reach Ft. Mohava, and if it comes all in the first hundred miles we shan't be dreading rapids afterwards, for if it should continue at this rate much more than a hundred miles, we should have to go the rest of the way *uphill*, which is *not often the case with rivers*. Major estimates that we shall fall fifty feet in the next mile, and he always underestimates. We have as yet found no place on the Colorado where we could not land on either side of the river, for though the walls come quite close to the water yet there has always been a strip of fallen rocks or a sand bank. Where we lay yesterday there was a sand beach half a mile long and much of the way more than a hundred yds. wide.

July 29. 69. Run 20 miles with ease. Found many small rappids or what we call *small* ones now but which would pass for *full-grown cataracts* in the States. We like them much for they send us along fast and easy and lower our altitude very much.

Major named the new stream "Dirty Devil Creek" and as we are the only white men who have seen it, I for one feel quite highly complimented by the name, yet it is in keeping with his whole character, which needs only a short study to be read like a book.

Those mountains we saw last night are not snow clad. We passed them today, leaving them on our right. They have considerable wood on them and are quite grand in appearance as they contain harder rocks than any we have before seen on the trip. Bazalt Granite &c. which wears away slowly and gives them a very rough appearance. Hope we shan't meet any such right in our way but expect to do so before we get through for all its explorers of the lower Colorado predict that there are Bazaltic & Granite walls to the unknown cañon from 3,000 to 6,000 ft. high. If so we ought to meet them pretty soon for we are fast making distance into the unknown.

We found an old ruin of a Moqui house today. It was built in a dessolate place where they could find a little grass and a little low land in which to raise a few vegetables. It must be one or two hundred years since it was inhabited as every trace of path or roof timbers are blotted out. It was built of stone with a thick strong wall some of which is still standing, but most has fallen down. It contained four rooms of the following dimensions: 13 x 16 — 13 x 18 — 13 x 16 — 13 x 28. There was also another not so well preserved built under the bluff as if for a sort of kitchen or shelter for their cattle. We found many specimens of curiously marked fragments of crockery some of which I have saved but may not be able to even get them home. I would like very much to find one of their villages along the river for they are a hospitable people and retain more of the former customs of the old race than any other living tribe.

August 1st. 69. Just saw three sheep this AM but failed to get one of them. The rocks are so smoothe it is impossible to follow them for they can run right up the side of a cliff where man can get no foothold. Their feet are made cupping and the outer surface of the hoof is as sharp as a knife. They seem to have no fear of falling but will leap from rock to rock, never stumbling nor slipping, though they will be a thousand ft. above us and a single miss-step

would dash them to atoms. They are very good eating and we need meat very much, not having over 15 lbs. of bacon in the whole outfit. We are short of everything but flour, coffee, and dried apples, and in a few days our rations will be reduced to that.

Aug. 2nd. 69. In the same camp, doomed to be here another day, perhaps more than that, for Major has been taking observations ever since we came here and seems no nearer done now than when he began. He ought to get the Latitude & Longitude of every mouth of a river not before known and we are willing to face starvation if necessary to do it but further than that he should not ask us to waite and he must go on soon or the consequences will be different from what he anticipates. If we could get game or fish we should be all right but we have not caught a single mess of fish since we left the junction. Major has now agreed to move on in the morning so we feel in good spirrits tonight.

Aug 11. 69. Have been in camp all day for I have nothing to wear on my feet but an old pair of boots in which I cannot climb the mountains and which are my only reliance for making portages. In the boat and much of the time in camp I go bare-foot. But I have a pair of camp moccasins to slip on when the rocks are bad or the sand is too hot. I have given away my clothing until I am reduced to the same condition of those who lost by the shipwreck of our boat. I cannot see a man of the party more destitute than I am. Thank God the trip is nearly ended for it is no place for a man in my circumstances, but it will let me out of the Army and for that I would almost agree to explore the River Styx. I have rigged a stone table and chair and have commenced again to copy my notes. Have copied some from time to time and find it much easier than to do it all at once. Shall get them copied to date if we stay here tomorrow and I fear we shall have to stay several days, though Jack got one set of observations today which gives us time once more. And if it is not cloudy, Major will get Latitude on the North Star tonight, but it is generally cloudy at night. He is going to get Longitude by the sun & moon, which he can probably get tomorrow as it don't cloud up generally until two or three PM.

Our camp is under the shelving edge of a cliff on the south side of the Chiquito and is protected from both sun and rain by overhanging rocks, though it is filthy with dust and alive with insects. If this is a specimine of Arrazona a very little of it will do for me. The men are uneasy and discontented and anxious to move on. If Major does not do something soon I fear the consequences. But he is contented and seems to think that biscuit made of sour and musty flour and a few dried apples is ample to sustain a laboring man. If he can only study geology he will be happy without food or shelter, but the rest of us are not afflicted with it to such an alarming extent.

Aug. 27. 69. Run 12 miles today but at noon we came to the worst rapid yet seen. The water dashes against the left bank and then is thrown furiously back against the right. The billows are huge and I fear our boats could not ride them if we could keep them off the rocks. The spectical is appalling to us. We have only subsistance for about five days and have been trying half a day to get arround this one rappid while there are three others in sight below. What they are we cannot tell, only that they are huge ones. If we could get on the cliff about a hundred yards below the head of this one, we could let our boats down to that point and then have foothold all the rest of the way, but we have tried all the PM without success. Shall keep trying tomorrow and I hope that by going farther back in the mountains and then coming down opposite we may succeed. Think Major now gone to try it.

There is discontent in camp tonight and I fear some of the party will take to the mountains but hope not. This is decidedly the darkest day of the trip but I don't dispair yet. I shall be one to try to run it rather than take to the mountains. "Tis darkest just before the day" and I trust our day is about to dawn.

Aug. 28. 69. Tried in vain to get arround or down the cliff and come to the determination to run the rappid or perish in the attempt. Three men refused to go farther (two Howlands & Wm. Dunn), and we had to let them take to the mountains. They left us with good feelings though we deeply regret their loss for they are as fine fellows as I ever had the good fortune to meet.

We crossed the river and carried our boats arround one bad point with great labor. And leaving the "*Emma Dean*" tied to shore, all the remainder of the party (six all told) got into the two large boats and dashed out into the boiling tide with all the courage we could muster. We rowed with all our might until the billows became too large to do anything but hold on to the boats, and by good fortune both boats came out at the bottom of the rappid,

well soaked with water of course but right side up and not even an oar was lost. The three boys stood on the cliff looking at us and, having waved them adieu, we dashed through the next rappid and then into an eddy where we stopped *to catch our breath* and bail out the water from our now nearly sunken boats. We had never [run] such a rappid before but we have run a worse one since that, this PM.

THE FATE OF GEORGE YOUNG BRADLEY

While the Powell brothers rode north to Salt Lake City, where the major would lecture the locals with stories about his conquest of the Colorado, George Bradley continued downriver from the mouth of the Virgin River with William Hawkins, Andy Hall, and Jack Sumner. Their easy float was a bit of a holiday, although plagued perhaps by growing disillusionment over the significance of their thousand-mile journey from Green River. These men formed a very elite fraternity, the first professional Grand Canyon river guides, yet none of them wanted to see the place again.

Bradley rode northwest from Fort Yuma to San Francisco by stage. Ten months later, on July 29, 1870, the California census listed a George Y. Bradley from New England living alone without real estate in El Monte Township, Los Angeles County, where he worked as a laborer. Because land there was limited for agriculture, he may have drifted south to become a rancher near San Diego. In the 1940s, Bradley's great nephew E. L. Morss mentioned that his mother could not recall whether Bradley's property was a small ranch or an orchard, nor could she remember where in California he had settled (Morss 1947a). My own search through the San Diego Historical Society turned up no record. City and county directories of 1870–1921 failed to list him, as did biographical files, homestead records, deed books, 1880 census records, and the *San Diego Union*. In short, neither I, nor Darrah some fifty years before me (Owen 1947; Darrah 1946, 1957; Morss 1946, 1947b), found anything to indicate that George Y. Bradley ever lived in San Diego County. The records do show a George Bradley who filed a homestead there in 1882 and 1884, but he may have been the same man who already resided in Ballena on April 17, 1869, five weeks *before* the 1869 expedition launched at Green River. Hence, George Y. Bradley's whereabouts in the Golden State after 1875 remain a mystery.

At any rate, an accident sabotaged Bradley's modest success as a rancher. He began to suffer increasing paralysis, and in the summer of 1885, wrote to his nephew, George E. Morss, who lived in Haverhill, Massachusetts, asking him to come to California to help Bradley return home to Newbury, Massachusetts. He and Morss returned to New England, where Bradley spent his last few months with his family, possibly in West Newbury with his sister, Lucy A. Watson. On November 13, 1885, he died of complications from his injury and was buried in the family plot in the Bridge Street Cemetery in West Newbury. Apparently Bradley's sisters Lucy and Elizabeth (Mrs. Jacob C.) Morss did not recognize the significance of his epic journey down the canyons of the Green and the Colorado. Neither notified the local papers with the news or a fitting obituary. When Bradley died, he did so silently.

This silence was broken thirty years later by Bradley's nephew, Charles Morss, who offered Bradley's journal to the Library of Congress with no restrictions on its publication. Newly transcribed, the journal is a priceless document for the quality of light it sheds on America's quintessential river exploration. Maybe it will help finally break the silence of Bradley's death and gain him that long delayed obituary:

GEORGE Y. BRADLEY

Soldier, Patriot, Geologist, Explorer, & Boatman
A Key Member of the First Six Explorers to
Successfully Traverse
The Great Unknown of the Canyons of the Green and
Colorado Rivers
of the American Southwest in 1869
And Chief Chronicler of the Expedition

As we float along on a muddy stream walled in by huge sandstone bluffs that echo back the slightest sound, hardly a bird save the ill-omened raven or an occasional eagle screaming over us, one feels a sense of loneliness as he looks on the little party, only three boats and nine men, hundreds of miles from civilization bound on an errand the issue of which everybody declares must be disastrous. Yet if he could enter our camp at night or our boats by day, he could read the cool deliberate determination to persevere that possesses every man of the party and would at once predict that the issue of all would be success.

George Y. Bradley was not merely a witness to this success; he was a primary reason for it.

WORKS CITED

Anderson, Martin J. n.d. John Wesley Powell's reporting of history: Fact? Fiction? or Fantasy? Manuscript, MS77, box 1, pp. 10–11. Martin J. Anderson Collection. Cline Library Special Collections, Northern Arizona University, Flagstaff.

Bass, William Wallace, ed. 1920. *Adventures in the canyons of the Colorado by two of its earliest explorers, James White and W. W. Hawkins, with introduction and notes.* Grand Canyon, Ariz.: privately printed.

Bradley, George Young. 1869. Journal, May 24–August 30, 1869. U.S. Library of Congress, Manuscript Division.

Darrah, William Culp. 1946. Letter to E. L. Morss. January 23. William Culp Darrah Collection, Utah State Historical Society, Salt Lake City.

———. 1947a. The Powell Colorado River expedition of 1869. *Utah Historical Quarterly* 15:9–18.

———. 1947b. George Young Bradley 1836–1885. *Utah Historical Quarterly* 15:29–30.

———. 1947c. Letters to Louise Bradley. July 3, July 25. William Culp Darrah Collection, Utah State Historical Society, Salt Lake City.

———. 1957. Letter to E. L. Morss. June 18. William Culp Darrah Collection, Utah State Historical Society, Salt Lake City.

Morss, E. L. 1946. Letter to W. C. Darrah. November 27. William Culp Darrah Collection, Utah State Historical Society, Salt Lake City.

———. 1947a. Letter to W. C. Darrah. February 11. William Culp Darrah Collection, Utah State Historical Society, Salt Lake City.

———. 1947b. Letters to W. C. Darrah. March 21, June 30. William Culp Darrah Collection, Utah State Historical Society, Salt Lake City.

Owen, A. G. (Supervising Reference Librarian, the City of San Diego). 1947. Letter to W. C. Darrah. July 22. William Culp Darrah Collection, Utah State Historical Society, Salt Lake City.

Sibussat, St. G. L. (Chief, Division of Manuscripts, Library of Congress). 1947. Letter to W. C. Darrah. February 7. William Culp Darrah Collection, Utah State Historical Society, Salt Lake City.

Stanton, Robert Brewster. 1932. *Colorado river controversies.* Repr., Boulder City, Nev.: Westwater, 1982.

———. n.d. The river and the cañon: The Colorado River of the West, and the exploration, navigation, and survey of its cañons, from the standpoint of an engineer. Unpublished manuscript. Cline Library Special Collections, Northern Arizona University, Flagstaff.

Worster, Donald. 2001. *A river running west: The life of John Wesley Powell.* New York: Oxford University Press.

Chapter Twenty-Five

AN APPOINTMENT WITH DEATH:
THE HOWLAND-DUNN TRAGEDY REVISITED

BY FRANK M. BARRIOS

For decades a mystery, more recently a heated controversy, the "desertion" and disappearance of Oramel Howland, Seneca Howland, and Bill Dunn from the first Powell expedition haunts riverside campfires to this day. Frank M. Barrios reexamines the evidence and tracks the three men from Green River, Wyoming, to one of the most remote landscapes in the United States in the 1860s, the Arizona Strip.

On August 28, 1869, Oramel Howland, his brother Seneca Howland, and Bill Dunn stood on a high ridge overlooking the Colorado River and watched in amazement as two small, wooden boats, *Kitty Clydes Sister* and *Maid of the Canyon*, fell into a muddy, churning mass of water. The boats momentarily disappeared in the tumultuous rapid below them only to reappear downstream, springing from the turbulent flow as if shot from a cannon. No doubt the men glanced at each other and agreed that they had made the correct decision to go no farther on Major John Wesley Powell's now famous Colorado River expedition through the Grand Canyon.

Much of what happened to these three men may never be known. We have an excellent written record of events leading up to the moment that the Howlands and Dunn left the expedition and began their trek northward from the mouth of what has long been called Separation Rapid. We have a written record of the meeting between Powell, his Mormon guide Jacob Hamblin, and Shivwits Indians who claimed to have killed the three men. There is also a volcanic rock at the top of Mount Dellenbaugh with the chiseled inscription, "Dunn." Nevertheless, many unanswered questions remain to fuel the controversy of what happened to these men.

They began their ill-fated journey at the mouth of Separation Canyon, but this canyon has many side drainages and no one knows for certain which they chose

to ascend, nor do we know the route they took to reach Mount Dellenbaugh. Since their bodies were never found, we have no idea where they were killed. This remote segment of Arizona remains almost as wild as it was in 1869, in some ways hampering the search for answers.

Today I will review what is known of this historical event and examine several subsequent incidents and explorations that may help fill in some historical gaps. I begin at the start of the expedition in Green River, Wyoming, but dwell on the probable route taken by Dunn and the Howlands through Separation Canyon and on to Mount Dellenbaugh. My proposed route is largely based on that taken by three local men stranded at the mouth of Separation in 1931 who did manage to make their escape, unlike Powell's men.

The first Powell expedition began at 1:00 PM on May 24, 1869, at Green River, Wyoming, in four boats: the *Emma Dean, Kitty Clydes Sister, Maid of the Canyon*, and *No Name*. The crew consisted of Major John Wesley Powell, his brother Walter, and eight other men accustomed to the out-of-doors, an ad hoc collection of hunters, trappers, mountain men, drifters, and pickups. Oramel Howland was the only formally educated man other than Major Powell. Although Powell does not mention friction among the crew, later interviews with some of the men and their journals reveal that friction did exist.

It took more than three months for the party to reach the spot where Dunn and the Howlands left the others. It had been a perilous journey. The *No Name* was destroyed in Lodore Canyon on the Green River, and even earlier, one of the pickups, Frank Goodman, had simply walked away. So by the time they reached Arizona Territory, the expedition had already been reduced by one man, one boat, much of their equipment and food, and a good deal of their enthusiasm. Their experiences through the Grand Canyon were, if anything, worse, and we may surmise that whatever friction existed among the crew had not lessened. When they reached Separation Rapid near the end of the canyon, the Howlands and Dunn informed Powell that they would attempt to climb out rather than proceed in the boats. Today a bronze plaque marks the location where the men separated; the name given the side canyon and rapid also commemorates the event.

Just before noon on August 27, 1869, the expedition reached this point of decision. Powell decided to camp here for the night, which gave the men time to ponder their limited options. Powell himself may have questioned the advisability of continuing on the river, but by morning, only Dunn and the Howland brothers had decided to leave. Powell left the *Emma Dean* in case the three men changed their minds and gave them a duplicate set of records, two rifles, a shotgun, and a letter from Powell to his wife. The remaining six men cleared the perilous rapid, fired weapons to signal their successful run, and waited two hours for the three to follow before continuing downriver. Three days later Powell and his remaining crew made it to the mouth of the Virgin River and were assisted by Mormon residents. Dunn and the Howlands vanished, but a Salt Lake City newspaper on September 7, 1869, published an unconfirmed report that three men had been killed by the Shivwits band of Southern Paiutes on the Arizona Strip.

In September 1870 Powell returned to the Arizona Strip to prepare for his second expedition and to find out what had happened to his men. Mormon missionary and guide Jacob Hamblin agreed to guide Powell and help him learn of the men's fate. He led Powell to a remote corner of the Strip and arranged a meeting with the Shivwits, who freely admitted killing the men. Their story, translated by Hamblin, was that when three men had arrived in one of their camps exhausted and nearly starved, they were given food and sent on their way. Shortly after their departure, an Indian from the east side of the Colorado River arrived in camp and reported that miners had killed one of their women in a drunken brawl. The Shivwits considered this information, as well as the story the men had told of boating through the Grand Canyon where no one had boated before, and decided that they had lied to cover their guilt. Consequently, the Shivwits pursued, ambushed, and killed all three. They apologized to Powell

and told him that if they had known the truth they would have aided instead of killed the men. Both Powell and Hamblin wrote about this meeting, and although the versions are very similar, Hamblin wrote that the men had been killed as they slept while Powell wrote that they were killed while obtaining water from a spring.

Another version of how and by whom the men were killed is found in Robert Brewster Stanton's *Colorado River Controversies* (1932). Stanton summarized an interview with Jack Sumner, one of the 1869 crew members, wherein Sumner claimed that the three men were killed by whites, presumably local Mormons. Sumner in later years claimed to have seen the silver watch he had entrusted to the men at Separation Rapid in the hands of a white man. When the man boasted of how he had acquired the watch, Sumner tried to get a look at it for positive identification but could not get his hands on it. Although Sumner knew the evidence was not conclusive, the incident was enough to convince him that the Shivwits were not responsible for the killings and may in fact have had nothing to do with them.

Authors of a recently published book supply further evidence that tends to support Sumner's theory. A letter written in 1883 and found recently near Hurricane, Utah, remarks on the killing of three men by local Mormon residents, but does not identify the men as Dunn and the Howlands. The book also relates the theory of the late local author and retired professor, Wesley Larson, who identified the killer, or one of the killers, as Eli N. Pace, a son-in-law of John D. Lee. This controversial alternative to the killings is intriguing, but it is likely that most of the historical community still supports the story that the men were killed by the Shivwits acting alone.

Whatever the details of the men's fate, their exact route from Separation Rapid to the place of their deaths remains a mystery. Very little documentation or physical evidence has been found concerning their final journey. Separation Canyon is a large, steep, and rugged side canyon that drains a large portion of the Shivwits Plateau. It contains several

"Dunn 1869" inscription atop Mount Dellenbaugh. Photograph by the author

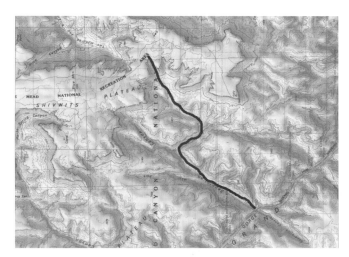

Map showing the probable route the Howlands and Dunn took out of Separation Canyon, from the Colorado River to Kelly Tanks.

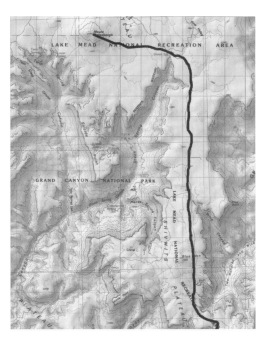

Map showing the probable route the Howlands and Dunn took from Kelly Tanks to Mount Dellenbaugh.

tributaries of its own that are delineated by sheer cliffs impassable to the average hiker. The topography could have doomed the men to death by thirst or starvation, but we know from the two disparate accounts of their deaths that they at least made it out of the Grand Canyon to the Shivwits Plateau. Atop Mount Dellenbaugh, a seven-thousand-foot-high mountain on the canyon's rim, there is a black rock with a heavily faded inscription that reads "Dunn" and "1869." It is very difficult to read, but may at one time have included the word "water" with an arrow pointing north. If authentic, it seems reasonable to conclude that the inscription was made by William Dunn.

The country where the Howland-Dunn trek took place remains remote today. It is bounded on the south by the Grand Canyon and on the north by isolated ranches and the town of Saint George. It is now part of the recently designated Parashant National Monument. The North Rim in the vicinity of Mount Dellenbaugh is typical of the immediate canyon area—relatively flat until plunging several hundred feet to the Esplanade layer of the Supai Group. Below the Esplanade is a near vertical plunge of up to several thousand feet to the river below. Roughly five miles southeast of Mount Dellenbaugh an asymmetrical finger measuring about two miles wide and twenty miles long extends out over the abyss. It is bounded by sheer cliffs on the east, west, and south but connected to the Shivwits Plateau to the north. It is commonly believed that the Howlands and Dunn emerged from Separation Canyon somewhere along this finger, and espied Mount Dellenbaugh as a beacon amidst the flat plateau terrain. It is logical that the men would have headed for the mountain to get their bearings and perhaps see signs of civilization, perhaps smoke from the Mormon community of Saint George. If they did emerge here, they would have hiked

north several miles until reaching the head of what is called today Green Spring Canyon, then headed northwest about five miles to reach the mountain.

To reach Mount Dellenbaugh today, you must drive from Saint George about ninety miles atop a dirt road that is impassable at times. It is common to drive the entire 180-mile round-trip without seeing another vehicle. The land is primarily administered by the Bureau of Land Management as cattle allotments, and there are scattered ranches along the way, many with absentee owners. On the road from Saint George, about ten miles from Mount Dellenbaugh, you encounter one of the oldest and largest cattle operations in this area, the Wildcat Ranch, and the only closed gate you must pass. On the south side of the gate there is a four-foot wooden sign erected by residents of Saint George in 1992. It reads "William Dunn, O. G. Howland and Seneca Howland after leaving Major Powells [*sic*] party came up Separation Canyon and crossed over Mt. Dellenbaugh[. T]hey were killed by Indians east of this marker the last of August, 1869."

This bold proclamation is based on a statement by an old Kaibab Paiute named Toab who in the early part of the twentieth century lived near the Wildcat Ranch. He claimed to have been a small boy when the incident occurred, and he once pointed to a landmark and told local cowboy Jimmy Guerrero that this was where his people had killed the three men from the Powell expedition, and that they had pleaded for mercy as his people killed them. Since Toab was known as a scoundrel who had once admitted to killing a woman near Wolf Hole and to having personally been a part of the ambush on Dunn and the Howlands, his story may be rubbish, but the sign assumes that Toab told the truth. Frederick Dellenbaugh, who accompanied Powell on his second expedition of 1871–72, considered the three men cowards and deserters. Dellenbaugh was later instrumental in having their names omitted from the Powell Memorial at the Grand Canyon's South Rim. He was quoted as saying that this was "correct, leaving off the names of two Howlands and of Dunn because of desertion," but continued that it would be "a graceful thing perhaps to put up on Shivwits Plateau near Mount Dellenbaugh a simple monument to them for they went within a day or two of the end of the voyage and the Major was never condemnatory." Perhaps the wooden sign near Wildcat Ranch serves as such a monument.

In 1931 three young local men found themselves stranded at the mouth of Separation Canyon in a situation similar to the men of 1869. Chester Bundy, Floyd Iverson, and Pat Bundy had launched a small, galvanized-metal boat upstream in search of the body of Iven Bundy, a twenty-three-year-old friend and relative who had drowned many miles upstream. After several days on the river they reached and tried to run Separation Rapid, severely damaging their boat. They decided to climb out Separation Canyon as Powell's men had done sixty-two years earlier, probably the first to try this route since 1869. Their ordeal is described in the history written by Nellie Cox and Helen Russel entitled *Footprints on the Arizona Strip* (1973). The three men walked up the side canyon until reaching a point where three tributaries come together. Pat went up the western tributary and returned in an hour claiming that even a bird

Separation Canyon viewed from the north on top of the Shivwits Plateau. Photograph by the author

could not escape that canyon. Floyd tried the middle canyon with the same result. They knew the eastern tributary had to work or they would all die, and it did provide a way out; all three reached the Shivwits Plateau at nightfall.

Iverson and the Bundys emerged just south of Kelly Tanks, located in the lower southern half of the elongated finger of the plateau previously described. Once on top they walked to safety. This incident suggests that Powell's men may well have taken the same route, the only plausible route according to the young men. In 1978, using this account as their guide, Dr. Michael Belshaw of Prescott led a party of four to retrace the young men's escape. They began at Separation Rapid on May 2, successfully negotiated Separation Canyon, and reached the top of Mount Dellenbaugh on May 5, once again affirming the probable route of William Dunn and the Howland brothers. Dr. Belshaw's story was published in the winter 1979 issue of the *Journal of Arizona History*. Harvey Butchart, in his *Grand Canyon Treks II* (1975), describes a short hike from Kelly Tanks down Separation Canyon to the Colorado River, presumably along the same route.

Butchart mentions no other route out of Separation Canyon, and in all probability, if one existed, he would have tried it and mentioned the attempt. The eastern arm may well be the only possible way out of the canyon. Once atop the Esplanade, Powell's men may have chosen one of several routes to the Shivwits Plateau, but it is logical that they would have stuck to the eastern arm to emerge near Kelly Tanks as others have done since. If you decide to try this route yourself, keep in mind that the entire area is just as arid, difficult, and dangerous—and almost as remote—as in 1869.

HARD HULLS, HARD KNOCKS, HARD HEADS: THE EVOLUTION OF HARD-HULLED ROWBOATS IN THE GRAND CANYON

BY BRAD DIMOCK

Brad Dimock spent twenty-five years as a commercial boatman in the Grand Canyon and on rivers in Utah, Alaska, Mexico, Guatemala, Chile, Ethiopia, and Tanzania. He recently settled down as a writer in Flagstaff, Arizona, "obsessed," he says, with river history. He built a replica of Glen and Bessie Hyde's Idaho sweepscow, piloted it through the Grand Canyon with his wife, Jeri Ledbetter, and parked it at the community building for the enjoyment of symposium participants. Dimock also replicated Buzz Holmstrom's boat, the Julius F., *which he launched at Lees Ferry in March 2002, then used to trace Holmstrom's river-running exploits. Here, Dimock recounts the various types of crafts used on the Colorado River through the Grand Canyon before the advent of inflatable rafts.*

In simple terms, rigid rowboats used in the Grand Canyon over the past century and a half can be categorized into two basic types: the keeled boats of John Wesley Powell and those who emulated him, and the revolutionary flat-bottomed boats that supplanted the Powell type. Flat-bottomed boats are represented by three distinctive styles: Galloway, Nevills cataract, and Oregon drift boat, or "dory."

These boats were rowed in one of two basic ways. Powell and his followers faced upriver and pulled hard, propelling the boat down the river. Later flat-bottomed boats, by and large, used a method generally credited to Nathaniel Galloway in the 1890s, wherein the boatman faced downriver and rowed upstream against the current to increase maneuverability.

As with any gross generalization, there are many variations and a few glitches that defy these categories. The following is a summary of hard-hulled boats and methods used on the Colorado River.

POWELL

Major John Wesley Powell opened exploration on the Colorado in an eastern, flatwater-style boat called a Whitehall. Whitehalls were round-sided boats rising from a full-length keelboard, built in caravel fashion; that is, the thin planks that formed the sides butted tight against one another, forming a smooth, tight seam. They were designed for speed on relatively smooth water, and when loaded with weight in the bottom (ballasted), they were quite stable, even in rough water. Unfortunately, these craft could not turn corners quickly or effectively.

Whitehalls were rowed with one or two oarsmen facing upstream, pulling hard downstream. Steering was usually aided by a sweep oar off the stern, operated by another boatman who stood facing downstream. With the deep draft of the keelboard, accelerated downstream speed, and lack of maneuverability, these boats were poorly adapted to shallow,

A precise replica of a twenty-two-foot Whitehall boat used on the 1869 Powell expedition. Photograph by Tim Cooper

rocky whitewater. In spite of that, they were popular for many years. The classic size was twenty-one-feet long by four-feet wide, with watertight hatches at each end and a large open cockpit. They were rowed with eight-foot oars and steered with a much longer twelve- to fourteen-foot sweep oar.

Expeditions that used Powell-type Whitehalls:

FIRST POWELL EXPEDITION, 1869: Three twenty-one- to twenty-two-foot boats and one sixteen-foot boat, with a sweep oar likely. Although there are no known photographs or definitive descriptions of the boats on Powell's first expedition, most researchers believe they were similar to those of Powell's much-photographed second expedition.

SECOND POWELL EXPEDITION, 1871–72: Three twenty-one- to twenty-two-foot boats with sweep oars and a central hatch to reduce cockpit size. These are featured in nearly all images of the Powell expeditions. They were built by Bagley Boat Works in Chicago.

BROWN-STANTON EXPEDITION, 1889: Brown chose light cedar boats for ease of portaging. They were very brittle, much like canoes, and fared poorly. These were abandoned after Brown and two other party members drowned in Marble Canyon.

STANTON EXPEDITION, 1890: Stanton returned to complete his railway survey through the Grand Canyon with stouter boats. As an interesting safety measure, he added emergency barrels loaded with supplies, sealed tight and built into the boats, in hopes they could be salvaged after the inevitable wrecks. They were.

LOPER/RUSSELL/MONETT, 1907: Apparently Charles Russell, Edwin Monett, and Bert Loper ordered their wood-framed, steel-skinned Whitehalls from a boat fabricator. Just how they rowed them is uncertain, and only one boat survived the trip.

CLYDE EDDY, 1927: Eddy ordered oversize Powell boats and operated each with five men—two pairs sitting abreast, each with one oar, and one sweep oarsman in back. This arrangement might have worked okay if they had used the Powell rowing method, but instead they chose the Galloway technique, which works poorly if at all with a keeled boat. Fortunately, they had very high water and wallowed through.

A woodcut showing the launch of the 1889 Brown/Stanton expedition, published in Scribner's Magazine *in 1890*

GALLOWAY

Nathaniel Galloway is credited with introducing a light-weight, flat-bottomed (flat from side to side and keel-less) boat with upturn, or "rocker," at either end. Construction was of thin, narrow planks, sometimes jointed caravel fashion, sometimes lapstrake (individual sideboards overlap each other). Although not as fast as Whitehalls, the Galloway boat pivoted easily and drafted little water. Galloway is also credited with introducing the stern-first technique of descending the river, rowing upstream, and ferrying laterally to avoid obstacles. Galloway's boats and his rowing style made river running far more practical, and, with some modifications, his boats and methods are still used today.

Expeditions that used Galloway-style boats:

GALLOWAY, 1897: Galloway began designing, building, and rowing wooden boats on the upper Green River in the 1890s. Those he built himself no longer exist. River historians assume that the boats he built for his 1907 expedition with Julius Stone are based on his homebuilt prototypes.

GALLOWAY/STONE, 1907: Julius Stone financed these boats and Galloway oversaw their construction. They were sixteen feet long by four feet wide and had six inches of rocker. They were built of thin lumber with caravel-jointed sides. One of these boats survives and is presently being restored at Grand Canyon National Park—the oldest extant Galloway-style boat known to have run the river through the Grand Canyon.

Nathaniel Galloway rowing his boat through Split Mountain Canyon, 1909. Photograph by Raymond Cogswell. Courtesy of Cline Library, Special Collections, Northern Arizona University, Flagstaff (NAU.PH.97.34.46)

KOLB, 1911–12: The Kolb brothers, after obtaining designs from Julius Stone, ordered two boats built in Racine, Wisconsin. Like Stone's and Galloway's, they were sixteen feet long and four feet wide with six inches of rocker, but they were of lapstrake construction and therefore stronger. Both boats still exist, the *Edith* at Grand Canyon National Park and the *Defiance* at the Powell Museum in Green River, Utah.

RUSSELL/CLEMENT/ TADJE, 1914: Bert Loper built the *Ross Wheeler*, the only survivor of this trip. It is galvanized steel over a steel frame, and today rests on the left bank of the Colorado River near Mile 108 in the Grand Canyon.

Ellsworth Kolb's Defiance, *built by the Racine Boat Company using specifications supplied by Julius F. Stone. Photograph by the author*

UNITED STATES GEOLOGICAL SURVEY, 1921–23: The rugged boats used by the Birdseye expedition were over-sized Galloways. They measured twenty-one feet long by four feet, six inches wide with six inches of rocker and lapstrake sides. One of these, the *Glen*, now resides at Grand Canyon National Park.

PATHE-BRAY, 1927: A fleet of five or six of these boats was built for this 1927 motion-picture trip. When the trip ended prematurely at Hermit Rapid, one was dragged out by cable and shipped to Hollywood; the rest were abandoned near the rapid. One of these, the *Bright Angel*, was later run by Francy and Harbin, then Ervin and Paine in 1928.

HATCH/SWAIN/FRAZIER, 1934: The so-called Colorado River Club began building Galloway-style boats from ply-wood in the 1930s. Members often rowed in a mock Powell style, backing willy-nilly down the rapids. Their boat names reflected their cavalier attitude: *What's Next, Don't Know,* and *Who Cares.*

CARNEGIE-CAL TECH EXPEDITION, 1937: This trip lead by Frank Dodge used large, very heavy mahogany Galloway boats. Some of these had been constructed for the Fairchild trips in lower Grand Canyon earlier in the 1930s.

BUZZ HOLMSTROM, 1937: Holmstrom hybridized the Galloway style from drift boats he saw in Oregon, creating a much stronger, quicker craft. It was fifteen feet long by four-and-one-half feet wide, and had an increased rocker of ten inches. Holmstrom built his boat, the *Julius F.*, out of Port Oxford cedar with lapstrake construction. The *Julius F.* was the last of the wooden-plank boats and the finest iteration of the Galloway style.

Holmstrom rowed in classic Galloway style in 1937, but by 1938 had begun incorporating elements of the Hatch backing-into-the-rapid entry. By combining the two styles, he was able to bust out of the initial violence of the rapid in Hatch style, then spin into the more controlled Galloway style for the remainder of the rapid. By doing so, Holmstrom presaged the modern rowing technique.

BERT LOPER, 1939–49: Loper continued to build boats in the Galloway style, similar in lines to his earlier *Ross Wheeler* but made of plywood. His final boat, *Grand Canyon*, was crudely built but got him far enough downstream to die of a probable heart attack just three weeks short of his eightieth birthday. The mostly decayed remains of the *Grand Canyon* rest near River Mile 41.

NEVILLS

In 1938 Norman Nevills introduced the cataract boat. Built of plywood, it was considerably wider than a Galloway with a pointed bow behind the boatman while the wide, blunt stern faced downstream. The cockpit was very large, like a Galloway, and cataracts were rowed in the Galloway style, but being far wider they were both more stable and able to carry a greater load. Cataracts remained popular until inflatables and motorized travel were introduced in the 1950s.

In the 1950s Nevills's boatman P. T. Reilly made a series of modified cataract boats, decking over much of the oversized footwell and bringing the blunt stern to a point to penetrate waves. Although Reilly's boats swamped less because of their smaller cockpits, they went under as many waves as they went over because of their low, flat decks.

River trips that used Nevills-style cataract boats:

NEVILLS, 1938–49: Nevills built three boats—*WEN*, *Botany*, and *Mexican Hat*—in the winter of 1937–38, and continued adding to his fleet until his death in 1949. Nevills rowed in the Galloway style, but sometimes used Holmstrom's hybrid entry. Although the cataract was the best passenger boat built up to the 1930s, it still could not take on the largest waves. Consequently, Nevills and his ilk became proficient at sneaking to the sides of bigger rapids,

Buzz Holmstrom in his boat at Hoover Dam, 1938. Photograph by Bill Belknap. Courtesy of Cline Library, Special Collections, Northern Arizona University, Flagstaff (NAU.PH.96.4.113.6)

Norman Nevills's cataract boats, 1949. Photograph by P. T. Reilly. Courtesy of Cline Library, Special Collections, Northern Arizona University, Flagstaff (NAU.PH.97.46.2.55)

From left: Chet Kelvin, Bert Loper, Bill Gibson, and Don Harris, in Galloway-style boats, 1939. Photograph by Bill Belknap. Courtesy of Cline Library, Special Collections, Northern Arizona University, Flagstaff (NAU.PH.96.114.10)

or "cheating" them, creating a generation of excellent technical boatmen.

MEXICAN HAT EXPEDITIONS, 1950–69: After Nevills's death in 1949, Frank Wright and brothers Jim and Bob Rigg continued to operate his company as Mexican Hat Expeditions. The company later passed to Gaylord Staveley and his wife (Nevills's daughter), Joan. In 1969 they ran their last trip in cataract boats. The *Wen* and *Mexican Hat* still survive, the former at Grand Canyon National Park, the latter at the Powell Museum in Green River, Utah.

REYNOLDS/HALLACY: These were copies of the Nevills boats, run on the upper stretches of the Green until its damming in 1963.

HARRIS/BRENNAN, 1950s: Don Harris, who helped Nevills build the original three cataract boats, received the *Mexican Hat* in trade for his labor. After separating from Nevills, he began running private trips with Bert Loper, then commercial trips with Jack Brennan, who built another cataract boat. Harris abandoned wooden rowboats for powered aluminum skiffs in the 1950s, then moved on to large inflatable pontoon rafts before retirement in the 1970s.

P. T. REILLY, 1949–64: Reilly built modified cataract boats in the late 1950s and ran several trips in them. He was often plagued by high water, which battered his fiberglass boats until they finally became unseaworthy. Midway through a high-water trip in 1959, he scuttled the boats near Phantom Ranch and hiked out.

LITTON

In 1962 Martin Litton, who had rowed the Grand Canyon with P. T. Reilly in 1954–55, imported an Oregon drift-boat hull to the Grand Canyon. These boats had a high ten-inch rocker, extremely high ends, and radically flared sides for stability in rough water (the evolution of this hull is another story). Flared sides widened the distance between oarlocks, allowing boatmen to go from a stubby eight-foot oar to a much more efficient ten-foot oar. Litton teamed with Reilly to incorporate Reilly's full decking of the boat. This boat was able to carry more passengers and cargo than prior hard-hulls.

Drift boats, more often called dories, were the first Grand Canyon boats designed to withstand the big waves of center current. Formerly, boaters had tried to avoid the biggest waves by "cheating" to the sides of the current near shore. This led to a modified Galloway rowing style, wherein boatmen still faced downstream, rowing upstream or across current to make the toughest moves. But for easier moves or less critical runs, they began pushing the boat downstream into rapids, something like motorboat runs. The push technique in rapids has been taken to remarkable extremes by some dory and raft boatmen in the last two decades.

LITTON, GRAND CANYON DORIES, 1962–87: Litton began running dories as a small private enterprise, but by 1970, he had become a full-fledged commercial outfitter. By the time he sold the company, he had put more than four dozen dories on the river, bringing the hard-hulled boat back into prominence in the Grand Canyon. Although most of his craft were built of plywood in Oregon, he also experimented with aluminum hulls.

GRAND CANYON DORIES, GRAND CANYON EXPEDITIONS, AND OTHERS, 1980S–PRESENT: Litton's old company still runs dories under the ownership of OARS, Inc. Meanwhile, the hard-hulls have spread to other companies as well, with Grand Canyon Expeditions, Arizona River Runners, Tour West, and others running them periodically. Private boaters are now buying and running (and wrecking) them as well. Modern dories are usually made of wood/epoxy laminate, although some have a foam core and others consist of aluminum.

GLITCHES AND MISFITS

JAMES WHITE, 1867: White was likely the first person to float the entire length of the Grand Canyon, and he did it on a log raft two years before Powell's first expedition. White's design of driftwood and rope has had few adherents since that time.

GEORGE FLAVELL, 1897: Flavell's boat was fifteen feet long, took eight days to build, and had little if any decking. He was described as rowing it facing downstream pushing on the oars (in flat water at Green River, Utah), but in his journal he describes pulling in rapids and adding a second set of oars for the Grand Canyon. Not enough is known to classify his boat or rowing style with certainty.

HUM WOOLLEY, 1903: Woolley left no record of his boat type or rowing style. However, both he and Flavell must rate extremely high as self-taught boatmen.

GLEN AND BESSIE HYDE, 1928: Glen and Bessie Hyde built an Idaho sweep-scow for their 1928 honeymoon trip. Although the scow was a popular and viable craft in Idaho at that time, and Hyde had mastered sweepscow technique on the Salmon in 1926, the scow is poorly suited to the pool-and-drop rapids of the Grand Canyon. Their trip proved fatal, and sweepscows gained no following in the Grand Canyon.

P. T. Reilly's double-ended cataract boats at Deer Creek Falls, 1958. Photograph by P. T. Reilly. Courtesy of Cline Library, Special Collections, Northern Arizona University, Flagstaff (NAU.PH.97.46.29.35)

Martin Litton rowing an aluminum drift boat (dory), 1994. Photograph by Richard Jackson. Courtesy of Cline Library, Special Collections, Northern Arizona University, Flagstaff (NAU.PH.94.37.221)

Chapter Twenty-Seven

Evolution of the Printed Colorado River Guide in Grand Canyon, Arizona

by Richard D. Quartaroli

The third edition of Larry Stevens's guide The Colorado River in Grand Canyon *has served me well during five Grand Canyon river trips. As Richard D. Quartaroli reveals, everyone since John Wesley Powell has had some form of printed material to tell them where they were and what they might expect downstream.*

Although many of today's twenty-five thousand annual Colorado River runners carry a guide, the evolution of printed guides over the past 135 years is not widely known. The purpose of my presentation is to offer a comprehensive bibliography and chronology, realizing space limitations and the possibility of as yet unknown variations. Guides may be roughly categorized into four groups: published accounts of previous river runners, the Birdseye Plan and Profile maps from the 1923 U.S. Geological Survey (USGS), publications containing information but not intended specifically as guides, and maps/guides based on the Birdseye maps and other USGS topographic maps.

PUBLISHED ACCOUNTS OF PREVIOUS RIVER RUNNERS

If James White indeed floated through the Grand Canyon on a cottonwood raft in 1867, he certainly did not have prior geographic information, printed or otherwise (Adams 2001; Dawson 1917). Major John Wesley Powell's 1869 expedition had the latest government map—an 1868 Warren/Freyhold—as well as a Mormon map identified in my other presentation ("GPS in 1869," page 129) at this symposium (Bradley 1947, 56–57). Powell's 1872 half-trip through the canyon benefited, of course, from his 1869 maps, accounts, and personal experience (Rusho 1969, 208;

Exploration of the Colorado River 1948–49). Frank Mason Brown's and Robert Brewster Stanton's river trips in 1889 and 1890 "had with [them] a transcript of Major Powell's [1875] report of his '69 journey" (Stanton 1965, 39–40). On November 15, 1896, George F. Flavell wrote Stanton, "I had your report of the Colorado which was of great value to me (in *Scribner's Magazine* [Stanton 1890, 591–613]). . . . I thought I would write to you and ask you about the Upper River in your report" (Stanton 1906–09, 999).

Julius F. Stone wrote during his run in 1909, "Before starting this morning I gave Coggswell all the maps, as well as Powell's [1875] and Dellenbaugh's [1908] books" (Stone 1932, xv, 48, 55). He also carried USGS maps, inferred by Stone's reference to "the Shinumo Quadrangle [Douglas et al. 1908] of the government map" (Stone 1932, 95).

On their 1911–12 trip, brothers Ellsworth and Emery Kolb remarked, "We got out our guide-book—Dellenbaugh's 'A Canyon Voyage' [1908]. . . . This book has been our guide down to this point; we could not have asked for a better one. Below here we had a general idea of the nature of the river, and had a set of the government maps, but we had neglected to provide ourselves with detailed information such as this volume gave us." They probably referred to USGS topographical or geological maps, ones they described at the confluence of the Green and Grand rivers as "the contour maps we carried" (Kolb 1914, 135, 249, 121).

PLAN AND PROFILE OF THE COLORADO RIVER

Prior to, and as a direct result of, battles over western water leading to the Colorado River Compact, the USGS under Colonel Claude H. Birdseye surveyed western rivers and potential damsites and published a series of maps (Jones and Helland 1948). When Birdseye's 1923 Grand Canyon party, with Emery Kolb as head boatman, reached Topographical Engineer R.W. Burchard's 1920 upstream "tie" at River Mile 251 (Westwood 1992, 217), they had completed the major portion of the survey of the Colorado River system. Birdseye and Burchard's *Plan and Profile of Colorado River from Lees Ferry, Ariz., to Black Canyon, Ariz.-Nev., and Virgin River, Nev.* (1924)—in twenty-one sheets of fourteen plans (maps) and seven profiles—increased the information about the course of the river within the Grand Canyon so appreciably that eighty years later it is still the basis for all subsequent river guides. In fact, even with today's state-of-the-art surveying technology, it is only recently that improvements in the Birdseye work have become possible (Brod 1997; Gonzales 2002).

Birdseye's "plan" is the course of the river laid out in sections horizontally with land-contour intervals of fifty feet; like a topographic map, it is a top-down view showing the course of the river. The "profile" is the elevation of the river with river-surface-contour intervals of five feet, a side view wherein the river's descent is shown continuously for calmer stretches (pools) and the steeper descents (drops) in rapids. As the "Plan and Profile" became available, many post-1923 river runners referred to them or carried them down the river.

During Clyde Eddy's 1927 trip, with Galloway's son Parley as head boatman, Eddy "reviewed Dellenbaugh's [1908] account of Powell's expeditions." He worked on and referred to maps many times without naming them. Map confirmation may be implied when Eddy wrote just above Granite Narrows, "Perhaps Birdseye and the Geological Survey were right, after all, in marking the stretch of river as a rapids," and wrote farther downstream, "Indecision Rapids is what I called it in my diary although the government map commemorates Kolb's adventure with the name 'Upset' instead" (Eddy 1929, 100–101, 226, 233).

The 1937 Carnegie-Cal Tech expedition had the express purpose of mapping geological formations. Head boatman Frank Dodge had been with Birdseye, and he and boatman Owen Clark had recently boated below Diamond Creek as part of the Fairchild surveys (Dodge n.d., 69–70). Although they mapped geology directly onto Fairchild aerial photographs, they also did so on the Plan and Profile. Geologist Bob Sharp wrote, "Today have noted similar areas of land slide masses near 135$^1/_2$ mile point and for a half mile downstream from Deer Cr—depression contour on profile map. #E" (Sharp 1937, 44). Buzz Holmstrom caught up with the Carnegie-Cal Tech trip at Diamond Creek and boated with them for several days. Previously "Holmstrom wrote to Colonel Claude Birdseye in Washington, D.C. for more pointers. . . . Birdseye supplied USGS survey maps of the river, an invaluable gift" (Welch et al. 1998, 84).

On Norm Nevills's first commercial Grand Canyon run in 1938, Lois Jotter, a graduate student from the University of Michigan, became one of the first two women to complete a canyon traverse. Although Lois and her father had read the 1924 *National Geographic* account of the Birdseye survey (Freeman 1924, 471–530, 547–548), she had to convince him to let her participate. They visited Birdseye in Washington, D.C., and "he gave her a set of his *Plan and Profile Maps of the Green and Colorado Rivers*—those stretches that the expedition would cover. . . . Norm was able to determine their location accurately by referring to the maps Colonel Birdseye had given to Lois, which Norm kept conveniently at hand in the map holder he had included as an extra feature in the *Wen*" (Cook 1987, 15, 28).

After Nevills died in 1949, Nevills Expeditions partners Frank Wright and Jim Rigg renamed the company Mexican Hat Expeditions. They and Jim's brother Bob continued to carry the Plan and Profile on their river trips (Rigg 2002). Nevills's oldest daughter, Joan, married Gaylord Staveley, who partnered with Wright in 1957, soloed in 1958, and renamed the company Canyoneers in 1962. Staveley commented, "By late 1954 I had seen Norm's scrolled versions . . . a rather heavy-duty brown 'wrapping paper' cut in a strip 11 inches wide . . . of the Plan and Profile sheets among the Nevills papers (and still have a couple of them) but I carried the full sheets in a metal canister" (Staveley 2002). In 1949 Nevills's boatman P. T. Reilly wrote that Nevills had "pasted these cutouts . . . from the sections of the 1923 Survey's maps . . . on a roll of brown wrapping paper and wrote events and dates on the edges of the roll" (Reilly 1992).

Georgie White Clark had a set of the Plan and Profile mounted on brown paper and folded into sixths for easier portability (Clark 1994). Reilly, with Mexican Hat Expeditions from 1950 to 1952, started leading his own noncommercial trips in 1953 (Quartaroli 1999, 462). He also had photocopies of the Plan and Profile and supplied his boatmen with a list of mileages and drops in rapids, developed "from [the] 1923 Survey" (Reilly 1964).

INFORMATIVE PUBLICATIONS THAT ARE NOT SPECIFICALLY RIVER GUIDES

Primarily geological descriptions, the following contain river mileages and descriptions of rapids that are sometimes erroneous. Several were published to celebrate the 1969 centennial of Powell's first trip, including:

- Péwé's geology, which covered the river from Lees Ferry to Phantom Ranch (Péwé 1968, 1969, 1974, 1983)
- Hamblin and Rigby's documentation in three parts—to Phantom Ranch, from Phantom Ranch, and in Cataract Canyon (Hamblin and Rigby 1968, 1969, 1971)
- The Powell Society set. Volume III covered Marble Gorge and the Grand Canyon (Simmons and Gaskill [1969])
- Hamblin and Rigby's work. Served as the "river log" for *Geology and Natural History of the Fifth Field Conference,* a result of the Powell Centennial River Expedition in 1969 (Baars 1969)

USGS Professional Paper 669's "The Rapids and the Pools—Grand Canyon" lists the ten steepest rapids in the first 150 miles in order of decreasing water-surface gradient (Leopold 1969, 138), a manner of rating of rapids I have always found interesting. The Geological Society of America's field guide (Beus 1974, 408–412) contained only a four-page list of geology stops, the mileages taken from Hamblin and Rigby. The International Geological Congress's 1989 *Field Trip Guidebook* incorporated a "Geologic Log" and a "Hydraulic Log" with geology, river miles, and rapid information (Billingsley and Elston 1989, 1–36; Graf et al. 1989, 37–47).

In the 1980s the USGS published Susan Kieffer's work on hydraulics and geomorphology of major rapids. She discussed river rapids and waves, defining terms and mathematical concepts, and her maps of ten major Grand Canyon rapids are both artistic and informative. Beginning in the 1990s, the publications of Melis, Webb, et al—primarily for USGS and the *Boatman's Quarterly Review*—discussed recent and historical debris flows and sediment transport, as well as physical events and actions that change rapids and river running.

Escape Routes from the Colorado River (Davis 1958) is self-explanatory, and its revision, *River to Rim Routes* (Butchart 1970a), covers similar ground. *Information for Running the Colorado through the Grand Canyon* (Davis 1974, 14–15) contains some of the escape routes, minimum impact and resource hints, as well as information now found in commercial and private boating requirements. The three *Grand Canyon Treks* (Butchart 1970b, 1975, 1984, combined reprint 1998) have been joined by *Day Hikes from the River* (Martin 1999, 2002) and *Grand Canyon River Hikes* (Williams 2000).

River Runners Guide through the Marble and Grand Canyons (Grand Canyon Natural History Association 1969) lists mileages, drops in rapids, and rapid ratings. The Sierra Club's *Grand Canyon of the Living Colorado* (Braun 1970, 142) contains an almost exact replication of Reilly's list. When the Sierra Club waged its battle against dams in the Grand Canyon in the 1960s, Reilly and Martin Litton took photographers and writers down the Colorado, accounting for the transfer of Reilly's list to the Sierra Club publication.

Two books called *Grand Canyon Place Names* (Granger 1960; McNamee 1997, 2004) include explanations for names along the Colorado River but only *River to Rim* (Brian 1992) emphasizes them. *Past and Present Biotic Communities of the Lower Colorado River Mainstem and Selected Tributaries*, vol. 2, *Lees Ferry to Lake Mead* (Ohmart 1982) uses a river corridor map to plot vegetation. Sunrise and sunset times for months of the year at popular camp and attraction sites are found in *The Boatman's Almanac* (Sorensen 1998, 1999, 2000), which also helps boatmen find sun in winter. *Looking for Early Shade* (Sorensen and Niemi 2000) helps boatmen find shade in summer.

A River Runner's Guide to the History of the Grand Canyon (Crumbo 1981, 1994) has geographical rather than chronological descriptions of historical events. Along the same line, but also including geology and "little-known facts," is "Coop's Plausible Guide to the River at the Bottom of the Canyon" (Cooper 1996, 16–17), a preliminary "teaser" for the first 12.8 river miles, soon to be expanded to book length (Cooper, forthcoming). Representative of the popular items found are *Recreation on the Colorado River* (Dirksen and Reeves 1985), "River Guide Bandannas and T-Shirts" (Rivers and Mountains [1986]) so that you can "Wear the River!," and *Grand Canyon Colorado River Trip* (Thomas 2000), a laminated card with 108 numbered rapids and locations along the river.

MAPS/GUIDES BASED ON THE BIRDSEYE MAPS AND OTHER USGS TOPOGRAPHIC MAPS

River runners used the Birdseye Plan and Profile maps and altered their structure to make them more practical while actually on the river. The first such variation published was the so-called "Les Jones' Scroll" in 1962. Leslie Allen Jones ran a western river for the first time when his son, Don Hatch, and cousin, Bus, who boated the Grand Canyon in

1934, got him involved with a 1953 Sierra Club trip through Dinosaur National Monument. In 1994 Jones reflected, "I'd noticed when I'd run with the Sierra Club the rapids all kind of ran together as a blur, and I couldn't remember the details well enough, and I didn't have any identification points. So I started my scroll maps—I didn't like the wind on the U.S. Geological [Survey] maps, so I started building my scroll maps.

"The outline of the maps was taken either from aerial photographs and drawn artfully, or traced directly from the contour maps of the U.S. Geological Survey, putting the river end-to-end, instead of cut up in segments like the USGS did, . . . so I could line the river out on a seven-inch scroll strip and then take it from one end to the other, without having to run off the scroll. . . . And then putting a profile of the river . . . wherever it fit best. . . . We had to put them on paper, for lack of mylar. Then we put them on mylar" (Jones 2001, 23–25).

Jones was one of a group of primarily Utah river runners who began Western River Guides Association (WRGA), with bylaws dated February 24, 1954. "Jones, a civil engineer and WRGA officer in charge of 'maps and reconnaissance,' created scroll maps of western rivers that the association made available to members, park rangers, and the public" (Webb 1992, 261, 264). One scroll stated "these maps are not a profit venture but a public service of the Western River Guides Association Inc. . . . Leslie A. Jones, Western River Guides Exec. Sec." (Jones 1964).

Most of the scrolls have 1960s dates; the scroll map for the upper Green River has a 1955 copyright (Jones 1955), but also a 1964 copyright for "River Ratings and Strip Maps." The Dock Marston Collection contains undated copies of Jones's report lists of his 1953 and 1954 trips and a copy, noted 1957, of a preliminary Grand Canyon scroll map, one with only brief historical notations (Marston n.d.). It shows the cuts of the Plan and Profile and the splices making up the scroll, with typewritten notations as opposed to the 1962 lettering in Jones's hand.

With variations in the Grand Canyon scroll, the 1962 copyright is not updated, so one must look for additional notes and trip data to determine the variant. Reilly owned an early seven-inch paper scroll with an end discourse on ratings (Reilly 1999). An eleven-inch paper Grand Canyon scroll, mailed in 1971, contains notes on Jones's 1962 trip and an additional caveat, but lacks the end discourse (Jones 1962a). A greater than seven-inch Mylar scroll purchased in 1983 has notes on his 1963 trip (Jones 1962b). After the 1994 "Old Timers Trip," wherein contemporary scientists and boatmen, as part of the Glen Canyon Environmental Studies, accompanied pre-dam river runners to record their impressions of environmental changes (Webb et al. [2002]),

Jones issued an updated scroll as well as "The Grand Canyon Continuous Photo Album Set" (Jones 1962 [1995]). Originally in paper, Jones made his scroll "water-resistant" by enclosing it in a plastic bag, sealed and scrolled within the bag.

American River Touring Association, an outfitting company, reproduced and sold the Plan and Profile in a smaller format. An introductory page and two additional sheets of "Mileage Schedule" indicate "they are particularly valuable to the Riverman" and compilation is by L. C. B. McCullough with "Range of ratings of rapids given by L. A. Jones, Dock Marston, Don Harris and P. T. Reilly" (American River Touring Association [1966]; McCullough [1966]).

The Belknaps, a longtime river-running family, created the next innovation with their "Powell Centennial" *Grand Canyon River Guide* by making a "Special River Runners Waterproof Edition" (Belknap 1969), following the Jones layout but in a flip-paged book format and sized to fit a standard .30-caliber ammo can. Affectionately nicknamed the "Buzzmap" (Riebeek 1980) after originator Buzz Belknap, this guide included quotes from Powell's 1875 *Report*, historical information, and now-classic photo captions. Buzz and sister Loie completely revised the "Buzzmap" in 1989 into an "All New Color Edition" (Belknap and Evans 1995), still available and one of the most-used guides on the river.

Another outfitter's guide, *Pictorial Color Map of Grand Canyon* (Kingsley et al. 1972), was also "waterproof" with a larger format and foldout maps. Based on geology rather than topography, Jack Currey's Western River Expeditions produced this guide, which acknowledged both the "Buzzmap" and Jones's Scroll. Prior to 1973, outfitter Tour West distributed *Colorado River Map of the Grand Canyon*, containing diagrams of maneuvering strategy through rapids superimposed on the Plan and including the Profile (Hansen [1973]; Whitney 1996). In 1974 Museum of Northern Arizona Curator of Zoology Steven Carothers and an associate began "preparation of a guidebook to the natural history of the Grand Canyon along the Colorado River, as well as to points of scenic and historic interest of the area." Never published, it would have included "Notes on Parking and Maneuvering Rafts, [and] Maps of Major Rapids" (Carothers 1974).

The Bureau of Reclamation and the USGS prepared a series of river mile indexes for most streams in the Pacific Northwest and Southwest. *River Mile Index: Lower Colorado River and Selected Tributaries, Arizona, California, Nevada, and Utah* is distinguished by having, instead of Lees Ferry as Mile 0, "[t]he starting point for the Lower Colorado River mile index . . . at the southerly international boundary with Mexico," with mileages running upstream

(Pacific Southwest Interagency Committee 1976, [ii]).

River runners witnessed releases from Glen Canyon Dam approaching pre-dam volumes in 1983, the same year Larry Stevens released his river guide, *The Colorado River in Grand Canyon* (Stevens 1983a). The "Stevens" was the same format as the "Buzzmap," but added information on a variety of topics such as geology and history. In addition, the river map indicated campsites and drops in rapids, two aspects that created some controversy. First editions included a one-page insert, "Postscript: A River Once More" because "[a]s this book was being printed, Glen Canyon Dam released 92,000 cfs into the Grand Canyon," so "[f]or a free update on these changes in river campsites, send a self-addressed, stamped envelope" (Stevens 1983a). With this request, you received "Grand Canyon Update: 1 November 1983" (Stevens 1983b). Now in its sixth edition, it is one of the two most popular river guides.

In 1984 *Colorado River Briefs for a Trip through Grand Canyon* appeared, containing "points of interest, camps [with size ratings], and background history of Colorado River place names [and was] a collection of excerpts from various river guides" in an ammo-can size. Rapid ratings were from Buzz Belknap's guide and maps were furnished by the USGS (Lindemann 1984, 5). Updated in its third printing in 1993, it is now in its eighth printing. Modern technology allowed the production of *Colorado River in the Grand Canyon*, color-printed on water-resistant paper, spiral-bound with laminated covers, in an oversize format. The hope of the authors was to show "the detail of the USGS topo maps" and to have the "map books 'go with the flow,'" that is, "where the river is oriented flowing upward" (Martin and Whitis 2004). Almost thirty years before, *Pictorial Color Map of Grand Canyon* was the first to show this orientation (Kingsley et al. 1972).

Both the *Pictorial Color Map* and our final entry (U.S. Geological Survey 2002) show where modern cartographic design and surveying techniques may take us. Personnel at the Grand Canyon Monitoring and Research Center under the USGS are involved in "a solution based on GPS-derived ellipsoid heights" since "the elevations in 1923 were not a concentric solution" (Gonzales 2002). This has led to development of "atlases with the new river miles and the centerline on them," by "development of digital GIS layers of three of the most popular river mile systems: Stevens, Belknap, and Birdseye USGS." (Mietz 2002). "What was produced was less of a river guide and more of a 'river mile system.' It exists in electronic form and each [hard-copy] map [page] consists of a half-mile section of the river corridor displayed at approximately 1:4000 scale" (Wyse 2002).

Electronically assisted and computer-generated mapping makes for more accurate and complete products—probably better in some aspects; possibly worse in others. The joy of discovery, the fun of exploring the little known, is perhaps diminished with too much preparation. Do we see what others have experienced and written, unfold a map, interpret the lines, look for esoteric facts, unscroll an innovator's log, or toss them all in the river and "go with the flow?" On August 18, 1869, Powell reported, "The book is open, and I can read as I run" (Powell 1875). That is still a grand way to experience a river.

Works Cited

Adams, Eilean. 2001. *Hell or high water: James White's disputed passage through Grand Canyon.* Logan: Utah State University Press.

American River Touring Association. [1966]. *Grand Canyon: A series of maps and profiles of the Colorado River from Lees Ferry, Arizona, to Temple Bar on Lake Mead.* Oakland, Calif.: American River Touring Association.

Baars, Donald L., ed. 1969. Geology and natural history of the Fifth Field Conference, Powell centennial river expedition, 1969. Durango, Colo.: Four Corners Geological Society.

Belknap, Buzz. 1969. *Grand Canyon river guide.* Special River Runners Waterproof ed. New York: Canyonlands Press.

Belknap, Buzz, and Loie Belknap Evans. 1995. *Belknap's waterproof Grand Canyon river guide,* 2nd ed. Evergreen, Colo.: Westwater Books.

Beus, Stanley S. 1974. River guide of Colorado River: Lee's Ferry to Phantom Ranch. In *Geology of northern Arizona,* part 2, eds. Thor N. V. Karlstrom, Gordon A. Swann, and Raymond L. Eastwood. Geological Society of America, Rocky Mountain Section.

Billingsley, George H., and Donald P. Elston. 1989. Geologic log of the Colorado River from Lees Ferry to Temple Bar, Lake Mead, Arizona. In *Geology of Grand Canyon, northern Arizona (with Colorado River guides),* eds. Donald P. Elston, George H. Billingsley, and Richard A. Young. Washington, D.C.: American Geophysical Union.

Birdseye, C. H., and R. W. Burchard. 1924. *Plan and profile of Colorado River from Lees Ferry, Ariz., to Black Canyon, Ariz.-Nev., and Virgin River, Nev.* Washington, D.C.: U.S. Geological Survey.

Bradley, George Y. 1947. George Y. Bradley's journal, May 24–August 30, 1969. Ed. William Culp Darrah. *Utah Historical Quarterly* 15.

Braun, Ernest. 1970. *Grand Canyon of the living Colorado.* San Francisco: Sierra Club Books/New York: Ballantine Books.

Brian, Nancy. 1992. *River to rim: A guide to place names along the Colorado River in Grand Canyon from Lake Powell to Lake Mead.* Flagstaff, Ariz.: Earthquest Press.

Brod, Chris. 1997. Personal communication.

Butchart, Harvey. 1970a. *River to rim routes: Marble and Grand canyons.* Grand Canyon, Ariz.: Inner Canyon Unit.

———. 1970b. *Grand Canyon treks: A guide to the inner canyon routes.* Glendale, Calif.: La Siesta Press.

———. 1975. *Grand Canyon treks II: A guide to the extended canyon routes.* Glendale, Calif.: La Siesta Press.

———. 1984. *Grand Canyon treks III: Inner canyon journals.* Glendale, Calif.: La Siesta Press.

———. 1998. *Grand Canyon treks: 12,000 miles through the Grand Canyon.* Bishop, Calif.: Spotted Dog Press.

Carothers, Steven W. 1974. Colorado River natural history guide. Unpublished manuscript. Carothers and Associate, Flagstaff, Ariz.

Clark, Georgie White. 1994. Maps: Topographic and profile. Series 5. Georgie White Clark Manuscript Collection 270. Cline Library, Northern Arizona University, Flagstaff.

Cook, William. 1987. *The* Wen, *the* Botany, *and the* Mexican Hat: *The adventures of the first women through Grand Canyon, on the Nevills Expedition.* Orangeville, Calif.: Callisto Books.

Cooper, Tim. 1996. Coop's plausible guide to the river at the bottom of the canyon. *Hibernacle News.*

———. Forthcoming. *Coop's plausible guide to the river at the bottom of the canyon.* Ed. Brad Dimock. Flagstaff, Ariz.: Fretwater Press.

Crumbo, Kim. 1981. *A river runner's guide to the history of the Grand Canyon.* Boulder, Colo.: Johnson Books.

———. 1994. *A river runner's guide to the history of the Grand Canyon.* 2nd ed. Boulder, Colo.: Johnson Books.

Davis, D. E. 1958. *Escape routes from the Colorado River, Lees Ferry to Lake Mead; Grand Canyon Natl Park.* Grand Canyon, Ariz.: National Park Service.

———. 1974. *Information for running the Colorado through the Grand Canyon; or How to have a minimum impact on yourself and the resource.* Grand Canyon, Ariz.: National Park Service and Grand Canyon Natural History Association.

Dawson, Thomas Fulton. 1917. *The Grand Canyon: An article giving the credit of first traversing the Grand Canyon to James White, a Colorado gold prospector, who, it is claimed, made the voyage two years previous to the expedition under the direction of Maj. J. W. Powell, in 1869.* Repr., Prescott, Ariz.: Five Quail Books, 2002.

Dellenbaugh, Frederick S. 1908. *A canyon voyage: The narrative of the second Powell expedition down the Green-Colorado River from Wyoming, and the explorations on land, in the years 1871 and 1872.* New York and London: G. P. Putnam's Sons/The Knickerbocker Press.

Dirksen, Greg, and Renee Reeves. 1985. *Recreation on the Colorado River.* Aptos, Calif.: Sail Sales Publishing.

Dodge, Frank B. n.d. *The saga of Frank B. Dodge: An autobiography.* Tucson: privately printed.

Douglas, Edward Morehouse, Richard T. Evans, H. L. Baldwin, and John T. Stewart. 1908. *Arizona (Coconino County), Shinumo quadrangle.* Washington, D.C.: U.S. Geological Survey.

Eddy, Clyde. 1929. *Down the world's most dangerous river.* New York: Frederick A. Stokes.

Exploration of the Colorado River and the high plateaus of Utah, by the second Powell expedition of 1871–72. 1948–49. Special issues, *Utah Historical Quarterly* 16–17.

Freeman, Lewis R. 1924. Surveying the Grand Canyon of the Colorado. *National Geographic Magazine* 45 (May):471–530, 547–548.

Gonzales, Mark. Personal communication. 2002

Graf, Julia B., John C. Schmidt, and Susan W. Kieffer. 1989. Hydraulic log of the Colorado River from Lees Ferry to Diamond Creek, Arizona. In *Geology of Grand Canyon, northern Arizona (with Colorado River guides),* eds. Donald P. Elston, George H. Billingsley, and Richard A. Young. Washington, D.C.: American Geophysical Union.

Granger, Byrd Howell. 1960. *Grand Canyon place names.* Tucson: University of Arizona Press.

Hamblin, W. Kenneth, and Keith J. Rigby. 1968. Guidebook to the Colorado River, part 1: Lee's Ferry to Phantom Ranch in Grand Canyon National Park. *Brigham Young University, Geology Studies* 15 (5).

———. 1969. Guidebook to the Colorado River, part 2: Phantom Ranch in Grand Canyon National Park to Lake Mead, Arizona-Nevada. *Brigham Young University, Geology Studies* 16 (2).

———. 1971. Guidebook to the Colorado River, part 3: Moab to Hite, Utah through Canyonlands National Park. Provo, Utah: Department of Geology, Brigham Young University.

Hansen, Russell H. [1973]. *Colorado River map of the Grand Canyon.* Orem, Utah: Tour West. Photocopy in Arizona River Runners Manuscript Collection 30, Cline Library, Northern Arizona University, Flagstaff.

Jones, Benjamin E., and Randolph O. Helland. 1948. *Index to river surveys made by the United States Geological Survey and other agencies; revised to July 1, 1947.* Washington, D.C.: U.S. Geological Survey.

Jones, Les. 2001. Les Jones. *Boatman's Quarterly Review* 14 (2):22–31.

Jones, Leslie Allen. 1955. *Green River.* Heber City, Utah: Western Whitewater.

———. 1962 [1995]. *The Grand Canyon continuous photo-album set.* Midway, Utah: Western Whitewater.

———. 1962a. *Grand Canyon.* Heber City, Utah: Western Whitewater.

———. 1962b. *Colorado River runner's scroll map.* Heber City, Utah: Western Whitewater.

———. 1964. *San Juan R.. and San Juan Sector of L. Powell.* Heber City, Utah: Western Whitewater.

———. 1994. Les Jones. Grand Canyon River Guides Oral History Collection, Cline Library, Northern Arizona University, Flagstaff.

Kingsley, John, Rodney G. Colvin, Joseph McIntyre, Betty Ann Currey, Thomas Menasco, and Jack L. Currey. 1972. *Pictorial color map of Grand Canyon: Geology, history, points of interest, river and rapids.* Salt Lake City: Paragon Press.

Kolb, E. L. 1914. *Through the Grand Canyon from Wyoming to Mexico.* New York: Macmillan.

Leopold, Luna B. 1969. The rapids and the pools: Grand Canyon. In The Colorado River region and John Wesley Powell. Paper 669, U.S. Geological Survey, Washington, D.C.

Lindemann, Linda Lou. 1984. *Colorado River briefs for a trip through the Grand Canyon.* Tucson, Ariz.: Lundquist Press.

Marston, Otis R. "Dock." n.d. Marston Papers. Huntington Library. San Marino, Calif.

Martin, Tom. 1999. *Day hikes from the river: A guide to 75 hikes from camps on the Colorado River in Grand Canyon National Park.* Flagstaff, Ariz.: Vishnu Temple Press.

———. 2002. *Day hikes from the river: A guide to 100 hikes from camps on the Colorado River in Grand Canyon National Park,* 2nd ed. Flagstaff, Ariz.: Vishnu Temple Press.

Martin, Tom, and Duwain Whitis. 2004. *Guide to the Colorado River in Grand Canyon: Lees Ferry to South Cove.* Buda, Tx.: Rivermaps.

McCullough, L. C. B. [1966]. [Rapids and ratings]. In: *Grand Canyon: A series of maps and profiles of the Colorado River from Lees Ferry, Arizona, to Temple Bar on Lake Mead.* Oakland, Calif.: American River Touring Association.

McNamee, Greg. 1997. *Grand Canyon place names.* Seattle, Wash.: The Mountaineers.

———. 2004. *Grand Canyon place names,* 2nd ed. Seattle, Wash.: The Mountaineers.

Mietz, Steven. Personal communication. 2002.

Ohmart, Robert D. 1982. *Past and present biotic communities of the lower Colorado River mainstem and selected tributaries: Lees Ferry to Lake Mead,* vol. 2. Boulder City, Nev.: U.S. Bureau of Reclamation.

Pacific Southwest Inter-Agency Committee. 1976. *River mile index: Lower Colorado River and selected tributaries; Arizona, California, Nevada, and Utah.* Report of the Water Management Technical Subcommittee.

Péwé, Troy L. 1968. *Colorado River guidebook: Lee's Ferry to Phantom Ranch.* Tempe: Arizona State University.

———. 1969. *Colorado River guidebook: A geologic and geographic guide from Lees Ferry to Phantom Ranch, Arizona,* 2nd ed. Tempe, Ariz.: Troy L. Péwé.

———. 1974. *Colorado River guidebook: A geologic and geographic guide from Lees Ferry to Phantom Ranch, Arizona,* 3rd ed. Tempe, Ariz.: Troy L. Péwé.

———. 1983. *Colorado River guidebook: A geologic and geographic guide from Lees Ferry to Phantom Ranch, Arizona,* 3rd ed., 2nd printing, with updates. Tempe, Ariz.: Troy L. Péwé.

Powell, John Wesley. 1875. *Exploration of the Colorado River of the West and its tributaries. Explored in 1869, 1870, 1871, and 1872, under the direction of the Secretary of the Smithsonian Institution.* Washington: Government Printing Office.

Quartaroli, Richard D. 1999. Epilogue in *Lee's Ferry: From Mormon crossing to national park* by P. T. Reilly. Logan: Utah State University Press.

Reilly, P. T. 1964. Series 6 map, Leslie Allen Jones scroll map. Cline Library, Northern Arizona University, Flagstaff.

———. 1992. Letter to Thorn Mayes. November 12. Mayes Collection, Cline Library, Northern Arizona University, Flagstaff.

———. 1999. Mileage and schedules. P. T. Reilly Manuscript Collection, Cline Library, Northern Arizona University, Flagstaff.

Riebeek, Michael "Bake." 1980. Personal communication.

Rigg, Bob. 2002. Personal communication.

River runners guide through the Marble and Grand Canyons: Conservation through cooperation. 1969. Grand Canyon, Ariz.: Grand Canyon Natural History Association.

Rivers and mountains. [1986]. Wear the river! Palo Alto, Calif.: Riverguide Bandannas and T-Shirts.

Rusho, W. L. 1969. Francis Bishop's 1871 river maps. *Utah Historical Quarterly* 37(2): 207–213.

Sharp, Robert P. 1937. Diary 2, 1937 Carnegie-Cal Tech Grand Canyon Expedition. Carnegie-Cal Tech Collection. Cline Library, Northern Arizona University, Flagstaff.

Simmons, George C., and Gaskill, David L. [1969].

Marble Gorge and Grand Canyon. Vol. 3 of *River runners' guide to the canyons of the Green and Colorado rivers, with emphasis on geologic features.* Flagstaff, Ariz.: Northland Publishing.

Sorensen, Jeff. 1998. *The boatman's almanac: A compilation of monthly sunrise and sunset times for various camps and popular sites in Grand Canyon.* July ed. Phoenix: privately printed.

———. 1999. *The boatman's almanac: A compilation of monthly sunrise and sunset times for campsites and cool places in Grand Canyon.* March ed. Phoenix: privately printed.

———. 2000. *The boatman's almanac 2000: A compilation of monthly sunrise and sunset times for campsites and cool places in Grand Canyon.* July ed. Phoenix: privately printed.

Sorensen, Jeff, and Nelbert Niemi. 2000. *Looking for early shade: Selected campsites for summer boating in Grand Canyon.* n.p.: privately printed.

Stanton, Robert Brewster. 1890. Through the Grand Cañon of the Colorado. *Scribner's Magazine* 8 (November):591–613.

———. 1906–09. The river and the cañon: The Colorado River of the West, and the exploration, navigation and survey of its cañons, from the standpoint of an engineer. Manuscript. New York Public Library.

———. 1965. *Down the Colorado.* Norman: University of Oklahoma Press.

Staveley, Gaylord. 2002. Personal communication.

Stevens, Larry. 1983a. *The Colorado River in Grand Canyon: A comprehensive guide to its natural and human history.* Flagstaff, Ariz.: Red Lake Books.

———. 1983b. *The Colorado River in Grand Canyon: A comprehensive guide to its natural and human history.* Grand Canyon Update: November 1, 1983. Flagstaff, Ariz.: Red Lake Books.

Stone, Julius F. 1932. *Canyon country: The romance of a drop of water and a grain of sand.* New York: G. P. Putnam's Sons.

Thomas, Jim. 2000. *Grand Canyon: Colorado River trip.* Flagstaff, Ariz.: Design and Sales Publishing.

U.S. Geological Survey. 2002. *A guide to the Colorado River in the Grand Canyon (from Glen Canyon Dam to Pierce Ferry).* March 2000 contours and river-mile systems. Flagstaff, Ariz.: U.S. Geological Survey, Grand Canyon Monitoring and Research Center.

Webb, Robert H., Theodore S. Melis, and Richard A. Valdez. [2002]. *Observations of environmental change in Grand Canyon.* Tucson, Ariz.: U.S. Geological Survey.

Webb, Roy. 1992. Until dissolved by consent: The Western River Guides Association. *Utah Historical Quarterly* 60 (3):259–276.

Welch, Vince, Curt Conley, and Brad Dimock. 1998. *The doing of the thing: The brief, brilliant whitewater career of Buzz Holmstrom.* Flagstaff, Ariz.: Fretwater Press.

Westwood, Richard E. 1992. *Rough-water man: Elwyn Blake's Colorado River expeditions.* Reno: University of Nevada Press.

Whitney, Tim. 1996. Personal communication.

Williams, Tyler. 2000. *Grand Canyon river hikes.* Flagstaff, Ariz.: Funhog Press.

Wyse, Stephanie. Personal communication. 2002.

Hydropolitics in the Far Southwest: Carl Hayden, Arizona, and the Fight for the Central Arizona Project, 1952–68

by Jack L. August Jr.

Dr. Jack L. August Jr. was one of three excellent presenters funded by the Arizona Humanities Council's speaker grant program. Together, he, Doug Kupel, and Bill Swan spent an entire morning unraveling some of the knots in western water law. Jack's presentation was extracted from his book, Vision in the Desert: Carl Hayden and Hydropolitics in the American Southwest *(Fort Worth: Texas Christian University Press, 1999), with an introduction by Bruce Babbitt.*

According to former U.S. Secretary of the Interior Bruce Babbitt, we are approaching the last phase of a productive century of federally sponsored reclamation in the American West. With the development of a few remaining authorized dams and delivery systems, the era of the construction of great reclamation projects will end.

A major contributor to the process of water-resource development in the American West was longtime senator Carl Hayden of Arizona (1877–1972). A native of Arizona's Salt River valley, Hayden, in his earliest years, experienced the often-cruel vicissitudes of flood and drought in the arid Southwest. He saw Arizona grow from a raw territory of a few thousand hardy pioneers to a desert oasis of millions. Central to his efforts in the service of his constituents was the development and use of the Colorado River, the controversial interstate stream that serves the needs of seven states (Wyoming, Colorado, Utah, New Mexico, Nevada, California, and Arizona) and Mexico. Moreover, while he devoted his public career to the residents of his state, the man who became known as the "Silent Senator" had an impact and significance far beyond the borders of the Grand Canyon State.

The most striking feature of Hayden's political career was its longevity. He spent sixty-seven of his ninety-four years of life in public office. Between 1900 and 1912, he learned the art of politics by serving in a variety of local and county offices. When statehood was achieved in the latter year, voters elected their native son to the House of Representatives, kept him there for seven terms, and in 1926 promoted him to the U.S. Senate, where he remained until retirement in 1969. During his fifty-seven years in the federal government, he served with ten presidents, beginning with William Howard Taft and ending with Lyndon Baines Johnson.

Water and its use and distribution, more than any other issue, lay at the heart of Hayden's public career. Unquestionably, the fortunes of his Arizona pioneer family were tied to water, or more specifically, to its diversion onto land. As a local politician he lobbied for one of the first and most successful federal reclamation projects, the Salt River Project. During his first term in the House he further revealed his understanding of the importance of water to his home state by obtaining authorization for an engineering study that led to the construction of Coolidge Dam on the Gila River and the San Carlos Reclamation Project. He also helped shape federal reclamation policy in its early years by writing and securing passage of the provision that allows local water-user associations throughout the country to take over the care, maintenance, and operation of federal reclamation projects. In nearly six decades in Congress, reclamation issues occupied more of his attention than any other legislative subject.

Hayden's longest, hardest fought congressional battle unfolded in the struggle for the Central Arizona Project (CAP), which today channels Arizona's share of the Colorado River to central portions of the state, particularly to the metropolitan areas of Phoenix and Tucson. Although Hayden's thirst for the Colorado can be traced to his youth, this story begins at 1:30 PM on August 13, 1952, when the senator welcomed a small group of somber-faced Arizonans to his office on Capitol Hill. After a brief exchange of pleasantries he stuck a battered, white straw hat on his bald head, strode to the door and beckoned, "come on boys, let's get this done." Together the group walked to the U.S. Supreme Court building. Among them was J. H. "Hub" Moeur, chief counsel for the Arizona Interstate Stream Commission, who filed a bill of complaint against California asking for judicial apportionment of the waters of the lower Colorado River basin. After witnessing the filing, the seventy-four-year-old senator issued a short statement to the press. "I believe this action," he told those gathered on the steps of the Supreme Court, "will make possible the settlement of a most serious controversy which is delaying the development of the Colorado River basin. If the Californians are sincere in their oft-repeated demands for court action, then they will welcome the opportunity to present their side of the case." With that, Arizona launched the monumental *Arizona v. California* Supreme Court case.

As several case students have noted, it was one of the most complex and fiercely contested in the history of the Court. Before its resolution, 340 witnesses and fifty lawyers had produced twenty-five thousand pages of testimony before a special master. The case dragged on for nearly eleven years and cost nearly $5 million. In addition, when a sharply divided Court announced its opinion on June 3, 1963, followed by the decree on March 9, 1964, the river possessed a greatly modified legal framework governing its apportionment and use among the basin states.

Arizona's contentions had changed little since the late 1910s and early 1920s, when the basin states focused their attentions on the Colorado River Compact and river development. The state asserted that California had made contracts for annual delivery of more than 5.3 million acre-feet of water in spite of laws limiting it to 4.4 million acre-feet. The limitation notwithstanding, Arizona's attorneys argued that California had built reclamation works capable of diverting eight million acre-feet per year, thereby posing a

threat to Arizona and other basin states. According to its attorneys, Arizona required 3.8 million acre-feet of Colorado system water per year just to sustain its existing economy. Furthermore, Arizona relied on and asserted its rights to water under a variety of federal and state actions, including the Colorado River Compact, Boulder Canyon Project Act, and California Limitation Act of 1929.

California registered no objection to Arizona's motion. Its substantial team of attorneys, led by the brilliant and indefatigable Northcutt "Mike" Ely, agreed with the U.S. solicitor, who advised the Supreme Court that the federal government had an interest in the case and would move to intervene if Arizona's motions were granted. On January 19, 1953, the Court granted Arizona's original motion, and the bill of complaint was filed. Hayden hoped for prompt action because he knew that no further progress could be made on CAP, or any other lower-basin project, until the Court reached its decision.

On May 20, 1953, California responded to Arizona's bill of complaint. In nearly five hundred pages of narrative and supporting documentation, California's attorneys contended that the state had a right to the beneficial and consumptive use of 5,362,000 acre-feet of Colorado River system water per year under the terms of the Boulder Canyon Project Act and the state's contracts with the secretary of the interior. Moreover, the state claimed prior appropriative rights to that amount of water, and that these rights were senior to Arizona's and therefore superior. Finally, California argued that Arizona, by failing to ratify the Colorado River Compact within the specified six months when the other six states had done so in 1923, and by its subsequent attempts to have the agreement declared invalid and the Boulder Canyon Project Act declared unconstitutional, abdicated its right to interpret these statutes.

Hearings on *Arizona v. California* began on January 14, 1956. When the Supreme Court at last announced its opinion on June 3, 1963, Hayden considered it a tremendous victory for Arizona while local newspapers considered it "a personal triumph for Carl Hayden." The Court, Hayden was pleased to note, centered its opinion on the Boulder Canyon Project Act rather than the Colorado River Compact. Moreover, Congress, the justices reasoned, "intended to and did create its own comprehensive scheme for . . . apportionment." In addition, Congress had authorized the secretary of the interior to use his contract power to implement a lower-basin agreement.

Each state retained exclusive rights to its tributaries, which meant Arizona's exclusive right to the Gila River. Concerning mainstream apportionment, the Court gave Arizona what it and Hayden had argued for since negotiations over the 1922 compact: 4.4 million acre-feet to California, 2.8 million to Arizona, and 300,000 to Nevada. "That formula," wrote Ben Cole of the *Arizona Republic*'s Washington Bureau, was "a personal triumph for Carl Hayden because the decision referred back twenty-five years to the December 12, 1928, debate in which Hayden pointed out that the Boulder Canyon bill and its allocation formula settled the dispute over lower basin waters." After reading the ninety-five pages of opinion and dissent, Hayden informed newsman Cole, "naturally I am pleased that the Supreme Court has in general followed the Special Master's recommendations with reference to the division of the waters of the Colorado River. This is especially gratifying because it makes possible at last for us to put our rightful share of our waters to use in the Colorado River Basin."

On June 4, 1963, one day after the Court's ruling, Senators Hayden and Goldwater and Arizona's three members of the House of Representatives introduced legislation (S 1658; HR 6796, HR 6797, and HR 6798) to authorize CAP, one of the largest water project proposals ever to come before Congress. Hayden's bill authorized a diversion of 1.2 million acre-feet per year of water to provide supplemental irrigation and municipal water to central and southern Arizona. To do this, it provided for the construction of five dams and reservoirs, two power plants, and transmission and distribution facilities on the Colorado and its tributaries in Arizona and western New Mexico. A key feature of this first bill was a 740-foot-high dam at Bridge Canyon at the headwaters of Lake Mead. Bridge Canyon Dam promised to be the highest dam in the Western Hemisphere. Its power plant would have a capacity of 1.5 million kilowatts, one-third of which would be transmitted south to pump water over a canal and aqueduct system from the existing Parker Dam on the Colorado to Phoenix (219 miles distant) and to Tucson (341 miles distant).

Hayden knew well that Congress historically delayed final action on reclamation projects until leaders and all sections of the state and region had arrived at a consensus. Looking for the broad support necessary for his bill, he advertised his past support for several big packages of upper-basin projects, including the Colorado River Project Act of 1956, which had led to the construction of Glen Canyon Dam. He had also played a prominent role in backing individual state proposals such as New Mexico's San Juan-Chama Project, which passed Congress in 1962.

In light of these and other previous efforts in support of regional water-resource development, Hayden believed he deserved the same kind of consideration for CAP within his state and throughout the region. Yet between 1960 and 1963, anticipation of a Supreme Court decision favorable to Arizona prompted federal administrators and representatives in the basin states to begin formulating a regional

plan for the entire basin, not just Arizona. In January 1962 Secretary of the Interior Stewart Udall, an Arizonan and former congressman, encouraged Wayne Aspinall (D-CO), chairman of the influential House Interior and Insular Affairs Committee, to ask the Department of the Interior to conduct a comprehensive study on development of the Colorado River. The study would prepare officials for the expected pressure for authorization of individual state projects, including CAP, as soon as the decision in *Arizona v. California* was handed down.

Indeed several such studies were already underway, and in November 1962, Aspinall asked Udall for an outline of the Department of the Interior's plans for a regional approach to water development in the basin. In an effort to practice "constructive water statesmanship," Secretary Udall and Undersecretary James Carr of California adopted the regional approach, and by January 1963, revealed an $8 billion plan that included projects in five western states. In announcing his regional program—the Pacific Southwest Water Plan (PSWP)—Udall hoped to "erase the outmoded concept limited by state lines, and concentrate on meeting the total water needs of a region." In addition to this lofty goal, he also sought to reconcile diverse interests and several multiple-use water projects into one harmonious and comprehensive plan. Beyond this, Udall tried to exploit common interests in PSWP by proposing huge hydroelectric dams at Bridge Canyon and Marble Canyon flanking Grand Canyon National Park. Revenues derived from these cash-register dams would underwrite the cost of the entire plan and guarantee the future growth and development of the Southwest.

To Hayden, PSWP and the comparatively simple CAP bill were competing legislative initiatives, and the senator and Arizona's political leadership were particularly incensed with the Kennedy administration in general and Secretary Udall in particular for their regional approach. During 1963 and 1964, in several exchanges between Hayden's office and Interior, an agitated Hayden let it be known in vivid and uncompromising language that he considered the overdrawn PSWP a method for delaying consideration of CAP that played into the hands of California and upper-basin opponents of CAP, particularly Colorado. Arizona Governor Paul Fannin added that he considered PSWP "a plot against Arizona born in California and formalized in the Interior Department by California's undersecretary." Fannin advocated that they "go it alone with the CAP as proposed by Hayden in S 1658." Udall insisted that the regional approach would benefit Arizona, and he informed Hayden in December 1963 that he could not file a favorable report on a separate CAP bill. Hayden shot back, "I vigorously protest your failure to keep your commitment to me and to other officials of this state. I insist that language be included in the PSWP which will be a clear endorsement of the CAP as embodied in S 1658 and/or as a separate first segment in any regional program."

Not surprisingly, Stewart Udall took a great deal of editorial abuse within Arizona over his "federalized regional project" that "placed all water and power of the Colorado under control of his department." One highly charged editorial in the *Arizona Republic* of August 18, 1963, asked "Udall, Where Are You?" suggesting that the grandiose PSWP meant that he had written off Arizona for his political future and that he had come under the influence of the California water lobby headed by Undersecretary of the Interior James Carr. Younger brother and Arizona Congressman Morris Udall was the focus of similar harsh criticism. Observers questioned whether he supported CAP or the "empire-building plan" unveiled by his brother. As the influential *Arizona Republic* editorialized in that 1963 piece, "Voters know where Stewart Udall stands—he's against the Central Arizona Project. . . . Will Morris Udall align himself with the rest of the Arizona delegation, which unanimously supports the project? Or, will he, in deference to his brother, sit on the sidelines and refuse to help Arizona?"

Despite the threat to CAP posed by a more complicated regional solution and the editorializing, as Arizona's quest for CAP shifted to Congress and as several proposals and counterproposals made their way through the maze of subcommittee and committee hearings, Hayden knew that his accumulated power and influence in the Senate boded well for the legislation. In 1966, moreover, an Arizona "task force" arrived in Washington to lend support to the legislative effort, drawing staff and expertise from the state's water establishment, consisting of the Arizona Interstate Stream Commission, Arizona Public Service, Central Arizona Project Association, and Salt River Project. Additionally, Hayden chaired the Senate Appropriations Committee, and he could, if he wanted to use this club, hold up every other water project in the country.

As usual, Hayden appeared before a variety of congressional committees, adding to his already considerable record of testimony on behalf of CAP. Typical of his statements between 1963 and 1968 was his testimony in support of his bill (S 1658) before the Senate Subcommittee on Irrigation and Reclamation of the Committee on Interior and Insular Affairs on August 27, 1963. "Arizona's efforts to obtain her full share of Colorado River water have been frustrated by the deliberate delaying tactics of California," he told the subcommittee, and "after fifteen years of separate consideration by Congress, the effort is being made to absorb the simple and readily understood

Central Arizona Project into one of the most controversial, complex, and confusing water resource development plans ever presented to Congress." Hayden told this and other groups of legislators in subsequent testimony that he believed in a regional concept of water resource development, that he could support any features of a regional plan that were sound, but that he was opposed to anything that would complicate and delay authorization of CAP. Hayden correctly predicted that legislators would hear testimony that there would be insufficient water in the river to sustain CAP. Anticipating these arguments, he quoted Commissioner of the Bureau of Reclamation Floyd Dominy, who stated that despite rumors to the contrary, "there is certainly enough water in the river for the CAP of 1.2 million acre-feet" per year under the *Arizona v. California* ruling.

Hayden also criticized the portion of the PSWP proposal to import 1.2 million acre-feet per year of water from northern California to southern California at a cost of billions of dollars while ignoring an equal amount of water that could be developed at a minimal cost through adequate conservation practices within the area. "This committee," he inveighed, "is being requested to provide funds for the import of water from northern California at a great cost to protect the right of southern California to waste water."

What especially irked Hayden about PSWP or other regional initiatives that emerged over the $4^1/_2$ years of legislative wrangling leading to the Colorado River Basin Project Act of 1968 was the obvious efforts of certain interests within California to delay CAP or nullify *Arizona v. California*. He bemoaned the solemn assurances of California's former governor Earl Warren, who, in 1948, told Hayden "whenever it is finally determined that water belongs to Arizona, it should be permitted to use that water in any manner or by any method considered best by Arizona." Moreover, Governor Edmund G. "Pat" Brown had announced that California, having lost the Supreme Court case, would not try to accomplish by obstructionism what she had failed to accomplish by litigation. Yet as Hayden stated on August 4, 1963, and reiterated on several occasions thereafter, for "forty years I have witnessed the thwarting of Arizona's effort to put to use its share of Colorado River water. At every turn Arizona has encountered the deliberate delaying tactics of California and there is every reason to believe that this plan of obstructionism will continue." Thus, as he told lawmakers at the outset of legislative consideration of CAP, "I think all of you know that I have always attempted to help in any way possible with every project of our western resources—even when I was being fought on my own project—but quite frankly my patience has been exhausted."

In spite of California's continued opposition, Hayden had powerful allies in the Senate. His close and respected friend, Henry Jackson (D-WA), chaired the Senate Interior Committee. Jackson, whose state owed much of its postwar prosperity to Hayden-supported reclamation programs, carefully monitored natural-resource development and federal reclamation. Moreover, Jackson's valued relationship with Hayden and firm alliance with President Kennedy served Arizona well during CAP's journeys through the Senate between 1963 and 1968. During the course of arriving at a measure suitable to all contending and conflicting interests, however, California and the upper basin looked to the Northwest and the Columbia River system for additional Colorado River water supplies, an effort to avoid water shortages they felt would be made worse by CAP. At one point during the process, several senators and representatives contemplated the importation of 8 million acre-feet of water per year from the Columbia River Basin and even from as far north as Canada. Naturally, Jackson saw fit to protect the interests of his region and took actions to eliminate trans-basin transfers of water during final consideration of the CAP bill. In final form the legislation provided for a ten-year ban on inter-basin transfer feasibility studies.

Hayden also counted on support from Clinton Anderson (D-NM), chairman of the Power and Reclamation Subcommittee of the Interior Committee. Anderson enjoyed considerable stature in the Senate as well as with groups concerned with water resource development and had a stake in the bill, as it pertained to protecting and extending water entitlements for his state. Moreover, his especially close relationship with Senator Jackson made Anderson an important ally in the CAP fight. Indeed, throughout his last term in office, Hayden relied on these two powerful men to counter the opposition arguments of California senators Thomas Kuchel, ranking Republican member of the Senate Interior Committee, and Claire Engle, who helped engineer the 1951 defeat of CAP in the House of Representatives.

Thankful for his senatorial support, Hayden and his staff nevertheless knew the real fight for passage lay in the House. Between 1963 and 1968, Arizona, fortunately, had capable and bipartisan representation. John Rhodes was a respected and influential leader among House Republicans who served on the Appropriations Subcommittee that would ultimately provide money to build the project. George Senner, a northern Arizona Democrat from Arizona's Third District, was untested, but he soon lost his seat to the inimitable Sam Steiger of Prescott, a Republican. And Morris Udall, a member of the key Committee on Interior and Insular Affairs, maintained special responsibilities over the bill. Importantly for Arizona, the three-man team in the House worked well together during the bill's final 4^1/$_2$-year legislative history.

Although Arizona's House delegation introduced CAP bills identical to Hayden's the day after the Supreme Court decision, nine out of ten congressional bills typically introduced and referred to committee never made it to a floor vote. The power of congressional committees, moreover, could not be overstated, and the committee chairmen were of special importance. Bills opposed by the chairman rarely emerged for a floor vote. He controlled the schedule of hearings on legislation, and undecided members often followed his lead. Since the principal obstacle to passage of CAP was in the House, the House Interior Committee—and its Irrigation and Reclamation Subcommittee, where the CAP bill was referred—held vital importance for CAP proponents.

For Hayden this meant CAP passing through the gauntlet of the committee chaired by Wayne N. Aspinall. According to most observers of Colorado River basin affairs, Aspinall—a former schoolteacher with a testy disposition—distrusted expansionist California and felt similarly about Arizona. In fact, the river ran under the window of his home on Aspinall Drive in Palisade, Colorado, and he sought to conserve every acre-foot before the lower-basin states would take it and never give it back. Mo Udall considered the sixty-seven-year-old chairman, who had served in Congress since 1948, "a superb legislative tactician." Of utmost concern to Aspinall was the obvious fact that although entitled to 2.8 million acre-feet of water annually, Arizona's use of this amount through CAP might cut sharply into water destined for upper-basin use that had not yet been developed. During one crucial phase of CAP's consideration in the House Interior Committee in 1967, Hayden, in an uncharacteristic display of power, had to threaten to eliminate funding for the Frying Pan-Arkansas Project in Colorado, and allowed that he would hold up other projects important to the House Interior chairman if he did not move the bill forward.

In addition to Aspinall, John Saylor of Pennsylvania, ranking Republican on the House Interior Committee, continued to frustrate Arizona as he had in the 1950s. Described by one colleague as a "dynamic, hard-hitting protagonist" who had earned respect in the House, Saylor was an ardent conservationist who supported expansion of the National Park System and advocated programs for outdoor recreation. Saylor, moreover, backed a strong wilderness bill and the integrity of the national parks, and complained vigorously about the Bridge Canyon Dam provision of CAP because it threatened to back water into Grand Canyon National Park. While not opposed to sound reclamation projects he opposed public power development, spotty financing, and poor planning in "marginal reclamation projects." He had voted against the Upper Colorado project in 1956, thereby gaining support among environmentalists.

Indeed in 1966 and 1967 environmentalists' opposition to the construction of dams in and around the Grand Canyon threatened to derail the CAP. By 1966 virtually everyone favorable to the legislation knew that the river was over-allocated, and most wanted to see augmentation from the Northwest, so they generally favored the Grand Canyon dams. As expressed in his first Supreme Court CAP bill, Hayden still advocated construction of Bridge Canyon Dam, as he had since 1947, and he indicated that he also supported a Marble Canyon Dam if revenues were needed to finance augmentation and other development. Yet the previously fragmented environmentalist movement, representing diverse interests and a wide array of organizations, consolidated in this instance to bring significant pressure on Congress and the Johnson administration. They contended that the dams would flood scenic areas and inundate portions of Grand Canyon National Park and Grand Canyon National Monument, and they wanted hydroelectric power dams removed from the bill.

By early 1966 the public seemed convinced that the most controversial aspect of the legislation involved the two proposed dams. And in the spring of that year, after *Reader's Digest*, *Life*, and even *My Weekly Reader* ran stories attacking the Grand Canyon dams, Hayden realized they posed insurmountable political obstacles. In a July 1967 memorandum to President Johnson advising him that the Senate Committee on Interior and Insular Affairs had recommended passage of S 1004, he added that this legislation contained "no new Colorado River dams." As Hayden aide Roy Elson interpreted the outcome of the dam fight: "Most people in the East and other places were for CAP, but they were against the dams because they had been informed by [David] Brower and his operatives that within the region there existed adequate amounts of alternative energy sources, notably low-grade coal." As a result Hayden and Arizona were forced to accept the alternative to hydroelectric power. As historian Donald Worster explained in his analysis of this "environmentalist victory," energy required for CAP was derived instead from coal strip-mined on Hopi lands at Black Mesa and burned in the Navajo Generating Station near Page, "polluting crystalline desert air with ash and poison gas." As one reclamation official explained the paradox, "it didn't solve a damn thing except it gave us power to pump water to central Arizona."

If acquiescing on the dam issue, incorporating aspects of Secretary Udall's regional plan, and jousting with Aspinall's upper-basin demands proved difficult, Hayden was galled by yet another compromise. From the start of congressional negotiations, California's senators had made it clear that a central condition for dropping opposition to CAP would be California's first priority to 4.4 million acre-feet each year. In other words, California wanted Arizona to regulate her mainstream diversions so that California would never receive less than 4.4 million acre-feet out of the 7.5 million acre-feet lower-basin allocation. At first an intransigent Hayden refused to negotiate the issue with California Senator Kuchel. By 1965, however, as time seemed to get shorter and the issue more complex, the bill in the Eighty-eighth and Eighty-ninth congresses provided for twenty-five- and twenty-seven-year guarantees for California's 4.4 priority. In the final version of the bill, Arizona promised California that CAP diversions "shall be so limited as to assure the availability" of 4.4 million acre-feet annually in perpetuity.

As Hayden neared the last year of his final term in office and CAP remained stalled in the House Interior Committee in spite of numerous concessions, Arizona's frustrated state leaders triggered another complication. Rumor of an Arizona "go-it-alone" CAP, promoted by state conservatives and elements within the Arizona Power Authority, first surfaced in 1963. A prominent feature of the state-financed and -operated plan included successful application of the Arizona Power Authority to the Federal Power Commission to finance, construct, and manage a hydroelectric power dam on the Colorado River. Hayden quickly thwarted this untimely effort by shepherding through Congress a bill (S 502) that preserved the jurisdiction of Congress over the construction of hydroelectric power works below Glen Canyon Dam on the Colorado River. With the passage of S 502 on June 23, 1964, those Arizonans calling for a state-owned and operated CAP were effectively prohibited from taking action, although they lobbied the senator and threatened continuously to take action as late as 1967. While the state plan reflected lack of consensus within Arizona over CAP strategy, it also illustrated the high degree of frustration over repeated legislative delays.

By the end of 1967, after seemingly endless negotiations among and within states—implementing selected provisions from more than thirty Department of the Interior studies and discarding others, crafting suitable and appropriate legal language, and including the time-honored pork barrel benefits for those politicians who needed to "bring home the bacon"—CAP was finally ready to move. Key in breaking the political logjam in California was Republican Governor Ronald Reagan, who began productive negotiations with Arizona's Republican Governor Jack Williams.

Another crucial element in prompting final action was Hayden's pressure on Wayne Aspinall, who was virtually forced to hold final hearings on the bill and report it out of committee. The legislation, depending on one's perspective, was either light enough or heavy enough to move. Most of the key players who participated in creating the measure that emerged from Congress—even opponents of CAP like California's Thomas Kuchel—could not disguise their profound pleasure that Senator Hayden came away from the momentous struggle with one last political victory. On September 12, 1968, when the Senate agreed to the House version of the Colorado River Basin Project Act, the ninety-year-old Hayden received glowing tributes for his persistent efforts. The senator quietly acknowledged the accolades with nods of appreciation.

On September 30, 1968, President Johnson, at a ceremony attended by Hayden and other Arizona dignitaries, signed CAP into law. Besides CAP, the legislation included authorization of several other controversial reclamation projects, including Hooker Dam in New Mexico, an aqueduct from Lake Mead to Las Vegas, the Dixie Project in Utah, and the Uintah Unit of the Central Utah Project. The act also authorized San Miguel, Dallas Creek, West Divide, Dolores, and Animas-La Plata projects in Colorado. Additionally, it authorized the Lower Colorado River Development Fund to build a yet-to-be-defined augmentation project. Finally, the bill made delivery of Mexico's 1.5 million acre-feet of water per year a national, not regional, responsibility. This legislation, signed into law two days before Hayden's ninety-first birthday, was the most expensive single congressional authorization in history when it was passed, containing $1.3 billion for program implementation.

On May 6, 1968, shortly before final touches were completed on CAP, Hayden was led into the Appropriations Committee chamber, which was jammed with senators, friends from Arizona, and a few reporters. President Johnson arrived bearing a pair of walnut bookends and issued a short, grandiloquent tribute. Senator Richard Russell of Georgia, Hayden's best friend in the Senate, then chaired a brief ceremony and introduced Hayden. The Arizona senator walked slowly to the dais and announced, "Among other things that fifty-six years in Congress have taught me is that contemporary events need contemporary men. Time actually makes specialists of us all. When a house is built there is a moment for the foundation, another for the roof, the walls, and so on. Arizona's foundation includes fast highways, adequate electric power, and abundant water, and these foundations have been laid. It is time for a new building crew to report, so I have decided to retire from office at the close of my term this year." As cameras clicked, Hayden burst into tears, as did nearly everyone else in the crowded room. With his typically brief announcement, Hayden signaled the end of his congressional service.

Most accounts of the political and legal history of CAP dutifully acknowledge Hayden's preeminent role in bringing water to central Arizona. Yet the veteran senator's influence has been obscured by the length of the process, the legendary *Arizona v. California* Supreme Court case, and thousands of pages of mind-numbing testimony in the Congressional Record. Hayden, more than any other CAP proponent, fashioned the legislative strategies that shaped CAP's configuration in the public mind. His actions and statements before innumerable congressional committees not only provide an important perspective for assessing CAP's broader economic, social, and environmental significance, but also reveal Arizona's profound role in fashioning solutions to vexing regional and national issues. Indeed, the hundreds of miles of canals, pumping stations, and water-delivery systems that today wind their way through the desert stand as a testament, for better or worse, to Hayden's towering public career.

The realization of Carl Hayden's dream raises some fundamental questions. Will the desert bloom in the twenty-first century with renewed agricultural activity and urban expansion? Or is this water-based civilization in a fragile ecosystem doomed to flourish briefly then disappear? Will Las Vegas and southern California, both pressing environmental limits and desperately seeking a greater share of lower-basin water, succeed in forcing Arizona back to the federal bargaining table? Certainly Hayden foresaw these questions and sensed their implications even as he fought mightily for the beneficial implementation of federal reclamation in the arid West.

Put another way, Hayden focused much of his considerable energy on the most important factor confronting his arid constituents: the search for large quantities of freshwater. Throughout his congressional career he represented the "heart of the West," which was to historian Walter Prescott Webb "a desert unqualified and absolute . . . a gigantic fire" that defied human settlement and economic development yet vividly defined the region as a unique place on the American landscape. From Hayden's perspective, Arizona and the Southwest were deficient in comparison with other parts of the country, most notably in water. Much of his public career, as exemplified in the legislative fight for CAP, was devoted to rectifying that deficiency.

Underlying the mad scramble for Colorado River water was the peculiarly western obsession with economic growth and development. This myopic quest in the environmentally sensitive central Arizona desert has come under close scrutiny in recent years. Scholars from a variety of disciplines have revisited the era of western water wars and dam-building orgies, and they have come away with profound questions regarding the long-term effects of environmental manipulation and the ultimate fate of the Colorado River, which one interpreter describes as "A River No More." As scholars and politicians reassess and revise their economic and environmental interpretations of federal reclamation, Carl Hayden will stand out as one public figure who in many ways symbolized this critical movement in the American West. Without question, water was among the region's most critical concerns in the nineteenth and twentieth centuries. No doubt the environment will continue to influence the direction of public policy in the region in the twenty-first century as well.

Parens Patria[1]: Issues Relating to the Colorado River Boundary between Grand Canyon National Park, the Hualapai Reservation, and the Navajo Nation

by Andrew Majeske

We were fortunate to have Andrew Majeske take time from his doctoral studies in Davis, California, to present his essay on Hualapai and Navajo boundary disputes "along" the Colorado River. As he points out in his afterword, the presentation led to lengthy discussion among participants, but as they say in both the legal and history professions, he is making an argument.

The critical question I address in this paper is whether the Navajo Nation and the Hualapai Tribe should have ownership, use and occupancy, and/or access rights to the Colorado River at the northern boundary of their reservations. The critical argument I make is that the Department of the Interior's Office of the Solicitor has issued opinions indicating that, for *different* reasons, these tribes do not have ownership, use and occupancy, or access rights even though in the case of both it was once recognized that the Colorado River was their reservations' northern boundary.[2]

Let me begin by drawing attention to the stretches of the Colorado River in the Grand Canyon relevant to this paper. The Navajo Nation boundary runs from the mouth of the Little Colorado River at River Mile 61 (measuring downstream from Lees Ferry, which is considered River Mile 0) to the Glen Canyon Dam at River Mile -15, a total of seventy-six miles of river frontage. The site for the proposed Marble Canyon Dam, a dormant project, is in the middle of this stretch at River Mile 39. The reservoir behind Marble Canyon Dam, if the dam were built, would extend all the way to Lees Ferry, leaving the Navajos

approximately twenty-two miles of frontage on the Colorado River between the mouth of the Little Colorado and the Marble Canyon Dam site that would be neither dam sites nor parts of reservoirs.

Except for a miniscule stretch of river between the proposed Hualapai Dam site and the spillway elevation of Lake Mead, the entire Hualapai Reservation's northern boundary is either an existing reservoir or potential reservoir for a proposed, though dormant, dam project. The tribe's river boundary begins at River Mile 165, just east of National Canyon, and extends downstream to Mile 273 in what is now Lake Mead. The site of the proposed Hualapai Dam (also known as the Bridge Canyon Dam) is at River Mile 235. The reservoir behind this dam would extend nearly to Kanab Creek (River Mile 144), well beyond the eastern edge of the reservation. The dam site

---

[1] A doctrine pursuant to which the United States makes critical decisions on behalf of American Indian tribes—literally the fatherland acts as parent. See Thomas 1994, at Section 57.07(a) (citing *Cherokee Nation v. Georgia*, 30 U.S. [5 Pet.] 1, 17 [1831]).

[2] It is beyond the scope of this paper to address how these tribes might want to use such access if their rights to it were recognized.

is at an elevation of 1,225 feet above sea level while the Hoover Dam spillway elevation is 1,221—a difference of only four feet.

THE NAVAJO BOUNDARY

These dams and reservoirs are relevant to the boundary issue because certain lands relating to the dams and reservoirs were carved out of these reservations: namely, "all lands designated by the Secretary of the Interior . . . as being valuable for water-power purposes and all lands withdrawn or classified as power-site lands" (Navajo Boundary Act [NBA])(73 Stat. L. 961). The Hualapai Dam site, the Marble Canyon Dam site, and the reservoirs they would create represent lands excluded from the reservations.[3] The NBA goes on to say that "the Indians . . . [have] the exclusive right to occupy and use such designated and classified lands until they shall be *required* for power purposes *or other uses* under the authority of the United States" (emphasis added). This language means that "the Indians" have the right to use and occupy these lands *until* the lands are *required* for (1) power purposes or (2) "other uses." The critical issue here is whether the "or other uses" language is limited by the reasons for which the land was excluded in the first place. That is, can the government do whatever it wants with the excluded lands, or is it restricted in any way to using the lands for the reasons it excluded the lands? These reasons were clearly set forth in the Arizona Enabling Act (61 Stat L. 575), which created the state of Arizona. This legislation is unambiguous; it describes the excluded lands as "actually or prospectively valuable for hydro-electric use or transmission." Thus, the question is, should the United States have, and did it intend to have, carte blanche to use these lands however it pleased? Given the specific purposes for which the lands were taken, should the United States be able to terminate the Indians' use and occupancy only for the specified reasons? I am inclined to think that if the matter were litigated, and if the arbiter of fact was a neutral party, the "or other uses" language would be limited to the stated reasons for the taking, particularly since, according to the Office of the Solicitor, "well founded doubt should be resolved in favor of the Indians" (1976 Hualapai Opinion).[4] What I have just described is the critical issue with respect to the Navajo boundary, namely, whether the "or other uses" language must be read in light of the reasons for which the land was taken. However, this was not the basis upon which the solicitor decided in favor of Marble Canyon National Monument (MCNM) and against the Navajos on the boundary issue.

Before turning to the solicitor's reasons for deciding the way he did, let me provide some background. The NBA was enacted in 1934 and was subject to the 1914 "water power" carve-outs. Nonetheless, Navajo occupation and use of these lands date to before 1900, when an Executive Order was issued that set aside the portion of the Navajo Reservation that borders on the Colorado River until at least 1969, when MCNM was formed.[5] After 1934 they used and occupied the land pursuant to the express provisions of the NBA. In 1969 the solicitor issued his Opinion regarding the boundary. In this Opinion he determined that the boundary was located one-quarter mile south of the river (at the 3,150-foot contour line), which is the South Rim for all practical purposes. The solicitor relied upon the "or other uses" language from the NBA, indicating that the creation of MCNM was a legitimate reason for terminating the Navajos' rights of use and occupancy. He ignored the uses for which the land was excluded that were clearly set forth in the Arizona Enabling Act.

The solicitor's reasoning is a prime example of what gives the practice of law such a bad reputation. As I will show, his interpretation appears to be the result of either outright deception, at worst, or at best, gross incompetence. Superficially, his decision appears simply to interpret the words of the NBA. Upon only slightly closer examination, however, it is clear that the decision is fatally flawed and distorts the language of the statute completely away from its reasonable meaning. The key to unraveling his Opinion is his interpretation of the word "required" in the NBA.

The solicitor's Opinion states "it is apparent that the President's proclamation setting aside the land for Park Service purposes would be a *required use* under the authority of the United States" (Solicitor's Opinion 1969,

---

[3] I assume for purposes of this presentation that (1) the exclusions were all performed correctly, and that (2) the exclusions apply to the Hualapai Reservation with equal force as they apply to the Navajo Reservation. If the exclusion language stopped here, so would this paper, at least with respect to the Navajo Boundary, but it does not.

[4] We should keep in mind that the Department of the Interior has a well-documented conflict of interest in relation to its fiduciary duty as trustee for American Indian interests and property. For example, see McCool 1987, 180–181; Thomas 1994, Sections 57.07 & 57.07(c). It is difficult to understand how the Department of the

Interior's solicitor could possibly avoid violating this duty when deciding a dispute between the BIA and another Department of the Interior division. Most certainly the solicitor is not a neutral judging body.

[5] While the solicitor's 1969 Opinion seemed to terminate Navajo use and occupancy, it is clear that it did not. As late as 1979, the Navajos apparently continued to enjoy use and occupancy of these lands according to Grand Canyon National Park's 1979 Colorado River Management Plan, as described in more detail below.

3) (emphasis added). The word "required" in the NBA, however, must be read in context: "until . . . *required* for power purposes or other uses" (emphasis added). The following is the relevant passage from the Navajo Boundary Act:

There are hereby reserved from the reservation . . . all lands heretofore designated by the Secretary of the Interior pursuant to section 28 of the Arizona Enabling Act . . . as being valuable for water-power purposes and all lands withdrawn or classified as power-site lands, saving to the Indians, nevertheless, the exclusive right to occupy and use such designated and classified lands until they shall be *required* for power purposes *or other uses* under the authority of the United States. . . . (emphasis added).

It is a mystery what the solicitor meant by a "required use." No such term is used in the NBA. The word "required" appears in the NBA, but it is used in the sense of preventing the United States from taking away the Navajos' "use and occupancy" rights *until* the excluded land is "required," i.e., necessary, for "power purposes or other uses." The issue is not whether taking the land to add to MCNM was a permissible "required use" (whatever the solicitor thought this might mean), but whether the "or other uses" language permitted the termination of the Navajos' right of "use and occupancy." If it did (highly unlikely, as argued above), the question becomes whether the land was necessary ("required") for whatever this "other use" might be. So, assuming that the solicitor did not need to show that the land was needed for dam or reservoir purposes, he would still have to show the land was necessary ("required") for the use for which it was taken.

The next critical question in my analysis of this issue and critique of the solicitor's Opinion is the question of whether the legislation establishing MCNM needed ("required") the use of these excluded lands. Clearly, it did not. By its own admission in 1979, ten years after the solicitor's 1969 Opinion, Grand Canyon National Park (GCNP) (into which MCNM was incorporated through the Grand Canyon National Park Enlargement Act of 1975) unequivocally stated in its Colorado River Management Plan both that it did not need ("require") the land, and also that it did not even consider it was entitled to it:

The 12.5 million acre reservation of the Navajo Nation borders the east bank of the Colorado River in the Marble Canyon Section of the park from River Mile 0 at Lee's [sic] Ferry to River Mile 61.8 at the confluence of the Little Colorado River. *The area from the river to and beyond the rim is undeveloped tribal park.* (National Park Service 1979, 34) (emphasis added).

We can conclude the following from the foregoing analysis: (1) regardless of what the solicitor said in his 1969 Opinion, the land was not necessary ("required") for MCNM; and (2) in the view of GCNP, the Navajos continued their rights of use and occupancy at least through 1979.

In summary, I believe the "or other uses" language in the NBA needs to be interpreted in light of the purposes for which the land was excluded from the Navajo Reservation in the first place—for a dam or reservoir. And even if this interpretation is not adopted, the language of the NBA explicitly states that the excluded property must be "required" for the "other use" before the Navajos' exclusive right to use and occupy the excluded lands can be terminated. That the lands carved out from the Navajo Reservation are not necessary is clear. Congress established that the land is not necessary for dam or reservoir purposes. The National Park Service admitted in 1979 that it did not need the land and did not even believe it was entitled to it. Therefore, the Navajo Nation at the very least should have the right to access the Colorado River from the mouth of the Little Colorado River to at least Lees Ferry and to use and occupy the land between the river and the 3,150-foot elevation contour along this stretch.

The Hualapai Boundary

We should first note that the solicitor addressed the Hualapai boundary differently from the Navajo boundary. His 1976 Opinion, issued in conjunction with the westward expansion of GCNP, while addressing the Hualapai Colorado River boundary issue, does not assert that the Hualapai are precluded from access by virtue of the 1914 legislation excluding hydropower lands. In fact, the 1976 Opinion does not even mention excluded hydropower lands. Instead, the deciding factor in the Opinion involves the language of the 1883 Executive Order creating the Hualapai Reservation.

The Executive Order describes the northern boundary as running "along" the Colorado River. The solicitor distinguishes the word "along" from other river-boundary descriptions using words such as "up" and "down" a river. "Up" and "down" a river, he explains (citing cases dealing with these precise words), intend a grant to the *center line* of the river (5).[6] But since the Executive Order uses "along" rather than "up" and "down," the solicitor asserts that the Hualapai were granted title only to

---

6 This point should be of great interest to the Navajo Nation, as their Colorado River boundary descriptions use "up" and "down."

the line of the Colorado River's high-water mark.[7]

Remarkably, the solicitor cited no case law to support his interpretation of "along." This point is critical: if there is a generally accepted principle of law establishing how the word "along" is to be interpreted in a stream/river boundary situation, and if "along" is to be interpreted according to this principle in the same way "up" and "down" are interpreted, then the solicitor implicitly admits the Hualapai Reservation boundary is the center of the Colorado River.[8] The convoluted analysis contained in both the 1976 and 1997 opinions dealing with the meaning of "along" is necessary, according to the solicitor, to determine what the legal meaning of "along" is in a boundary description. He asserts that no generally accepted legal rule exists, thereby justifying his interpretive analysis. The necessary corollary of this is that the analysis the solicitor undertakes is meaningless, or should be, if such a legal rule *does* exist.

Before addressing whether a legal rule in fact exists on this point, let us examine the analysis the solicitor did use. He determined that the Hualapai could not have been granted title to the center of the Colorado River because the Hualapai were required in 1881 to acknowledge that the reservation lands they were receiving were worthless wastelands. If these lands were indeed worthless, his reasoning continues, the word "along" cannot be interpreted as granting title to the center of the river since title extending to the center of the river would be of some value. Any value would mean that the Hualapai Reservation consisted of something more than worthless wasteland.

We should now ask why the Hualapai made the 1881 statement that the reservation lands were valueless: they did it to obtain their reservation. They were required by the federal government to acknowledge that the land they were being given was economically worthless to "whites" (Solicitor's Opinion 1976, at 2). It is difficult to believe that in the relatively enlightened year of 1976, the solicitor could consider it conscionable to attempt to use such an obviously coerced statement against the Hualapai. And

even more unbelievable, in 1997, he approved this aspect of the reasoning of the 1976 Opinion. For clarification, the Hualapais' 1881 statement, in relevant part, states:

> They urge that the following reservation be set aside for them while there is still time; that the land can never be of any great use to the whites; that there are no mineral deposits upon it, as it had been thoroughly prospected; *that there is little or no arable land; that the water is in such small quantities*, and the country is so rocky and void of grass, that it would not be available for stock raising (Walapai Papers, S. Doc. No. 273, 74th Cong. 2nd Sess. (1936) at 135-136) (emphasis added—this is the language the solicitor relied upon).

Legally, there are at least two critical difficulties with the solicitor's reliance on this statement. Courts do not enforce unconscionable provisions,[9] nor do they give weight to statements that have been coerced. Presumably, if his opinions were to be published widely, the solicitor would not have dared to use such an unconscionable argument. Again we see a consequence of a judging body that is neither neutral nor accountable.

Let us return now to the question about the legal meaning of the word "along" in a stream/river boundary description, keeping in mind that if there is a generally accepted legal meaning, then we must conclude that the solicitor's analysis is moot. Contrary to what the 1976 Opinion suggests, there is in fact a generally accepted legal interpretation for the word "along" in a stream/river boundary situation. This was very easy to determine. Section 30 of the "Boundaries" entry in the widely used legal encyclopedia *Corpus Juris Secundum* specifically lists the words "with," "along," "by," "on," "up," and "down," and indicates that cases construe all of these words "to carry title to the center" of a nonnavigable stream/river.[10] Apparently, the solicitor failed to perform even the most rudimentary legal research before he prepared his 1976 Opinion, and the

---

[7] The high-water mark is the relevant point on a "navigable river"—the solicitor, according to his 1976 Opinion, believes that the Colorado is navigable. In the question-and-answer session following the presentation of this paper at the Grand Canyon History Symposium, Jan Balsom, who is in charge of Grand Canyon National Park's relations with American Indian tribes, confirmed that the park considers the high-water mark to be the "historical" high-water mark, that is, the high-water mark *before* the construction of Glen Canyon Dam, a height that will not be reached unless the dam fails or is decommissioned. Even if the high-water mark is the boundary, the solicitor neglects to address an additional problem: "A conveyance to [the] 'high water mark,' as a general rule, vests in the grantee the right to the soil between ordinary high and ordinary low water mark, as incident or appurtenant to adjacent lands" (Ephraim Creek Coal & Coke Co. v. Bragg, 83 S.E. 190, 191 [W.Va. 1914]). Thus, even if the Hualapai do not hold title to the land below the high-water mark, they appear to have the right to use and occupy it.

[8] Assuming, of course, the Colorado River is considered nonnavigable in Grand Canyon—see the discussion of this issue below.

[9] Consider the way courts have dealt with racial restrictions in contracts, deeds, and covenants.

[10] Accord: 12 Am.Jur.2nd Boundaries Section 24. This rule pertains to the case of a "nonnavigable" stream. The legal significance for boundary purposes of what is and is not legally considered a "navigable" stream is discussed below. The generally accepted rule is that property that borders on a nonnavigable stream/river, unless an intention to the contrary is manifest, grants title to the center of the river. This has been the generally accepted legal principle since before the 1883 Executive Order establishing the Hualapai Reservation. See Drake v. Russian Land Co., 103 P. 167, 169 (Ca Ct of Appeals 1909) "[this] common law rule . . . has been adopted generally throughout the United States." Cases following this rule include Rowland v. Shoreline Boat & Ski Club, 544 N.E.2nd 5, 7 (Ill. App. 1989); McDonald v. Alexander, 388 S.W.2nd 725, 727 (Tex. App. 1965); Rollan v. Posey, 126 S.2nd 464, 466 (Ala. 1961); Kelley v. King, 36 S.E.2nd 220, 223 (N.C. 1945); and Conner v. Jarrett, 200 S.E. 39, 45 (W.Va. 1938). Cases following this rule *and* interpreting the word "along" include Westmoreland v. Buetell, 266 S.E.2nd 260, 261 (Ga. App. 1980) and Rowe v. Cape Fear Lumber Co., 38 S.E. 896 (N.C. 1901).

1997 Opinion was no better researched. Now that their shortcomings have been pointed out, these decisions should not be allowed to stand.

The final point I will address with respect to the Hualapai boundary dispute is whether the Colorado River should be considered navigable or nonnavigable for title purposes. This distinction is important because if it is considered navigable, the *entire* riverbed belongs to the State of Arizona to the extent it was not excluded for hydropower purposes; and if Arizona owns it, the Hualapai have no claim to the center of the river, regardless of how their title documents may read.[11] If the river is considered nonnavigable, however, the Hualapai boundary is the center of the Colorado River, assuming, of course, that the accepted legal method of determining navigability is used. I noted earlier that the solicitor stated in his 1976 Opinion that the Colorado River was navigable; however, he cited no support for this assertion. In 1997 the solicitor issued an updated Opinion on the Hualapai boundary issue. In this updated Opinion, he acknowledges that he had no basis for the determination and explicitly takes back the 1976 assertion of navigability. He goes on to say that he refuses to opine one way or the other as to the Colorado River's navigability.[12] Remarkably, the 1997 Opinion completely fails to address perhaps the most critical consequence of taking back the Opinion as to navigability: that the "high-water mark" is considered the boundary only if the river is navigable (see Solicitor's Opinion 1976, at 7-8). The 1976 and 1997 opinions, therefore, provide no legal basis for GCNP to assert that the high-water mark is the appropriate boundary for the Hualapai Reservation.

Let us examine the issue of navigability. For title purposes, the determination of whether the Colorado River in the Grand Canyon is navigable depends on whether the river was navigable in 1912, when Arizona became a state. The test of navigability, according to a leading boundary law treatise of the time, was whether the Colorado River was "susceptible of being used in [its] ordinary condition as [a] highway for commerce, over which trade and travel are or may be conducted in the customary modes of trade and travel on water" (Taylor 1876, 46–47).[13] Needless to say, in 1912 river runners could barely run the river; trade or travel in "the customary mode" was unimaginable. To reiterate,

the significance of the Colorado River being nonnavigable for title purposes is that, if it is, the Hualapai boundary extends to the center of the Colorado River (assuming that the accepted legal interpretation of "along" is employed).

I argue one additional point. Even assuming that the Colorado River was navigable in the Grand Canyon in 1912, the Hualapai people would still have a clear right to access the river since "the [property] owner has . . . a property right of access from the front of [the] land to the navigable part of the stream" (Skelton 1876, 322). Unfortunately, neither the 1976 nor 1997 Solicitor's Opinion addresses this access issue.

In summary, the portion of the Hualapai Reservation that is not subject to hydropower exclusion should extend to the middle of the Colorado River if the clear legal standards relating to the interpretation of "along" and "navigability" are used. Even if the Colorado River in the Grand Canyon is considered navigable, the Hualapai have a clear right of access to the navigable part of the river from their land. The 1976 and 1997 solicitor's opinions must be reviewed by a neutral and accountable judging body, preferably one that can thoroughly and competently perform the necessary legal research.

Conclusion

On a commercial paddle trip on the Colorado River in the Grand Canyon in the summer of 2000, our trip leader told us that the National Park Service was taking hard-line positions with the neighboring American Indian tribes with respect to the Colorado River boundary. The trip leader indicated that the park service's objective was to gain full control of Colorado River access in the Grand Canyon. To accomplish this, at least with respect to the Hualapai, the park service had taken the position that the boundary was the historic high-water mark (pre–Glen Canyon Dam). Effectively, this position eliminated the Hualapais' access to the river without the park's consent since, barring a catastrophic failure of Glen Canyon Dam or its decommissioning, the pre-dam high-water mark will never again be reached by the river. I continue to wonder how the right-to-access issue was handled (or avoided) by the park service in their dealings with the Hualapai.[14] Meanwhile, I have learned

---

[11] This is based on the assumption that the 1912 Act of Congress establishing Arizona overrides the 1883 Executive Order establishing the Hualapai Reservation, at least to this extent.

[12] Citing the United States Supreme Court Opinion *Arizona v. California*, 283 U.S. 423, 452-53, the Solicitor's Office in 1997 indicates that the Colorado River was navigable upstream as far as the Virgin River at Black Canyon, well short of the Hualapai Reservation. No legal determination appears ever to have been made with respect to the navigability of the Colorado River in Grand Canyon.

[13] See *Hanes v. State*, 973 P.2nd 330, 334 (Ok. App. 1998) for a discussion of the navigability test. See also *United States v. Cress*, 243 U.S. 316, 323 (1916).

[14] The highest officials of Grand Canyon National Park appear to have believed in good faith, and without any reservation, in the validity of the solicitor's opinions, and have acted accordingly. See Burnham 2000, 292–293.

that upriver, the National Park Service has in recent years taken a rather hard-line position with the Navajos. They now contend that the South Rim is the Navajo Nation's northern boundary. Again, it is difficult to understand how the park service can justify this position in light of their 1979 Colorado River Management Plan in which they say the Navajos continue to use and occupy the hydropower carve-out lands.[15]

AFTERWORD

I am no longer a practicing attorney and nothing I say in this paper can be considered a "legal opinion." If anyone wishes to take a legal position based on what I say in this paper, be sure to consult first with a practicing attorney. This paper has already generated controversy. I shared my research and conclusions with Stanley Pollock in the Navajo Nation's Attorney General's Office, and Clay Bravo and Cisney Havetone in the Hualapai Tribal Offices in Peach Springs, as early as June 2001 (prior to presenting an earlier version of this paper at the Association for the Study of Literature and the Environment Conference at Northern Arizona University in late June 2001). At that time, the Hualapai were not represented by counsel. My relations with the representatives of both tribes were pleasant, if not very productive. When I submitted a revised paper for the Grand Canyon History Symposium, personnel at GCNP also became aware of my research and conclusions. In November 2001 I sent a revised version of the paper to Stanley Pollock and to Louise Benson, Hualapai chairwoman. After she misplaced the paper, I sent her another copy in early January 2002. She gave the paper to the attorneys hired by the tribe (the Hualapai Tribe had hired new counsel in the intervening months). I then proceeded to trade numerous phone and e-mail messages with one of the tribe's attorneys—we never did speak directly. The attorney suggested that I might want to consider not presenting the paper at the conference—that it was full of problems, and that I might not be aware of the sensitive nature of the political arena. The attorney's final message, which I received after the beginning of the conference, even suggested that the Hualapai Tribe would need to send a delegation to present an opposing point of view. No such delegation materialized, and I have not heard from the tribe's attorney since.

My presentation at the conference went smoothly, but the question-and-answer session was unique in my experience. Jan Balsom, the park's liaison with neighboring tribes, introduced the panel and remained as an audience member. During the question-and-answer session, a number of questions arose as to the relationship of the park with the Hualapais that I could not answer. Jan was as qualified as anyone to answer these questions, however, given her job and experience. There proceeded a lively discussion between the audience and Jan—an exchange that consumed virtually all of the remaining time. Never before have I experienced such a lively Q & A session following a talk—a session in which audience members talked almost exclusively among themselves.

Several weeks after the conference I received an e-mail from Jeffrey Ingram, the Sierra Club's Southwest representative during the late 1960s and a man who was instrumental in the crafting and passing of the Grand Canyon National Park Enlargement Act of 1975, asking if he could read my paper. I sent him a copy and asked if he had any comments. I soon received an e-mail with his comments, which were longer than my paper. It was very useful to get the benefit of his firsthand experience with many of the issues I dealt with in the paper. I end this presentation by quoting the final paragraph from Ingram's letter:

> Andy, I have no idea if anyone other than you has tried to grapple with these river boundary issues. As I hope you can tell, I think they are worthwhile because they can point the way toward fruitful cooperation between NPS and the Navajo & Hualapai. Put in the context of enhancing the wilderness & natural qualities of the Canyon while avoiding the degrading activities, your work can be extremely valuable. GCNP has been ordered to proceed with a [Colorado] River Management Plan ([C]RMP) over the next couple of years. The subject we have been discussing here could be a vital and positive contribution to a soundly-based, Canyon-friendly, [C]RMP.

---

15 One final note: What should happen to the lands excluded for hydropower, if, as seems likely, these dams are not built? I have not specifically researched this issue from a legal standpoint, but general principles of fairness suggest that some sort of reversion theory should apply—that is, the land eventually should revert to the reservations from which it was taken.

Casinos of Stone: Monsoon Gambling and Playing the Slot Canyons

by Tom Myers

The canyon community was saddened in 2001 with the news that George Mancuso and his companion, Linda Brehmer, had died in a flash flood on the Little Colorado River. Dr. Myers, who has spent the last twelve years treating injuries incurred in the canyon and writing of the dangers and deaths to be found there, was Mancuso's friend. He was moved to write and present this caution concerning flash floods, interwoven with the story of the tragic deaths of Mancuso and Brehmer. Tom hopes that the essay will prevent others from gambling their lives on their next visit to the Grand Canyon.

It is pure serendipity, and it is pure joy—those trysts of chance, when you unexpectedly run into a friend in a place for which you share a passion. A timeless moment of connection, although often fleeting, can be so genuine and so sincere that it remains with you always, long after each has traveled entirely different journeys. For lovers of canyons and rivers, when the rendezvous is beside flowing water deep within a sculpted gorge, there is nothing quite like it.

Approaching the confluence of the Little Colorado and Colorado rivers, I was hoping for such a rendezvous. It was mid-June and very hot for foot travel, but I knew it was his favorite place on Earth, a place he loved to frequent. I was running the river, but he would be walking, probably alone. And although somewhat eccentric, to me, George was the epitome of Grand Canyon passion.

Pulling in, I walked upstream, bankside and opposite the measured current of

George Mancuso at the Little Colorado River confluence with the Colorado in 2000. Photograph by Lea Jane Parker

blue-green water, but part of a steady flow of other river runners. A busy day. Lots of people. If he was there, I thought it unlikely that I would be able to spot him amid those frolicking in the water and sunning on the ledges. Then, looking across the Little Colorado, one person did stand out. Lean and tan, he walked swiftly with a seasoned hiker's confidence and a recognizable hint of urgency. I knew it was George.

Calling him over, he introduced me to his new hiking companion, who trailed behind. Linda was soft-spoken, in her early fifties. It was her first canyon hike. George, on the other hand, was a bona fide canyon hiker and professional photographer. I knew he had plodded at least 6,000 miles in roughly twenty-five years. Where we now stood was his favorite spot in his favorite place, the inspiration for his annual pilgrimages and source of his livelihood.

George was his usual bundle of nervous energy and did most of the talking.

Like always, his enthusiasm rivaled the setting, his passion as deep as the canyon itself. Still, as we parted, I sensed he felt a twinge of loneliness at being left behind. Having been in his boots many times before, I knew exactly how he felt. I smiled softly, left them some cold beer and soda, and waved goodbye.

It is really more a question of when, not if. Near misses are already numerous, and hundreds, many unknowingly, continue to put themselves at risk every day during the monsoon season, usually for reasons that are almost understandable. The Grand Canyon is famous for its scenic side canyons, many of which are spectacular slots found in few places other than the American Southwest. For many hikers and river runners a trip in the canyon is not complete without stops at these locations; indeed, it is sacrilegious not to stop. They become trip-long expectations and "must-sees." Often the intense pressure from fellow trip members and high-paying clients to enter slot canyons despite warning signs of potential flooding supersedes good judgment by commercial guides, private boaters, and hiking leaders. The "we may never get this chance again" mentality spurs a gambler's dilemma: should we stay out or go in? In the gambler vein—bearing in mind the odds of flash flooding and the sheer numbers of backcountry users—it thus seems inevitable that one day an entire river or hiking party will be swept into oblivion unless they learn how to play those odds.

In many ways, flash floods are the southwestern equivalent of midwestern tornadoes. The product of natural meteorological phenomena, they are fast and furious, and they have incredible destructive potential. Both are fascinating spectacles of sound, wind, water, and power. To see one, just once, is not uncommon in either region; getting caught in one and living to tell about it is rare. For most people, however, the destructive potential of flash floods remains vague. Most occur in remote washes and drainages where there are no buildings to level or inhabitants to wash away. The reality is, even for lifelong residents of the American Southwest, where evidence abounds, flash floods will seldom be seen and rarely appreciated. Again, the problem is partly because it is harder to relate to deeply carved arroyos or boulder-choked drainages produced by flash floods than to demolished homes or twisted automobile wreckage left by tornados. Consequently, flash floods are often underestimated and unanticipated by those who venture into their domain at the wrong time, even if the adventurer is a seasoned canyon hiker.

"Have you heard the news about George Mancuso yet? You know he's missing."

Up until that point, my phone conversation with ranger Bil Vandergraff about an upcoming National Park Service river trip had been lighthearted. "So what else is new?" was my reply.

Monsoon rains in September 1997 produced flash flooding along the Inner Gorge rock face below Kanab Creek. Photograph by Jerre Sears

I had known George for years. He was notorious for showing up late after a long canyon excursion. "How long has he been missing?" I asked.

"Ten days. He was reported missing by the son of a woman he was hiking with. She's missing too. A woman named Linda . . ."

My heart went to my throat. I swallowed hard. "Damn it, George," I thought aloud.

"Monsoons" are typically a welcome and expected reprieve from the intense summer heat in the arid Southwest. The gradual buildup of moisture-laden clouds from wind-driven air masses migrating up from the south produces afternoon thundershowers that render temporary but priceless respite to unrelenting heat. Unfortunately, most of the water leaves as quickly as it arrives, sometimes quicker. This is especially true in the high desert of the Colorado Plateau. Rain falls on the rocky, barren terrain and, with nothing to hold it back, begins a frenzied race toward the nadir in elevation. Gathering mass, momentum, and debris, it careens like an out-of-control freight train down dry streambeds and washes, blasting over anything in its path. By the time it gets to the bottom of the drainage it can become a debris-choked tidal wave of mud, rock, cacti, cow manure, basketballs, and tires. All this can occur from a single storm cell over a miniscule area, while just a few miles away conditions remain blue skied and bone dry. Therein lies the biggest problem inherent to canyon river running and side-canyon exploration during stormy weather.

On the plateaus, one can see monsoon activity for miles. Within the confines of the Grand Canyon, a limited rift of sky may be all that is visible. The deeper one goes, the narrower this perspective becomes. Consequently, one can easily be lulled into a false sense of security about entering. If the sky above is invitingly blue, it is easy to naively venture into the drainage, oblivious to a potentially lethal juggernaut emanating from an unseen deluge at the head of the drainage. To complicate things, these monsoon events peak during July through September, a period which coincides with the peak period of river travel and canyon hikes. Whether or not these travelers appreciate the monsoon pattern and their limited ability to anticipate flash floods, they are there and therefore involved in a potentially high-stakes gamble.

What is the solution? Simply to avoid Phantom, Deer, and Havasu creeks or any other slot canyon at all times during the monsoon season seems extreme. After all, thousands of hikers and river runners have been in such canyons over the years yet there have been only eleven flash-flood–related deaths in the Grand Canyon involving hikers and none involving river runners. Still, close calls have been countless. So what is reasonable advice, and can advice make the "monsoon gamble" a little more calculated, not just a reflex throw of the dice?

For starters, if ominous black thunderheads litter the sky, plainly announcing that a downpour is imminent, or if

A flash flood in Indian Canyon on July 18, 2002. Photographs by Linda Jalbert

it is already raining, the decision about entering or not entering should be obvious. Stay out. Fold your hand. Mother Nature just showed you hers and she is holding a Royal Flush—literally. But suppose she is wearing her poker face, and that slice of sky is invitingly blue or the clouds are fluffy-white? The decision is obviously tougher, but there are some important "tells," as they say in Las Vegas.

First, again, the monsoon season usually begins in July and ends in September. Second, monsoon storms by definition and atmospheric physiology are afternoon events. Third, it usually takes large flash floods from one to four hours to

reach the river because they originate well up the side drainages on the plateaus or above the rims (floods that begin nearer the river tend to be much smaller). Given these facts, how vital might this information be to the canyon-country trekker? The reality check is telltale.

All but one of the known thirteen flash-flood deaths in the Grand Canyon occurred in July, August, or September. These twelve victims in the Grand Canyon, as well as eleven victims in nearby Antelope Canyon in 1997, all died during the afternoon. And since 1990, of eleven flash floods recorded in the depths of the Grand Canyon at Bright Angel Creek between July and September, nine (more than 80 percent) occurred during afternoon or early evening hours. The facts are clear, although the life-saving admonition—entering any narrow canyon that is part of a large drainage area during the typical monsoon season is risky—is more subtle; venturing into one of these canyons during afternoon or evening hours may be substantially riskier.

Afternoon thunderstorms had been showering the Little Colorado River gorge for days. George and Linda had seen at least two flash floods surge below their campsite at the confluence of Salt Trail Canyon and the Little C., which they had carefully selected above the flood plain. Their camp was found abandoned. Personal items and sleeping gear remained unpacked and exposed, as though they planned to return at any moment.

On August 7 Linda wrote in her journal that today they would go to "Emerald Pool" in Big Canyon, a tributary of the Little Colorado. She hoped to wash her hair in clean water. This was her final journal entry.

Given the monsoon pattern, if it seems absolutely necessary to explore that side canyon and the skies are clear, consider doing it in the morning then get out. If there is any hint of rain, forget it. Again, it sounds simple, but it is usually not that black and white. The pressure may be on, and the timing may be off. Nevertheless, this simple rule of thumb could save your life. But understand this holds true only for "typical" monsoon activity. If weather patterns are unusual, all bets are off. Flash floods occur year-round, and the largest—the ones that create rapids on the river with their huge debris flows—tend to occur at night in late winter or early spring when rain causes the snowpack to melt. These floods, as well as those produced by low-pressure storm systems at any time of year, do not fall into the same category as monsoons. It all comes down to a best guess.

So what if you guess wrong?

Fortunately, you are not necessarily doomed if a flash flood arrives when you are stuck in a drainage. You may still have an ace up your sleeve. Most flash floods are "telegraphed" to some degree and are perceptible if you remain alert. For example, with large floods (the lethal kind), a deep roar typically precedes the flow by as much as a minute, sometimes even more. Like a train, it warns people to get out of the way—or else. Yet as loud as this roar may be, it can be masked or muffled by creek babble until the flood is on top of you. So think about keeping someone posted as a lookout just upstream, away from the din of the creek or waterfall but within earshot and eyesight of those in the creek. Also look for potential escape routes as you hike. Many people do not know that while most flash floods could be outrun by a healthy adult in an open-field sprint (flash floods typically flow at maximum speeds averaging six to twelve miles per hour), the race would be lost if it were down a drainage that required tricky climbing or boulder hopping. Luckily, many floods can be outmaneuvered by side scrambling out of the drainage bottom if the walls are not too steep, and sometimes a couple of seconds is all that is needed.

Think about these options when you are about to enter an especially steep, long and narrow, boulder-choked drainage; ponder how those boulders got there. Seriously consider not going beyond anything that you could not run through or climb out of in a hurry, or stay in the wide-open section, especially when napping or camping. Above all, remain vigilant for subtle clues, such as sudden muddying of

Mancuso's tripod found at Emerald Pool shortly after the flash flood. Photograph by Elias Butler

a creek (some floods present this way rather than with a large tumbling wave), the earthy smell of clay and other minerals, a sudden shift of wind or sound.

None of this is meant to dissuade or discourage off-river hiking. Exploring side canyons is truly rewarding, the best way to really "experience" the Grand Canyon, and should be part of every Grand Canyon backcountry trip. But take time to heed Mother Nature's mood before you ante into the monsoon gamble. Look for signs of permission before rummaging through her canyon home and its spectacular, narrow corridors. Always contemplate and respect the natural forces that formed and still form the canyon. And save your real gambling for the slot machines, where you have a lot less to lose.

Searchers Scott Thybony and Tony Williams found Linda's body tightly wrapped around the base of a tamarisk tree on August 22, four days after the search began. She was found below "Emerald Pool" about one-quarter mile up Big Canyon, and less than one mile from their campsite. Still wearing boots, most of her clothing and hair were gone, having been stripped away by the flash flood's debris. A Teva shirt was also found snagged in a tamarisk about eight feet above the streambed. Film found at the campsite showed that George had been wearing the shirt.

A few days later, Grand Canyon boatman Greg Woodall found George's body during a routine river patrol. Arriving at the confluence, Greg was tipped off by some ravens hovering above a rocky bar beside the main island near the Little Colorado mouth. The body was found about five feet above river level, covered with driftwood debris. Ironically, and perhaps fittingly, this resting place was George's most beloved and photographed spot in the canyon.

"The ravens," Woodall said, "showed him to us. And he's where he wanted to be, and the ravens kind of guaranteed he'd be there forever."

GEORGE LAMONT MANCUSO
1954–2001

AND

LINDA BREHMER
1950–2001

Appendix A
Symposium Participants

Marilyn Abraham	*Tucson, Arizona*	Mary J. Straw Cook	*Santa Fe, New Mexico*
Bruce Aiken	*Grand Canyon, Arizona*	Pam Cox	*Grand Canyon, Arizona*
Stewart Aitchison	*Flagstaff, Arizona*	Nancy Dallett	*Phoenix, Arizona*
Leland C. "Lee" Albertson	*Tempe, Arizona*	Chuck Davis	*Sedona, Arizona*
Shirley Albertson	*Tempe, Arizona*	Jan Davis	*Sedona, Arizona*
Joe Alston	*Grand Canyon, Arizona*	Rich Della Porta	*Grand Canyon, Arizona*
Judy Alston	*Grand Canyon, Arizona*	Brad Dimock	*Flagstaff, Arizona*
Michael Amundsen	*Flagstaff, Arizona*	Michael Dom	*Kingman, Arizona*
Mike Anderson	*Grand Canyon, Arizona*	Denise Donofrio	*Carefree, Arizona*
Linda Anderson	*Grand Canyon, Arizona*	Cameron Doss	*Prescott Valley, Arizona*
Robert Audretsch	*Grand Canyon, Arizona*	Minette Doss	*Prescott Valley, Arizona*
Jack L. August Jr.	*Prescott, Arizona*	Brian Doyle	*Grand Canyon, Arizona*
Val Avery	*Flagstaff, Arizona*	Jacque Doyle	*Phoenix, Arizona*
John S. Azar	*Fredonia, Arizona*	Elizabeth Drake	*Scottsdale, Arizona*
Jim Babbitt	*Flagstaff, Arizona*	Susan Eubank	*Grand Canyon, Arizona*
Doug Bale	*Hungerford, England*	Helen Fairley	*Flagstaff, Arizona*
Janet R. Balsom	*Grand Canyon, Arizona*	Ed Farnam	*Stockton, California*
Gale Barg	*Kingman, Arizona*	Phoebe Farnam	*Stockton, California*
Frank Barrios	*Phoenix, Arizona*	David C. Frauman	*Indianapolis, Indiana*
Bryan Bates	*Flagstaff, Arizona*	John Frazier	*Grand Canyon, Arizona*
Emma P. Benenati	*Flagstaff, Arizona*	Pam Frazier	*Grand Canyon, Arizona*
Bruce Benware	*Peoria, Arizona*	Shelley Friscia	*Scottsdale, Arizona*
Edna Benware	*Peoria, Arizona*	Stew Fritts	*Grand Canyon, Arizona*
Bill Bishop	*Flagstaff, Arizona*	Elmer Fuchs	*New Mexico*
Peter MacMillan Booth	*Wickenburg, Arizona*	Dora Fuchs	*New Mexico*
Dorothy Boulton	*Flagstaff, Arizona*	Brad Fuqua	*Grand Canyon, Arizona*
Stephen Bridgehouse	*Grand Canyon, Arizona*	Michael P. Ghiglieri	*Flagstaff, Arizona*
Neita Bridger	*Flagstaff, Arizona*	Susan Golightly	*Flagstaff, Arizona*
Joe Brindle	*Philadelphia, Pennsylvania*	Christi Goll	*Tucson, Arizona*
Patty Brookins	*Grand Canyon, Arizona*	Debbie Goll	*Tucson, Arizona*
Bonnie Brune	*Pinetop, Arizona*	Keith Green	*Grand Canyon, Arizona*
Michael Buchheit	*Grand Canyon, Arizona*	Nancy Green	*Grand Canyon, Arizona*
Tom Carmony	*Tempe, Arizona*	Karen Greig	*Menlo Park, California*
Dan Cassidy	*Phoenix, Arizona*	Mickey Hahnenkratt	*Phoenix, Arizona*
Diane Cassidy	*Phoenix, Arizona*	Judy Hellmich	*Grand Canyon, Arizona*
Carolyn Castleman	*Peoria, Arizona*	Lois Henderson	*Grand Canyon, Arizona*
Bradford Cole	*Flagstaff, Arizona*	Rita Hicks	*Phoenix, Arizona*
Mike Coltrin	*Tucson, Arizona*	Betsy Hilgendorf	*Grand Canyon, Arizona*
Sue Ellen Coltrin	*Tucson, Arizona*	Amy Horn	*Grand Canyon, Arizona*
Paul Conn	*Flagstaff, Arizona*	J. Donald Hughes	*Denver, Colorado*
Edward Cook	*Santa Fe, New Mexico*	Mrs. Don Hughes	*Denver, Colorado*

Charles House	Tucson, Arizona	Fred Schick	Sedona, Arizona
Bill Johnston	Grand Canyon, Arizona	Jean Schick	Sedona, Arizona
Paul Julien	Tucson, Arizona	Hank Schneider	Prescott, Arizona
Henry Karpinski	Grand Canyon, Arizona	B. J. Schroeder	Mesa, Arizona
Jan Koons	Grand Canyon, Arizona	John Schroeder	Mesa, Arizona
Richard Koopman	Longmont, Colorado	Charles Schulz	Carefree, Arizona
Rosemary Koopman	Longmont, Colorado	Gus Scott	Prescott, Arizona
Michelle Krezek	Boulder, Colorado	Sandra Scott	Prescott, Arizona
Doug Kupel	Phoenix, Arizona	Elizabeth Sharp	Flagstaff, Arizona
Gary Ladd	Page, Arizona	Jim Shea	Tucson, Arizona
Don Lago	Flagstaff, Arizona	Sharon Shea	Tucson, Arizona
Bill Larson	Burbank, California	Linda Sheppard	Tucson, Arizona
Mrs. Bill Larson	Burbank, California	Dan Shilling	Tucson, Arizona
Pat Lauzon	Flagstaff, Arizona	Ron Short	Grand Canyon, Arizona
Robert Lauzon	Flagstaff, Arizona	Fred Simonelli	Los Angeles, California
Mary Layman	Flagstaff, Arizona	Mary Simpson	Flagstaff, Arizona
Roy Lemons	Belen, New Mexico	Joan Slater	Tucson, Arizona
Edna Lemons	Belen, New Mexico	Philip Slater	Tucson, Arizona
George Lubick	Flagstaff, Arizona	Drifter Smith	Flagstaff, Arizona
Andrew Majeske	Davis, California	Ed Spicer	Santee, California
Don Mattox	Albuquerque, New Mexico	John Stark	Flagstaff, Arizona
Vivian Mattox	Albuquerque, New Mexico	George Steck	Albuquerque, New Mexico
Jim McCarthy	Peoria, Arizona	Larry Stevens	Flagstaff, Arizona
Shannon McCloskey	Grand Canyon, Arizona	Bill Suran	Kachina Village, Arizona
Mona Lange McCroskey	Prescott, Arizona	Bill Swan	Scottsdale, Arizona
Gretchen Merten	Flagstaff, Arizona	John Sudar	Grand Canyon, Arizona
David Meyer	Grand Canyon, Arizona	Julie Tackenberg	Tucson, Arizona
Ellen Miller	Grand Canyon, Arizona	William Tackenberg	Tucson, Arizona
Tom Miller	Flagstaff, Arizona	Henry Taylor	Kirtland, New Mexico
Sandra Munoz-Weingarten	Phoenix, Arizona	Denise Traver	Flagstaff, Arizona
Tom Myers	Flagstaff, Arizona	Richard Ullman	Grand Canyon, Arizona
Brian Nordstrom	Prescott, Arizona	Sally Underwood	Dewey, Arizona
Jim Ohlman	Kayenta, Arizona	Steve Verkamp	Flagstaff, Arizona
Janice Ohlman	Kayenta, Arizona	Suzie Verkamp	Abiquiu, New Mexico
Sue Ordway	Flagstaff, Arizona	Jennie Valentine	Page, Arizona
Stephen Owen	Chandler, Arizona	Demica Vigil	Grand Canyon, Arizona
Lynn Perkins	Howard, Kansas	Andrew Wallace	Prescott, Arizona
Marge Post	Grand Canyon, Arizona	Bernice Wallace	Prescott, Arizona
Louis Purvis	Brownwood, Texas	Carl Wargula	Goodyear, Arizona
Marie Purvis	Brownwood, Texas	Eve Watson	Grand Canyon, Arizona
Richard D. Quartaroli	Flagstaff, Arizona	Todd Weber	Prescott, Arizona
Mike Quinn	Grand Canyon, Arizona	Mike Weaver	Grand Canyon, Arizona
Donn Reynard	Grand Canyon, Arizona	Donna Weissenborn	Tucson, Arizona
Al Richmond	Flagstaff, Arizona	John Westerlund	Flagstaff, Arizona
Rich Richmond	Flagstaff, Arizona	John Wharton	Boulder, Colorado
Andrea Ross	Davis, California	Dotti Willis	Gold Canyon, Arizona
Anne Rosen	Grand Canyon, Arizona	Guy Willis	Gold Canyon, Arizona
Hal Rothman	Las Vegas, Nevada	Juti Winchester	Fresno, California
Melissa Ruffner	Prescott, Arizona	Marjorie Woodruff	Chandler, Arizona
Christa Sadler	Flagstaff, Arizona	John Zanotti	Peoria, Arizona

Grand Canyon
History
Symposium

January 24 - 27, 2002

Grand Canyon Village
South Rim — Grand Canyon National Park

You are cordially invited to the Grand Canyon History Symposium, the first such gathering to address historical topics specific to Grand Canyon National Park! One of our goals is to introduce NPS administrators and interested members of the public to the history of issues confronting the park today. Another is simply to learn more of the legacy of this crown jewel of the National Park System.

The following is an up-to-date schedule of presentations and events, intended to peak your interest and convince you to sign on for this inaugural historical event. At the end, please follow our step-by-step registration procedure. There may be minor adjustments as the first day nears, but you can count on the dates, meals, accommodations, prices, and general symposium flow presented here. Please register now, since, because of meeting room limitations, participation is limited to the first 100 registrants.

Presentations and Events

Thursday, January 24, 2002

9:15 a.m.   **Train Departs Williams**
Symposium participants meet at the Williams Depot and will be seated together, accompanied by historian Al Richmond who will relate the history of the Grand Canyon Railway en route. (You may, of course, drive to the South Rim if you do not want to take the train)

12:15 a.m.   **Train Arrives at Grand Canyon Station**
Participants have several hours to check into their hotel, eat lunch, and acclimate.

2:30-6:00 p.m.   **Registration, Reception & Programs at Kolb Studio**
• Conference registration/packets
• Complimentary refreshments
• Art exhibit

3:30 - 4:15 p.m.   **Women of Grand Canyon**
Interpretive program with Denise Traver

4:30 - 5:30 p.m.   **Women of Grand Canyon**
Interpretive program with Denise Traver

There are no scheduled evening activities. For National Park Service interpretive programs and restaurant information, participants should reference *The Guide*, the National Park Service newspaper, which is supplied in your packet and available throughout the park.

Friday, January 25, 2002 at the Historic Community Building

7:00-8:30 a.m.   **Registration Continues Complimentary Refreshments**

Open All Day   **Book Booth**

8:30-9:45 a.m.   **Superintendent's Welcome**
Joe Alston

Conference Orientation
Mike Anderson

9:45-10:00 a.m.   **Break**

10:00-Noon   **Colorado River — Room A**

Rafting for People with Disabilities
Sandra Munoz-Weingarten

Historic River Running
Bonnie Brune

Research on the Colorado River
Emma Benenati

10:00-Noon   **Anecdotes & More — Room B**

Grand Canyon on Postage Stamps
Bill Bishop

Hoover Dam Castings
Fred Simonelli

Grand Canyon National Park Tramway Survey of 1919
Jim Ohlman / Lon Ayers

12:00-1:30 p.m.   **Buffet Lunch & Keynote Speaker**
Professor Hal Rothman
University of Nevada, Las Vegas

Maswik Dining Room (Pre-registration required)
The menu includes prickly pear chicken, carved beef au jus with horseradish sauce, baked cod with lemon paprika butter, garlic mashed potatoes, wilted spinach and honeyed carrots, rice pilaf, house salad, and dessert.

1:30-3:15 p.m.   **Backcountry — Room A**

Whatever Happened to Jazz?
George Steck

GCNP Toll Roads & Trails
Mike Anderson

Building the Yaki Trail
Henry Karpinski

1:30-3:15 p.m.   **Anecdotes & More — Room B**

Shrine of the Ages
Juti Winchester

Kolb Airfield, 1926
Lee Albertson

Mystery Cabins of Buckskin Mtn.
John Azar

3:30-5:15 p.m.   **Civilian Conservation Corps — Room A**

A Hard Rocky Road to Nowhere
Roy Lemons

Blue Denim University
Peter Booth

The Ace in the Hole
Louis Purvis

3:30-5:15 p.m.   **Colorado River — Room B**

Boats, Oars, and Lore
Brad Dimock

Dunn-Howland Murders Revisited
Frank Barrios

The Geographic Powell Survey
Richard Quartaroli

There are no scheduled evening activities. Please consult *The Guide* for NPS interpretive programs and restaurant information.

2

Presentations and Events

Saturday, January 26, 2002 at the Historic Community Building

7:00-8:30 a.m.	Complimentary Refreshments
Open All Day	Book Booth
8:30 - 12:15 p.m.	**Colorado River Issues — Room A**

River Law and Rights
Bill Swan

Carl Hayden and the
Central Arizona Project
Jack August

Lee's Ferry Revisited
Doug Kupel

8:30 - 10:15 a.m.	**Grand Canyon Historic Photography — Room B**

Lantern Slides, c. 1900
Jim Babbitt

Photographs of Amelia &
Josephine Hollenback, 1897
Mary Jean Cook

Photographic Prints of the 1920s
Mona McCroskey

10:30 - 12:15 p.m.	**Grand Canyon Research — Room B**

Grand Canyon Geomorphology
Gretchen Merten

A Little Knowledge
Goes a Long Way
Jan Balsom

Biological Research at Grand
Canyon
Larry Stevens

12:15-1:30 p.m.	**Lunch** is not provided. Please consult *The Guide* for restaurant information.

1:30-3:15 p.m.	**Colorado River — Room A**

Colorado River Printed Guides
Richard Quartaroli

Secret Journal of George Bradley
Michael Ghiglieri

Flash Flood! Lethal Histories
Tom Myers

1:30-3:15 p.m.	**Ethnic/American Indian - Room B**

Grand Canyon's Railroad Culture
Al Richmond

National Park Service and
Tribal River Issues
Andrew Majeske

3:30-5:15 p.m.	**Tourism Session - Room A**

Railroads at Both Rims
Al Richmond

The CCC's Role in Tourism
Peter Booth

Mary Colter:
Grand Canyon Architect
David C. Frauman, PhD.

3:30-5:15 p.m.	**Preservation and Development — Room B**

Grand Canyon National Park:
Scenery or Habitat
Don Hughes

Bert Lauzon's Grand Canyon
Brad Cole

Orphan Mine
Mike Amundson

7:00-9:00 p.m.	**Awards Banquet & Featured Speaker** *Jim Babbitt*

Arizona Room (Pre-registration required)

The menu includes roast striploin of beef with shitake demi-glace, Caesar salad, horseradish mashed potatoes, seasonal squash medley, vanilla ice cream in tortilla bowl with prickly pear glaze.

Sunday, January 27, 2002

Field Trips
(Pre-registration required)

7:30-8:30 a.m.	**Orientation for the Day's Trips** Meet at Community Building. Complimentary coffee and tea will be available.
8:30-10:30 a.m.	**Historic Village Walking Tour with Mike Anderson** 25 persons maximum
11:00-Noon	**Historic Boat Tour with Brad Dimock** 10 persons maximum
11:00-3:00 p.m.	**Bus tour, Hermits Rest to Desert View with Denise Traver** 45 persons maximum
2:15-3:30 p.m.	**Bright Angel History Room Talk with Maxine Edwards** 30 persons maximum

Mule Trips

Participants may make individual arrangements for a mule ride to Plateau Point by calling (303) 297-2753.

3

Sponsorship

Cooperating organizations including Grand Canyon Association, Grand Canyon Field Institute, Arizona Humanities Council, Grand Canyon National Park Lodges, Grand Canyon Pioneers Society, and the National Park Service have contributed staff, time, money, and services to make this conference as afford-able as possible for attendees.

Special Thanks

All of us involved in planning the symposium offer our special gratitude to the **Arizona Humanities Council** and the **National Endowment for the Humanities** for their generous grants and support. Our gathering is associated with the NEH program entitled *Moving Waters: the Colorado River and the West,* which is sponsoring events throughout the Southwest during early 2002.

Steering Committee

Michael Anderson, National Park Service; John Azar, Grand Canyon Pioneers Society; Jan Balsom, National Park Service; Michael Buchheit, Grand Canyon Field Institute; Pam Frazier, Grand Canyon Association; Judy Hellmich, National Park Service; Bill Johnson, Grand Canyon National Park Lodges; Jon Sudar, National Park Service; Bill Suran, Grand Canyon Pioneers Society.

Program Committee

Michael Anderson, National Park Service; Valeen Avery, Northern Arizona University; Andy Wallace, Northern Arizona University—emeritus.

Registration Procedure

Reservations can be made only by telephone. Please use the following worksheet prior to telephone

1. registration to determine the events and programs in which you wish to participate.

Item	Unit Cost	Number	Total Cost	
Grand Canyon Railway round trip	$27.50		_____	
Registration Fee*	$35.00		_____	(non-refundable)
Friday buffet lunch	$13.00		_____	
Saturday awards banquet	$30.00		_____	
Sunday Bus Tour with Box Lunch	$11.00		_____	(limited to first 45)
Sunday Historic Walking Tour	No Fee		_____	(limited to first 25)
Historic Boat Tour	No Fee		_____	(limited to first 10)
Bright Angel History Room Talk	No Fee		_____	(limited to first 30)

* Note: Park entrance fees are waived for all presenters and registrants.

2. Call Grand Canyon Field Institute at (928) 638-2485. GCFI accepts Visa, Mastercard, or American Express.
Payment by check must be received by GCFI within two weeks of registration or your registration will be can-celed automatically. The $35 registration fee is non-refundable. All other items listed above may be cancelled for a full refund up to 15 days prior to the symposium. No refunds will be made after January 9, 2002.

3. To reserve lodging, call Grand Canyon National Park Lodges at (928) 638-2525. This is a quick and easy call—sufficient rooms have been set aside to accommodate all participants.

Special Symposium Rates

Maswik Lodge North . . . . . . First night $40.00, second night $40.00, third night free.
Rimside Accommodations . . . First and second nights at standard rate, third night free.

Confirmation

A confirmation letter and other necessary materials will be mailed to you within three weeks of registration/payment.
Upon registration at the symposium, you will receive name tags, event tickets, and symposium updates.

Grand Canyon History Symposium
Grand Canyon Association, P. O. Box 399, Grand Canyon, AZ 86023

Grand Canyon History Symposium is published by Grand Canyon Association (GCA) in cooperation with Grand Canyon National Park. Michael Anderson, Symposium Director/Editor; Ron Short, GCA Art Director. Photos: Michael Quinn, GCNP Museum Collection. © 2001 Grand Canyon Association. Printed by *Arizona Daily Sun* on recycled paper, using soy inks.

CONTRIBUTORS

Leland C. "Lee" Albertson is a retired engineer who lives in Tempe, Arizona, with his wife, Shirley, and diminutive dog, Lady. He has long been an active member of the Grand Canyon Historical Society, serving as its president more than once, and organizes the society's annual Easter Sunrise Service at the canyon. His interests include Grand Canyon backpacking, river running, and history, and he is currently looking for his next research project.

Michael F. Anderson, PhD, earned his doctoral degree in history from Northern Arizona University in Flagstaff in 1999. He has been a researcher and writer of canyon history since 1990, a teacher and guide for the Grand Canyon Field Institute since 1993, and the Grand Canyon National Park's trails archaeologist since 2001. Dr. Anderson is the author of three canyon histories, all published by the Grand Canyon Association: *Living at the Edge: Explorers, Exploiters, and Settlers of the Grand Canyon Region* (1998); *Polishing the Jewel: An Administrative History of Grand Canyon National Park* (2000); and *Along the Rim: A Guide to Grand Canyon's South Rim from Hermits Rest to Desert View* (2001).

Jack L. August Jr., PhD, lives in Prescott, Arizona, and is a historian and expert witness in the Natural Resources Section of the Arizona Attorney General's Office, where his work focuses on water issues and state trust lands. He also teaches graduate courses in water policy and the New American West, as well as courses on the history of the American West and the environment via the Web, satellite, and Interactive Instructional Television, for Northern Arizona University. Dr. August is presently completing a book on Evan Mecham and the rise of the conservative right in the West. He is a former Fulbright Scholar and Pulitzer Prize nominee, and was recently named director of the Dennis DeConcini Project at the James E. Rogers College of Law at the University of Arizona in Tucson.

John S. Azar is an avid long-distance hiker and eclectic historian of Grand Canyon. His most recent hike with canyon resident Rich Della Porta and several others nearly spanned the length of Grand Canyon, a seventy-eight-day trek from Lees Ferry to Diamond Creek. He has researched the history of the World War II crew that parachuted from their disabled bomber into Grand Canyon, and is a world expert on pioneer cabins of the Grand Canyon region, which he occasionally rehabilitates in cooperation with federal land managers. Azar recently moved from Albuquerque, New Mexico, to Fredonia, Arizona, to be closer to his favorite place on Earth, the Arizona Strip.

Janet R. Balsom received her bachelor's degree in anthropology from the State University of New York at Buffalo in 1980 and master's degree in anthropology from Arizona State University at Tempe in 1984. She worked as an archaeological consultant when she signed on as a volunteer at the North Rim in 1981, the beginning of her long career at Grand Canyon. Balsom served as park archeologist from 1984 until 1995, and she now directs the park's cultural resource program, which includes the museum collection, historic preservation program, and archaeological and American Indian consultation programs.

Frank Barrios descends from a pioneer Phoenix family and spent his working career on water issues affecting the State of Arizona. After graduating from Arizona State University in 1966, he worked for the Bureau of Reclamation and Arizona Department of Water Resources until his retirement in 1995. He remains active in community affairs and retains his certification as a Professional Civil Engineer and Registered Land Surveyor.

Emma P. Benenati, PhD, is an adjunct professor at Northern Arizona University and a research Coordinator/Ecologist at Grand Canyon National Park. Her doctoral research addressed the ecology and management of the aquatic resources in the Colorado River, and the effect Glen Canyon Dam has on them. Research she has pursued during the past twelve years encompasses the Colorado River Basin from Canyonlands National Park in Utah to Lake Mead National Recreation Area on the Arizona-Nevada border, with an emphasis on the river in Grand Canyon.

Bill Bishop, a former river guide, developed his interest in the history of the rivers of the Colorado Plateau while working the river. Most of Bishop's fellow guides had degrees in geology, archeology, or similar disciplines, and since his degree in forestry did not exactly lend itself to the canyonlands, he decided to focus on history. In 1995 he started Canyon Books, a business specializing in out-of-print books, papers, and other materials pertaining to Grand Canyon, the Colorado River, and the Colorado Plateau.

Peter MacMillan Booth, PhD, a fifth-generation westerner, was born in Denver, grew up in south Texas, and moved to Arizona as a young man. He earned a bachelor of arts from the University of Texas, master of arts from the University of Arizona, and doctorate from Purdue University, all in history, with a focus on modern American, Western, and American Indian history. Dr. Booth was formerly assistant director of education at the Arizona Historical Society in Tucson, and education director at the Desert Caballeros Western Museum in Wickenburg, Arizona. He is a promoter of local history, public history, and historic preservation.

Bonnie Brune spent twenty-five years as a librarian in Washington, D.C., public schools; Oregon's Klamath County schools; and Arizona schools in Sanders, Yuma, and San Carlos. Since 1979 she has been viewing, walking, boating, photographing, and learning about Grand Canyon at every opportunity. In 1992 Brune began serving as a Grand Canyon associate naturalist, or volunteer ranger, leading walks, giving talks, and presenting evening programs in the summer seasons.

Bradford Cole grew up in Pocatello, Idaho; earned a bachelor of arts degree from Idaho State University; and finished his master of science degree at Utah State University. He is a member of the Academy of Certified Archivists, and has served as curator of manuscripts for Cline Library at Northern Arizona University. Rather than dwell on himself, Cole chose to thank the Lauzon family for their generous donation of family archival material to the Cline Library and for their support for this project, especially Loren "Tiny" Lauzon for his time and comments.

Mary J. Straw Cook is a classical concert musician and historian living in Santa Fe, New Mexico. She is currently writing the biography of Gertrudis Barcelo, La Tules, the notorious Santa Fe gambler. She is the author of *Loretto: The Sisters and Their Santa Fe Chapel* (Santa Fe: Museum of New Mexico Press, 1984) and is the editor of *Immortal Summer: The 1897 Letters & Photographs of Amelia Hollenback* (Santa Fe: Museum of New Mexico Press, 2002). She is also founder of the Friends of the Palace of Governors.

Brad Dimock earned a bachelor of arts degree from Prescott College, then proceeded, as he put it, to "squander his education for more than twenty-five years as a commercial boatman." He is now an "aspiring hermit," living in Flagstaff. Dimock coauthored *The Doing of the Thing: The Brief, Brilliant Whitewater Career of Buzz Holmstrom* (Flagstaff, Ariz.: Fretwater Press, 1998), and authored *Sunk Without a Sound: The Tragic Colorado River Honeymoon of Glen and Bessie Hyde* (Flagstaff, Ariz.: Fretwater Press, 2001). Both won the National Outdoor Book Award, and the latter won the Arizona Highways Nonfiction Book Award.

David C. Frauman, PhD, is a clinical psychologist on the faculty of Indiana University School of Medicine and in private practice in Indianapolis. He is interested in the psychology of creativity, art, and artists and has written psychobiographical articles on southwestern painter Maynard Dixon and Depression-era photographer Dorothea Lange, as well as Picasso, Mozart, and Monet.

Michael P. Ghiglieri, PhD, earned his doctoral degree in biological ecology from the University of California–Davis. He has run commercial whitewater trips and treks in America, Ethiopia, Kenya, Tanzania, Uganda, Rwanda, Sumatra, Java, Papua New Guinea, Peru, Turkey, and Canada. Since 1974 Dr. Ghiglieri has spent 1,700 days inside the canyon, guiding 630 river trips overall and rowing or paddling 38,000 miles. A former NPS river ranger and president of the Grand Canyon River Guides Association (2002–03), his books on Grand Canyon include *Canyon* (Tucson: Univ. of Arizona Press, 1992), and, with coauthor Tom Myers, the much-acclaimed *Over the Edge: Death in Grand Canyon* (Flagstaff, Ariz.: Puma Press, 2001).

J. Donald Hughes, PhD, is John Evans Professor of History at the University of Denver. Dr. Hughes worked a number of summers in the 1960s as a ranger-naturalist at Grand Canyon National Park. In 1976 he became a founding member of the American Society for Environmental History, and he edited its journal, *Environmental Review*, in the early 1980s. His books include *In the House of Stone and Light: A Human History of the Grand Canyon* (Grand Canyon, Ariz.: Grand Canyon Natural History Association, 1978) and *An Environmental History of the World: Humankind's Changing Role in the Community of Life* (London: Routledge, 2001).

Roy Lemons resided in Belen, New Mexico, at the time of his death in the summer of 2002. He was born in 1918 and enlisted in the Civilian Conservation Corps in April 1936 at the age of seventeen. He served in Company 819 at Grand Canyon Village through September 1938, primarily as assistant to park naturalist Eddie McKee. He also worked at Grand Canyon shortly thereafter, manning the Signal Point fire lookout at Pasture Wash. In later years, Lemons promoted the CCC on a national and international level, traveling to the Solomon Islands in 1991 to speak at the dedication of a memorial plaque for CCC men who died at Guadalcanal and elsewhere in World War II, and serving as vice president of Chapter 141 of the National Associates of the Civilian Conservation Corps Alumni.

Andrew Majeske is currently writing his doctoral dissertation in the English Department at the University of California–Davis, following the completion of degrees from John Carroll University (BA, 1983), Loyola University of Chicago School of Law (JD, 1986), and Duquesne University (MA, 1995). From 1986 to 1992, he practiced law in the real estate department of McDermott Will & Emery in Chicago. From 1992 until 1997 he was in general legal practice at Picadio McCall Miller & Norton in Pittsburgh, where his legal representation included regional land trusts. Majeske was awarded the Francis Bacon Fellowship to the Huntington Library in 2002 and the Woodrow Wilson Foundation's Charlotte Newcombe Dissertation Fellowship for 2002–03. He resides in Davis, California, with his wife, Andrea Ross, a poet and former interpretive ranger at Grand Canyon.

Mona Lange McCroskey is a fourth-generation Arizonan with bachelor's and master's degrees in history and a master's in library science. She has published extensively in periodicals such as *Smoke Signal*, *Journal of the West*, *Sharlot Hall Museum Gazette*, and the *Cornell H.R.A. Quarterly*. She has conducted approximately 150 oral-history interviews for the Sharlot Hall Museum in Prescott and is the editor of *Summer Sojourn to the Grand Canyon: The 1898 Diary of Zella Dysart* (Prescott, Ariz.: Holly Bear Press, 1996).

Gretchen Merten is a doctoral student in the Department of History at Northern Arizona University (NAU) in Flagstaff. She fell in love with Grand Canyon's geological and human history when she first backpacked the canyon with her science club in eighth grade, and she "has never been the same since." Merten thanks the Department of History at NAU, especially George Lubick, Susan Deeds, Karen Powers, Andy Wallace, and Val Avery for their intellectual support and friendship, and Lance and Maggie "for everything."

Tom Myers, MD, has been exploring in and around Grand Canyon since 1973. He has a bachelor's degree in history from Northern Arizona University, but after earning an MD from the University of Arizona, he worked full time as a physician at the Grand Canyon Clinic from 1990 to 1999. His current practice is in Williams, Arizona. Dr. Myers has hiked the canyon backcountry extensively and rowed the Colorado River many times. He is coauthor of two Grand Canyon books: *Fateful Journey: Injury and Death on Colorado River Trips in Grand Canyon* (Flagstaff, Ariz.: Red Lake Books, 1999), with Christopher C. Becker and Lawrence E. Stevens, and *Over the Edge: Death in Grand Canyon* (Flagstaff, Ariz.: Puma Press, 2001), with Michael Ghiglieri.

Jim Ohlman has worked as a hydrogeologist for Peabody Western Coal Company since 1986, overseeing groundwater and surface-water monitoring at the Kayenta and Black Mesa mines in northeastern Arizona. He was a guide and manager for Grand Canyon Trail Guides when they operated from the Grand Canyon Railroad Depot in the 1970s, and he has also worked as an exploration geologist. At Northern Arizona University, he earned a bachelor of science degree in geophysics (1975) and a master of science degree in structural geology (1982). He is a Registered Geologist with the State of Arizona, but with thirty years of canyon hiking and climbing experience under his soles, he is also fast becoming one of the "grand old men" of the Grand Canyon backcountry. Ohlman lives with wife, Janice; sons T. J., Chris, and John; and daughter, Sarah in Kayenta, Arizona.

Louis Purvis was born in Callahan County, Texas, in 1910. He served in the Civilian Conservation Corps from 1934 through 1937, working in several companies in Arizona, including Grand Canyon's Company 818. He earned a bachelor of arts degree from Howard Payne College in 1941, served in the U.S. Navy in the South Pacific throughout World War II, and returned to earn a master's degree at Texas Technological College in 1951. He worked for thirty years as a teacher, and he has been active in the affairs of CCC alumni since the 1980s, organizing (with wife Marie and others) the first reunion of Arizona CCC personnel in 1985 and acting as chair of the committee to write the history of the CCC in Arizona.

Richard D. Quartaroli first glimpsed the canyon in 1971, has been boating the Colorado River since 1973, and was president of Grand Canyon River Guides in 2001–02. Formerly research librarian at Glen Canyon Environmental Studies, he is now special collections librarian (or "keeper of the books") for Northern Arizona University's Cline Library. He credits river running for fueling his fascination with southwestern history in general and with the Grand Canyon and Colorado River in particular. Quartaroli, like Bradford Cole, thanks all who helped with his research for this symposium and the Cline Library for its active participation in the proceedings.

Al Richmond retired from Air Force Pararescue as a chief master sergeant in 1981 after twenty-seven years of service. He thereafter completed bachelor's and master's degrees at Northern Arizona University in Natural Resources Interpretation and Quaternary Studies—multidisciplinary fields that include geology, biology, anthropology, geography, and history. Richmond is currently president of the Arizona State Railroad Museum Foundation and historian for the Grand Canyon Railway. He also lectures on the Colorado Plateau and climate history, transportation, and the American Civil War. He has published in regional journals and is the author of two books: *Cowboys, Miners, Presidents & Kings: The Story of the Grand Canyon Railway* (Flagstaff, Ariz.: Grand Canyon Pioneers Society, 1985) and *Rails to the Rim: Milepost Guide to the Grand Canyon Railway* (Williams, Ariz.: Grand Canyon Railway, 1990).

George Steck, PhD, was born in Berkeley, California, in 1925 B.T. (before television), served in the U.S. Navy, and earned his doctorate in statistics from the University of California–Berkeley. He moved to New Mexico in 1955 (with wife, Helen, and two sons) to work for Sandia National Laboratories, and in the following year did a float trip with Georgie White through Glen Canyon. He has been rafting the river, hiking the canyons, and accumulating stories ever since. Dr. Steck completed a six-week trek from Lees Ferry to Lava Falls in 1977 and a canyon-length hike from Lees Ferry to the Grand Wash Cliffs in 1982. One of the "grand old men" of canyon hiking, climbing, and backpacking, he published two books on canyon loop hikes and was honored by the Grand Canyon Historical Society for a lifetime of contributions to the canyon community. Dr. Steck passed away in 2004.

INDEX